W9-BAG-430

STUDY GUIDE

TO ACCOMPANY

PRINCIPLES OF
MANAGERIAL FINANCE

TWELFTH EDITION

LAWRENCE J. GITMAN

THOMAS M. KRUEGER
UNIVERSITY OF WISCONSIN, LA CROSSE

PEARSON
Prentice
Hall

Boston San Francisco New York
London Toronto Sydney Tokyo Singapore Madrid
Mexico City Munich Paris Cape Town Hong Kong Montreal

Executive Editor: Donna Battista
Editorial Assistant: Kerri McQueen
Production Editor: Heather McNally
Manufacturing Buyer: Carol Melville

Pearson Prentice Hall™ is a trademark of Person Education, Inc.

1 2 3 4 5 6 BB 11 10 09 08

ISBN-13: 978-0-321-52523-9
ISBN-10:   0-321-52523-X

Table of Contents

Preface

This study guide is intended to supplement the accompanying textbook, *Principles of Managerial Finance, 12th edition*. As a supplement, it will review the concepts presented in the text and reinforce the application of these concepts through practice problems and sample exams. The best way to be successful in learning finance is to try working through many different problems that will test your ability to use the concepts you have learned. The field of finance, similar to accounting, is one that requires practice, practice, practice!

This study guide is organized as follows:

Chapter Summary

Learning Goals with a brief description of each

Chapter Outline with the specific learning goal noted in each section. The learning goals are highlighted on the left side of the page. For example, learning goal 1 is highlighted as follows:

Sample Problems and Solutions

Study Tips

Student Notes—a place where you can make your own notes as you work through the chapter

Sample Exam—10–16 True/False questions, 15–26 Multiple Choice questions, and 2–3 Essay questions

Answer Sheet for the Sample Exam

After reading the chapter outline, see if you can work through the sample problems without looking at the solution. Once you have attempted a problem, check your answer with the given solution.

Additionally, a sample exam is given to test your knowledge and the application of the presented material. Try taking the exam and then check your answers on the answer sheet. Many of the questions have an explanation for the answer. If you are still unsure of the reason for the answer, review the study guide and/or the textbook.

I wish you great success in learning this material! Your ability to understand the field of finance will greatly advance your career potential regardless of your major. Additionally, the field of finance is an exciting one with many potential career opportunities. In fact, this field is expected to see significant continued growth for employment in the near future. I wish to thank Larry Gitman for producing a truly outstanding managerial finance textbook, my family (Debi, Joshua, Sarah, and Philip) for their support, and the editorial assistance of Heather McNally and Mina Kim.

Thomas M. Krueger, D.B.A.
Professor of Finance
University of Wisconsin- La Crosse

Chapter 1
The Role and Environment
of Managerial Finance

■ Chapter Summary

The *Principles of Managerial Finance* text used in your finance course is organized around learning goals. Each chapter lists the learning goals and they are repeated throughout. Each chapter in this study guide will begin by listing these learning goals along with a brief summary discussion. After reading the chapter outline that follows, see if you can answer the questions raised by the learning goals.

Define finance, its major areas and opportunities and the legal forms of business organization. The financial services area encompasses financial product design and the delivery of financial advice. Loan officers, bank managers, and stock brokers are some of the many financial services positions. The managerial finance area encompasses the duties of the financial manager in the business firm. Financial analysts, cash managers, and credit analysts perform managerial finance roles. Corporations dominate sole proprietorships and partnerships in terms of receipts and net profits. Corporate owners cannot lose more than their investments, while sole proprietors and partners have unlimited liability. The primary emphasis of the text is on corporations.

Describe the managerial finance function and its relationship to economics and accounting. Finance functions involve analyzing the proper allocation of financial assets. The financial analysis applies to business decision making. Accounting and finance are closely related; however, accounting is generally responsible for data collection and presentation, while the financial manager uses this data for decision making.

Identify the key activities of the financial manager. The key activities of the financial manager are analyzing and planning, making investment decisions, and making financing decisions.

Explain the goal of the firm, corporate governance, the role of ethics, and the agency issue. The primary goal of the financial manager is to maximize the wealth of the firm's shareholders. This is not the same thing as maximizing profits. Maximizing profits may result in a short-term management viewpoint and a failure to properly consider risk.

Understand financial institutions and markets, and the role they play in managerial finance. Financial managers constantly interact with financial institutions and financial markets. An understanding of these institutions will increase the financial manager's success.

Discuss business taxes and their importance in financial decisions. Since taxes are often 40% or more on corporate income, many financial decisions are made with an eye toward lowering this large expense.

■ Chapter Notes

Definition of Finance and Major Areas in Finance

Finance is the art and science of managing money. All individuals and organizations earn or raise money. Finance is concerned with the process, institutions, markets, and instruments involved in the transfer of money among and between individuals, businesses, and governments.

Career opportunities in finance can be broken down into two broad areas:

1. Financial services deal with the design and delivery of advice and financial products to individuals, business, and government. Career opportunities center on banking, financial planning, investments, real estate and insurance.

2. Managerial finance is concerned with the duties of the financial manager in the business firm. The financial manager is responsible for such tasks as budgeting, financial forecasting, cash management, credit administration, investment analysis, and funds procurement.

Three Basic Forms of a Business

There are three basic legal forms of business organizations, each with its own unique characteristics.

1. A sole proprietorship is owned and operated by one individual. The profits from the sole proprietorship are taxed as the owner's personal income, and the sole proprietor has unlimited liability.

2. Partnerships are formed when two or more individuals enter into a business relationship for the purpose of profits. Like the sole proprietorship, partnerships are taxed as the personal income of each partner, according to that partner's percentage of ownership. Partnerships also have unlimited liability to the creditors of the business.

3. A corporation is a form of business organization that is treated as a separate legal entity from the owners of the business. A corporation can sue and be sued, be party to contracts, and engage in any business function that would normally be performed by individuals. A corporation has limited liability, in that the owners' wealth is protected from the corporation's creditors.

    The owners of a corporation are its stockholders whose ownership is evidenced by either common or preferred stock. Stockholders benefit from either an appreciation in the value of their shares or from receipt of dividends.

    Other organizational forms blend the characteristics of corporations with those of partnerships.

Relationships in Managerial Finance

Managerial finance has similarities to both economics and accounting.

Finance is closely related to the field of economics, in that the financial manager must understand economic theory and be aware of the consequences of varying levels of economic activity and changes in economic policy.

The fields of finance and accounting are closely related in that both are concerned with the calculation and reporting of information that helps in measuring the performance of a business and assessing its financial position. The main difference between the two fields is that the financial manager must go one step further and make decisions based on the accountant's financial data.

Accountants compute income using generally accepted procedures, while financial managers are more concerned with cash flows.

Roles of the Financial Manager

The roles of the financial manager can be broken down into three primary activities:
1. Perform financial analysis and planning
2. Make investment decisions
3. Make financing decisions

Goals of the Financial Manager

The goal of the financial manager is not to maximize the profits of the firm, but to maximize the shareholder's wealth. Profit maximization fails to recognize the timing of returns, cash flows and risk. The financial manager increases shareholder wealth by taking these issues into account:
1. *Timing of returns*: Because a firm can earn returns on funds it receives, a dollar that is received sooner is much more valuable than a dollar that is received later.
2. *Cash flows available to stockholders*: Financial managers should make decisions that increase the cash flows available to the shareholders. Financial managers can increase cash flows to the stockholders by adopting policies that lead to increased dividends or increased stock prices.
3. *Risk*: The financial manager should examine the trade-off that exists between risk and return. The higher the risk of a particular project, the higher the return should be to the firm, which leads to increased cash flows for the stockholders.

Economic value added (EVA) measures whether an investment contributes to owners' wealth.
EVA = After tax operating profits – cost of funds

Consider Ethics

Financial managers should consider ethical issues when making decisions. For instance:

1. Are stakeholder rights being violated?

2. Does one stakeholder benefit to the detriment of another?

3. If a stakeholder will be hurt, how can it be remedied?

The Agency Problem

The agency problem can be defined as the likelihood that managers may place personal goals ahead of corporate goals. There are two factors that work to contain the agency problem.

1. Market forces constantly monitor the weaknesses of a firm, and any weaknesses that arise due to the agency problem will be corrected by the outside forces.

2. Agency costs, borne by the stockholders of a company, attempt to prevent or minimize the agency problem. There are four main types of agency cost.
    a. Monitoring expenditures
    b. Bonding expenditures
    c. Opportunity costs
    d. Structuring expenditures

Incentive plans such as stock options reduce agency costs by aligning managers' interests more closely to those of stockholders.

The Sarbanes-Oxley Act of 2002 focuses on eliminating many disclosure and conflict of interest problems that were uncovered by the corporate misdeeds of late 1990s. This act did the following:

1.   established an oversight board to monitor the accounting industry

2.   tightened audit regulations and controls

3.   toughened penalties against executives who commit corporate fraud

4.   strengthened accounting disclosure requirements

5.   established board structure and membership guidelines

6.   required instant disclosure of stock sales by corporate executives

7.   increased security regulation authority and budgets for auditors and investigators

Finance Relation with Market and Institutions

Financial institutions serve as intermediaries by channeling the savings of individuals, businesses, and governments into loans or investments. In order to assure that the public trust is maintained, markets and institutions are heavily regulated and supervised. The major financial institutions in the U.S. are commercial banks, savings and loans, credit unions, savings banks, insurance companies, pension funds, and mutual funds.

The financial markets are a forum where suppliers of funds and demanders of funds can transact business. Broker markets consist of national and regional securities exchanges, while broker markets include Nasdaq and the over-the counter market. In the latter, all trades include a market maker.

One way to view the markets is as either money markets or capital markets. Money markets are where securities trade that have less than one year to maturity. Securities with greater than one year to maturity trade in the capital markets. So treasury bills are found in the money markets and stock is traded in the capital markets.

Business Taxes

Ordinary income is income earned through the sale of goods or services. The more that is earned the greater the percentage of tax that is owed. The average tax is the amount of tax paid divided by total income. The marginal tax rate is the percentage of tax owed on the last dollar earned. Marginal rates usually exceed average rates.

Capital gains are income earned due an increase in the value of an asset. Currently, capital gains are added to ordinary income and taxed at the regular corporate rate, with the maximum rate of 39%. To simplify tax calculations, a fixed rate of 40% will be used throughout this text regardless of whether it is ordinary or capital gain income.

■ Sample Problem Solutions

In this section of the study guide, I will demonstrate how to solve the problems presented in the text. There will be warnings about what mistakes students usually make and detailed explanations about why a particular method is used. Review the problems shown here carefully before working on your homework assignments or the sample test.

Chapter one is unique in that it contains few mathematical models. Most of the rest of the text will have many more.

Example 1.   Solving for Earning per Share

Profits are commonly expressed in terms of earnings per share (EPS), which represents the amount earned during the period (typically a quarter or a year) on each share of common stock outstanding.

EPS = Total earnings during the period/the number of shares outstanding

If the firm's net income after tax is $100,000 for the year and there are 50,000 shares of common stock in the public's hands, what are the annual earnings per share?

Solution

EPS = $100,000/50,000 = $2

Notes:

1.   The total earnings represent the period's earnings that are available for common stockholders. This means that taxes and preferred stock dividends should already be subtracted from the total.

2.   The number of shares in the denominator should be only those held by *common stockholders* since preferred stockholders usually receive constant dividends regardless of what the firm earns.

Example 2.   Solving for economic value added

A firm is evaluating a new product expected to generate total benefits measured in today's dollars of $100,000. The production of the new product will free up a machine used to make its predecessor. The old machine can be sold for $10,000. The cash investment required to launch and produce the product is $75,000 in today's dollars. Should the product be produced?

Solution

Compute the EVA

EVA = $100,000 – ($75,000 – $10,000) = $25,000

Since EVA is positive, shareholder wealth is increased. The product should be produced.

Example 3.   Income tax calculation

A firm has $1,000,000 in ordinary and capital gains income. What will this firm owe in taxes according to the figures in Table 1.4 of the text?

Solution

Total taxes due = $113,900 + [0.34 × ($1,000,000 − $335,000)]

Total taxes due = $113,900 + (0.34 × $665,000)

Total taxes due = $113,900 + $226,100 = $340,000

■ Study Tips

This is the place in this workbook where you will find notes, tips and warnings about the chapter that will help you complete assignments and prepare for exams. These helping notes are the result of teaching finance to thousands of students over many years. Most students have trouble with the same things. In this section I will try to help you over these tougher parts and to point out areas that justify extra attention because they often show up on exams.

1. Most students learn about the various forms of business in their business law and accounting classes and so are tempted to skim this material. Test your knowledge by seeing if you can list the strengths and weaknesses of each form. For example, a primary advantage to the corporate form of business is that the corporation can raise money more easily due to limited liability.

2. The difference between accounting and finance can be summarized quite easily. There are two main factors to remember.
    a. The accountants use an accrual approach to determining income, while financial managers measure cash flows.
    b. The accountants' primary focus is on the collection of data, while the financial managers use the data to make decisions.

3. Know the goal of the financial manager. It is to maximize shareholder wealth. Note that this goal does not say that the financial manager is concerned with bondholder wealth. Shareholder wealth is maximized by maximizing the firm's stock price. This means that the financial manager must pay attention to the factors that affect stock price. These include the timing, the risk, and the size of the firm's cash flows.

4. Understand that the actions firms take to prevent managers from maximizing their own wealth and happiness at the expense of the firm are themselves agency costs. For example, the costs of audits is an agency cost because audits would not be necessary if agents were not running the firm.

■ Student Notes

■ Sample Exam—Chapter 1

True/False

T F 1. A corporation is considered to be a separate "legal entity" from the owners and has the power of an individual in that it can sue and be sued.

T F 2. The treasurer in medium-to-large-size firms handles the accounting activities, such as tax management, data processing, and financial accounting.

T F 3. The main goal of the financial manager is to increase the firm's overall profits.

T F 4. In a corporation, profits are generally measured in terms of earnings per share.

T F 5. There is a positive correlation between risk and return. The higher the risk of an investment, the higher the required return will be on that investment.

T F 6. The primary role of the accountant in a corporation is to develop and provide financial data that will allow the financial manager to make decisions about the firm's financial position.

T F 7. A firm's earnings are a true representation of cash flows available to the stockholders.

T F 8. Economic value added measures the difference between the benefits from investment and the cost of the investment, all in today's dollars.

T F 9. Agency costs are fees that are paid by the management of a corporation to compensate any investor feels that he has suffered a loss due to the agency problem.

T F 10. The accrual method of accounting recognizes revenues at the time of sale and expenses when they are incurred.

T F 11. Because of tax benefits, financial managers prefer cash flows later rather than sooner.

T F 12. In general, stockholders wish to incur higher risk in order to ensure higher returns.

T F 13. The stakeholders of a corporation are those that would be employees, customers, suppliers, and creditors.

T F 14. The ethical behavior of the financial manager has a substantial impact on the shareholder's wealth maximization concept.

T F 15. A sole proprietor has limited liability, which means that his or her personal wealth is protected from creditors.

T F 16. The capital expenditure manager evaluates and recommends proposed long-term investments.

Multiple Choice

1. Which of the following is not one of the primary activities of the financial manager?
    a. Make financing decisions
    b. Prepare financial statements
    c. Make investment decisions
    d. Perform financial analysis

2. A _____ is a form of business organization that is considered an artificial being and has limited liability.
    a. partnership
    b. professional group
    c. corporation
    d. sole proprietorship

3. The main goal of the financial manager is to
    a. maximize profit.
    b. maximize stakeholder wealth.
    c. minimize cost.
    d. maximize shareholder wealth.

4. _____ can be defined as the art and science of managing money.
    a. Economics
    b. Finance
    c. Accounting
    d. Banking

5. Determine earnings per share for Company XYZ in 2009.

    Financial Data of XYZ

Earnings for 2009	$30,000
Outstanding shares of common stock	10,000
Outstanding shares of preferred stock	5,000
Price of stock	$30

    a. $3.00
    b. $2.00
    c. $0.30
    d. $6.00

6. When the risk of an investment is high, the rate of return required by the investor will be
    a. moderate.
    b. low.
    c. high.
    d. equal to the thirty day T-bill.

7. A market force that has, in recent years, threatened management to perform in the best interest of the shareholder is the _____ in which a firm is acquired by another firm without the support of management.
   a. fidelity bond
   b. market collapse
   c. incentive plan
   d. hostile takeover

8. _____ are groups of individuals such as employees, customers, suppliers, creditors, and others that have a direct economic link to a firm.
   a. Shareholders
   b. Stakeholders
   c. Environment
   d. Market forces

9. The _____ has/have the ultimate authority in guiding corporate affairs and in making general policy for the corporation.
   a. chief executive officer
   b. shareholders
   c. stakeholders
   d. board of directors

10. Which of the following is a career opportunity in the field of financial service?
    a. Investment advisor
    b. Cash manager
    c. Credit analyst
    d. Corporate financial analyst

11. The most expensive form of business to organize is the
    a. limited partnership.
    b. sole proprietorship.
    c. corporation.
    d. general partnership.

12. _____ recognizes revenues and expenses only with respect to actual inflows and outflows of cash.
    a. Cash method
    b. Assignment method
    c. Accrual method
    d. Revenue realization method

13. The wealth of the shareholders of a corporation is represented by
    a. price of stock.
    b. earnings per share.
    c. profits.
    d. cash flows.

14. If the managers of a company are not the owners of the company, they are considered
    a. directors.
    b. shareholders.
    c. insiders.
    d. agents.

15. The controller of a company is typically responsible for
    a. financial planning.
    b. strategic planning.
    c. accounting activities.
    d. managing cash.

16. The main economic principle used in managerial finance is
    a. pricing theory.
    b. marginal analysis.
    c. cash flow analysis.
    d. supply and demand.

17. The manager responsible for monitoring and managing the firm's exposure to loss from currency fluctuations is the
    a. foreign exchange manager.
    b. hedge analyst.
    c. currency control manager.
    d. foreign currency analyst.

18. The calendar year for Company XYZ has just ended. During this year, XYZ sold an airplane for $200,000 that cost them $100,000 to manufacture. XYZ has not received payment for the sale. Net profit and cash flow for XYZ are
    a. $100,000 and $100,000 respectively.
    b. $200,000 and $200,000 respectively.
    c. $100,000 and –$100,000 respectively.
    d. $100,000 and –$200,000 respectively.

19. Pizzas by Mail sold $100,000 of pizzas in January and $150,000 in February. Sixty percent of sales are collected the month of the sale and forty percent are collected the following month. Cash expenditures are $80,000 each month. What is the cash flow for February?
    a. $170,000
    b. $50,000
    c. $40,000
    d. $70,000

20. Investors that are _____ generally want to avoid risk.
    a. risk-averse
    b. market makers
    c. risk-tolerant
    d. paranoid

21. Which of the following is not included in making investment decisions?
    a. inventory
    b. fixed assets
    c. accounts receivable
    d. notes payable

22. Firms should maximize wealth rather than profits because maximizing profits ignores
    a. the timing of returns.
    b. earnings per share.
    c. cash flows available to stockholders.
    d. risk.

23. While evaluating decision alternatives or potential actions, financial managers must consider which of the following?
    a. only risk
    b. only return
    c. both risk and return
    d. risk, return, and the impact on share price

24. Which of the following is not included in agency costs?
    a. bonding and structuring costs
    b. cost of goods sold
    c. monitoring expenditures
    d. opportunity costs

25. A more recent issue within the business community that is causing major problems is
    a. the privatization of ownership.
    b. short-term versus long-term financial goals of management.
    c. ethical problems.
    d. environmental concerns.

26. Joshua Gilbertstein had the following cash flows in February of this year.

Item	Amount
Car payment	$ 415
Dividend received	$ 25
Gas	$ 125
Groceries/food	$ 255
Interest received	$ 44
Net pay received	$3,500
Rent	$ 650
Stock purchase	$1,200

Joshua's net cash flow for the month was:
    a. $855
    b. $924
    c. $2,124
    d. $3,569

Essay

1. Briefly explain the trade-off between risk and return.

2. Explain why the primary goal of the financial manager should be owner wealth maximization and not profit maximization for the corporation. Give reasons why profit maximization does not work.

3. Contrast broker and dealer markets.

■ Chapter 1 Answer Sheet

True/False	Multiple Choice	
1. T	1. B	16. B
2. F	2. C	17. A
3. F	3. D	18. C
4. T	4. B	19. B
5. T	5. A	20. A
6. T	6. C	21. D
7. F	7. D	22. D
8. T	8. B	23. D
9. F	9. D	24. B
10. T	10. A	25. D
11. F	11. C	
12. F	12. A	
13. T	13. A	
14. T	14. D	
15. F	15. C	
16. T		

$$NP = \$200{,}000 - \$100{,}000$$
$$CF = -100{,}000$$

$$\$30{,}000/10{,}000 = \$3$$

26. B

$$(0.4 \times \$100{,}000) + (0.6 \times \$150{,}000) - \$80{,}000$$
$$= \$40{,}000 + \$90{,}000 - \$80{,}000 = \$50{,}000$$

Essay

1. Since investors are risk averse, a security must provide a higher level of return to induce investors to accept a higher level of risk. As a result, increasing risk will be associated with increasing return.

2. Profit maximization may result in maximizing profits in each period at the expense of maximizing the stock price. This is because some investments may take a long time to pay off or may have high risk. Ultimately, all that stockholders really care about is the return they earn on holding the stock. Efforts by managers to maximize this return will maximize shareholder wealth. Profit maximization may not work because managers may be tempted to accept more risky projects to increase earnings, or to reduce or delay research and development to increase current period earnings.

3. The key difference between broker and dealer markets is the way in which trades are executed. The broker market consists of national and regional securities exchanges. With the assistance of brokers, the buyer and seller are simultaneously brought together on the floor of this exchange. In contrast, the dealer market, there are essentially two trades in every transaction with the buyer purchasing shares from a dealer and the seller selling shares to a dealer. Broker markets include the New York Stock Exchange, while the dealer market includes Nasdaq and the over-the-counter market.

Chapter 2
Financial Statements and Analysis

■ Chapter Summary

This chapter demonstrates the use of ratios to help examine the health of a firm. Ratio analysis is useful for identifying both problem areas and areas of strength for a firm. One ratio by itself is usually not very useful. It is when ratios are compared—both across time and to those of similar firms—that the benefits are realized. By the end of this chapter, you will find yourself much more familiar with balance sheets and income statements.

LG 1 *Review the contents of the stockholders' report and the procedures for consolidating international financial statements.* The stockholders' report contains the letter to stockholders, four key financial statements, and notes to the financial statements.

LG 2 *Understand who uses financial ratios, and how.* Both insiders and outsiders use financial ratio analysis to compare a firm's performance and status to that of other firms or to itself over time. Financial statement analysis takes two forms: cross-sectional analysis, where firms are compared to other similar firms, and time-series analysis, where firms are compared to themselves at different points in time.

LG 3 *Use ratios to analyze a firm's liquidity and activity.* It is best to perform ratio analysis by grouping ratios together that examine a common issue. For example, activity ratios measure the speed with which various accounts are converted into sales or cash. Liquidity ratios measure the firm's ability to pay its bills by examining the net working capital, current ratio, or quick ratio.

LG 4 *Discuss the relationship between debt and financial leverage and the ratios used to analyze a firm's debt.* The debt ratio and the debt/equity ratio measure indebtedness. Coverage ratios, such as times interest earned and fixed payment coverage, measure the ability to service fixed contractual requirements such as interest, principal or sinking-fund payments.

LG 5 *Use ratios to analyze a firm's profitability and its market value.* The common-size statement can be used to examine the gross profit margin, the operating profit margin, and the net profit margin. Other measures of profitability include the return on assets, the return on equity, earnings per share, and the price/earnings ratio.

LG 6 *Use a summary of financial ratio and the DuPont system of analysis to perform a complete ratio analysis of a firm.* The DuPont system provides a framework for dissecting the firm's overall financial statements and assessing its condition. The focal point of the DuPont system is the return on total assets. This is explained by the net profit margin and total asset turnover. If the ROA indicates a problem, subordinate ratios can be examined to identify the source of the problem.

■ Chapter Notes

Stockholders' Report

Corporations are required to produce annual stockholders' reports that are sent to all shareholders. It will usually begin with a letter from management to stockholders that summarizes the state of the firm and management's views as to its future. This letter is then followed by the four basic statements:

1. *Income statement*: A financial summary of the firm's operating results during a specified period.
2. *Balance sheet*: A summary of the firm's financial position at a given time.
3. *Statement of retained earnings*: Reconciles the net income earned during a given year, and any cash dividends paid, with the change in retained earnings between the start and the end of that year.
4. *Statement of cash flows*: A summary of the cash flows over the period of concern.

The stockholders report will conclude with notes to the financial statement. These provide detailed information on the accounting policies, procedures, calculations, and transactions underlying entries in the financial statements.

Use of Financial Ratios

Ratio analysis is used to compare a firm's performance and status with that of other firms or to itself over time.

There are two types of ratio comparisons: cross-sectional and time-series.

1. Cross-sectional analysis compares different firms' financial ratios at the same point in time. It involves comparing the firm's ratios to those of an industry leader or to the industry averages.
2. Time-series analysis is the evaluation of a firm's performance over time. Time-series allows the firm to compare its current performance to past performance.

Cautions about using ratio analysis.

1. Do not use a single ratio to judge the overall performance of the firm.
2. The financial statements being compared should be dated at the same point of time during the year.
3. Audited financial data should be used to ensure relevant financial information.
4. The financial data being compared in the ratio analysis should be developed in the same manner.
5. When performing time-series analysis, inflation should always be taken into account.

Liquidity Ratios

The liquidity of a corporation measures its ability to satisfy its short-term obligations. In other words, liquidity measures the ease with which it can pay its bills. The three basic measures of liquidity are net working capital, the current ratio, and the quick (acid-test) ratio.

Net working capital is used to measure the firm's overall liquidity.

$$\text{Net Working Capital} = \text{Current Assets} - \text{Current Liabilities}$$

The current ratio measures the firm's ability to meet its short-term obligations.

$$\text{Current Ratio} = \frac{\text{Current Assets}}{\text{Current Liabilities}}$$

The quick (acid-test) ratio is similar to the current ratio except that the quick ratio excludes inventory, which is generally the least liquid current asset.

$$\text{Quick Ratio} = \frac{\text{Current Assets} - \text{Inv}}{\text{Current Liabilities}}$$

Activity Ratios

Activity ratios are used to measure the speed with which various accounts are converted into sales or cash.

Inventory turnover measures the liquidity of a firm's inventory.

$$\text{Inventory Turnover} = \frac{\text{Cost of Goods Sold}}{\text{Inventory}}$$

The average collection period is useful in evaluation of credit and collection policies.

$$\text{Average Collection Period} = \frac{\text{Accounts Receivable}}{\text{Average Sales Per Day}}$$

The average payment period measures the average amount of time needed to pay accounts payable.

$$\text{Average Payment Period} = \frac{\text{Accounts Payable}}{\text{Average Purchases Per Day}}$$

The total asset turnover indicates the efficiency with which the firm uses all its assets to generate sales.

$$\text{Total Asset Turnover} = \frac{\text{Sales}}{\text{Total Assets}}$$

Analyzing Debt

Creditors' claims must be satisfied before earnings are distributed to the shareholders, so it is in the best interest of the present and prospective shareholders to pay close attention to the indebtedness of a corporation.

Financial leverage is a term that is used to describe the magnification of risk and return introduced through the use of fixed cost financing such as debt and preferred stock. A firm that is heavily leveraged will have a large proportion of debt financing in relation to its assets.

The debt ratio measures the proportion of total assets financed by the firm's creditors. The higher this ratio, the more financial leverage the firm has.

$$\text{Debt Ratio} = \frac{\text{Total Liabilities}}{\text{Total Assets}}$$

The times-interest-earned ratio measures the firm's ability to make interest payments.

$$\text{Times Interest Earned} = \frac{\text{Earnings Before Interest and Taxes}}{\text{Interest}}$$

The fixed payment coverage ratio measures the firm's ability to meet all fixed payment obligations, such as loan interest and principal, lease payments, and preferred stock dividends.

$$\text{Fixed Payment Coverage} = \frac{\text{Earnings Before Interest and Taxes} + \text{Lease Payments}}{\text{Int} + \text{Lease} + \{(\text{Prin} + \text{Pref Stock Div}) \times [1/(1-T)]\}}$$

where: $T = \text{Corporate Tax Rate}$

Analyzing Profitability

Measures of profitability relate the returns of the firm to its sales, assets, equity, or share value. These measures allow the analyst to evaluate the firm's earnings with respect to a given level of sales, a certain level of assets, the owners' investment, or share value.

Common-size income statements express each item in the income statement as a percentage of sales. Common-size income statements are useful when comparing the performance of a firm for a particular year with that of another year.

The gross profit margin measures the percentage of each sales dollar remaining after the firm has paid for its goods.

$$\text{Gross Profit Margin} = \frac{\text{Sales} - \text{Cost of Goods Sold}}{\text{Sales}} = \frac{\text{Gross Profits}}{\text{Sales}}$$

The operating profit margin measures the percentage of profit earned on each sales dollar before interest and taxes.

$$\text{Operating Profit Margin} = \frac{\text{Operating Profits}}{\text{Sales}}$$

The net profit margin measures the percentage of each sales dollar remaining after all expenses, including taxes, have been deducted.

$$\text{Net Profit Margin} = \frac{\text{Earnings Available for Common Stockholders}}{\text{Sales}}$$

The return on total assets (ROA) measures the overall effectiveness of management in generating profits with its available assets. The ROA is also called the return on investment.

$$\text{Return On Total Assets} = \frac{\text{Earnings Available for Common Stockholders}}{\text{Total Assets}}$$

The return on equity measures the return earned on the owners' (and common stockholders') investment in the firm.

$$\text{Return On Common Equity} = \frac{\text{Earnings Available for Common Stockholders}}{\text{Common Stockholders' Equity}}$$

The earnings per share represent the number of dollars earned on behalf of each outstanding share of common stock.

$$\text{Earnings Per Share} = \frac{\text{Earnings Available for Common Stockholders}}{\text{Number of Shares of Common Stock Outstanding}}$$

The price/earnings (*P/E*) ratio reflects the amount that investors are willing to pay for each dollar of earnings. The higher the *P/E* ratio, the higher the investor confidence in the firm.

$$P/E \text{ Ratio} = \frac{\text{Market Price Per Share of Common Stock}}{\text{Earnings Per Share}}$$

The market to book ratio reflects the level of return on equity and the degree of investor confidence.

Complete Ratio Analysis

Complete ratio analysis includes a large number of liquidity, activity, debt, and profitability ratios. There are two popular approaches to complete ratio analysis: DuPont system of analysis and summary analysis.

1. The DuPont system of analysis merges the income statement and the balance sheet into two summary measures of profitability: return on total assets (ROA) and return on equity (ROE).

$$\text{ROA} = \frac{\text{Earnings Available for Common Stockholders}}{\text{Sales}} \times \frac{\text{Sales}}{\text{Total Assets}} = \frac{\text{Earnings Available for Common Stockholders}}{\text{Total Assets}}$$

$$\text{ROE} = \frac{\text{Earnings Available for Common Stockholders}}{\text{Total Assets}} \times \frac{\text{Total Assets}}{\text{Common Stock Equity}} = \frac{\text{Earnings Available for Common Stockholders}}{\text{Stockholders' Equity}}$$

2. A firm's performance should not be judged on a single ratio, but rather groups of ratios. To fully evaluate a corporation, four aspects need to be analyzed on a cross-sectional and time-series basis: liquidity, activity, debt, and profitability.

■ Sample Problems and Solutions

Use the balance sheet and income statements for Pizzas by Mail, Inc. that follow on this and the next page to answer the example questions.

Example 1.   Basic ratio calculation

Calculate the ratios indicated using the financial statements that follow.

Ratio	Answer	Ratio	Answer
Net Working Capital		Debt-Equity Ratio	
Current Ratio		Times Interest Earned	
Quick Ratio		Fixed Payment Coverage	
Inventory Turnover		Gross Profit Margin	
Average Collection Period		Operating Profit Margin	
Average Payment Period		Net Profit Margin	
Fixed Asset Turnover		Return on Assets	
Total Asset Turnover		Return on Equity	
Debt Ratio		Earnings per Share	

Pizzas by Mail, Inc.
Income Statement
Year Ending December 31, 2009

Net Sales Revenue		$30,000,000
Less: Cost of Goods Sold		21,000,000
Gross Profits		9,000,000
Less: Operating Expenses:		
Selling Expense	$2,500,000	
General and Administration Expense	1,500,000	
Depreciation Expense	1,000,000	
Total Operating Expense		$ 5,000,000
Operating Profits		$ 4,000,000
Less: Interest Expense		2,000,000
Net Profits Before Tax		$ 2,000,000
Less: Taxes (40%)		800,000
Net Profits After Tax		$ 1,200,000

Pizzas by Mail, Inc.
Balance Sheet
December 31, 2009

Assets

Current Assets	
Cash	$ 1,000,000
Marketable Securities	3,000,000
Accounts Receivable	12,000,000
Inventories	7,500,000
Total Current Assets	23,500,000
Gross Fixed Assets	
Land and Buildings	$11,500,000
Machinery and Equipment	20,000,000
Furniture and Fixtures	8,000,000
Total Gross Fixed Assets	$39,500,000
Less: Accumulated Depreciation	$13,000,000
Net Fixed Assets	$26,500,000
Total Assets	$50,000,000

Pizzas by Mail, Inc.
Balance Sheet
December 31, 2009 (Continued)

Liabilities and Stockholders' Equity

Current Liabilities:

Accounts payable	$ 8,000,000
Notes payable	8,000,000
Accruals	500,000
Total current liabilities	$16,500,000
Long-term debt (annual payments required of $800,000)	$20,000,000
Total liabilities	$36,500,000

Stockholders' equity

Preferred stock (100,000 shares, Div = $2.00/share)	$ 2,500,000
Common stock (1 million shares @ $5.00 par)	5,000,000
Paid in capital in excess of par on common stock	4,000,000
Retained earnings	2,000,000
Total stockholders' equity	$13,500,000
Total liabilities and stockholders' equity	$50,000,000

Solution

Ratio	Answer	Ratio	Answer
Net working capital	23.5 − 16.5 = 7,000,000	Debt-equity ratio	20/13.5 = 1.48
Current ratio	1.42	Times interest earned	4/2 = 2
Quick ratio	0.97	Fixed payment coverage	4,000,000/(2,000,000 + (800,000 + 200,000 × 1/(1 − 0.4))) = 1.09
Inventory turnover	2.80	Gross profit margin	9/30 = 0.3
Average collection period	12,000,000/ (30,000,000/365) = 146	Operating profit margin	4/30 = 0.13
Average payment period	8,000,000/(21,000,000/365) = 139	Net profit margin	(1.2 − 0.20)/30 = 0.033
Fixed asset turnover	30/26.5 = 1.13	Return on assets	(1.2 − 0.2)/50 = 0.02
Total asset turnover	30/50 = 0.6	Return on equity	13.5 − 2.5 = 11 (1.2 − 0.2)/11 = 0.091
Debt ratio	36.5/50 = 0.73	Earnings per share	1,200,000 − 200,000/ 1,000,000 = 1

Example 2.   Common-Size Income Statement

Pizzas by Mail, Inc.
Income Statement
Year Ending December 31, 2009

Net sales revenue
Less: Cost of goods sold
Gross profits
Less: Operating expenses:
    Selling expense
    General and administration expense
    Depreciation expense
        Total operating expense
Operating profits
Less: Interest expense
Net profits before tax
Less: Taxes (40%)
Net profits after tax

Prepare a common-size income statement for Pizzas by Mail Inc. for the year
ending 2009.

Solution

Pizzas by Mail, Inc.
Common Size Income Statement
Year Ending December 31, 2009

Net sales revenue		100.00%
Less: Cost of goods sold		70.00%
Gross profits		30.00%
Less: Operating expenses:		
Selling expense	8.33%	
General and administration expense	5.00%	
Depreciation expense	3.33%	
Total operating expense		16.67%
Operating profits		13.33%
Less: Interest expense		6.67%
Net profits before tax		6.67%
Less: Taxes (40%)		2.67%
Net profits after tax		4.00%

Example 3.   Evaluating Ratios

Pizzas by Mail has decided that it should expand nationally despite some limited complaints that pizzas
are arriving cold. It has contacted Joe Flattop at the Last Chance National Bank for a $2,000,000 loan to
fund the expansion. Mr. Flattop collected the following industry information to use in evaluating the loan
request.

Industry Averages for Mail Order Food Businesses	
Current ratio	1.95
Debt ratio	0.46
Debt-equity ratio	1.07
Times interest earned	7.30
Fixed payment coverage ratio	1.85

Evaluate whether or not Last Chance National should extend the loan to Pizzas by Mail.

Solution

Begin by setting up a chart to compare the critical ratio with the industry ratios. If more than one year of data is available, the last several years should be included in the chart as well.

	Company vs. Industry Comparison		
Ratio	**Industry**	**Pizzas by Mail**	**Evaluation**
Current ratio	1.95	1.42	worse than industry
Debt ratio	0.46	0.73	worse than industry
Debt-equity ratio	1.07	1.48	worse than industry
Times interest earned	7.30	2.00	worse than industry
Fixed payment coverage	1.85	1.09	worse than industry

The firm has a much higher degree of indebtedness and a much lower ability to service debt than the average firm in the industry. The firm has a low current ratio. Even Last Chance National would have to decline this loan.

Example 4.   Evaluating Ratios

Use the following ratios to evaluate the health of Bogus Baked Goods.

	Time Series and Cross-Section Ratios Bogus Baked Goods					
	2009		**2010**		**2011**	
Ratio	**Bogus**	**Industry**	**Bogus**	**Industry**	**Bogus**	**Industry**
Current ratio	2.00	1.90	1.78	1.85	2.05	1.95
Quick ratio	1.00	0.95	0.89	0.95	0.95	0.95
Average collection period	72 days	65 days	93 days	70 days	90 days	71 days
Average payment period	80 days	70 days	117 days	75 days	106 days	75 days
Inventory turnover	3.00	4.00	2.87	3.80	2.62	4.00
Fixed asset turnover	1.33	1.50	1.11	1.55	1.42	1.60
Total asset turnover	0.80	0.90	0.69	0.93	0.78	0.95
Debt ratio	0.25	0.27	0.28	0.25	0.26	0.25
Debt-to-equity ratio	0.50	0.48	0.57	0.49	0.55	0.49
Gross profit margin	25%	24%	21%	25%	19%	27%
Operating profit margin	15%	14.8%	12%	14.9%	8.8%	15%
Net profit margin	6.7%	7.0%	5.0%	6.7%	3.5%	6.8%
Return on equity	7.15%	8.63%	4.79%	8.31%	3.69%	8.61%
Return on assets	5.3%	6.5%	3.5%	6.5%	2.8%	6.4%
Times interest earned	9.0	8.0	5.8	8.0	5.0	8.0

Solution

There are many acceptable ways to analyze financial ratios. One way that will help keep your thoughts organized and assure that you are considering every issue is to separate the ratios into categories based on what they tell us. In other words, review the liquidity ratios first, then the activity ratios, the debt ratios, and finally the profitability ratios. Review and summarize how the firm is doing in each of the four areas, then conclude how the firm is doing overall.

Liquidity: Bogus's liquidity appears to be slightly better than the industry and relatively consistent over time. Be careful not to read too much into small deviations from norms or to read a trend into normal variations that occur over time.

Activity: The activity ratios suggest there may be some problems in the firm's management. The average collection period is increasing and much longer than the industry average. It is possible that the firm is using its credit terms as a marketing tool. This could be easily determined by asking management. The longer payment period usually indicates that the firm is having liquidity problems, but this does not appear to be the case here. It may be due to sloppy accounting systems or may be the result of negotiated terms with suppliers. Again, management should be asked to explain. The inventory turnover, fixed asset turnover, and total asset turnover are all well below the industry average. There is no evidence of improvement over the last several years. This indicates that the inventory is being mismanaged. There may be too much or obsolete inventory.

Debt Ratio: The debt ratio suggests that the firm's level of debt is in line with others in its industry and that it has not changed significantly. The times-interest-earned ratio has a declining trend. This may be due to falling profitability.

Profitability Ratios: Many analysts think that the profitability ratios are the most important since if the firm is making a fair profit, the other ratios are inconsequential. Bogus's gross profit margin is falling and it is well below the industry average. The other profitability ratios are below the industry average and show similar falling trends. This is a *serious* problem. There are many reasons why this may happen. There may be low cost competitors that are forcing Bogus to lower prices, or Bogus may be finding it difficult to buy its supplies as cheaply as competitors. The reason for this problem must be found and rectified.

Overall: The firm's problems seem to result from excessive levels of inventories, accounts receivable, accounts payable, and its inability to earn sufficient profits. A trend of rising costs and expenses without corresponding increases in the selling price may explain the declining returns on sales and assets. A loan officer considering extending a loan to Bogus would need to discuss the problems identified here with management.

Example 5. DuPont Analysis

Use the ratios given for Bogus Baked Goods to perform a DuPont Analysis.

Solution

ROA = Net profit margin × Total asset turnover
ROE = 3.5% × 0.78 × (1/(1 − 0.26) = 3.69%

Since the ROE is below the industry, the analyst will want to determine whether the problem is due to the profit-on-sales component, efficiency-of-asset-use component, or a use-of-leverage component.

Example 6.

Terri Spiro, an experienced budget analyst at XYZ Corporation, has been charged with assessing the firm's financial performance during XXX3 and its financial position at year-end XXX3. To complete this assignment, she gathered the firm's XXX3 financial statements, which follow. In addition, Terri obtained the firm's ratio values for XXX1 and XXX2, along with the XXX3 industry average ratios (also applicable to XXX1 and XXX2). These are presented in the table on the following page.

XYZ Corp. Financial Statements

	Income Statement (in Thousands)		
Fiscal Year End	**01/29/XXX3**	**01/30/XXX2**	**01/31/XXX1**
Net sales	30,762,000	36,151,000	37,028,000
Cost of goods	26,258,000	29,853,000	29,732,000
Gross profit	4,504,000	6,298,000	7,296,000
Selling, general & administrative expenses	6,544,000	7,588,000	7,366,000
Operating income	–2,040,000	–1,290,000	–70,000
Non-operating income/expense	–1,067,000	–978,000	89,000
Income before interest and tax	(3,107,000)	(2,268,000)	19,000
Interest expense	155,000	344,000	287,000
Income before tax	–3,262,000	–2,612,000	–268,000
Net income before extraordinary items	–3,262,000	–2,612,000	–268,000
Extraordinary items & discontinued operations	43,000	166,000	—
Net income	–3,219,000	–2,446,000	–268,000
Outstanding shares	519,124	503,295	486,510

XYZ Corp. Financial Statements
Balance Sheet

	Assets (in Thousands)		
Fiscal Year End	**01/29/XXX3**	**01/30/XXX2**	**01/31/XXX1**
Cash	613,000	1,245,000	401,000
Accounts receivable	664,000	800,000	1,300,000
Inventories	4,825,000	5,796,000	6,051,000
Total current assets	6,102,000	7,841,000	7,752,000
Property, plant & equipment	4,892,000	6,093,000	6,557,000
Deposits & other assets	244,000	249,000	523,000
Total assets	11,238,000	14,183,000	14,832,000

XYZ Corp. Financial Statements
Balance Sheet (Continued)

Fiscal Year End	Liabilities (in Thousands)		
	01/29/XXX3	01/30/XXX2	01/31/XXX1
Accounts payable	1,248,000	89,000	2,159,000
Current long term debt	—	—	68,000
Accrued expenses	872,000	563,000	1,774,000
Total current liabilities	2,120,000	652,000	4,001,000
Long term debt	8,150,000	8,555,000	2,918,000
Non-current capital leases	623,000	857,000	943,000
Total liabilities	10,893,000	10,064,000	7,862,000
Minority interest	646,000	889,000	887,000
Common stock net	519,000	503,000	487,000
Capital surplus	1,922,000	1,695,000	1,578,000
Retained earnings	–2,742,000	1,032,000	4,018,000
Shareholders equity	345,000	4,119,000	6,970,000
Total liabilities & net worth	11,238,000	14,183,000	14,832,000

XYZ Corporation
Historical Ratios

Ratio	Actual XXX1	Actual XXX2	Actual XXX3	Industry Average XXX3
Current ratio	1.938	12.026		1.1
Quick ratio	0.43	3.14		0.3
Inventory turnover (times)	4.91	5.151		7.2
Average collection period	72.462	8.077		
Total asset turnover (times)	2.496	2.549		2.7
Debt ratio	0.53	0.71		0.44
Times interest earned ratio	0.066	–6.593		
Gross profit margin	19.70%	17.42%		24.9
Net profit margin	–0.72%	–6.77%		3.2
Return on total assets (ROA)	–0.018	–0.172		8.1
Return on common equity (ROE)	–0.038	–0.594		19.6
Price/earnings (P/E) ratio				22.9
Market/book (M/B) ratio				10.21

a.   Calculate the firm's XXX3 financial ratios, and then fill in the preceding table.

b.   Analyze the firm's current financial position from both a cross-sectional and a time-series viewpoint. Break your analysis into evaluations of the firm's liquidity, activity, debt, profitability, and market.

c.   Summarize the firm's overall financial position on the basis of your findings in part **b.**

Solution

a.   Ratio Calculations

Financial Ratio	XXX3
Current ratio	$6,102,000 ÷ $2,120,000 = 2.878
Quick ratio	($6,102,000 − $4,825,000) ÷ $1,277,000 = 0.60
Inventory turnover (times)	$26,258,000 ÷ $4,825,000 = 5.442
Average collection period (days)	$664,000 ÷ ($30,762,000 ÷ 365) = 7.879
Total asset turnover (times)	$30,762,000 ÷ $11,238,000 = 2.737
Debt ratio	$10,893,000 ÷ $11,238,000 = 0.969
Times interest earned	−$3,107,000 ÷ $155,000 = −20.045
Gross profit margin	(30,762,000 − 26,258,000) ÷ 30,762,000 = 14.64%
Net profit margin	−$3,219,000 ÷ $30,762,000 = −10.46%
Return on total assets	−$3,219,000 ÷ $11,238,000 = −0.286
Return on equity	−$3,219,000 ÷ $345,000 = −9.330

XYZ Corporation
Historical Ratios

Ratio	Actual XXX1	Actual XXX2	Actual XXX3	Industry Average XXX3
Current ratio	1.938	12.026	2.878	1.1
Quick ratio	0.43	3.14	0.60	0.3
Inventory turnover (times)	4.91	5.151	5.442	7.2
Average collection period	72.462	8.077	7.879	
Total asset turnover (times)	2.496	2.549	2.737	2.7
Debt ratio	0.53	0.71	0.969	0.44
Times interest earned ratio	0.066	−6.593	−20.045	
Gross profit margin	19.70%	17.42%	14.64%	24.9
Net profit margin	−0.72%	−6.77%	−10.46%	3.2
Return on total assets (ROA)	−0.018	−0.172	−0.286	8.1
Return on common equity (ROE)	−0.038	−0.594	−9.330	19.6
Price/earnings (P/E) ratio				22.9
Market/book (M/B) ratio				10.21

b.   *Liquidity:* The firm has sufficient current assets to cover current liabilities. The firm's liquidity is higher than the industry average. The trend is downward from years XXX2 to XXX3 and getting closer to the industry average.

Activity: The inventory turnover is stable, but lower than the industry average, which could indicate the firm is holding too much inventory. The average collection period is decreasing due to a decrease in accounts receivable. Total asset turnover is stable and matches the industry average. This indicates that the sales volume is sufficient for the amount of committed assets.

Debt: The debt-equity ratio has increased and is substantially higher than the industry average. This places the company at high risk. Typically industries with heavy capital investment and higher operating risk try to minimize the financial risk. XYZ Corporation has positioned itself with both heavy operating and financial risk. The times-interest-earned ratio is decreasing and also indicates a potential debt service problem.

Profitability: The gross profit margin is decreasing slightly and is well below the industry average. The next profit margin is also decreasing and far below the industry average. This is an indicator that the firm does not have sufficient sales dollar remaining after expenses have been deducted. The high financial leverage has caused the low profitability.

Market: Return on equity and return on assets are both decreasing and are well below the industry average. This indicates a problem of management in generating profits with its available assets, as well as a problem with the return earned on the owner's investment in the firm.

c.   XYZ Corporation has a problem with sales not being at an appropriate level for its capital investment. As a consequence, the firm has acquired a substantial amount of debt which, due to the high interest payments associated with the large debt burden, is depressing profitability. These problems may be picked up by investors and reflect in market ratios.

■ Study Tips

This chapter presents and explains the more common financial ratios used to analyze firms. A few points need to be emphasized.

1.   Seldom will ratios answer questions. Most of the time they raise questions. This is valuable because by raising questions they give the analyst a direction to continue study. For example, a loan officer will be able to ask the *right* questions of a loan applicant.

2.   Do not get too excited over small annual deviations from the industry or from historical values. This is natural to businesses. Look for trends that indicate a problem that is more than just an annual anomaly.

3.   Do not put too much faith in one ratio by itself. There are several ratios in each major area of analysis. Use them all and view all of them together to get the big picture.

■ Student Notes

_____

_____

_____

_____

_____

■ Sample Exam—Chapter 2

True/False

T   F   1.   The more financial leverage that a firm uses, the greater will be its risk and expected return.

T   F   2.   Scantron Corporation's inventory turnover ratio is twice as fast as the industry average. It is safe to assume that Scantron is a profitable corporation.

T   F   3.   The creditors of a firm must be satisfied before any earnings can be distributed to the common shareholders.

T   F   4.   Common-size income statements restate each item in the statement as a percentage of net income.

T   F   5.   The operating profit margin must take into account interest and taxes.

T   F   6.   A *P/E* ratio of 20 indicates that investors are willing to pay $20 for each $1 of earnings.

T   F   7.   Earnings per share is calculated by dividing retained earnings by the number of shares of common stock outstanding.

T   F   8.   Return on total assets (ROA) is sometimes called the return on investment.

T   F   9.   Liquidity ratios are used to measure the speed with which various accounts are converted into sales.

T   F   10.   Generally, inventory is considered the most liquid asset that a firm possesses.

T   F   11.   The current ratio measures the firm's ability to meet short-term obligations.

T   F   12.   When referring to ratio comparisons, time-series analysis compares a firm to that of an industry leader.

T   F   13.   When ratios of different years are being compared, inflation should be taken into consideration.

T   F   14.   Standard Corporation reported a gross profit margin of 28% in 2009. Parker Inc. reported a gross profit margin of 15% in 2009. It is safe to assume that Standard Corporation generated higher operating profits than Parker in 2009.

T   F   15.   The DuPont system of analysis merges a firm's income statement and balance sheet into a summary measure of profitability.

T   F   16.   Personal financial statements are necessary for the establishment and monitoring of your progress towards personal financial goals.

Multiple Choice

1. Carter Corporation has current assets of $120 million and inventory equal to $30 million. If Carter's current liabilities are $100 million, what will the current ratio be?
   a. 0.90
   b. 1.20
   c. 4
   d. 1.71

2. An increased debt position will be accompanied by _____ risk.
   a. undetermined
   b. unchanged
   c. less
   d. greater

3. _____ refers to the overall solvency of the firm—the ease with which it can pay its bills.
   a. Liquidity
   b. Turnover
   c. Leverage
   d. Coverage

4. Stanton Inc. reported annual sales of $400,000 in 1999. At year end the balance in accounts receivables was reported to be $10,000. What was the average collection period for Stanton based on a 360 day year?
   a. 2.5 days
   b. 40 days
   c. 4 days
   d. 9 days

5. _____ are used to measure the speed in which various accounts are converted into sales or cash.
   a. Liquidity ratios
   b. Activity ratios
   c. Debt ratios
   d. Profitability ratios

6. A company's fixed assets are termed its _____ assets.
   a. short-term
   b. earning
   c. financed
   d. equity

7. The _____ ratio measures the financial leverage of the firm.
   a. current
   b. times interest earned
   c. debt-equity
   d. acid test

For question 8, refer to the following information.

ABC Corporation	
Sales Revenue	XX%
Less: Cost of Goods Sold	XX%
Gross Profit Margin	25%

8. What will ABC's cost of goods sold be if expressed as a percentage of sales?
    a. 125%
    b. 25%
    c. 100%
    d. 75%

9. _____ is/are generally the least liquid current asset that a corporation possesses.
    a. Marketable securities
    b. Cash
    c. Inventory
    d. Accounts receivable

10. _____ involves comparing a firm to the industry leader or to an industry average.
    a. Coverage analysis
    b. Cross-sectional analysis
    c. DuPont analysis
    d. Time-series analysis

11. Inventory values and asset values can differ year to year due to
    a. inflation.
    b. increased cost of capital.
    c. recessions.
    d. depressions.

12. Net working capital is calculated as current assets minus
    a. inventory.
    b. cost of goods sold.
    c. fixed assets.
    d. current liabilities.

13. A firm with sales of $500,000, net profits after taxes of $20,000, total liabilities of $200,000, and stockholders' equity of $100,000 will have a return on equity of
    a. 5%.
    b. 20%.
    c. 10%.
    d. 40%.

14. The _____ ratio indicates the amount of money that investors are willing to pay for $1 of earnings.
    a. EPS
    b. times interest earned
    c. *P/E*
    d. earnings

15. The DuPont system of analysis allows firms to break down their return on equity down into all of the following components EXCEPT
    a. inventory usage.
    b. profit in sales.
    c. efficiency of asset usage.
    d. use of leverage.

16. Starbuck Corporation reported EPS of $2.30 for 2009. In 2009 Starbuck had earnings available to common stockholders of $1,380,000. How many outstanding shares of common stock did Starbuck have in 2009?
    a. 3,174,000
    b. 600,000
    c. 400,000
    d. 3,600,000

17. The _____ ratio measures the firm's ability to meet payment obligations such as loan interest and principal, and preferred stock dividends.
    a. times interest earned
    b. debt-equity
    c. current ratio
    d. fixed payment coverage

18. In the _____ income statement, each item is expressed as a percentage of sales.
    a. pro forma
    c. common-size
    b. second stage
    d. sales based

For questions 19 and 20, refer to the following information.

Reeves Enterprises			
Year Ended December 31, 2009			
Sales	$ 400,000	Stockholder's Equity	$200,000
Total Assets	1,000,000	Cost of Goods Sold	100,000
Total Liabilities	900,000	Net Profit After Taxes	70,000
EPS	4.3	Long-term Debt	400,000

19. What will Reeves' ROA be for 2009 under the DuPont system?
    a. 7%
    b. 10%
    c. 4%
    d. 14%

20. What will Reeves' ROE be for 2009 under the DuPont system?
    a. 14%
    b. 35%
    c. 18%
    d. 10%

21. What is the net worth of Carl and Carol Luedtke, a retired couple who live in their RV on rented property in Florida, have the following assets and liabilities.

Item	Amount
Checking account	$ 1600
Money market fund	$ 2200
Stocks	$ 22,000
Bonds	$ 19,000
2008 Nissan Altima	$ 23,000
2001 Winnebago RV	$134,000
Furnishings	$ 2,100
Jewelry	$250
Bank card balance	$880
Unpaid utility bill	$170
Auto loan	$ 26,000

    a. $20,100
    b. $43,100
    c. $177,100
    d. $231,200

22. Which of the following is not considered when calculating the personal liquidity ratio:
    a. annual mortgage payments
    b. bank card balances
    c. auto loan balances
    d. savings account balances

Essay

1. Explain why financial leverage is associated with risk.

2. List some of the precautions that should be taken when performing ratio analysis.

■ Chapter 2 Answer Sheet

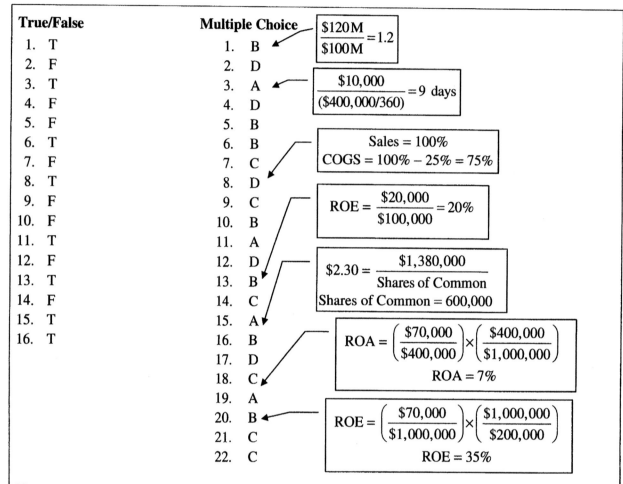

True/False

1. T
2. F
3. T
4. F
5. F
6. T
7. F
8. T
9. F
10. F
11. T
12. F
13. T
14. F
15. T
16. T

Multiple Choice

1. B
2. D
3. A
4. D
5. B
6. B
7. C
8. D
9. C
10. B
11. A
12. D
13. B
14. C
15. A
16. B
17. D
18. C
19. A
20. B
21. C
22. C

$$\frac{\$120M}{\$100M} = 1.2$$

$$\frac{\$10,000}{(\$400,000/360)} = 9 \text{ days}$$

Sales = 100%
COGS = 100% − 25% = 75%

$$ROE = \frac{\$20,000}{\$100,000} = 20\%$$

$$\$2.30 = \frac{\$1,380,000}{\text{Shares of Common}}$$
Shares of Common = 600,000

$$ROA = \left(\frac{\$70,000}{\$400,000}\right) \times \left(\frac{\$400,000}{\$1,000,000}\right)$$
$$ROA = 7\%$$

$$ROE = \left(\frac{\$70,000}{\$1,000,000}\right) \times \left(\frac{\$1,000,000}{\$200,000}\right)$$
$$ROE = 35\%$$

Essay

1. Financial leverage is a term that is used to describe the ratio of debt financing to the stockholders' equity. Debt financing is considered to carry a greater risk than equity financing because creditors must be satisfied before any earnings can be distributed to the stockholders. The larger the amount of debt to equity that a firm carries, the greater the chance that the common shareholders will not receive any of the firm's earnings. Because of this risk associated with debt financing, a firm that is heavily leveraged is considered to be risky.

2. a. Do not use a single ratio to judge the overall performance of the firm.
    b. The financial statements being compared should be dated at the same point of time during the year.
    c. Audited financial data should be used to ensure relevant financial information.
    d. The financial data being compared in the ratio analysis should be developed in the same manner.
    e. When performing time-series analysis, inflation should always be taken into account.

Chapter 3
Cash Flow and Financial Planning

■ Chapter Summary

Financial planning is an important part of every financial manager's job. By accurately projecting future cash surpluses and shortfalls, timely arrangements can be made. For example, bankers will look much more favorably on a loan request to fund a temporary cash need anticipated two months in the future than it will on a loan request for funds needed right now. Two methods are provided to compute the external funds needed by a firm.

Accurate financial planning is difficult because of the need to project uncertain future events. A developer may not need cash if his properties sell but may be in deep trouble if they do not. Financial planning under uncertainty is addressed in this chapter.

 Understand tax depreciation procedures and the effect of depreciation and on the firm's cash flows. Depreciation represents the systematic charging of a portion of the costs of fixed assets against annual revenues over time. A firm will often use different depreciation methods for financial reporting than for tax calculations. When estimating cash flows, depreciation and any other noncash charges are added back to operating profits. Under the MACRS procedure, the depreciable value of an asset is its full cost, including outlays for installation. No adjustment is required for expected salvage value. The MACRS procedures classify assets other than real estate into property classes based on recovery periods of 3, 5, 7, 10, 15, and 20 years. Each recovery period has a schedule of depreciation percentages for each year of the recovery period.

 Discuss the firm's statement of cash flows, operating cash flows, and free cash flows. The statement of cash flows summarizes the firm's cash flow over a given period of time. Managers must identify all corporate sources and uses of funds, and then classify these items as operating, investment, or financing cash flows. The statement of cash flows allows financial managers to analyze and explain the firm's sources and uses of cash over time.

 Understand the financial planning process, including long-term (strategic) financial plans and short-term (operating) plans. There are two key elements to the financial planning process, cash planning and profit planning. Cash planning involves preparation of the firm's cash budget. Financial planning begins with the preparation of a long-term strategic plan that guides the preparation of short-term operating plans.

 Discuss the cash-planning process and the preparation, evaluation, and use of the cash budget. The cash budget is a tool for forecasting the firm's cash flow in the future. The cash budget is even important to firms who have surplus cash because it will let them take advantage of higher returns on longer term investments. Cash budgets usually begin with a sales forecast. Projected disbursements are subtracted from the receipts to arrive at the ending cash balance. The cash balance is rolled forward from period to period. Once the cash budget has been prepared, it must be interpreted. Most cash budgets represent a best effort to project the future. But since it involves a projection, there will usually be an element of uncertainty. Some firms choose to compute best-case, most-likely, and worst-case scenarios. Others use computer simulation to deal with this uncertainty.

Explain the simplified procedures used to prepare and evaluate the pro forma income statement and the pro forma balance sheet. The judgment approach to pro forma balance sheet and income statement preparation involves estimating some account values and calculating others, thereby requiring a "plug" figure to bring the statement into balance. If a plug figure must be added to the right side of the balance sheet, additional external funds are needed.

Evaluate the simplified approaches to pro forma financial statement preparation and the common uses of pro forma statements. Pro forma statements are based on the assumption that the firm's past financial condition is an accurate indicator of its future and that certain variables, such as cash, accounts receivable, and inventories, can be forced to take on certain desired values. These assumptions may not always reflect the truth, and the financial manager must be careful to monitor the accuracy of the projections.

■ Chapter Notes

Depreciation

Business firms are allowed to systematically charge a portion of the costs of fixed assets against revenues. This is called depreciation. Depreciation lowers the tax base and is beneficial to corporations from a tax standpoint. Depreciation is computed using straight line or MACRS. To compute straight line depreciation, add together all costs associated with putting the asset into service, subtract the salvage value, and then divide by the expected life of the asset.

Depreciation for tax purposes is determined by the modified accelerated cost recovery system (MACRS).

Remember from chapter 1 that the financial manager is only concerned with cash flows rather than the operating profit that is reported in the income statement. To adjust the income statement to show cash flows from operation, all noncash charges must be added back to the firm's net profits. These noncash charges include depreciation, amortization, and depletion allowances.

Under the MACRS procedure, an asset is depreciated at its full cost, including outlays for installation. No adjustment for salvage value is needed.

Under MACRS, an asset's depreciable life is broken down into 6 property classes. The recovery periods are 3, 5, 7, 10, 15, and 20 years. Assets such as research equipment and specialty tools would fall into the 3-year recovery class. More expensive items such as buildings would fall into the 20-year recovery class.

Compute depreciation by multiplying the original asset value by the percentage listed for each year under the asset's class life. For example, if the asset has a 5 year class life and originally cost $10,000, the first year's depreciation is computed by multiplying $10,000 \times 0.20 = 2000$.

Cash flow

A firm's cash flow can be broken down into three divisions:
1. *Operating flows* are cash flows directly related to the production and sale of the firm's products.
2. *Investment flows* are cash flows associated with the purchase and selling of both fixed assets and business interest.
3. *Financing flows* result from the debt and equity financing transactions.

The statement of cash flows summarizes the sources and uses of cash for the firm. For example, an increase in accounts payable by $100 is a source of cash. An increase in a firm's inventory by $200 is a use of cash, since an additional $200 would be tied up in the firm's inventory.

The **statement of cash flows** can be developed in a five step process:

1. Calculate the changes in assets, liabilities, and stockholders' equity.
2. Determine if the change is a source or a use of funds.
3. Separately sum all the sources and uses of funds. If done correctly, these figures should be equal.
4. Net profit after taxes, depreciation and any other noncash charges, and dividends need to be determined. Depreciation and the other noncash charges can be then added to the net operating profit after taxes in the cash flows from operations, and the dividends can be taken out of the cash flows from financing activities.
5. The relevant data from steps 1, 2, 3 and 4 need to be broken down into cash flows from operating activities, investing activities, or financing activities. Once the five steps are completed, the cash flow statement can be prepared.

Uses and Sources of Funds Statement: To prepare the uses and sources of funds statement, evaluate each balance sheet line item to determine whether it is a source of cash or a use of cash. Sources and uses of cash are determined as follows:

Sources:

1. Decrease in an asset account, and/or
2. Increase in a liability account.

Uses:

1. Increase in an asset account, and/or
2. Decrease in a liability account.

Free cash flows represent the amount of cash flow available to investors—the providers of debt and equity—after the firm has met all operating needs and paid for investments in net fixed assets and net current assets.

Financial planning

Financial planning guides the actions of a firm toward the achievement of immediate and long-term goals. The financial planning process begins with long-term, or strategic, financial plans that in turn guide the formulation of short-term, or operating, plans and budgets.

Long-term (strategic) financial plans: Long-term financial plans are planned long-term financial actions and the anticipated financial impact of those actions. These plans tend to cover periods of 2- to 10-years and typically deal with such things as proposed fixed-asset outlays, research and development activities, and major sources of financing.

Short-term (operating) financial plans: Short-term financial plans are short-term financial actions and the anticipated financial impact of those actions. These plans tend to cover a 1- to 2-year period and are centered on key inputs, which include sales forecasts and various forms of operating and financial data, and key outputs, which include a number of operating budgets, the cash budget, and pro forma financial statements.

Cash planning: Cash budgets

The cash budget allows the firm to forecast its short-term cash requirements, typically over a year, divided into monthly intervals. In planning the cash budget, the firm pays particular attention to surplus cash and cash shortages.

Sales forecasts

The main component in the financial planning process and therefore any cash budget is the firm's sales forecast. Based on the sales forecast, the financial manager estimates the monthly cash flows that will result from projected sales receipts and from production-related, inventory-related, and sales-related outlays. The financial manager also determines the level of fixed assets required and the amount of financing needed to support the forecasted level of sales. The sales forecast may be based on an analysis of external or internal data or a combination of both.

External forecast: An external forecast is based on the relationship that can be observed between the firm's sales and certain key external economic indicators, such as the gross domestic product (GDP), new housing starts, and disposable personal income.

Internal forecast: Internal forecasts are based on a consensus of forecasts made by the firm's salespeople in the field.

Combined forecast: Firms most often use a combination of external and internal forecasts. The internal data provides insight into sales expenditures, and the external data provides a means of adjusting these expenditures to take into account general economic factors.

Preparing the cash budget

The general format for the cash budget is presented in the following table:

	Jan.	**Feb.**	**...**	**Nov.**	**Dec.**
Cash Receipts			...		
Less: Cash disbursements	___	___	...	___	___
Net cash flow			...		
Add: Beginning cash	___	___	...	___	___
Ending cash	↗	↗	... ↗	↗	
Less: Minimum cash balance	___	___	...	___	___
Required total financing			...		
Excess cash balance			...		

Cash receipts: These include all items from which cash inflows result in any given financial period. Examples are cash sales, collection of accounts receivable, and other cash receipts.

Cash disbursements: These include all outlays of cash in the period covered. Examples are cash purchases, payment of accounts payable, rent payments, and tax payments.

Net cash flow, ending cash, financing and excess cash: A firm's net cash flow is found by subtracting the cash disbursements from cash receipts in each period. By adding beginning cash to the firm's net cash, the ending cash for each period can be found. Finally, subtracting the desired minimum cash balance from ending cash yields the required total financing or the excess cash balance.

Evaluating the cash budget

The cash budget can determine whether an excess of cash or a shortage of cash will result in each period. Excess cash can be invested in marketable securities, and shortages of cash can be financed with short-term borrowing (notes payable).

In evaluating the cash budget, a level of uncertainty does exist. One way to cope with this uncertainty is for the financial manager to prepare a best-case forecast, a most-likely forecast, and a worst-case forecast. An evaluation of these cash flows allows the financial manager to determine the amount of financing necessary to cover the most adverse situations. A second way that a financial manager can cope with uncertainty when preparing a cash budget is to use computer simulation. By simulating the occurrences of sales, the firm can develop a probability distribution of its ending cash flows for each month.

Profit planning: Pro forma statement fundamentals

 Profit planning typically involves the preparation of a pro forma (projected) income statement and balance sheet. The two key inputs that are required for preparing pro forma statements are (1) the financial statements from the preceding year and (2) the sales forecast for the coming year.

Pro forma income statement

A simple method for developing a pro forma income statement is to use the percent-of-sales method. This method for preparing the pro forma income statement assumes that the relationship between expenses and sales in the coming year will be identical to those in the immediately preceding year.

Example

The following percent-of-sales figures were taken from Encore Inc.'s 2009 income statement:

$$\frac{\text{COGS}}{\text{Sales}} = 75\%$$

$$\frac{\text{Operating Expenses}}{\text{Sales}} = 15\%$$

$$\frac{\text{Interest Expense}}{\text{Sales}} = 2\%$$

Assuming the relationship between expenses and sales is the same for 2010 as for 2009, Encore's pro forma income statement for 2010 based on sales is as follows:

Sales revenue	$160,000
Less: Cost of goods sold (0.75)	120,000
Gross profits	$ 40,000
Less: Operating expenses (0.15)	24,000
Operating profits	$ 16,000
Less: Interest expense (0.02)	3,200
Net profit before taxes	$ 12,800
Less: Taxes (0.40 × 12,800)	5,120
Net profits after taxes	$ 7,680

A strict application of the percent-of-sales method assumes that all costs are variable. Nearly all firms have fixed costs, and ignoring this in the pro forma income statement usually results in the misstatement of the firm's forecast profit. It is advisable when using the percent-of-sales method to break down costs into fixed and variable components. Fixed costs do not vary with differing levels of sales and should be estimated by the financial manager based on upcoming capital expenditures and historic fixed costs.

Pro forma balance sheet

The most popular method for developing a pro forma balance sheet is the judgmental approach. This approach estimates the values of certain balance sheet accounts while calculating others and uses the firm's external financing as a balancing figure. A positive value for the balancing figure, which is stated on the balance sheet as "external funds required," indicates that the firm must raise external funds through debt and/or equity in order to support the firm's forecasted level of sales. If a negative value exists for external funds required, the firm's forecasted financing is in excess of its needs.

Evaluation of pro forma statements

 The percent-of-sales method and judgmental approach to pro forma preparation are popular because of their simplicity, but they do contain weaknesses.

The weakness of the simple pro forma approaches lies within two of their basic assumptions:

1. The firm's past financial condition is an accurate indicator of its future financial performance, and
2. certain variables, such as cash, accounts receivable, and inventories, can be forced to take on certain "desired" levels.

■ Sample Problems and Solutions

Example 1.   Cash Budgets

Prepare a cash budget for the first quarter for With-It Wonderwear Inc., given the following data.

Management has projected total and credit sales for the first three months of 2009 as follows:

Month	Year	Total Sales	Credit Sales
December	2008	$825,000	$770,000
January	2009	730,000	690,000
February	2009	840,000	780,000
March	2009	920,000	855,000

Based on historical data, 25% of the credit sales are collected in the month the sales were made, and 75% are collected the next month. Purchases are estimated to be 60% of the next month's total sales, but are paid for in the month following the order. This means that the expenditure for inventory in each month is 60% of that month's sales. The beginning and target cash balance is $100,000. Other disbursements are as follows:

Expense Item	January	February	March
Wages	$250,000	$290,000	$290,000
Rent	27,000	27,000	27,000
Other Expense	10,000	12,000	14,000
Taxes	105,000		
Dividends			40,000
Capital Expenditures		75,000	

Prepare your solution on the table on the next page:

	CASH BUDGET		
	January	**February**	**March**
SALES	730,000	840,000	920,000
Credit Sales	690,000	780,000	855,000
RECEIPTS			
Cash sales			
Collections			
Total Cash			
DISBURSEMENTS			
Payments of A/P			
Wages			
Rent			
Other Exp			
Taxes			
Dividends			
Cap Expense			
TOTAL EXPENSE			
Begin Cash			
CASH IN-OUT			
Ending Cash			
TARGET BALANCE			
LOAN REQUIRED			

Solution

CASH BUDGET

	January	February	March	
SALES	730,000	840,000	920,000	$730,000 - 690,000$
Credit Sales	690,000	780,000	855,000	
RECEIPTS				$(0.25 \times 690,000) +$
Cash sales	40,000	60,000	65,000	$(0.75 \times 770,000)$
Collections	750,000	712,500	798,750	
Total Cash	790,000	772,500	863,750	
DISBURSEMENTS				$0.60 \times 730,000$
Payments of A/P	438,000	504,000	552,000	
Wages	250,000	290,000	290,000	
Rent	27,000	27,000	27,000	
Other Exp	10,000	12,000	14,000	
Taxes	105,000			
Dividends			40,000	Total cash receipts –
Cap Expense		75,000		total expense
TOTAL EXPENSE	830,000	908,000	923,000	
Begin Cash	100,000	100,000	100,000	$(100,000 - 60,000)$
CASH IN-OUT	(40,000)	(135,500)	(59,250)	The amount needed
Ending Cash	60,000	(35,500)	40,750	to bring the balance
TARGET BALANCE	100,000	100,000	100,000	up to 100,000.
LOAN REQUIRED	(40,000)	(135,500)	(59,250)	

Note: Cash budgets tend to be varied due to the different types of projections available and the needs of the firm. The cash budget presented here is similar to, but not exactly like, the one presented in the text. You may have developed a still different model. The important concept is to estimate total cash receipts, and outflow and to determine how much additional cash will be required to reach the target cash balance.

Example 2.   Scenario Analysis

Joe Blow has invented a toe exerciser that he expects to sell by mail-order. He projects sales of $200,000 during each of the months of January, February, and March. His monthly purchases during this time will be $140,000; wages and salaries will be $20,000 per month; and a monthly rent of $5,000 must be paid. Taxes of $30,000 are due in January. A $25,000 payment for the purchase of capital equipment is due in February. All sales are for cash, and beginning cash balances are assumed to be zero. Joe wants to maintain a $5,000 minimum cash balance. While Joe is certain of all other figures, he is a little nervous about the accuracy of his sales forecast. He feels a pessimistic sales figure of $180,000 per month and an optimistic figure of $220,000 is accurate. What are the minimum and maximum cash balances the company can expect for each of the next three monthly periods?

Solution

Summary of Disbursements

	January	February	March
Purchases	$140,000	$140,000	$140,000
Wages	20,000	20,000	20,000
Rent	5,000	5,000	5,000
Taxes	30,000		
Capital Equipment		25,000	
Total Cash Disbursements	$195,000	$190,000	$165,000

	January			February			March		
Cash Flow	**Pessi-mistic**	**Most Likely**	**Opti-mistic**	**Pessi-mistic**	**Most Likely**	**Opti-mistic**	**Pessi-mistic**	**Most Likely**	**Opti-mistic**
Total Cash Receipts	$180	$200	$220	$180	$200	$220	$180	$200	$220
Less: Total Cash Disbursements	195	195	195	190	190	190	165	165	165
Net Cash Flow	($ 15)	$ 5	$ 25	($ 10)	$ 10	$ 30	$ 15	$ 35	$ 55
Add: Beginning Cash	0	0	0	($ 15)	$ 5	$ 25	($ 25)	$ 15	$ 55
Ending Cash	$(15)	$ 5	$ 25	($ 25)	$ 15	$ 55	($ 10)	$ 50	$110
Less: Minimum Cash Balance	5	5	5	5	5	5	5	5	5
Required Total Financing	$ 20			$ 30			$ 15		
Excess Cash Balance		$ 20			$ 10	$ 50		$ 45	$105

During January, Joe Blow will need a maximum of $20,000 of financing, while at best, he will have $20,000 available for short-term investment. During February, the firm's maximum financing requirement will be $30,000; however, it could experience a surplus between $10,000 and $50,000. The March projections reflect a borrowing requirement of $15,000, with a surplus between $45,000 and $105,000. By considering the extreme values reflected in the pessimistic and optimistic outcomes, Joe should be able to plan his cash requirements more accurately.

Example 3.   Pro forma financial statements

The Kiddy Car Driving School wishes to use the percent-of-sales shortcut method to prepare their 2009 pro forma financial statements. Use the operating statements below and the additional information given to prepare a pro forma income statement and balance sheet.

1.   The firm has estimated that its sales for 2009 will be $1,350,000.
2.   The firm expects to pay $52,000 in cash dividends in 2009.
3.   Taxes payable will equal 25% of the tax liability on the pro forma income statement.
4.   All assets and all current liabilities change as a percentage-of-sales.

The balance sheet and income statement needed to complete this problem appear on the next page.

Prepare your solution here.

Kiddy Car Driving School
Pro forma Income Statement
January 2009–December 2009

Net Revenues
Less Cost of Goods Sold
Gross Profit
Less: Operating Expenses
Profits Before Taxes
Less: Taxes (40%)
Net Profits After Taxes
Less: Cash Dividend
Increase in Retained Earnings

Kiddy Car Driving School
Pro forma Balance Sheet
December 31, 2009

Assets	Liabilities and Owners' Equity
Cash	Accounts Receivable
Marketable Securities	Taxes Payable
Accounts Receivable	Other Current Liabilities
Inventory	Total Current Liabilities
Total Current Assets	Long-term Debt
Net Fixed Assets	Common Stock
	Retained Earnings
Total Assets	Total Liabilities and Equity

Kiddy Car Driving School
Income Statement
January 2009–December 2009

Net Revenues	$1,200
Less Cost of Goods Sold	900
Gross Profit	300
Less: Operating Expenses	150
Profits Before Taxes	150
Less: Taxes (40%)	60
Net Profits After Taxes	90
Less: Cash Dividend	30
Increase in Retained Earnings	$ 60

Kiddy Car Driving School
Balance Sheet
December 31, 2009

Assets		Liabilities and Owners' Equity	
Cash	$ 48	Accounts Receivable	$156
Marketable Securities	36	Taxes Payable	15
Accounts Receivable	216	Other Current Liabilities	0
Inventory	144	Total Current Liabilities	171
Total Current Assets	444	Long-term Debt	300
Net Fixed Assets	540	Common Stock	225
		Retained Earnings	288
Total Assets	$984	Total Liabilities and Equity	$984

Solution

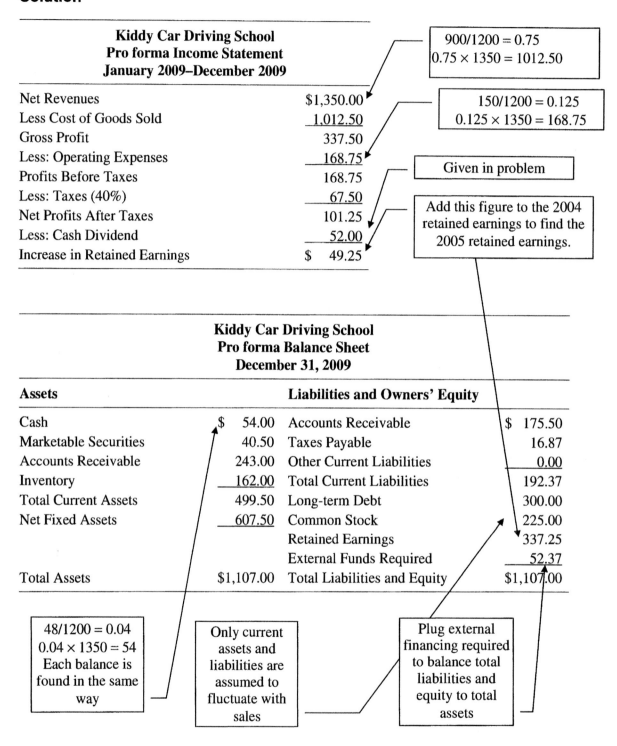

Based on the pro forma statements, the firm will have an external funding requirement of $52,375 to support its planned 2009 sales level.

■ Study Tips

1. Most instructors will emphasize the weaknesses of percentage-of-sales forecasting methods. Recognize that you are assuming that the firm's past financial condition is an accurate indicator of its future and that certain variables, such as cash, accounts receivable, and inventories, can be forced to take on certain desired values. The methods discussed in this chapter are only as valid as these assumptions. For established firms, they may be accurate. For newer, more volatile firms, they may not.

2. Cash budgets are projections about uncertain events. As such, even when the assumptions hold true, sales forecasts may be wrong. This is where scenario analysis becomes important. In more sophisticated models, probabilities will be assigned to various outcomes to aid in the selection of the right level of external financing. Still, in the final analysis, the manager's experience, intuition, and risk tolerance will play an important role in determining the borrowing level.

■ Student Notes

_____

_____

_____

_____

_____

■ Sample Exam—Chapter 3

True/False

T   F   1. The strategic financial plans are planned long-term financial actions and the anticipated financial impact of those actions.

T   F   2. Cash planning involves the preparation of the firm's income statement.

T   F   3. The sales forecast, cash budget, and pro forma financial statements are the key outputs of the short-run (operating) financial planning.

T   F   4. The excess cash balance is the amount available for investment by the firm if the desired minimum cash balance is less than the period's ending cash.

T   F   5. The cash budget gives the financial manager a clear view of the timing of the firm's expected profitability over a given period.

T F   6.   A firm's net cash flow is the mathematical difference between the firm's beginning cash and its cash disbursements in each period.

T F   7.   The financial planning process begins with short-run plans and budgets that in turn guide the formulation of long-run financial plans.

T F   8.   One weakness of the percent-of-sales method for developing pro forma income statements is that it assumes the past performance of the firm will be an indicator of future performance.

T F   9.   The financial manager may cope with uncertainty and make more intelligent short-term financial decisions by preparing several cash budgets, each based on differing assumptions.

T F 10.   If the net cash flow is less than the minimum cash balance, financing is required.

T F 11.   Due to the no-fixed-cost assumption in the percent-of-sales method, the use of cost and expense ratios generally tends to understate profits when sales are increasing and overstate profits when sales are decreasing.

T F 12.   A positive external funds requirement would indicate that the firm's financing is in excess of its needs and that funds would therefore be available for repaying debt, repurchasing stock, or increasing the dividend to stockholders.

T F 13.   The pro forma statements provide the financial manager with the amount of external financing required to support a given level of sales, as well as a basis for analyzing in advance the level of profitability and overall financial performance of the firm in the coming year.

T F 14.   One basic weakness of the judgmental approach to developing pro forma balance sheets lies in the assumption that certain variables, such as cash, accounts receivable, and inventories, can be forced to take on certain "desired" values.

T F 15.   The "plug" figure that is used as a balancing account in the pro forma balance sheet is retained earnings.

Multiple Choice

1. The financial planning process begins with _____ financial plans that in turn guide the formation of _____ plans and budgets.
   a. long-run; operating
   b. strategic; operating
   c. short-run; long-run
   d. long-run; short-run

2. The key aspects of the financial planning process are
   a. investment planning and profit planning.
   b. cash planning and financing.
   c. cash planning and investment planning.
   d. cash planning and profit planning.

3. Pro forma statements are used for
   a. profit planning.
   b. credit analysis.
   c. cash budgeting.
   d. all of the above.

4. Which of the following would be the least likely to utilize pro forma financial statements or a cash budget?
   a. top management
   b. middle management
   c. investors
   d. lenders

5. The _____ is a financial projection of the firm's short-term cash surpluses or shortages.
   a. operating plan
   b. cash budget
   c. strategic plan
   d. pro forma income statement

6. _____ forecast is based on the relationship between the firm's sales and certain economic indicators.
   a. A sales
   b. An internal
   c. A pro forma
   d. An external

7. Key inputs to short-term financial planning are
   a. leverage analysis.
   b. economic forecasts.
   c. sales forecasts; operating and financial data.
   d. financial budgets.

8. The key input to any cash budget is the
   a. sales forecast.
   b. current economic outlook.
   c. operating plan.
   d. pro forma income statement.

9. _____ forecast is based on a buildup of sales forecasts through the firm's own sales channels, adjusted for additional factors such as production capabilities.
   a. An external
   b. A pro forma
   c. An internal
   d. A sales

10. The firm's final sales forecast is usually a function of
    a. external indicators.
    b. both internal and external factors.
    c. internal forecast.
    d. top management's estimates.

11. Of the following, generally the easiest to estimate are
    a. cash sales.
    b. cash disbursements.
    c. cash receipts.
    d. short-term borrowings.

12. A projected excess cash balance for the month may be invested in
    a. marketable securities.
    b. junk bonds.
    c. long-term securities.
    d. secured bonds.

13. The percent-of-sales method of preparing the pro forma income statement assumes that all costs are
    a. fixed.
    b. independent.
    c. constant.
    d. variable.

14. All of the following accounts are used in the preparation of the cash budget EXCEPT
    a. cash receipts.
    b. depreciation.
    c. cash disbursements.
    d. excess cash.

15. If the firm expects short-term cash surpluses it can plan
    a. short-term investments.
    b. leverage decisions.
    c. long-term investments.
    d. short-term borrowing.

16. The _____ method of developing a pro forma balance sheet estimates values of certain balance sheet accounts, while others are calculated.
    a. accrual
    b. percent-of-sales
    c. judgmental
    d. cash

17. _____ generally reflects the anticipated financial impact of long-term actions.
    a.   An operating financial plan
    b.   A strategic financial plan
    c.   A pro forma income statement
    d.   A cash budget

18. The primary purpose in preparing a budget is
    a.   for profit planning.
    b.   for risk analysis.
    c.   to estimate sales.
    d.   for cash planning.

19. Generally, firms that are subject to a high degree of _____, relatively short production cycles, or both, tend to use shorter planning horizons.
    a.   financial planning
    b.   profitability
    c.   financial uncertainty
    d.   operating uncertainty

20. All of the following are key economic indicators EXCEPT
    a.   internal sales forecast.
    b.   disposable personal income.
    c.   GNP.
    d.   new housing starts.

21. Kein anticipates take-home pay of $2,750 in each of the next three months, plus a dividend of $75 in the second month. His primary expenses are housing at $556 per month and food which averages $345 per month. Other expenses are expected to be $1,045 per month. He anticipates spending $2,400 on a new plasma television in the 3rd month. What is his cash surplus (or deficit) in the second month?
    a. $729
    b. $879
    c. $1,705
    d. $1,780

22. Going back to the prior question, what is the cumulative cash surplus (or deficit) over the three months?
    a. $ 87
    b. $237
    c. $2,412
    d. $2,487

23. Which of the following is not correct about personal goals?:
    a. Personal goals should be clearly defined.
    b. Personal goals should have a priority.
    c. Personal goals should be the same throughout one's life.
    d. Personal goals should include a cost estimate.

Essay

1. Discuss the purpose of spending so much time and energy preparing cash budgets and pro forma financial statements. Is this effort well spent even in firms that have an obvious cash surplus?

2. Discuss the weaknesses of the simplified approaches to preparing pro forma financial statements.

■ Chapter 3 Answer Sheet

True/False		Multiple Choice	
1.	T	1.	D
2.	F	2.	D
3.	F	3.	D
4.	T	4.	C
5.	F	5.	B
6.	F	6.	D
7.	F	7.	C
8.	T	8.	A
9.	T	9.	C
10.	F	10.	B
11.	T	11.	C
12.	F	12.	A
13.	T	13.	D
14.	T	14.	B
15.	F	15.	A
		16.	C
		17.	B
		18.	D
		19.	D
		20.	A
		21.	B
		22.	A
		23.	C

Essay

1. Cash budgets and pro forma statements allow the financial manager to anticipate the need for funds well in advance. By having prior warning of an impending problem, actions can be taken to deal with it. For example, short-term lines of credit can be established. Additional equity can be sold, or the firm can choose a more moderate level of growth. Even in firms that have cash surpluses, cash budgeting is important. By determining how long funds can be invested, the financial manager can take advantage of the higher returns usually available on long-term securities.

2. The basic weakness of the simplified approaches relates to the underlying assumptions. The financial manager assumes that the past is a relevant and accurate predictor of the future. Additionally, because the financial manager must make projections, there is the risk that desired rather than real projections will be used.

Chapter 4
Time Value of Money

■ Chapter Summary

Without question, this is the most important chapter in the text. Not because the concepts are necessarily more important than those presented in other chapters, though they are fundamental to all of finance, but because most of the rest of the text will use the methods developed here. If you fail to really internalize this material, you will have a very difficult time with the rest of the course. On the other hand, by studying this chapter carefully, you will find that finance is both interesting and understandable. Because of the importance of this material, the study guide has more examples and practice problems than usual. **Do them all!**

 Discuss the role of time value in finance, the use of computational aids and the basic patterns of cash flows. The timing of cash flows must be considered because financial managers make decisions that affect cash flows that will occur over many years. A dollar received today is worth more than a dollar received tomorrow if for no other reason than because it could be invested. There are several tools available to help with time value calculations, including tables, calculators, and built-in functions on spreadsheet programs.

 Understand the concepts of future value and present value, their calculation for a single amount, and the relationship between them. Future values are amounts that will accrue by letting a sum of money earn income over time. The longer a balance is allowed to earn, the greater will be the future value. Compound interest is interest that is earned on interest. The more frequently the balance is compounded, the higher the effective interest rate. The concept of present value involves discounting future cash flows back to the present to determine what you would be willing to pay today for the right to receive the future cash flow. Present values are used extensively in business to analyze business opportunities and investments.

 Find the future value and the present value of both an ordinary annuity and an annuity due, and find the present value of a perpetuity. An annuity is a stream of payments where each payment is exactly alike and where the payments occur at exactly the same interval. For example, if you win the lottery, the 20 annual payments you receive is an annuity. The payments do not have to occur annually. An annuity can have payments received monthly, weekly, or even daily. Because annuities occur so often in business, there are time-saving techniques to finding their value.

 Calculate both the future value and the present value of a mixed stream of cash flows. A mixed stream of cash flows is one where the amounts to be received vary each period as opposed to an annuity where the cash flows are equal across periods. There is often a need to find the present value or future value of a stream of cash flows that varies. For example, a business opportunity may involve one stream of cash flows for the first five years and a different stream during the next ten years. When valuing assets, we will use the present value methodologies.

Understand the effect that compounding interest more frequently than annually has on future value and on the effective annual rate of interest. We frequently need to work with cash flows that are received more frequently than once per year or are paid more frequently than once per year. For example savings institutions compound interest monthly, daily or even continuously.

 Describe the procedures involved in (1) determining deposits needed to accumulate a future sum, (2) loan amortization, and (3) finding interest or growth rates (4) finding an unknown number of period. Another application of the time value of money is to determine how much must be set aside to accumulate some future balance. For example, suppose that you have determined that you will need $1 million to retire. If you have 20 years until retirement, you would need to know how much must be put into your retirement account each year to reach your retirement goal.

■ Chapter Notes

Time value of money

 Recall from Chapter 1 that the financial manager must make decisions based on cash flows. Because a firm can make positive returns on these cash flows, the financial manager must take into consideration the time value of money. There are two common views in which a financial manager can measure the time value of money: future value and present value.

1. Future value techniques are used to find future values which are measured at the end of a project's life. The future value technique uses compounding to find the future value of each cash flow at the end of the investment's life and then sums them to find the future value of the project.

2. Present value techniques are used to find present values which are measured at the beginning of a project's life. The present value technique uses discounting to find the present value of each cash flow at time zero and then sums them to find the investment's present value.

Computational aids

The calculation of future and present value is aided by the use of financial tables and calculators. There are financial tables at the end of this handbook as well as in the textbook. These tables contain factors that simplify the arithmetic involved in the calculations.

Financial calculators are an alternative to financial tables. There are a variety of inexpensive and very powerful calculators available and they are highly recommended. The Financial Calculator section of this handbook provides some tips on the use of the more popular models.

Personal computers using spreadsheet programs can also perform TVM calculations.

Future value of a single amount

 The future value of a present amount is found by applying compounded interest over a specified period of time.

Example

If Tom places $100 into a savings account that earns 6% interest compounded annually, at the end of year 1 he will have $100 in principal and $6 in interest for a total of $106.

$$FV \text{ at end of year } 1 = \$100 \times (1 + 0.06) = \$106$$

If Tom leaves the $106 in the account for another year, the principal plus the interest earned in year 1 will be compounded for an additional year. The new amount at the end of year 2 will be $112.36.

$$FV \text{ at end of year } 2 = \$106 \times (1 + 0.06) = \$112.36$$

The $112.36 is the future value of $100 compounded annually at 6% for 2 years.

The calculation of future values can be simplified in several ways.

1. To avoid compounding interest at each year's end, the following equation can be used to find the future value for a single amount of money, over any number of periods.

$$FV_n = PV \times (1 + r)^n$$

where:

FV_n = the future value at the end of period

PV = initial principal, or present value

r = the annual rate of interest paid

n = the number of periods, typically years

Using the previous example, the future value for $100 compounded annually at 6% for 2 years can be found by:

$$FV_n = \$100 \times (1 + 0.06)^2$$
$$FV_n = \$112.36$$

2. Future value interest tables provide a pre-calculated future value interest factor (FVIF). The FVIF is simply the $(1 + r)^n$ portion of the future value formula.

Nominal and effective annual rates of interest

The nominal rate of interest is the contractual or stated interest rate. The effective annual rate reflects the impact of compounding. The following formula converts the nominal rate (r) to its effective rate with m compounding periods per year.

$$EAR = \left(1 + \frac{r}{m}\right)^m - 1$$

3. Financial calculators are available today at very reasonable prices and can ease solving many types of time value problems. It is best to begin by learning to solve the problems using the equations, then to progress to using the calculator. By using the formulas, you learn to adjust for nonannual compounding and other issues that will surface later in the chapter. These issues do not disappear when you begin using a calculator.

A financial calculator is distinguished by a row of buttons that correspond to the inputs to TVM problems.

where:

N = the number of periods

I = the interest rate per period

PV = the present value or the initial deposit

MT = the payment (this button is used only when there is more than one equal payment)

FV = the future value

These buttons appear either on the face of the calculator or on the calculator's screen.

There are a few common errors students make when using financial calculators. First, be sure that the number of compounding periods is set correctly. The default is usually 12 periods per year. If the number of periods is set to 12 periods per year, the calculator divides the interest rate by 12 before performing calculations. Most new calculators are preprogrammed to divide the interest rate by 12. Additionally, whenever the batteries are replaced the calculator will revert to dividing by 12. (Check your calculator now and set it to one period per year. Refer to your owner's manual.)[3]

Using the previous example, the future value for $100 compounded annually at 6% for 2 years can be found using the calculator by:

$$N = 2$$
$$I = 6$$
$$PV = 100$$
$$PMT = 0$$
$$\text{CPT } FV = \$112.36$$

Example: What is the effective annual rate if the nominal rate is 12% and deposits are compounded monthly?

Solution

$$EAR = \left(1 + \frac{0.12}{12}\right)^{12} - 1$$

$$EAR = 0.1268 = 12.68\%$$

Future value of an annuity

An annuity is a stream of equal cash flows. The two basic types of annuities are the ordinary annuity and the annuity due. With an ordinary annuity, payments occur at the end of each period, and with an annuity due, payments occur at the beginning of each period.

The future value of an annuity can be found by summing the future value of each year's cash flow. It is important to remember that with an ordinary annuity, payment is made at the end of the period, so in the last period no interest will be received.

---

[3]To check the number of periods on the TI BA-II plus press the 2nd key and then the I/Y button. Your calculator should display P/Y = 1.00. If not, enter 1 on the keypad and press Enter.

To simplify the future value of an ordinary annuity calculation, a pre-calculated future value interest factor for an annuity is provided. The $FVIFA_{r,n}$, when interest is compounded annually at r percent for n periods is multiplied by the amount to be deposited annually at the end of each year. This will give the future value of an annuity.

$$FVA_n = PMT \times FVIFA_{r,n}$$

where:

FVA_n = the future value of the annuity at the end of period n

PMT = the amount to be deposited annually at the end of each year

The payments for an annuity due are received at the beginning of each period. Because of this, the equation for finding the future value of an annuity must be converted to work for the future value of an annuity due. The $FVIFA_{r,n}$ is converted for an annuity due as follows:

$$FVIFA_{k,n} \text{ (annuity due)} = FVIFA_{r,n} \times (1 + r)$$

The $FVIFA_{k,n}$ for an annuity due can then be plugged into the future value of an annuity calculation.

Ordinary annuity versus annuity due

When payments fall at the end of each period, we have an ordinary annuity. If the payments fall at the beginning of the period, we have an annuity due. To solve annuity due problems, compute the *FV* or *PV* as you would for an ordinary annuity, then multiply the result by $(1 + r)$.

Perpetuity

A perpetuity is an annuity that never stops providing its holder with payment dollars at the end of each year. The present value interest factor used in determining the present value of a perpetuity is stated as:

$$PVIFA_{r,\infty} = \frac{1}{k}$$

Thus, to find the present value of a stream of payments that goes on forever, simply divide the payment amount by the interest rate.

$$PV_{perpetuity} = \frac{\text{Payment}}{r}$$

For example, the present value of a stream of payments of \$2 that will go on forever, assuming a 10% interest rate is \$2/0.1 = \$20.

Present value of a single amount

The present value of a single amount is found by discounting each year's cash flows back to time zero. The process of discounting is simply the inverse of compounding interest. The application of discounting is concerned with answering the question, "If I am earning r percent on my money, what will I be willing to pay today, in year zero, for the opportunity to receive FV_n dollars n periods from now?"

The equation for finding the present value of a single amount can be stated as:

$$PV = \frac{FV_n}{(1+r)^n} = FV \times \left[\frac{1}{(1+r)^n}\right]$$

Example

Harry wishes to find the present value of $500 that will be received 5 years from now. Harry is earning 10% on his money. What is the most that Harry is willing to pay today to receive the $500 five years from now?

1. **Equation Solution**

$$PV = \$500 \times \left[\frac{1}{(1+0.10)^5} \right]$$

$$PV = \$310.46$$

To simplify the present value calculation, a present value interest factor is provided. The $\text{PVIF}_{r,n}$, where cash flows are discounted annually at r percent for n periods, is simply the $\frac{1}{(1+r)^n}$ part of the present value equation.

$$PV = FV_n \times \text{PVIF}_{r,n}$$

2. **Calculator Solution**

$N = 5$

$I = 10$

$FV = 500$

$\text{CPT } PV = \$310.46$

Present value of an annuity

An annuity is a stream of equal payments that arrive at equal intervals. The present value of an annuity is found by multiplying the cash flow amount by the present value interest factor of an annuity.

$$PV = \text{PMT} \times \text{PVIFA}_{r,n}$$

Present value of cash flow streams

There are two possible types of cash flow streams. A mixed stream of cash flows reflects no pattern year after year. An annuity, as defined earlier, is a stream of equal cash flows.

The present value for a mixed stream of cash flows can be found by finding the present value of each future amount, and then summing them to find the present value of the investment.

The present value for an annuity can be found as described in the earlier section for finding the present value of an ordinary annuity.

Sometimes an annuity will be embedded within a mixed stream of cash flows. The following process will determine the present value of a mixed stream of cash flows with an embedded annuity.

1. Find the present value of the annuity by using the equation for finding the present value of an ordinary annuity.

2. Add the present value calculated in Step 1 to the cash flow immediately preceding the start of that annuity. Eliminate the annuity's cash flows to determine the revised cash flows.

3. Discount the revised cash flows back to time zero in the normal fashion.

Example

Texas Oil expects an investment to provide the following cash flows. Texas Oil requires a 10% return on its investments. What will be the present value of the investment?

		Step 1	Step 2		Step 3
			Revised Cash Flow		Present Value
Year (n)	Cash Flow	PV of Annuity	[(2) + (3)]	$PVIF_{10\%,n}$	[(4) × (5)]
(1)	(2)	(3)	(4)	(5)	(6)
1	$2,000	$7,461	$9,461	0.909	$8,600.05
2	3,000⎤	⇑	0	0.826	0
3	3,000⎮ ⟶ $PVIFA_{10\%,3}$		0	0.751	0
4	3,000⎦ ×2.487		0	0.683	0
5	1,000		1,000	0.621	621.00
			Present value of mixed stream		$9,221.05

The present value of the mixed stream of cash flows with an embedded annuity is $9,221.05.

Sometimes savings institutions compound interest more frequently than annually. If this is the case, the future value formula can be restated as:

$$FV_n = PV \times \left(1 + \frac{r}{m}\right)^{m \times n}$$

where: m = number of times per year interest is compounded

Referring to the preceding example, Tom's $100 compounded quarterly at 6% for 2 years will now be worth $112.65.

$$FV_n = \$100 \times \left(1 + \frac{0.06}{4}\right)^{4 \times 2}$$

$$FV_n = \$112.65$$

Occasionally interest is compounded continuously. The $FVIF_{r,n}$ used in the continuous compounding formula is found by:

$$FVIF_{k,n} \text{ (continuous compounding)} = e^{r \times n}$$

where: e = the exponential function which has a value of 2.7183

To compare loan costs or investment returns over different compounding periods, nominal and effective interest rates must be distinguished.

Special Applications of Time Value

There are three special applications of time value that are introduced in Chapter 5.

1. **Payments to Accumulate a Future Balance:** Often it is necessary to calculate the annual deposits needed to accumulate a certain amount of money n periods from now. The equation that makes it possible to find the necessary deposits is an alteration of the equation used to find the future value of an annuity.

$$FVA_n = PMT \times FVIFA_{r,n}$$

To find the necessary deposits, simply solve the equation to determine payments.

$$PMT = \frac{FVA_n}{FVIFA_{r,n}}$$

Example

You want to save the down payment for a house. If you need to accumulate $10,000 over the next 5 years, how much must you save every year?

$$PMT = \frac{\$10,000}{FVIFA_{5yrs,10\%}} = \frac{\$10,000}{6.105} = \$1,638.00$$

2. **Loan Amortization:** The term *loan amortization* refers to the determination of the equal annual loan payments necessary to provide a lender with a specified interest return and repay the loan principal over a specified period. To find loan payments, use the present value of an annuity formula and rearrange the terms.

$$PVA_n = PMT \times (PVIFA_{r,n})$$
$$PMT = \frac{PVA_n}{PVIFA_{r,n}}$$

Example

What is the annual payment due on a $10,000 loan repayable with annual payments over 10 years if interest is 10%?

$$PMT = \$10,000/PVIFA_{10\%,10yrs} = \$10,000/6.145 = \$1,627.34$$

3. **Interest Growth Rates:** It is often necessary to calculate the annual rate of growth exhibited by a stream of cash flows. For example, you may want to know the annual compounded rate of growth in the dividends paid by a firm. To do this, use only the **first and last** cash flows. Ignore all the cash flows in the middle. Determine how many periods there were when growth could occur, then use the present value equation to solve for the interest rate that will equate the present value with the future value.

Example

Assume that the dividend for Bogus Corp. was $2.00 in 2003, $2.25 in 2004, $2.35 in 2005, $1.90 in 2006, $2.00 in 2007, and $2.50 in 2008. What was the annual compounded growth rate of the dividends?

Remember to ignore all but the first and last cash flow. Thus the *PV* will be $2.00 and the *FV* will be $2.50. Then count the *intervals* over which the cash flow could grow. In this example the dividend could grow between 2003 and 2004, between 2004 and 2005, between 2005 and 2006, between 2006 and 2007, and between 2007 and 2008, which is 5 growth periods.

$$PV = FV(PVIF_{5yrs,g})$$
$$\$2 = \$2.5(PVIF_{5yr,g})$$
$$\$2/\$2.5 = 0.8 = PVIF_{5yr,g}$$

Now look up the factor in the table by finding the factor closest to 0.8 on the row across from the 5 periods. The value (0.8) falls between 4% and 5%, so estimate the growth rate as 4.5%.

4. **Rule of 72:** A useful rule of thumb to estimate how long it will take a deposit to double is to divide 72 by the interest rate. For example, it takes about 7 years for a deposit to double at 10% (72/0.10 = 7.2 years).

■ Sample Problems and Solutions

1. Future Value (Compounding)

$$FV_n = PV\,(1+r)^n$$

Example 1.   You deposit $150 in the bank and leave it for 5 years at an annual rate of 6%. Interest is paid annually. How much will be in your account at the end of the 5th year?

a. Equation Solution
Using the above equation, $\$150(1.06)^5 = \$200.73$.

b. Calculator Solution
Using the calculator,

$N = 5$

$I = 6$

$PV = 150$

CPT $FV = \$200.73$

Example 2.   When you were 2-years old, your grandmother left you a trust fund with $10,000 in it that has been earning 12% for 20 years. How much is in the fund now (assume annual compounding)?

a. Equation Solution
$\$10,000(1.12)^{20} = \$96,462.93$

b. Calculator Solution

$N = 20$

$I = 12$

$PV = 10,000$

CPT $FV = \$96,462.93$

Example 3.   Now assume that instead of annual compounding, the bank pays interest to you semi-annually (twice per year). Up until now we have assumed that n referred to the number of years. Actually it refers to the number of *periods*. If you have $100 on deposit, what is it worth at the end of 3 years if the annual interest rate is 12%?

a. Equation Solution
Convert the interest rate to the rate that will be earned during one period. Since each period is 1/2 of a year, then the interest rate must be 1/2 of the annual rate = 0.12/2 = 0.06. Next, determine how many periods there are. Since there are 2 periods per year and 3 years, there are 6 periods. The solution is $\$100(1.06)^6 = \$141.85$.

The formula for compounding more than once per year is:

$$FV = PV\left(1 + \frac{r}{m}\right)m \times n$$

where: m = the number of times per year you compound

b. Calculator Solution

$N = 6$

$I = 6$

$PV = 100$

$CPT\ FV = \$141.85$

Example 4. If the bank pays interest quarterly?

a. Equation Solution

$\$100(1.03)^{12} = \$142.58$

b. Calculator Solution

$N = 12$

$I = 3$

$PV = 100$

$CPT\ FV = \$142.58$

Example 5. If the bank pays interest monthly?

a. Equation Solution

$\$100(1.01)^{36} = \$143.08$

Notice that the ending balance increases as the number of compounding periods per year increases.

b. Calculator Solution

$N = 36$

$I = 1$

$PV = 100$

CPT $FV = \$143.08$

Example 6. *Using the tables:* In the back of the book are *FV* tables that simplify calculations. Repeat the Examples 1 and 2 above using the tables.

Solution   Below is an example of how to use a Future Value table. The value of $1 at 5 periods from now at 6% interest is highlighted.

Period (*n*)	4%	5%	6%
4	1.170	1.216	1.262
5	1.217	1.276	1.338
6	1.265	1.340	1.419

$\$150(1.338) = \$200.70$

2. Future Value of an Annuity

Frequently we are interested in computing how much a series of equal deposits will be worth in the future. For example, say you belong to a retirement program at your work where $1,000 is deposited on your behalf every year. You may want to know how much of a retirement this will provide. You could compute the future value by simply computing the future value of each deposit separately, then adding them all together. While this method can be extended to any number of periods, it becomes tedious after a while. The following formula is for computing the future value of an annuity.

$$FV \text{ of Annuity} = PMT \sum_{t=1}^{n}(1+r)^{t-1} = PMT\left(FVIFA_{r,n}\right)$$

These values have been computed for you in the tables in your book for various interest rates and time periods. These tables make finding any future value of an annuity easy and quick.

Example 1. Use the table to compute the future value of $1,000 put into a retirement account for 15 years that earns 10% per year.

a. Table Solution

$FV = \$1,000(FVIFA_{15yr,10\%}) = \$1,000(31.772) = \$31,772.00$

b. Calculator Solution

$PMT = 1,000$

$N = 15$

$I = 10$

$CPT\ FV = \$31,772.48$

Example 2. You make investments of $100 per month for 2 years. If you earn an average of 12% per year, assuming monthly compounding, how much will your investment be worth?

a. Table Solution

$FV = \$100(FVIFA_{24 \text{ periods, } 1\%}) = \$100(26.973) = \$2697.30$

b. Calculator Solution

$PMT = 100$

$N = 24$

$I = 1$

$CPT\ FV = \$2,697.35$

Example 3. Suppose that over the next 5 years you want to accumulate $45,000 to buy a used Porsche 911. How much must you deposit every year if you can earn 10% per year?

a. Table Solution

$FV = PMT(FVIFA)$

The FV must be $45,000, the future value interest factor for an annuity is

$FVIFA_{5yrs,10\%} = 6.105$

so $\$45,000 = PMT(6.105)$

$PMT = 7,371.01$

b. **Calculator Solution**

$FV = 45,000$

$N = 5$

$I = 10$

CPT PMT $= \$7,370.89$

3. **Present Value**

In earlier work we recognized that because of compound interest income money grows over time. If money grows over time, we would rather have a fixed amount now than that same fixed amount at some time in the future. This is because we can invest the money if we get it now and it will be worth more in the future. But suppose we can't get the money now and instead have to wait until the future before we get paid. That future payment is not worth as much to us as it would be had it been paid now. This is the concept behind present value. The present value calculation lets us determine how much a sum received in the future is worth today.

Example 1. Compute the present value of $1,000 to be received in 1 year if interest rates are 10%.

a. **Equation Solution**

$PV = FV/(1 + k)$

$PV = \$1,000/(1.1) = \$909.09$

b. **Calculator Solution**

$N = 1$

$I = 10$

$FV = 1,000$

CPT $PV = \$909.09$

Example 2. Compute the present value of $1500 to be received in 5 years if interest rates are 12%.

a. **Equation Solution**

$PV = \$1,500/(1.12)^5 = \$851.14$

b. **Calculator Solution**

$N = 5$

$I = 12$

$FV = 1,500$

CPT $PV = \$851.14$

Example 3. You get your taxes done at H&R Block and find that you are due a refund of $1,000. Suppose that the refund won't be paid by the IRS for exactly two months. If you feel that you can earn 12% on your money, how much does H&R Block have to offer you now for your future payment of $1,000?

a. **Equation Solution**

$PV = \$1,000/(1.01)^2 = \$980.30$

Since the payment will be received in 2 months, a monthly rate of interest must be used. Twelve percent per year converts to 1% per month. Since 2 months will pass, the exponent will be 2. The interpretation of the answer is that you will be satisfied if H&R Block offers $980.30 or more for an assignment of your refund.

b. Calculator Solution

$N = 2$

$I = 1$

$FV = 1,000$

CPT $PV = \$980.30$

Example 4. Your aunt dies and leaves you $100,000 to be delivered in 5 years. An attorney offers you $60,000 for an assignment of the trust. If your required rate of return is 12%, should you agree to the deal?

a. Equation & Table Solutions

$PV = \$100,000(\text{PVIF}_{5yrs,0.12}) = \$100,000(0.5674) = \$56,740$ or

$PV = \$100,000/(1.12)^5 = \$56,742.69$

Both methods of solving this problem are shown here. If you had $56,742.69 today, it could be invested so that at the end of 5 years you would have $100,000. If you had the $60,000 that the attorney was offering and invested it, you would have more than $100,000 at the end of 5 years. Take the offer.

b. Calculator Solution

$N = 5$

$I = 12$

$FV = 100,000$

CPT $PV = \$56,742.69$

Example 5. If multiple cash flows that arrive at different times are to be evaluated, compute the PV of each one separately and then add them together. For example, suppose you win a scholarship that pays $2,000 at the end of the first year, $2,500 at the end of the second year, and $3,000 at the end of the third year. What is the value of this scholarship if your required rate of return is 8%?

a. Equation Solution

$PV_{\$2,000} = \$2,000/(1.08) = \$1,851.85$

$PV_{\$2,500} = \$2,500/(1.08)^2 = \$2,143.35$

$PV_{\$3,000} = \$3,000/(1.08)^3 = \$2,381.50$

$PV_{all} = \$1,851.85 + \$2,143.35 + \$2,381.50 = \$6,376.70$

b. Calculator Solution

$PV = \$1,851.85$

$PV = \$2,143.35$

$PV = \$2,381.50$

$PV_{all} = \$6,376.70$

4. Present Value of an Annuity

An annuity is a stream of equal payments. Note that these payments do not have to be received annually. Twelve monthly payments of $100 is an annuity. In the last section we computed the present value of a stream of payments that were unequal. The PV of a stream of equal payments could be computed the same way, but as the number of payments increases, this becomes tedious. A short cut is to use formulas that compute the PV of annuities. The formula is

$PVA = PMT(\text{PVIFA}_{r,n})$.

Example 1. Compute the PV of a retirement benefit that pays $1500 per year for 20 years if your required rate of return is 12%.

a. **Table Solution**

$$PVA = \$1,500(PVIFA_{20yrs,12\%}) = \$1,500(7.4694) = \$11,204.10$$

b. **Calculator Solution**

$PMT = 1,500$

$N = 20$

$I = 12$

CPT $PV = \$11,204.17$

Example 2. A more difficult problem is where there is a delay before the annuity begins. For example, suppose the above 20 year annuity of $1,500 did not begin until the end of the 5th year. To solve problems like this, first find the PVA. Then, treat that PV at time 5 as if it were a lump sum and find its PV at time 0. Find the PV if the payment stream in part **c** did not begin for 5 years.

a. **Table Solution**

$$PVA_5 = \$1,500(PVIFA_{20yrs,12\%}) = \$1,500(7.4694) = \$11,204.10$$
$$PVA_0 = \$11,204.10\ (PVIF_{4yrs,12\%}) = \$11,204.10\ (0.6355) = \$7,008.16$$

In the first step, the present value of the annuity at the end of the 4th year is calculated. The second step discounts this sum back to time zero. This problem demonstrates one of the most difficult aspects of TVM calculations—keeping track of the timing of the cash flows. If the cash flows begin at the end of the 5th period, the present value of the annuity calculation will find the present value as of the end of the 4th period. The annuity equation discounts the annuity back 1 period from when the first payment is received. Since the annuity is discounted 1 period in the first step, you need to discount the balance back only 4 periods in the second step.

b. **Calculator Solution**

$N = 4$

$I = 12$

$FV = 11,204.17$

CPT $PV = \$7,120.45$

5. More on Annuities

The area of working with the time value of money that causes the greatest problems is annuities. Find the present value of the annuities in the following examples, using the timeline of payments and assuming a 10 percent rate of return.

Example 1.

a. **Table Solution**

$$PV = 100(PVIFA_{3,10\%}) = 100(2.487) = 248.7$$

Notes:
1. The number of periods in the annuity is *always* equal to the number of payments received.
2. The present value of annuity formula discounts the annuity one and *only one* period.

b. Calculator Solution

PMT = 100

$N = 3$

$I = 10$

CPT PV = \$248.69

Example 2.

a. Table Solution

$$PV = 100(\text{PVIFA}_{3,10\%})(\text{PVIF}_{1,10\%}) = 100(2.487)(0.909) = 226.07$$

Notes:
1. $100(\text{PVIFA}_{3,10\%})$ discounts the value of the annuity back one period to the end of the first period.
2. Multiplying by $(\text{PVIF}_{1,10\%})$ discounts the annuity back to time 0.

b. Calculator Solution

$N = 1$

$I = 10$

$FV = 248.69$

CPT PV = \$226.08

Example 3.

a. Table Solution

$$PV = 100(\text{PVIFA}_{5,100\%})(\text{PVIF}_{4,10\%}) = 100(3.791)(0.683) = 258.92$$

Notes:
1. Use the 5 period PVIFA because 5 payments of 100 are received.
2. Discount back 4 periods because using the annuity factor discounted the annuity back 1 period.

b. Calculator Solution

PMT = 100	$N = 4$
$N = 5$	$I = 10$
$I = 10$	$FV = 379.08$
CPT PV = \$379.08	CPT PV = \$258.92

Example 4.

a. **Table Solution**

$$PV = 100(\text{PVIFA}_{3,10\%})(\text{PVIF}_{1,10\%}) + 200(\text{PVIFA}_{5,10\%})(\text{PVIF}_{4,10\%})$$

$$= 100(2.487)(0.909) + 200(3.791)(0.683) = 743.92$$

Notes:

1. Find the *PV* of each annuity separately, then add together.

2. Instead of multiplying by $\text{PVIF}_{r,n}$, you could divide by $1/(1+r)^n$.

Be sure you thoroughly understand and can do each of these examples. The process will be repeated over and over in different sections of the course.

b. **Calculator Solution**

PMT = 100	$N = 1$
$N = 3$	$I = 10$
$I = 10$	$FV = 248.69$
CPT $PV = \$248.69$	CPT $PV = \$226.08$
PMT = 200	$N = 4$
$N = 5$	$I = 10$
$I = 10$	$FV = 758.18$
CPT $PV = \$758.18$	CPT $PV = \$517.85$

$\$226.08 + \$517.85 = \$743.93$

6. Loan Amortization

One application of the present value of an annuity formula is to compute payments or loan terms. Remember the formula is $PV = \text{PMT}(\text{PVIFA}_{r,n})$. When a bank makes a loan it must be indifferent to whether it has the money it loans out or it receives the payment stream that the borrower promises to pay. This means that the *PV* of the payment stream must equal the loan amount. To solve a loan amortization problem, fit the parts of the equation that are given.

Example 1.

What is the payment to amortize a $10,000 loan over 10 years if the interest rate is 12%?

a. **Table Solution**

$$\$10,000 = \text{PMT}(\text{PVIFA}_{10\text{yrs},12\%}) = \text{PMT}(5.6502)$$

$$\text{PMT} = \$10,000/5.6502 = \$1,769.85$$

b. **Calculator Solution**

$PV = 10,000$

$N = 10$

$I = 12$

CPT PMT = $1,769.84

7. Growth Rates

To compute the growth rate, put the *PV*, *N*, and *FV* into the *PV* formula. Solve for *r* (*r* is the growth rate).

Example 1. You have earnings in year 1 of $20, year 2 of $18, year 3 of $25, year 4 of $30, and year 5 of $40. What is the average annual compound earnings growth rate?

Solution

$PV = FV(\text{PVIF}_{r,n})$
$20 = 40(\text{PVIF}_{r,4})$
$0.5 = (\text{PVIF}_{r,4})$

Look up the factor 0.5 across from 4 periods. The factor is between the 18% and 20% factors. Note that the 4 period factor is used because there are only 4 compounding periods, not 5.

8. Annuity Due

An annuity due is a cash flow that begins at the beginning of each period rather than at the end of each period. For example, rent is usually paid in advance so it would be an annuity due. When using financial calculators, it is important to set the calculator correctly as to when payments are received (i.e., end vs. beginning mode). To convert from an ordinary annuity, multiply by $(1 + r)$.

Example. $500 rent payments are to be made at the beginning of months 1–12. What is the *PV* of the rental payment stream assuming a cost of capital of 12%?

a. **Table Solution**

Compute the PV of the annuity, then multiply by $(1 + r)$. $PV = \$500(\text{PVIFA}_{12mo,1\%}) = \$500$ $(11.2551) = \$5,627$

Now convert to annuity due: $\$5,627 \times (1.01) = \$5,683.83$

b. **Calculator Solution**

Before using your calculator to find the present value of an annuity due, depending on the specifics of your calculator, you must either switch it to BEGIN mode or use the DUE key. (*Note:* Because we nearly always assume end-of-period cash flows, *be sure to switch your calculator back to END mode when you have completed your annuity-due calculations.*)

$N = 12$
$I = 1$
$\text{PMT} = 500$
CPT $PV = \$5,683.81$

9. Continuous Compounding

So far we have only dealt with discrete compounding intervals, that is annual, semi-annual, quarterly, etc. It is possible to continue compounding beyond this. We could obviously go to daily compounding, then hourly, then by each minute and second. Using calculus, this can be extended into infinity. The resulting compounding equations for continuous compounding are:

$FV_n = PV(e^{r \times n})$ and
$PV_n = FV/(e^{r \times n}) = FV(e^{-r \times n})$

where $e = 2.71818182846$

Example

Compute the future value of $100 invested for 1 year with a compounded 10% return.

Solution

$FV = \$100(2.718181^{0.1(1)}) = \$110.5167$

Note that continuous compounding results in a higher ending balance than is possible with any other compounding frequency.

10. Effective Rate

As the number of compounding periods increases, the effective rate also increases. This means that you may be just as well off with a lower rate that is compounded more often than with an simple interest rate. To compare nominal rates to compounded rates, an effective rate must be computed. The formula for computing the effective rate is:

$$\text{Eff Rate} = \left(1 + \frac{r}{m}\right)^m - 1$$

where r = annual percentage rate and m = the number of compounding periods per year.

Example 1

What is the effective interest rate if a 12% annual rate is compounded 12 times per year?

Solution

Effective Rate $= (1 + (0.12/12))^{12} - 1 = (1.01)^{12} - 1 = 0.1268$

Example 2

Would you rather receive 8.5% compounded annually or 8% compounded quarterly?

Solution:

Effective Rate $= (1.02)4 - 1 = 0.0824$.

You would rather have the 8.5% rate that is compounded annually.

■ Quick Drill Problems

These are quick and easy problems to practice on. The answers follow.

1. What is the future value of a 10-year ordinary annuity of $15,000 per year assuming a discount rate of 10% per year?

2. What is the future value of a 2-year ordinary annuity of $500 per month, assuming an annual interest rate of 12% per year?

3. What is the future value of a $1,000 deposit made today that will be left on deposit for 5 years earning an annual rate of 10%?

4. What is the present value of an ordinary annuity of $1,500 per year that will be received for 5 years assuming an interest rate of 12%?

5. What is the present value of an annuity due of $1,500 per year that will be received for 5 years assuming an interest rate of 12%?

6. What is the present value of a lump sum of $300 that will be paid at the end of the 5th year assuming that the interest rate is 10%?

7. What is the future value at the end of year 3 of the following cash flow stream assuming a 10% interest rate? $100 will be received at the end of year 1, $200 will be received at the end of year 2, and $300 will be received at the end of year 3.

8. What will be the present value of the above cash flow?

9. If the present value of a 5-year ordinary annuity is $500, assuming that the discount rate is 10%, what are the annual payments?

10. What is the future value after 5 years of $1,000 that is placed in a savings account today that pays interest quarterly, assuming an annual interest rate of 8%?

11. What is the effective annual interest rate for an account that pays interest quarterly at the annual rate of 8%?

12. In today's dollars, you need $50,000 to retire. If you will retire in 30 years and if inflation will average 4% per year between now and when you retire, how much will you need during the first year of your retirement?

13. What will be the monthly payment on a loan of $15,000 that is amortized over 2 years at an annual interest rate of 12%?

14. What is the interest rate on a loan of $20,000 due in 5 years and requiring an annual payment of $5,686.29?

15. What is the present value of a perpetuity that pays $2 per quarter if the discount rate is 12% per year?

Quick Drill Answers

1. $239,061.37

2. $13,486.73

3. $1,610.51

4. $5,407.16

5. $6,056.02

6. $186.28

7. $641

8. $481.59

9. $131.90

10. $1,485.95

11. 8.24%

12. $162,169.88

13. $706.10

14. 13%

15. $66.67

■ Study Tips

One of the most difficult parts of solving time value of money problems is figuring out which equation to use. When you are doing your homework this is not too hard because most of the problems are grouped together by problem type. The difficulty arises when you go into your exam and the problems are all mixed up and not labeled. The following *rules of thumb* can be helpful for deciding how to go about finding a solution.

1.   Use the *PV* to analyze investments.

2.   Use *PV* to compute loan terms.

3.   Use *PV* to compute the nest egg needed to make a series of future payments (for example, how much must be saved before you can retire).

4.   Use *PV* to compute how much you will pay for something (valuation).

5.   Use *FV* to compute a future balance.

6.   Use *FV* to compute the payment needed to achieve a future balance.

One last time, this **chapter is critical to your success** in the rest of this course. A great deal of what follows in later chapters will use the methodology developed here. Attempt all of the sample problems. Mark the ones you miss, and come back and try them again later. Keep working these problems until you thoroughly understand how they are done.

■ Student Notes

_____

_____

_____

_____

_____

■ Sample Exam—Chapter 4

True/False

T   F   1.   Financial managers make their decisions at time zero, so they tend to use present value techniques.

T   F   2.   Future value techniques use future values which are usually measured at the end of a product's life.

T   F   3.   To find the future value of a single amount of money, the financial manager uses discounting.

T   F   4.   Quarterly compounding will result in a lower amount of money accumulated than continuous compounding.

T   F   5.   In personal finance, the nominal rate of interest is used synonymously with the annual percentage rate (APR).

T   F   6.   The future value of an ordinary annuity is always greater than the future value of an identical annuity due.

T   F   7.   The future value interest factor tables were developed for use with ordinary annuities.

T   F   8.   The effective rate of interest differs from the nominal rate in that it reflects the impact of compounding frequencies.

T   F   9.   An annuity due is an annuity for which the payments occur at the end of each period.

T   F   10.   The amortization of a loan involves creating an annuity out of a present amount.

T   F   11.   A dollar that is received in year two will be more valuable than a dollar received in year one, assuming a constant rate of interest.

T   F   12.   The future value interest factor for k percent and n periods is the inverse of the present value interest factor for k percent and n periods.

T   F   13.   The future value indicates the amount of money that would have to be invested today at a given interest rate over a specified period to equal some future amount.

T   F   14.   A mixed stream of cash flows consists of cash flows with no particular pattern.

T   F   15.   The $FVIFA_{k,n}$ tables cannot be used to find the future value of an annuity due.

Multiple Choice

1.   The rate of interest that is actually paid or earned is called the _____ interest rate.

   a.   real
   b.   effective
   c.   nominal
   d.   stated

2. The future value of $500 received today and deposited at 10% for 5 years is
   a. $500.
   b. $310.50.
   c. $805.50.
   d. $788.65.

3. At an 8% rate of interest, which will result in the greatest amount of money accumulated?
   a. annual compounding
   b. quarterly compounding
   c. semi-annual compounding
   d. continuous compounding

4. The present value of $800 received at the end of year 6, assuming an opportunity cost of 7%, is
   a. $532.80.
   b. $648.76.
   c. $1,200.80.
   d. $747.66.

5. _____ is an annuity that never stops providing its holder with payment dollars at the end of each year.
   a. An annuity due
   b. A warrant
   c. A perpetuity
   d. An ordinary annuity

6. Occasionally the financial manager will use _____ to roughly estimate how long a given sum must earn at a given annual rate to double that amount.
   a. time-to-double tables
   b. the rule of 72
   c. derivatives
   d. nominal interest rates

7. The future value of an ordinary annuity with $200 annual deposits into an account paying 6% interest over the next 10 years will be
   a. $2,120.
   b. $2,794.37.
   c. $1,987.56.
   d. $2,636.20.

8. The present value of a $10,000 perpetuity at an 8% discount rate is
   a. $125,000.
   b. $9,259.
   c. $10,000.
   d. $108,000.

9. The present value of $300 received at the end of year 1, $400 received at the end of year 2, and $200 received at the end of year 3, assuming an opportunity cost of 12%, is
   a. $803.57.
   b. $729.10.
   c. $1,008.
   d. $648.76.

10. _____ refers to the amount of money on which interest is paid.
   a. Capital
   b. APR
   c. Loan base
   d. Principal

11. Find the future value at the end of year 3 of the following stream of cash flows received at the end of each year. Assume that the firm can earn 9% on its investments.

Year	Amount
1	$600
2	800
3	900

   a. $1,918.77
   b. $2,484.86
   c. $2,708.40
   d. $2,507.00

12. The future value of an annuity due with $400 annual deposits into an account paying 7% interest over the next 8 years is
   a. $4,391.20.
   b. $3,200.75.
   c. $3,976.36.
   d. $2,800.

13. The future value of $3,000 deposited at 11% compounded quarterly for each of the next 6 years is
   a. $5,211.
   b. $5,611.
   c. $4,976.
   d. $5,751.

14. A young couple wishes to accumulate $35,000 at the end of 4 years so that they may make a down payment on a house. What should their equal end-of-year deposits be to accumulate the $35,000, assuming a 6% rate of interest?
   a. $7,718
   b. $8,000
   c. $6,915
   d. $8,765

15. The effective interest rate for a savings account that is compounded quarterly at 8% is
    a.   8.24%.
    b.   8.04%.
    c.   8.76%.
    d.   9%.

16. What will the equal annual end-of-year payments need to be to fully amortize a $25,000, 12% loan over a 5-year period?
    a. $3,953
    b. $6,354
    c. $4,283
    d. $6,935

17. The present value of $10,000 received in year 20, assuming an opportunity cost of 14%, is
    a. $480.
    b. $3,280.
    c. $730.
    d. $1,250.

18. The term _____ indicates that the amount earned on a given deposit has become part of the principal at the end of a specified period.
    a.   discounting
    b.   compounded interest
    c.   amortization
    d.   future value

19. The future value of an ordinary annuity of $3,500 each year for 25 years, deposited at 9%, is
    a. $95,375.
    b. $108,765.24.
    c. $326,486.76.
    d. $296,446.50.

20. Which of the following formulas will determine the future value of an annuity due?
    a. $FVA_n = PMT \times [FVIFA_{r,n} \times (1 + r)]$
    b. $FVA_n = PMT \times FVIFA_{r,n}$
    c. $FVA_n = PMT \times \dfrac{FVIFA_{r,n}}{(1+r)}$
    d. $FVA_n = PMT(1 + r) \times FVIFA_{r,n}$

21. Time value of money techniques can be applied to:
    a.   lump-sum amounts.
    b.   cash flows streams of varying amounts.
    c.   streams of similar cash flows.
    d.   all of the above.

22. In their professional life, _____ managers need to understand time-value-of-money concepts in order to accurately estimate the cost of investment in new equipment, processes, and inventory.
    a. accounting
    b. operations
    c. marketing
    d. sales

23. The least precise estimates of the personal value of future cash flows are likely to arise through the use of:
    a. financial calculators.
    b. spreadsheets.
    c. financial tables.
    d. trick question, all provide similar precision

Essay

1. Explain why the future value of an annuity due is always greater than the future value of an ordinary annuity with the same rate of return and the same amount of periods.

2. Why do financial managers tend to evaluate investment opportunities with present value techniques?

■ Chapter 4 Answer Sheet

(*Note:* calculator solutions will be slightly different than solutions prepared with tables)

True/False	Multiple Choice
1. T	1. B
2. T	2. C $FV = \$500 \times \text{FVIF}_{10\%,5}$
3. F	$FV = \$500 \times 1.611 = \$805.50$
4. T	3. D
5. F	4. A $PV = \$800 \times \text{PVIF}_{8\%,6}$
6. F	$PV = \$800 \times 0.666 = \$532.80$
7. T	5. C
8. T	6. B
9. F	7. D $FVA = \$200 \times \text{FVIFA}_{6\%,10}$
10. T	$FVA = \$200 \times 13.181 = \$2,636.20$
11. F	8. A $\text{PVIFA}_{8\%,\infty} = \dfrac{1}{0.08} = 12.5$
12. T	$PV = \$10,000 \times 12.5 = \$125,000$
13. F	9. B $PV_1 = \$300 \times \text{PVIF}_{12\%,1} = \$267.90$
14. T	$PV_2 = \$400 \times \text{PVIF}_{12\%,2} = \$318.80$
15. F	$PV_3 = \$200 \times \text{PVIF}_{12\%,3} = \$142.10$
	$PV = \$267.90 + \$318.80 + \$142.10 = \$729.10$

10. D

11. B $FV_3 = \$600 \times \text{FVIF}_{9\%,2} = \$712.86$

　　　$FV_2 = \$800 \times \text{FVIF}_{9\%,1} = \$872$

　　　$FV_1 = \$900$

　　　$FV = \$712.86 + \$872 + \$900 = \$2,484.86$

12. A $\text{FVIFA}_{7\%,8} = 10.260 \times (1 + 0.07) = 10.978$

　　　$FVA = \$400 \times 10.978 = \$4,391.20$

13. D $FV = \$3,000 \times \left(1 + \dfrac{0.11}{4}\right)^{4 \times 6}$

　　　$FV = \$3,000 \times 1.917 = \$5,751$

14. B $\text{PMT} = \dfrac{\text{FVA}_n}{\text{FVIFA}_{6\%,4}}$

　　　$\text{PMT} = \dfrac{\$35,000}{4.375} = \$8,000$

15. A $k_{eff} = \left(1 + \dfrac{0.08}{4}\right)^4 - 1$

　　　$k_{eff} = 8.24\%$

16. $\quad$ D $\quad PMT = \dfrac{PVA_n}{PVIFA_{12\%,5}}$

$$PMT = \dfrac{\$25,000}{3.605} = \$6,935$$

17. $\quad$ C $\quad PV = \$10,000 \times PVIF_{14\%,20}$

$$PV = \$10,000 \times 0.073 = \$730$$

18. $\quad$ B

19. $\quad$ D $\quad FVA = \$3,500 \times FVIFA_{9\%,25}$

$$FVA = \$3,500 \times 84.699 = \$296,446.50$$

20. $\quad$ A

21. $\quad$ D

22. $\quad$ B

23. $\quad$ B

Essay

1. Because an annuity due's cash flows are received at the beginning of the period, unlike the cash flows of an ordinary annuity which occur at the end of the period, they have more time to compound. The future value of a dollar received in year zero will always have a higher future value than a dollar received in year one.

2. Time value of money techniques are used by financial managers to assess the value of future cash flows. When evaluating the alternatives associated with these future cash flows, financial managers tend to rely on present value techniques because they are operating in time zero. When evaluating projects or investments, financial managers need to answer the question, "What are the future cash flows associated with this opportunity worth to me in present day dollars?"

Chapter 5
Risk and Return

■ Chapter Summary

Two of the most important concepts in finance are risk and return. Most of us realize that as risk increases, investors will demand a higher return as compensation. What you may not know is that there are different types of risk and only some risk results in increased returns. This chapter explores these concepts and develops the model that relates how much additional return is needed to compensate for added risk.

 Understand the meaning and fundamentals of risk, return, and risk preferences. Most people think of risk as the chance of taking a loss. This is not a sufficient definition of risk in a financial setting. A better definition of risk is that the cash flows are variable. This implies that assets can still be risky even when there is no chance of a loss. We assume that investors are risk averse. This means that they avoid risk and when risk increases, investors must be compensated with an increase in return.

 Describe procedures for measuring the risk of a single asset. If risk is defined as variability in returns, then to measure risk we need a statistic that increases as return variability increases. One such statistic is the standard deviation. An alternative measurement of risk for an asset held by itself is the coefficient of variation. These measures of risk are not appropriate for measuring the risk of an asset held in a portfolio.

 Discuss the measurement of return and standard deviation for a portfolio and the concept of correlation. The return on a portfolio of assets will be the weighted average of the return on the individual assets. The portfolio risk will not be the weighted average of the individual standard deviations because risk will be affected by the relationship between the different assets. Portfolio risk is measured with beta.

 Understand the risk and return characteristics of a portfolio in terms of correlation and diversification, and the impact of international assets on a portfolio. Combining assets with negatively correlated returns provides the best opportunity to minimize overall risk. When assets with positive and negative returns are put into the same portfolio, the variability in the portfolio return is reduced since when returns fall on one asset, returns increase on the other.

 Review the two types of risk and the deviation and the role of beta in measuring the relevant risk of both a security and a portfolio. In a perfect world, the only relevant risk is nondiversifiable risk because it cannot be eliminated. Diversifiable risk can be eliminated through diversification. Nondiversifiable risk, also called market risk, is measured by beta.

 Explain the capital asset pricing model (CAPM), its relationship to the security market line (SML), and the major forces causing shifts in the SML. The CAPM is a model that projects the required return on an asset given the asset's beta, the return on a risk-free asset, and the performance of the market. The required return is the sum of the return on the risk-free asset plus a risk premium sufficient to compensate an investor for incurring the extra risk of investing in the risky asset.

■ Chapter Notes

Risk and Return Fundamentals

There are two key determinants of share price: risk and return. Risk can be viewed in terms of an asset held in isolation or in terms of an asset held in a portfolio.

Risk defined

Risk is often defined as the chance of a loss. However, in a strict financial context, this is not right. Risk is synonymous with the term *uncertainty*. The more variable the returns to an asset, the more uncertain they are and the more risky they are.

Return defined

The return on an investment is measured as the total gain or loss experienced on behalf of its owner over a given period of time. Return is the change in the asset's value plus any cash distributions received while it is owned. The return is calculated using the following formula.

$$r_t = \frac{P_t - P_{t-1} + C_t}{P_{t-1}}$$

where

r_t = actual, expected, or required rate of return during period t

P_t = price (value) of asset at time t

P_{t-1} = price (value) of asset at time $t - 1$

C_t = cash received from the asset investment in the time period $t - 1$ to t

Risk Preferences

Investors can be either *risk indifferent, risk averse, or risk seeking.* A risk indifferent investor does not require any adjustment to the return as risk increases. A risk seeker actually prefers risky investments over less risky investments. The risk averse investor requires increased returns to compensate for increased risk. We assume that the usual, rational investor is risk averse.

Measuring the risk of a single asset

Scenario analysis, while not a method for measuring risk, can be used to get a feel for risk. When different scenarios are evaluated, the greater the difference in the outcomes, the greater is the risk. If changing sales, for example, has little impact on net income, the firm is less risky than one where a small change in sales greatly affects the bottom line. It is not unusual to use spreadsheets to create different scenarios as an aid to evaluating the riskiness of an investment.

Probability distributions describe the riskiness of an asset more precisely. A probability distribution is a model that relates probabilities to the associated output. Probability distributions can be shown as either simple bar charts or continuous graphs.

The most common measure of risk is the statistic called the *standard deviation.* The standard deviation measures the dispersion about the mean. To compute a standard deviation, the mean is found first. The actual outcomes are subtracted from this mean outcome to find the dispersion. This dispersion is squared to eliminate the negative signs.

The coefficient of variation is a measure of the relative dispersion. It should be used when comparing the risk of assets that have very different returns. The *CV* gives the risk per dollar of return. *CV* is computed by dividing the standard deviation by expected return.

Remember that the standard deviation and the coefficient of variation are useful in measuring the risk of an asset *only when it is held by itself.* Never use these measures when the asset is held as part of a diversified portfolio.

Risk of a portfolio

The risk of any single asset should not be viewed separately from other assets in the portfolio. The investor's goal is to create an efficient portfolio. This is one where the maximum return is achieved with the minimum level of risk. This will only occur in a fully diversified portfolio. Since risk must be viewed along with return, we first show how to compute the return for a portfolio.

Portfolio return

The return on a portfolio is computed as the weighted average of the returns on each asset in the portfolio.

Correlation

Correlation is a statistic that measures the relationship between the movement of one security to another. Securities can be either

1. *positively correlated;* if the series move in the same direction;

2. *negatively correlated;* if the series move in opposite directions; or

3. *uncorrelated;* if there is no relationship between the movement of one security and another.

As long as assets are not perfectly positively correlated, diversification can reduce the risk of the portfolio.

The above graph shows the returns to two perfectly negatively correlated securities. The horizontal dashed line shows the return to the holder of the portfolio. Notice that the portfolio return does not vary over time even though returns to each security do. When assets are perfectly positively correlated, there is no benefit from diversification. In general, the smaller the correlation (the less positive or the more negative), the greater is the benefit of diversification.

International diversification

Most securities in this country move together. This is because they are all affected by the same factors. For example, when interest rates rise, most firms do poorly because the costs of expansion and debt increase. If the cost of oil were to increase, most firms would suffer. One solution to this problem is to invest in different countries. Since the economies of different countries do not always move together, poor returns from one country may be offset by high returns from another.

There are several types of risk associated with international diversification that should be considered. Currency fluctuations and political turmoil can substantially increase the risk of an international investment.

Risk and return: The capital asset pricing model (CAPM)

The capital asset pricing model is the theory that links together risk *and* return. To develop this theory, we must first identify the different types of risk.

Total risk can be viewed as consisting of two types: *nondiversifiable risk* and *diversifiable risk*. Diversifiable risk represents the portion of an asset's risk that is associated with random causes that can be eliminated through diversification. For example, labor problems may affect one firm in a portfolio. This may increase the market share of other firms in the portfolio so that the net return to the investor remains unchanged. Nondiversifiable risk cannot be eliminated by diversifying. Factors such as war, inflation, international incidents, and political events tend to affect all firms in similar ways. This kind of risk is also referred to as the risk of the market.

It does not take a large number of securities to eliminate the bulk of the diversifiable risk. Refer to the following diagram. If an investor holds 15 to 20 securities, most diversifiable risk is eliminated. Since an investor can easily eliminate diversifiable risk, the only risk that is important and the only risk that influences the required return on a security is nondiversifiable or market risk.

The model: CAPM

Beta

The beta coefficient is used to measure nondiversifiable risk. It is found by determining how the return on a stock responds to different returns by a portfolio composed of all of the stocks in the whole market.

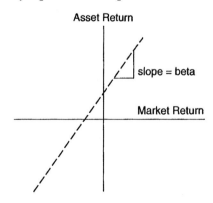

The market returns are on the *X*-axis and the asset returns are on the *Y*-axis. The slope of the line that best fits is the beta. This line is called the *characteristic line*.

Betas are widely available in many investment guides. The average beta of the whole market is 1. Firms with betas greater than 1 are more risky than the average stock and firms with betas less than one are less risky. For example, most utilities have low betas, say 0.50 to 0.75. Young, high growth stocks have higher betas, say 1.25 to 2.00.

Portfolio Beta

Asset	Amount invested	Weight	Beta	Weight × Beta
IBM	$25,000	25%	1.15	0.2875
WalMart	$25,000	25%	1.08	0.27
Apple	$50,000	50%	1.10	0.55
Portfolio Beta				1.1075 = 1.11

The beta of a portfolio is found by finding the weighted average of the betas of the firms in the portfolio.

$$b_p = (w_1 \times b_1) + (w_2 \times b_2) + \cdots + (w_n \times b_n)$$

where b_p = beta of the portfolio
w_1 = proportion of wealth invested in security 1
b_1 = beta of security 1

Compute the portfolio beta.

Example

The Equation

Using the beta coefficient to measure market risk, the capital asset pricing model is given by the following equation.

$$r_j = R_f + [b_j \times (r_m - R_f)]$$

where

r_j = required return on asset j
R_f = risk-free rate of return
b_j = beta coefficient for asset j
r_m = market return

View the equation as saying the required return on asset j, r_j, is equal to what could be earned with no risk, R_f, plus a risk premium to compensate the investor for choosing a risky investment instead of a risk-free investment. The market risk premium, $(r_m - R_f)$, represents the premium the investor receives for taking the average amount of risk. This average amount is adjusted by multiplying by beta.

Example

What is the required return on a stock with a beta of 1.25, if the return on the market is 0.10 and the risk-free rate is 0.04?

$$r_j = 0.04 + 1.25(0.10 - 0.04) = 0.04 + 0.075 = 0.115$$

The security market line

When the required returns on all stocks are graphed against their corresponding betas, the result is the security market line (SML). The SML will be a straight line.

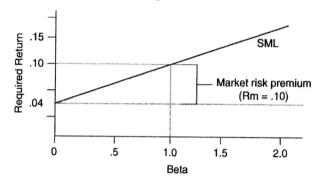

Shifts in the security market line

Market conditions will cause the security market line to shift up or down or to change in slope. For example, if inflation increases, the SML will shift up by the amount of the increase, while maintaining the same slope. If investors become more risk averse, the slope of the SML will increase. This results in offering investors a higher return to compensate them for incurring the risk of the market.

Efficient Markets

Suppose a security offered a return above the required return shown by the SML. As soon as other investors discovered this security, they would rush to purchase it since it represents a "good deal." As many investors attempted to buy, the price of the security would naturally rise. If the price rises, the return that the buyer receives falls. When the price rises enough that the return has fallen to what is offered by other securities of this risk, the buying activity will stop and the security will be in equilibrium.

■ Sample Problems and Solutions

Example 1

Suppose that you bought IBM stock at $45. Due to the strength of its mainframe business, its stock price rises to $75. Also suppose that $2.00 in dividends are paid. What is your return?

Asset	Amount Invested	Weight	Return	Weight × Return
IBM	$25,000	25%	0.15	0.0375
WalMart	$25,000	25%	0.18	0.0450
Apple	$50,000	50%	0.10	0.05
Return on Portfolio				0.1325

Solution

$$r = \frac{\$75 - \$45 + \$2}{\$45} = 0.7111 = 71.11\%$$

Example 2

What is the return on the portfolio of securities listed below?

Solution

In the last column the weight (computed by dividing the amount invested in the security by the total amount invested in the portfolio) is multiplied by the return. The product is then summed. The result is the return on the portfolio.

Example 3

For the stock listed in the following table, calculate the standard deviation. The economy is projected to either boom, be normal, or fall into a recession. Columns 2 and 3 list the probabilities of each of these events along with the stock price under each possibility.

State of Economy	Probability	Stock Price	$(\tilde{x}_i - \hat{x})$	$(\tilde{x}_i - \hat{x})^2$	$p_i(\tilde{x}_i - \hat{x})^2$
Boom	0.30	$50	25	625	187.50
Normal	0.50	20	−5	25	12.50
Depression	0.20	0	−25	625	125.00
$\hat{X}$	—	$25	—	—	—

Solution

$$\sigma_x = \sqrt{(187.50 + 12.50 + 125.00)} = 18.03$$

First compute the expected value or mean of the stock prices. You should get $25 for the expected value. You next take the outcome for the boom, $50, subtract the expected value ($25) square it and multiply by the probability of a boom (0.30). You do the same for normal and depression. Finally, sum them up and take the square root.

Example 4

Review the following and indicate which investment you would choose if you were risk indifferent, a risk seeker, or risk averse. You currently own a firm that earns 13% and has a risk index of 8%.

Investment	Expected Return	Expected Risk Index
Zero Inc.	10%	10%
Batman Enterprises	13%	12%
Spiderman Limited	20%	6%

Solution

a.   If you are risk indifferent, you do not care whether an increase in risk is accompanied by an increase in return. In the above example, you would choose Batman Enterprises because as the risk goes up, there is no increase in return.

b.   If you are a risk seeker, you want as much risk as possible given your level of return. This would lead you to choose Zero Inc. and Batman Enterprises because they give greater risk with lower return.

c.   If you are risk averse (normal), you will choose Spiderman Limited because it gives the highest return for the level of risk.

Example 5

Compute the coefficient of variation for Bongos Galore if the expected return is 20% and the standard deviation of the returns is 8%.

Solution

The coefficient of variation is a measure of the risk per unit of return earned.

$$CV = 0.08/0.20 = \mathbf{0.40}$$

Example 6

Given the following returns on the market portfolio and on Tony's Tune-up Shoppe, estimate Tony's beta graphically.

Year	2002	2003	2004	2005	2006	2007	2008
Tony's	5%	8%	10%	6%	4%	−2%	10%
Market	2.5%	4%	5%	3%	2%	−1%	5%

Solution

Begin by graphing the returns with the market return on the *X*-axis and Tony's returns on the *Y*-axis. Using the rise over the run method, estimate the slope of the line drawn that best connects the dots. The slope is the firm's beta. In this case, it is equal to **2**. A beta of two means that as the market moves by 1%, the return on the stock will move by 2%.

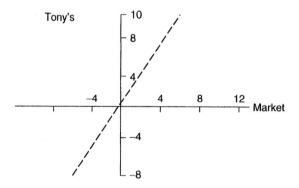

Example 7

If the risk-free rate of interest is 4% and the market return is 10%, what would be the required return for a security with a beta equal to 2?

Solution

The CAPM is $r_i = R_f + \text{Beta}(r_m - R_f)$. The expected return is then computed as $0.04 + 2(0.1 - 0.04) = 0.16 = 16\%$. The most common mistake made by students using the CAPM is to mix percentages together with decimals in the same equation. Second, make sure that you know where the plus sign is and where the minus sign is.

Example 8

Benjamin Corporation, a growing computer software developer, wishes to determine the required return on an asset that has a beta of 1.5. The risk-free rate of return is 7% and the expected return on the market is 11%.

Solution

$$7\% + 1.5(11\% - 7\%) = 13\%$$

Example 9

You are interested in investing $3,000 in asset x with beta of 1.0, $2,000 in asset y with beta of −0.5, and $5,000 in asset z with beta of 2.0. What is the beta of the portfolio?

Solution

First compute the asset weights. These are the percentages invested in each of the assets. There is a total of $10,000 invested in the three assets. 30% is invested in asset x ($3,000/$10,000), 20% is invested in asset y and 50% is invested in asset z. Now find the weighted average of the betas. $B_p = 0.3(1) + 0.2(-0.5) + 0.5(2) = 1.2$

Example 10

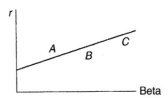

Which of the above assets would you select? Why?

Solution

A is above the security market line. This means that it provides a higher return for its level of risk than do other securities. For this reason you would select it. B and C are below the security market line and provide a lower return for their level of risk than do other securities. For this reason, reject B and C.

Example 11

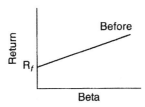

Remember that R_f includes the real rate of interest and inflation and that the market risk premium is a measure of risk aversion. If investors become more risk averse, what happens to the slope of the SML?

Solution

If investors become more risk averse, a higher premium will have to be paid to induce them to invest in risky securities. This implies that the market risk premium increases. Remember that the market risk premium is the slope of the security market line.

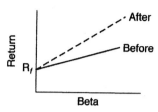

Example 12

If the inflation premium increases, what happens to the SML?

Solution

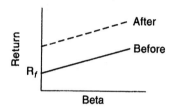

If expected inflation increases, r_m and R_f will both increase by a like amount. Since the slope of the security market line is $(r_m - R_f)$, there will be no change in the slope. The intercept (R_f) will increase.

■ Quick Drill Problems

The following are a sample of easy, quick practice problems you can use to test your risk and return skills. The answers follow.

1. Compute the holding period return for a security you bought for $30.00 two years ago and sold last week for $35.00. You received $1.00 in dividends while you owned the stock.

2. You believe that next year there is a 30% probability of a recession and a 70% probability that the economy will be normal. If your stock will yield −10% in a recession and 20% in a normal year, what is your expected return?

3. What is the standard deviation of the security discussed in Problem 2?

4. If the standard deviation of a security's returns is 14 and the expected return is 11%, what is the coefficient of variation?

5. You hold a portfolio composed of 20% security A and 80% security B. If A has an expected return of 10% and B has an expected return of 15%, what is the expected return from your portfolio?

6. Suppose you rebalance the portfolio discussed in Problem 5 such that it is now composed of 80% security A and 20% security B. If A has an expected return of 10% and B has an expected return of 15%, what is the expected return from your portfolio?

7. If you were to choose two of the firms listed in Table 7.2 to combine in a portfolio and if your only goal was to minimize risk, which two would you choose?

8. Estimate the beta of a firm assuming that when the market goes up 5% this firm's returns rise 20% and when the market falls 10% this firm's returns fall 40%.

9. Estimate the beta of a firm assuming that when the market goes up 5% this firm's returns rise 2.5% and when the market falls 10% this firm's returns fall 5%.

10. What is the beta of a portfolio composed of 40% security A with a beta of 2 and 60% security B with a beta of 0.75?

11. What is the beta of a portfolio composed of 40% security A with a beta of 1.5 and 60% security B with a beta of −0.25?

12. If the average return on the market is 21% and the risk free security has a return of 6%, what is the market risk premium?

13. Assume that the risk free rate is 5%, the return on the market is 15% and that a firm's beta is 0.5. What return must you earn to be satisfied that you are being fairly compensated for the risk of the firm?

14. Using the assumptions made above about the risk-free rate and the return on the market, what will be the required return for a security with a beta of 1.5?

15. You have analyzed the firm discussed in Problem 14 and determined that its expected return is 19.5%. Would you choose to buy it?

16. If investors in general agree that the market is less likely to post a loss, are market risk premiums likely to rise or fall?

17. The risk-free rate of interest is 5%. The market risk premium falls from 10% to 8%. How much does the required return fall for a security with a beta of 1.5?

18. The risk-free rate of interest is 5%. The market risk premium falls from 10% to 8%. How much does the required return fall for a security with a beta of 0.75?

19. You have become convinced that inflation has been tamed. You have been using a real rate of 2% and an inflation rate of 4% to estimate the risk free rate to be 6%. The market rate is also estimated using an assumed inflation rate of 4%. If you believe that inflation will be 3% in the future, how much will the required return on your portfolio change by if the return on the market is 10% and your portfolio's beta is 1.2? (Note that both the market rate and the risk-free rate will change.)

20. Refer to the data in Problem 19. How much will the required return on your portfolio change by if your portfolio's beta is 0.5? (Assume inflation is 4%.)

Answers to Quick Drill

1. 20%

2. 11%

3. 0.1374

4. 1.27

5. 14%

6. 11%

7. Fairchild and SWA

8. 4

9. 0.5

10. 1.25

11. 0.45

12. 15%

13. 10%

14. 20%

15. No

16. Fall

17. 3%

18. 1.5%

19. 1%

20. 2.8%

■ Study Tips

1. Remember that the firm's standard deviation and coefficient of variation measure total risk so are not appropriate measures of risk of securities held in a portfolio. In a portfolio, the only risk that matters is market risk because the rest is eliminated by diversification.

2. The CAPM provides a way of calculating the required return on a security. The required return is how much you must earn to feel fully compensated for holding a risky investment.

3. Be able to distinguish between the characteristic line and the security market line. The characteristic line relates one security to the market. The slope of the characteristic line is beta. The security market line relates the required return to risk. The slope of the security market line is the market risk premium.

4. Be able to distinguish between diversifiable and nondiversifiable risk.

■ Sample Exam—Chapter 5

True/False

T   F   1.   Most investors are risk averse, since for a given increase in return they require an increase in risk.

T   F   2.   The coefficient of variation is useful for evaluating the risk of a security held in a portfolio.

T   F   3.   Longer-lived assets usually are more risky because it is more difficult to accurately forecast cash flows that occur far into the future.

T   F   4.   Adding an asset to a portfolio that is perfectly positively correlated with existing portfolio returns will have no affect on portfolio risk.

T   F   5.   There is no possible way that combining assets into a portfolio will result in a portfolio that is riskier than its riskiest asset.

T   F   6.   Unless assets are negatively correlated, combining assets into a portfolio will not reduce portfolio risk.

T   F   7.   A firm with a negative beta may have high sales when the economy weakens and low sales when the economy recovers.

T   F   8.   Diversifiable risk is the only risk that influences the required return because nondiversifiable risk can be eliminated.

T   F   9.   Beta measures nondiversifiable, or market, risk.

T   F   10.   Beta is the slope of the security market line.

T   F   11.   The characteristic line maps the relationship between the return on the market and the return on a security. Its slope is beta.

T   F   12.   As investors become more risk averse, the market risk premium increases and the security market line becomes steeper.

T   F   13.   Fixed income securities, such as bonds or preferred stocks, usually have betas equal to zero.

T   F   14.   Risk can best be defined in finance as the chance of a loss.

T   F   15.   The standard deviation is a measure of relative dispersion and is used in comparing the risk of assets with differing expected returns.

T   F   16.   Standard deviation can be used to measure risk on an ex-ante basis using historical returns.

Multiple Choice

1. _____ is the variability in returns associated with an investment.
   a. Median
   b. Risk
   c. Coefficient of variation
   d. Profit

2. You compute the _____ on an asset by subtracting the beginning price from the ending price, adding any cash distributions, and dividing by the beginning price.
   a. return
   b. risk
   c. profit
   d. standard deviation

3. A person who prefers more risk to less risk and who does not require additional return to compensate for increased risk is
   a. risk averse.
   b. risk neutral.
   c. risk seeker.
   d. smart.

4. Assume that last year you purchased 100 shares of Rubber Ducky Inc. for $25 per share. The price 1 year later is $27 per share. If a $2.50 dividend was paid, what is the return?
   a. $50
   b. 8%
   c. 2.50%
   d. 18%

5. Assume that you purchased stock last year for $27. Today's price is $25. What is the return?
   a. $2.00
   b. 8%
   c. −7.41%
   d. $2.00

6. One method to evaluate the riskiness of an investment opportunity is to estimate the cash flows under the most optimistic, most likely, and most pessimistic set of assumptions. This type of analysis is called
   a. break-even analysis.
   b. marginal analysis.
   c. scenario analysis.
   d. probability analysis.

7. A measure of the dispersion of returns around the mean return is the
   a. probability distribution.
   b. standard deviation.
   c. coefficient of variation.
   d. student's *t*.

8. Given the following expected returns and standard deviations of assets A, B and C, which asset should the prudent financial manager select?

Asset	Expected Return	Standard Deviation
A	10%	10%
B	12%	10%
C	12%	8%

   a. A
   b. B
   c. C
   d. impossible to tell

9. What is the coefficient of variation for asset A if the standard deviation is 0.02, the expected return is 0.10, and the probability of a return equal to 0.10 is 25%?

   a. 0.02
   b. 0.20
   c. 0.05
   d.   5

10. A portfolio that provides the maximum return for a given level of risk is known as the

   a. optimal portfolio.
   b. risk averse portfolio.
   c. continuous portfolio.
   d. efficient portfolio.

11. If the returns on one asset move in the same direction as the returns on another asset then the assets are

   a. positively correlated.
   c. not correlated.
   b. negatively correlated.
   d. perfectly positively correlated.

12. If you put $26,000 in asset A, $33,000 in asset B, and $55,000 in asset C, and if the expected return to A is 10%, to B is 12% and to C is 14%, what is the expected return on the portfolio?

   a. 12%
   b. 0.125
   c. 0.228
   d. 0.1425

Use the following table to answer Questions 13–16.

Asset	Return	Beta	Proportion
A	10%	0.75	0.20
B	12%	1.00	0.40
C	14%	1.25	0.40

13. What is the expected return for the portfolio?
    a. 0.11
    b. 0.124
    c. 0.37
    d. 0.4

14. The portfolio beta is
    a. 0.75.
    b. 1.
    c. 1.05.
    d. 1.25.

15. Referring to the above table, which firm is most risky in a portfolio context?
    a. A
    b. B
    c. C
    d. impossible to tell

16. Referring to the above table, which firm is most risky if held in isolation (i.e. not part of a portfolio)?
    a. A
    b. B
    c. C
    d. impossible to tell

17. Combining several assets into a portfolio so that the risk of the portfolio is reduced is known as
    a. valuation.
    b. diversification.
    c. liquidation.
    d. risk aversion.

18. Another term for nondiversifiable risk is
    a. systematic risk.
    b. nonsystematic risk.
    c. firm specific risk.
    d. both b. and c.

19. The beta of the market portfolio is
    a. 0.
    b. 1.
    c. 1.5.
    d. variable according to the level of risk aversion.

20. The slope of the security market line increases when
    a.   inflation increases.
    b.   inflation decreases.
    c.   the risk premium increases.
    d.   investors become less risk averse.

21. When the capital asset pricing model is graphed, the resulting line is called the
    a.   characteristic line.
    b.   security market line.
    c.   standard deviation.
    d.   beta.

22. If the beta of an asset is 1.25, the risk-free rate of interest is 0.04, and the return on the market portfolio is 0.12, what is the required return on the asset?
    a.   0.12
    b.   0.14
    c.   0.16
    d.   0.24

23. What is the market risk premium for the asset discussed in Problem 22 above?
    a.   1.25
    b.   0.12
    c.   0.08
    d.   0.16

24. If the required return on a security is 10%, the risk-free rate is 0.05, and the return on the market is 0.14, what is the beta of the firm?
    a.   0.14
    b.   1
    c.   1.4
    d.   0.56

25. As risk aversion decreases, due to greater confidence in the long term health of the economy,
    a.   firms' betas will increase.
    b.   investors' required return will decrease.
    c.   investors' required return will increase.
    d.   firms' betas will decrease.

26. _____ analysis is a technique for assessing risk that uses several possible solutions in order to obtain a sense of the variability among returns.
    a.   Monte Carlo
    b.   Range
    c.   Scenario
    d.   Situation

27. Actual risk may be _____ the expected risk.
    a. greater than
    b. equal to
    c. less than
    d. all of the above

28. Vy Le will only accept companies that have a coefficient of variation of 0.82 or better. Which of the following companies is acceptable?
    a. AXEL: Return = 10%, Standard Deviation = 10%
    b. BENRIL: Return = 12%, Standard Deviation = 10%
    c. CAMPEN: Return = 8%, Standard Deviation = 10%
    d. DEMPSZY: Return = 14%, Standard Deviation = 10%

Essay

1. Distinguish between an investor's expected rate of return and the required rate of return. How is each computed? If the expected rate of return is 12% and the required rate of return is 10%, will investors buy the security?

2. Given the following information, should the asset be purchased?

State of the Economy	Probability	Return
Boom	0.25	0.16
Normal	0.5	0.14
Bust	0.25	0.12

The risk free rate of interest is 5%, the return on the market is 12%, and the beta of the firm is 1.0.

■ Chapter 5 Answer Sheet

True/False

1. F
2. F
3. T
4. T
5. T
6. F
7. T
8. F
9. T
10. F
11. T
12. T
13. T
14. F
15. F
16. T

Multiple Choice

1. B
2. A
3. C
4. D
5. C
6. C
7. B
8. C
9. B, $0.02/0.10 = 0.2$
10. D
11. A
12. B, $\$26{,}000/\$114{,}000 = 0.228$
    $0.228(0.10) + 0.289(0.12) + 0.482(0.14) = 0.125$
13. B, $0.1(0.2) + 0.12(0.4) + 0.14(0.4) = 0.124$
14. C, $0.2(0.75) + 0.4(1) + 0.4(1.25) = 1.05$
15. C
16. D, (need to see either SD or CV)
17. B
18. A
19. B
20. C
21. B
22. B, $0.04 + 1.25(0.12 - 0.04) = 0.14$
23. C, $0.12 - 0.04 = 0.08$
24. D, $0.10 = 0.05 + B(0.14 - 0.05), B = 0.55$
25. B
26. C
27. D
28. D

Essay

1. The expected return is what you think you will earn based on the different possible states of the economy and their associated probabilities. This is computed by finding the weighted average of the returns earned in each of the states of the economy. The required return is the return needed to fully compensate the investor for investing in a risky asset. It is computed by using the CAPM. If the expected return is greater than the required return, the investor will buy the security.

2. To solve this problem you must first compute the expected return. This expected return can then be compared to the required return computed from the CAPM.

   $Exp(R) = 0.25(0.16) + 0.5(0.14) + 0.25(0.12) = 0.14$

   $Req(R) = 0.05 + 1(0.12 - 0.05) = 0.12$

   Since the required return is less than the expected return, the security should be purchased.

Chapter 6
Interest Rates and Bond Valuation

■ Chapter Summary

All assets are valued the same way. Once you have learned the idea behind valuation, you can extend it to the valuation of anything. To value an asset, simply find the present value of any cash flows that will accrue to the holder of the asset. For example, to value a business, find the present value of the profits that the firm will generate. To find the value of a building, find the present value of the net cash flows that the building will generate. The valuation of stocks and bonds are the focus of this chapter. This is a good opportunity to practice your time value of money skills.

 Describe the interest rate fundamentals, the term structure of interest rates, and risk premiums. Interest rates and required returns represent the costs of using various forms of financing. The real rate of interest is that rate that would exist in the absence of risk and inflation. The nominal rate differs from the real rate in that it includes inflation and risk premiums. The term structure of interest rates refers to the way yields change depending on how long a security has until it matures.

 Review the legal aspects of bond financing and bond cost. There are certain legal arrangements that help protect bond investors. These contained in the bond indenture, which includes various provisions of the bond and the bond covenants.

 Discuss the general features, quotations, ratings, popular types, and international issues of corporate bonds. There are three features often included in bonds. These include a conversion feature, a call feature, and stock purchase rights. Bonds are rated by several agencies to reflect their risk of default. The ratings range from AAA to D.

 Understand the key inputs and basic model used in the valuation process. Every business asset that has value will generate cash flows by either providing profits or by reducing costs. In a later chapter we will focus on how these cash flows are computed. For now, be aware that it is these cash flows that make a business asset valuable. The required return that is used as the discount rate when valuing an asset reflects the riskiness of the cash flows.

 Apply the valuation model to bonds, and describe the impact of required return and time to maturity on bond values. Regardless whether you are valuing bonds, stock, or some other asset, you always find the present value of the cash flows. Models will be presented in this chapter for valuing bonds and stocks, but keep in focus that the models are just applications of the present value techniques you learned in Chapter 5.

Explain yield to maturity (YTM), its calculation, and the procedure used to value bonds that pay interest semi-annually. The yield to maturity is the return an investor will receive if the bond is held until it matures. It is the return that sets the current market value of the bond equal to the present value of the coupon payments and the maturity price. The YTM that is computed for semi-annual payments will have to be multiplied by two to get the annual yield.

■ Chapter Notes

Interest Rate Fundamentals

 When funds are lent, the cost of borrowing the funds is the interest rate.

When funds are obtained by selling ownership interest, as in the sale of stock, the cost to the issuer of the funds is commonly called the required return.

The real rate of interest is the rate that has not been adjusted for inflation, liquidity preferences, or risk. The real rate of interest is the most basic cost of money.

The nominal rate of interest is the actual rate of interest charged by the supplier of funds and paid by the demander. The nominal rate of interest, r, consists of the real rate of interest, r^*, plus an inflation premium, IP, and a risk premium, RP, that covers such things as default risk and contractual provisions.

Nominal Rate of Interest

$$r = r^* + IP + RP$$

where:

r = nominal rate of interest

r^* = real rate of interest

IP = inflation premium

RP = risk premium

The risk free-rate of interest, R_F, is the required return on a risk free asset. The risk free rate consists of the real rate of interest plus an inflation premium. The rate on the three-month U.S. Treasury bill (T-bill) is considered to be the risk-free rate of return.

Risk-Free Rate of Return

$$R_F = r^* + IP$$

where:

R_F = risk-free rate of interest

Term Structure of Interest Rates

The term structure of interest relates the interest rate to the yield to maturity.

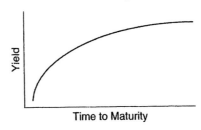

The yield curve is a graph of the term structure of interest rates. It is a graphical representation of the yield to maturity of a security (*y*-axis) and the time to maturity (*x*-axis). The yield curve can take on three different shapes: upward-sloping, flat, or downward-sloping.

There are three generally cited theories that help to explain the shape of the yield curve.

1. *The expectations hypothesis* reflects investor's expectations about future interest rates. The hypothesis is based on inflationary expectations. Expectations of higher future rates of inflation will result in higher long-term interest rates. The opposite is true for expected lower rates of inflation. If investors believe that inflation rates will be lower in the future, then long-term interest rates will be lower than short-term rates.

2. *Liquidity preference theory* suggests that investors require a premium for tying up funds for long periods of time. This premium is due to the reduced liquidity of long-term funds. To avoid having to repeatedly renew short-term debt, borrowers are willing to pay a premium to obtain long term funds. This helps to explain why the normal yield curve is upward-sloping.

3. *Market segmentation theory* is based on the law of supply and demand. The theory suggests that the market for loans is segmented by the length of maturity for different funds and that the supply and demand for loans within each segment determine the interest rate.

Risk

A risk premium is attached to the risk free rate to cover such things as default risk, maturity risk, liquidity risk, contractual provisions, and tax risk. In general, securities with the highest risk premiums are considered to either have a high rate of default, have a long maturity, contain unfavorable contractual provisions, or not be tax exempt.

There is a risk-return trade-off, in that investors must be compensated for accepting greater risk with the expectation of greater returns. The higher the risk, the higher the expected return.

Legal aspects

Certain legal arrangements are required to protect purchasers of bonds; bondholders are protected primarily through the indenture and the trustee. The bond indenture is a legal document that specifies both the rights of the bondholders and the duties of the issuing corporation. Included in the indenture are descriptions of the amount and timing of all interest and principal payments, various standard and restrictive provisions, and, frequently, sinking fund requirements.

The standard provisions require that the borrower:

1. maintain satisfactory accounting records

2. periodically supply audited financial statements

3. pay taxes and other liabilities when due

4. maintain all facilities in good working order

Bond indentures also contain the bond covenants that keep managers from increasing the risk of the issue. These include requirements that the firm maintain minimum levels of liquidity, limit the sale of accounts receivable to generate cash, constrain subsequent borrowing, and limit the payment of dividends.

There are three features of bonds that are frequently found.

1. A conversion feature allows the holder to convert the bond into stock. This is an option that bondholders will only exercise when the stock price has risen to a point where it is profitable to do so. The conversion feature allows bondholders to share in the good fortunes of the firm.
2. A call feature lets the firm force bondholders to sell the bond back to the firm at the firm's option. This lets the firm retire debt if it is no longer needed or to refinance debt if interest rates fall.
3. Stock purchase warrants are "sweeteners" that give holders the right to purchase shares of common stock at a specified price over a certain period of time.

Bond rating help investors interpret the risk of a bond issue. Moody's and Standard and Poor's rate bonds from AAA to D depending on the likelihood of default. The lower the rating the higher the interest rate the bond must pay to attract investors.

Valuation fundamentals

Valuation is the process that incorporates the time value of money with the concept of risk and return to determine the worth of an asset.

Key Inputs

The value of any asset depends on the cash flows it is expected to provide over time.

In addition to making cash flow estimates, the timing of the cash flows must be known. In combination with one another, the cash flow and its timing fully define the return expected from the asset.

The level of risk associated with a cash flow can affect its value. In general, the greater the risk of a cash flow, the lower its value. Therefore, in the valuation process the higher the risk, the greater the required return (discount rate).

The basic valuation model

The value of *any* asset is the present value of all future cash flows it is expected to provide over the relevant time period.

The value of an asset based on its cash flows is calculated using the following formula.

$$V_0 = \frac{CF_1}{(1+r)^1} + \frac{CF_2}{(1+r)^2} + \cdots + \frac{CF_n}{(1+r)^n}$$

or

$$V_0 = [CF_1 \times (PVIF_{r,1})] + [CF_2 \times (PVIF_{r,2})] + \cdots + [CF_n + (PVIF_{r,n})]$$

where:

V_0 = value of the asset at time zero

Cf_t = cash flow expected at the end of year t

r = appropriate required return (discount rate)

n = relevant time period

Bond valuation

Bonds are long-term debt instruments used by businesses and governments to raise large sums of money. The value of a bond is the present value of the contractual payments its issuers are obligated to make from the current time until it matures. The interest rate that the holder of the bond will receive is called the coupon rate. It does not change while the bond is outstanding. Most corporate bonds have a maturity, or par value, of $1,000. This is the amount that the firm pays to the holder when the bond matures. The discount rate used to value bonds is that rate of interest that bonds with similar risk are yielding in the market at the time the bond is being valued. This rate *will* change over time.

The following equation is used to find the value of a bond making annual coupon payments.

$$B_0 = I \times \left[\sum_{t=1}^{n} \frac{1}{(1+r_d)t} \right] + M \times \left[\frac{1}{(1+r_d)^n} \right]$$

or

$$B_0 = I \times (PVIFA_{rd,n}) + M \times (PVIF_{rd,n})$$

where:

B_0 = value of bond at time zero

I = annual interest in dollars

r_d = discount rate (required return)

n = years to maturity

M = dollar par value

Bond value behavior

There are certain external forces that constantly change the value of a bond in the marketplace. Since these forces are not controlled by bond issuers or investors, it is important to understand the impact that required return and time to maturity have on bond value.

When the required return on a bond differs from the bond's coupon interest rate, the bond's value will differ from its par value. Increases in the basic cost of long-term funds or in risk will raise the required return. Alternatively, decreases in the basic cost of long-term funds or in risk will lower the required return. When the required return is greater than the coupon interest rate, the bond value will be less than its par value. In this case, the bond will be selling at a discount. When the required return is less than the coupon, the bond value will be greater than par. In this case, the bond will be selling at a premium. In the following graph, the bond has a coupon interest rate of 10%. Notice that when the market rate is 10%, the bond sells at par ($1,000). When rates fall, the market price increases and when rates rise, the market price decreases.

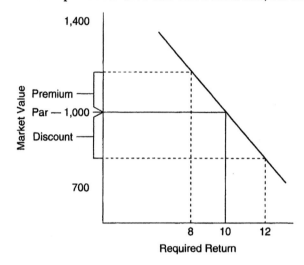

Whenever the required return of a bond is different from its coupon interest rate, the amount of time to maturity affects bond value. Constant required returns allow the bond's value to approach par as the bond moves closer to maturity.

The change in the value of a bond due to changing required returns is affected by time. A change in a bond's required return that has 10 years to maturity will have a greater impact on the bond's value than a change in required return on a bond with only 1 year left to maturity.

Yield to maturity (YTM)

The yield to maturity (YTM) is the rate that investors earn if they buy a bond at a specific price and hold it until maturity. There are three ways to calculate the YTM of a bond. The trial and error approach finds the value of the bond at various rates until the rate causing the calculated bond value to equal its current value is found. The approximation yield formula is given in the following equation.

$$\text{Approximate Yield} = \frac{I + \dfrac{M - B_0}{n}}{\dfrac{M + B_0}{2}}$$

where:

I = interest payment

B_0 = current market value

M = maturity value

n = periods to maturity

The hand-held business calculator provides the most accurate YTM value. Refer to your user's manual on how to calculate YTM values.

Semiannual interest and bond values

The valuation of a bond paying *semi-annual* interest can be found by performing a simple modification to the equation used to find the value of a bond with annual interest payments.

1. Convert the annual interest, I, to semiannual by dividing by two.

2. Multiply the years to maturity, n, by two.

3. Convert the required stated return from an annual rate, rd, to a semiannual rate by dividing it by two.

The equation used for finding the value of a bond paying semiannual interest is displayed in the following formula.

or

$$B_0 = \frac{I}{2} \times \left[\sum_{t=1}^{2n} \frac{1}{\left(1+\frac{r_d}{2}\right)^t} \right] + M \times \left[\frac{1}{\left(1+\frac{r_d}{2}\right)^{2n}} \right]$$

$$B_0 = \frac{I}{2} \times \left(PVIF_{\frac{r_d}{2},2n} \right) + M \times \left(PVIF_{\frac{r_d}{2},2n} \right)$$

■ Sample Problems and Solutions

Example 1   Valuation of any asset

Compute the value of a Picasso oil painting that is projected to sell for $15 million in 10 years if
the cost of capital is 20%.

a. **Equation Solution**

To find the value of any business asset, compute the present value of the cash flows that the asset will generate. In this case, the painting will only generate cash flow when it is sold at the end of 10 years.

$$P_{oil} = \$15,000,000/(1.20^{10}) = \$2,422,580$$

b.   Calculator Solution

$N = 10$

$I = 20$

$FV = 15,000,000$

CPT $PV = \$2,422,584$

Example 2

You are appraising a commercial office building that is fully leased and expected to stay that way. The net revenue off the building is $144,000 per year. The expected life of the building is 30 years. What is the value of the building if the required rate of return is 18%?

a.   Equation Solution

Again, all that you need to do is compute the present value of the cash flows. The net cash flows will be $144,000 per year for 30 years.

$$P_{\text{building}} = \$144,000(\text{PVIFA}_{30\,\text{yrs},18\%}) = \$144,000(5.517) = \$794,448$$

b.   Calculator Solution

$N = 30$

$I = 18$

$PMT = 144,000$

CPT $PV = \$794,420$

Example 3

How much would you pay for a business that is expected to lose $10,000 for each of the next 5 years and then to earn $15,000 each year from then on? Assume a required rate of return of 20%.

a.   Table Solution

To find the present value of this stream of payments, you must first find the present value of the annuity of negative payments, and then find the present value of the deferred annuity of positive payments. The two streams are then added together.

$$PV_{\text{neg cash flow}} = -\$10,000(\text{PVIFA}_{5\,\text{yrs},20\%}) = -\$10,000(2.991) = -\$29,910$$

$$PV_{\text{pos cash flow}} = (\$15,000/0.2)(\text{PVIF}) = \$75,000(0.402) = \$30,150$$

$$PV_{\text{all cash flows}} = -\$29,910 + \$30,150 = \$240$$

Note 1: The present value of the $15,000 that goes on forever is computed by dividing the cash flow by the discount rate. This is the formula for a perpetuity.

Note 2: Notice that the discount rate used to find the present value of these assets is high. The discount rate reflects the risk of the investment, and since paintings, real estate, and business ventures tend to be risky, it is appropriate to use a high rate when computing value.

b.   Calculator Solution

$N = 5$	$N = 5$
$I = 20$	$I = 20$
PMT = 10,000	$FV = 75,000$
CPT $PV_{\text{neg cash flow}} = -\$29{,}906$	CPT $PV_{\text{pos cash flow}} = \$30{,}141$

$PV_{\text{all cash flows}} = -\$29{,}906 + \$30{,}141 = \$235$

Example 4:   Bond Valuation

Compute the value of a bond that matures in three years and pays interest annually. The coupon rate is 10% and the face amount is $1,000. Assume a discount rate of 12%.

a.   Table Solution

If the coupon rate is 10%, the interest payment is 0.10($1,000) = $100. To value this bond you must find the present value of the interest payments, plus the present value of the final payment of $1,000 that will be received at maturity.

$$P_{\text{bond}} = \$100(\text{PVIFA}_{3\text{yrs},12\%}) + \$1{,}000(\text{PVIF}_{3\text{yrs},12\%})$$
$$= \$100(2.402) + \$1{,}000(0.712)$$
$$P_{\text{bond}} = \$952.20$$

b.   Calculator Solution

$N = 3$

$I = 12$

$PMT = 100$

$FV = 1{,}000$

CPT $PV = \$951.96$

Example 5

Compute the value in Example 4 above, if the bond matures in 20 years instead of in 3 years.

a.   Table Solution

$$P_{\text{bond}} = \$100(\text{PVIFA}_{20\text{yrs},12\%}) + \$1000(\text{PVIF}_{20\text{yrs},12\%}) = \$100(7.469) + \$1{,}000(0.104) = \$850$$

Note:

When the term to maturity increases, the effect of the increased discount rate is greater. In Example 4, the bond sells for $952.20, but in Example 5 it sells for $850.

b.   Calculator Solution

$N = 20$

$I = 12$

$PMT = 100$

$FV = 1{,}000$

CPT $PV = \$850.61$

Example 6

Review the following table. Explain what it implies about interest rate risk.

Term	Discount Rate 9%	10%	11%
1	1008.70	1000	991.00
10	1063.00	1000	940.00
20	1090.00	1000	920.30

Solution

As the discount rate increases, the value of the bond falls. This is interest rate risk. If market rates increase after you buy a bond, the value of the bond will decrease. If you sell it, you will suffer a loss. The magnitude of the effect on value of a change in interest rates increases as the term to maturity increases. Notice that a 1% increase in the discount rate results in about a $9 decrease in value for the bond that matures in 1 year, but an $80 decrease in value for the bond that matures in 20 years.

Example 7

A zero coupon bond pays no interest. How much would you pay for a zero coupon bond that pays $1,000 at maturity in 5 years, if the discount rate is 12%?

a.   **Table Solution:**

$$P_{bond} = \$1,000/(1.12^5) = \$1,000(PVIF_{5yrs,12\%}) = \$1,000(0.567) = \$567$$

b.   **Calculator Solution**

$N = 5$

$I = 12$

$FV = 1,000$

CPT $PV = \$567.43$

Example 8

Compute the value of a bond that matures in 3 years and pays interest *semi-annually*. The coupon rate is 10% and the face amount is $1,000. Assume a discount rate of 12%.

a.   **Table Solution**

If the coupon rate is 10%, the *semiannual interest payment* is 0.05($1,000) = $50.

$$P_{bond} = \$50(PVIFA_{6\ periods,6\%}) + \$1,000(PVIF_{6\ periods,6\%})$$
$$= \$50(4.917) + \$1,000(0.705)$$
$$P_{bond} = \$950.85$$

Note that now the number of periods has increased to 6 because there are 6 payments being made over the 3 years. The discount has been divided in half as well because the 6-month rate will be one half of the annual rate.

b.   Calculator Solution

$N = 6$

$I = 6$

$PMT = 50$

$FV = 1,000$

CPT $PV = \$950.83$

Example 9   Yield to Call

Citicorp bonds, which mature in 7 years, have a coupon rate of 9%, have a par value of $1000, and sell for $904.47. What is the yield to maturity?

a.   Equation Solution

To solve for the yield to maturity by hand, use the approximation formula. (The calculator solution is also 11.03%.)

$$\text{Approximate Yield} = \frac{I + \dfrac{M - B_0}{n}}{\dfrac{M + B_0}{2}}$$

$$\text{YTM} = \frac{90 + \dfrac{(1000 - 904.47)}{7}}{\dfrac{1000 + 904.47}{2}} = 0.1103$$

b.   Calculator Solution

$N = 7$

$PV = -904.47$

$PMT = 90$

$FV = 1,000$

CPT $I = 11.03$

Bond Valuation Quick Drill Problems

These problems are quick and easy practice to see how well you have understood the concepts in this chapter. The answers follow.

1. A building has an expected life of 30 years. Its net cash flows are projected to be $120,500 per year. If a discount rate of 17% is appropriate, what is the value of the building?

2. If the discount rate were to increase to 23% because of a perception of increased risk in the real estate market what would be the revised value of the building?

3. A bond's par value is $1000. It has 5 years until maturity. Its coupon rate is 7%. What is the value of the bond if the market rate is 10%, assuming annual compounding?

4. Given the bond in Problem 3, what would the current value be if the market rate were 5%?

5. Again use looking at the bond in Problem 3, what would the value be if it had 30 years to maturity instead of 5 years, assuming all other features are as given in Problem 3?

6. What is the price of a bond with features as are given in Problem 3 except that it matures in 1 year rather than in 5 years?

7. Review your solutions to Problems 5 and 6. Which bond is subject the greatest interest rate risk?

8. What would the value of the bond discussed in Problem 3 be if interest payments made were semi-annual rather than annually?

9. What would be the value of the bond discussed in Problem 4 if interest payments were made semi-annually rather than annually?

10. What will be the price of the bond discussed in Problem 3 when there are 4 years before it matures?

11. What is the percentage change in price of the bond discussed in problem 10 between when there are 5 years before it matures and when there are 4 years before it matures?

12. What is the current yield of the bond discussed in Problem 3?

13. Is the sum of the current yield and the change in price found in Problem 11 the same as the market rate?

14. A bond has a current market price of $1,125. It has a annual coupon rate of 6%, a par value of $1,000 and matures in 10 years. What is its yield to maturity?

15. A bond has a current market price of $825. It has an annual coupon rate of 6%, a par value of $1,000 and matures in 10 years. What is its yield to maturity?

16. What would be the yield to maturity for the bond discussed in Problem 14 if the payments were made semiannually rather than annually? If you use a calculator remember to multiply your answer by two.

17. What would be the yield to maturity for the bond discussed in Problem 15 if the payments were made semiannually rather than annually?

   *The solutions listed below were found using a financial calculator. Some of these problems require the use of a financial calculator since some of the interest rates are not in the tables.

Answers
1. $702,441.45

2. $522,860.82

3. $886.28

4. $1,086.59

5. $717.19

6. $972.73

7. Problem 5

8. $884.17

9. $1,087.52

10. $904.90

11. 2.10%

12. 7.90%

13. Yes

14. 4.43%

15. 8.69%

16. 4.44%

17. 8.65%

■ Study Tips

1. The principle behind valuation is simple. Any financial asset may be valued by finding the present value of all cash flows. The trick is (a) identifying the cash flows, (b) determining how to compute their present value. This later issue requires a thorough understanding of time-value-of-money mathematics. If you are struggling with this chapter go back and reread the TVM chapter, paying particular attention to the sections covering present value.

2. If you can possibly obtain a financial calculator, use it to check your work on these valuation problems. Financial calculators are especially useful for bond calculations.

3. You can check your work on bond valuation problems by applying the discount/premium method. You learned that as interest rates fall the price of the bond increases, and vice versa. When you value a bond, compare the discount rate to the coupon rate and decide whether the bond should be selling for more or less than $1,000. Compare your answer and see if it is reasonable. For example, say you are to find the value of a bond with a 10% coupon, 5 years to maturity and an 8% discount rate. Since the discount rate is below the coupon rate, rates have fallen. When rates fall, the bond price rises. Therefore you know that the value of the bond must be over $1,000. In fact, the value of this bond is actually $1,079.85.

■ Student Notes

■ Sample Exam—Chapter 6

True/False

T F 1. The value of any asset depends on the accounting profits it is expected to provide over the ownership period.

T F 2. If the value of a bond, B_0, is less than its par value, the bond is selling at a discount.

T F 3. The yield to maturity on a bond with a current price equal to its par value will always equal the coupon interest rate.

T F 4. A bond covenant contains a description of the call feature and the sinking fund for a bond.

T F 5. The bond indenture reports on the risk characteristics of the bond.

T F 6. Bond rating agencies provide investors a rating that reflects the default risk of a bond issue.

T F 7. Any action that increases the risk of an asset will also increase that asset's required return.

T F 9. Bonds with short maturities will have less interest rate risk than bonds with longer maturities and equal features.

T F 10. As market interest rates increase bond prices increase.

T F 11. The discount rate of a bond is synonymous with the bond's required return.

T F 12. The trial-and-error approach to bond valuation involves finding the value of the bond at various yield to maturity rates until the rate that causes the calculated bond value to equal its current value is found.

T F 13. The longer the period until a bond matures, the less a change in market interest rates will affect its market value.

T F 14. Longer-term bonds have lower interest rate risk than short-term bonds.

T F 15. The value of a bond is the present value of its coupon payments until maturity plus the present value of its par value at maturity.

Multiple Choice

1. _____ is the process that links risk and return in order to determine the worth of an asset.
   a. Depreciation
   b. Valuation
   c. Evaluation
   d. Discounting

2. The value of an asset is the _____ of all future cash flows it is expected to provide over a relevant time period.
   a. required return
   b. future value
   c. present value
   d. sum

3. Risk is generally incorporated into the _____ in the present value model.
   a. discount rate
   b. cash flows
   c. timing
   d. total value

4. A bond will sell at _____ if the required return is greater than the coupon rate.
   a. par
   b. a premium
   c. liquidation value
   d. a discount

5. The present value of a bond's _____ determines the value of the bond.
   a. dividend
   b. coupon payment
   c. maturity value
   d. coupon payment and maturity value

6. _____ is/are long-term debt instruments used by business and government.
   a. Preferred stock
   b. Retained earnings
   c. Bonds
   d. Common stock

7. Interest rate risk and the time to maturity have a relationship that is best characterized as
   a. inverse.
   b. unrelated.
   c. varying.
   d. direct.

8. What is the approximate yield to maturity for a $1000 par value bond selling for $1100 that matures in 5 years and pays a 10% coupon?
   a. 12.5%
   b. 7.6%
   c. 10%
   d. 13.6%

9. As market rates increase the value of a bond will _____, all other things equal.
   a. increase
   b. decrease
   c. remain unchanged
   d. cannot be determined

10. The longer the term a bond has before it matures, _____ will be the affect on its value due to a 1% change in market interest rates.
    a. the greater
    b. the lower
    c. either a or b, depending on the direction of the interest rate change.
    d. neither a or b, since bond maturity has no impact on interest rate sensitivity.

11. What is the value of a bond with 10 years to maturity, a 7% coupon rate, annual interest payments, $1000 par and a 7% market rate?
    a. $900
    b. $1000
    c. $1100
    d. $1150

12. The yield to maturity on a bond with a price equal to its par value will
    a. always be equal to the coupon rate.
    b. will be more than the coupon rate.
    c. will be lower than the coupon rate.
    d. will depend upon the required return.

13. What is the yield to maturity for the following bond (to the nearest full percentage)?

Current Price	Coupon Rate	Par Value	Frequency of Interest Payment	Years to Maturity
$954	12%	$1000	Annually	7

   a. 7%
   c. 12%
   b. 9%
   d. 13%

14. For an investor that plans to purchase a bond that matures in one year, the primary concern should be
    a. yield to maturity.
    c. interest rate risk.
    b. coupon rate risk.
    d. exchange rate risk.

15. A bond pays no interest. It has a $1000 par and matures in 5 years. What is its value if market rates are 10%?
    a. $0
    b. $500
    c. $1000
    d. $620.92

16. The key inputs to the valuation process include cash flows (returns), the required return (risk), and
    a. discount rates.
    c. timing.
    b. present value.
    d. expected return.

17. Corporate bonds usually have which of the following?
    a. face value of $1000
    b. an initial maturity of 10 to 30 years
    c. semi-annual interest payments
    d. all of the above

18. A firm has issued a bond that has a coupon of 11%, semi-annual interest payments, a required return of 14%, and 10 years left until maturity. What will the bond sell for today?
    a. $1000
    c. $843
    b. $841
    d. $895

19. A bond has a current market price of $1100. It is said to be selling at a
    a. premium.
    b. discount.
    c. bonus.
    d. reward.

20. Which of the following is not likely to be included in bonds' covenants?
    a. restriction on dividends
    c. minimum levels of liquidity
    b. limits on additional debt
    d. call provision

21. In early 2007, three-month Treasury bills were offering a return of approximately:
    a. 3 percent.
    b. 5 percent.
    c. 7 percent.
    d. 9 percent.

22. All of the following are measures of total return, except:
    a. current yield.
    b. yield to call.
    c. yield to maturity.
    d. Trick question, all are measures of total return.

23. Which of the following bonds has the highest cost per unit?
    a. Bond A, a $2,000 par value bond priced at $72.045
    b. Bond B, a $1,000 par value bond priced at $100.000
    c. Bond C, a $900 par value bond priced at $144.090
    d. You would pay the same amount for Bond A and Bond C.

Essay

1. What is interest rate risk? When is it greatest?

2. Under what conditions will an investor actually receive a return on a bond equal to the yield to maturity?

■ Chapter 6 Answer Sheet

True/False		Multiple Choice	
1.	F	1.	B
2.	T	2.	C
3.	T	3.	A
4.	F	4.	D
5.	F	5.	D
6.	T	6.	C
7.	T	7.	D
8.	F	8.	B
9.	T	9.	B
10.	F	10.	A
11.	T	11.	B
12.	T	12.	A
13.	F	13.	D
14.	F	14.	A
15.	T	15.	D
		16.	C
		17.	D
		18.	B
		19.	A
		20.	D
		21.	B
		22.	A
		23.	A

$$YTM = \frac{100 + \dfrac{1{,}000 - 1{,}100}{5}}{\dfrac{1{,}000 + 1{,}100}{2}} = 7.62\%$$

$$\frac{120 + \dfrac{1000 - 954}{7}}{\dfrac{1000 + 954}{2}} = 12.95\%$$

$$B_0 = \$55 \times (10.594) + \$1000(0.258)$$
$$= 840.67$$

Essay

1. Interest rate risk is the volatility in the price of a bond due to changing interest rates. It is greatest when the time to maturity is longest.

2. An investor will earn the yield to maturity only if the bond is held until it matures. The yield to maturity includes both interest income and changes in the value of the bond over time. The current yield is computed as the interest payment divided by the current market price. The yield to maturity will include this return plus any return from price changes in the bond over time. If the bond is not held until it matures these price changes will not be fully received.

Chapter 7
Stock Valuation

■ Chapter Summary

As we discussed in Chapter 6, all assets are valued as the present value of all future cash flows. The value of a bond was the present value of its interest and principal payments and the value of a building was the present value of its net cash flows. The value of stock is also found as the present value of its cash flows. The problem is that estimating these cash flows can be very difficult. We will investigate various methods for estimating cash flows and for computing their value in this chapter.

LG 1 *Differentiate between debt and equity capital.* Capital refers to a firm's long-term sources of funds. This capital can be either borrowed or equity. Borrowed capital is called debt capital or debt financing. Equity capital is obtained by selling shares of stock to investors who then have an ownership interest in the firm.

LG 2 *Discuss the rights, characteristics, and features of both common and preferred stock.* Common stock is the type of stock that you usually think of when discussing stock. It gives the holder the right to residual earnings and the right to vote in key company issues. Preferred stockholders neither vote nor share in company profits. They only receive a fixed dividend payment.

LG 3 *Describe the process of issuing common stock, including venture capital, going public, and the investment banker, and interpreting stock quotations.* Most firms do not issue stock very often, so must enlist the services of various professionals to help with the process.

LG 4 *Understand the concept of market efficiency and basic common stock valuation using zero growth, constant growth, and variable growth models.* The idea behind market efficiency is that all securities are priced correctly all of the time. If a stock was overpriced, investors would sell it. This would reduce its price and increase its return. When the return has risen to its correct level, the selling will stop. Stocks are valued based on the present value of their dividends. For firms that pay a constant dividend, the perpetuity formula is used. This chapter introduces other simplifying methods for valuing stock.

LG 5 *Discuss the free cash flow valuation model and the book value, liquidation value, and price/earnings (P/E) multiples approaches.* The book and liquidation value methods to stock valuation ignore the value of future cash flows. The *P/E* method involves multiplying the firm's expected earnings per share by the industry *P/E*.

LG 6 *Understand the relationships among financial decisions, return, risk and the firm's value.* Managerial decisions that decrease cash flows or increase risk will result in low stock prices. Similarly, if management can increase cash flows without increasing risk, stock prices can be increased. This is the goal of financial managers.

■ Chapter Notes

Valuation of stock is complicated by the fact that the future cash flows are not known with any certainty. This chapter discusses various ways analysts value stock despite this problem.

Debt versus Equity Capital

In the last chapter we discussed the characteristics of debt. This chapter focuses on equity. Investors who buy equity are called stockholders and they receive certain rights. These rights include:

1. A voice in management.
2. Claims on income and assets.

Stock can be distinguished from debt by two additional features:

1. The security does not mature.
2. Dividend income is subject to taxes.

The true owners of the firm are the stockholders. They are sometimes referred to as the residual owners because they receive whatever is left after all other claims on the business have been satisfied. Stockholders can share in the good fortunes of the firm if it does well. However, stockholders are not guaranteed anything except that they cannot lose more than they have invested.

Terminology

Par value: This is a useless term that refers to the value assigned to one share of stock for accounting purposed—usually $1.00.

Preemptive rights: This allows common stockholders to maintain their proportionate ownership in the corporation when new shares are issued by giving them the right to buy more shares in any future issue.

Authorized, outstanding and issued shares: The firm's charter will specify the maximum number of shares it may issue. More shares can only be issued if shareholders agree by a vote. The number of shares outstanding is the number that is held by the public. Issued shares are the shares of common stock that have been put into circulation: they represent the sum of outstanding shares and treasury stock.

Voting rights: Stockholders have the right to vote on key issues affecting the firm.

Dividends: Stockholders have the right to receive dividends at the discretion of the board of directors. Dividends are usually paid quarterly.

American Depository Shares: Securities backed by stocks of foreign companies that are held in bank vaults that facilitate U.S. investor purchase of non-U.S. companies and trade them in U.S. markets.

Preferred stock

Preferred stock is a much like debt as it is like common stock. Preferred stockholders receive a fixed dividend payment that does not change, even if the firm does extremely well. They are not allowed to vote, unless the firm has defaulted on its dividends payments. It is called preferred stock because preferred stock dividends are paid before common stock dividends.

Preferred stock is most often used by public utilities that want to increase their financial leverage without increasing risk, by acquiring firms in merger transactions, or by firms that are experiencing losses and need additional financing. Preferred stock is frequently combined with other special features, such as conversions or warrants, to enhance its attractiveness to investors.

Basic rights of preferred stockholders

Distribution of earnings: Preferred stockholders are given priority over common stockholders with respect to the distribution of earnings. If the stated preferred stock dividend is passed (not paid) by the board of directors, the payment of dividends to common stockholders is prohibited.

Distribution of assets: Preferred stockholders are usually given preference over common stockholders in the liquidation of assets as a result of a firm's bankruptcy, although they must wait until all creditors have been satisfied.

Voting rights: Since preferred stockholders are not exposed to the same amount of risk as common stockholders (distribution of earnings, distribution of assets, fixed dividend payment), they are not normally given voting rights.

Features of preferred stock

Restrictive covenants: Restrictive covenants are usually placed on preferred stock to ensure the continued existence of the firm and the regular payment of the stated dividend. Violation of a preferred stock covenant usually permits preferred stockholders either to obtain representation on the firm's board of directors or to force the retirement of their stock at or above its par, or stated value.

Cumulation: For preferred stock that is *cumulative*, all dividends in arrears must be paid along with the current dividend before payment of dividends to common stockholders. Preferred stock that is *noncumulative* does not accumulate dividends.

Participation: Most issues of preferred stock are *nonparticipating*, which means that preferred stockholders receive only the specified dividend payments. Occasionally, *participating* preferred stock is issued, which allows preferred stockholders to participate with common stockholders in the receipt of dividends beyond a specified amount.

Call feature: Preferred stock is usually callable, which means that the issuer can retire outstanding stock within a certain period of time at a specified price. The call price is usually set above the initial issuance price, but it may decrease according to a predetermined schedule as time passes.

Conversion feature: Preferred stock often contains a conversion feature that allows holders to convert each share into a stated number of shares of common stock.

Special types of preferred stock

ARPS: Instead of a fixed dividend payment, adjustable-rate preferred stock (ARPS) pays a dividend that is tied to interest rates on specific government securities.

PIK: Payment-in-kind (PIK) preferred stock, usually does not pay cash dividends, but rather pays in additional shares of preferred stock, which pay dividends in even more preferred stock. After a stated time period, PIK preferred are supposed to begin paying cash dividends or provide holders with a chance to swap for another, more traditional security. PIK preferred are equivalent to junk bonds, which are extremely risky, and are used to finance corporate takeovers.

Preferred stock advantages

Ability to increase financial leverage: Since preferred dividends are fixed payments to its holders, the use of preferred stock will help to increase the firm's financial leverage, which will magnify the effects of increased earnings on common stockholders' returns.

Flexibility: Although preferred stock is similar to debt, it differs from debt in that the issuer can pass a dividend payment without suffering the consequences that result when an interest payment is missed on a bond.

Use in corporate restructuring: Preferred stock is often exchanged for shares of common stock in the restructuring process of a corporation. The preferred stock allows for the payment of a fixed dividend and for the remaining funds to be reinvested to perpetuate the growth of the new enterprise.

Preferred stock disadvantages

Seniority of the preferred stockholder's claim: Preferred stockholders are given priority over common stockholders, which jeopardizes the returns of common stockholders.

Cost: Unlike the payment to debt holders, the payment to preferred stockholders is not guaranteed, and the holders of preferred stock must be compensated for this risk with higher interest rates. Also, preferred stock dividends are not tax deductible, unlike the interest payments on debt.

Difficult to sell: A large number of investors find preferred stock unattractive, and most often firms must include special features such as conversion or warrants to enhance its marketability.

 Most firms begin with an initial investment by its founders in the form of common stock. As the firm develops, venture capital firms may supply additional funds. These firms look for opportunities to get involved with companies that are in their early stage of product development. While many startup firms fail, when one is successful, the returns can be very high.

The term "going public" refers to selling company common stock to the public for the first time. The firm may make a (1) public offering, (2) a rights offering, or (3) a private placement.

The first time stock is offered to the public is called an initial public offering (IPO). This is a primary market transaction since the issuing firm is receiving the proceeds of the sale. An investment banking firm will usually be involved in an IPO. The main activity of the investment banker is underwriting. Underwriting involves purchasing the stock from the issuing firm and reselling it to the public, usually through its brokerage network. If the issue is large the investment banking firm may form a syndicate to spread the risk. A syndicate is a group of investment banking firms that join together temporarily to market a security to the public.

Common stock valuation

 To determine the value of a common stock, it is important to keep in mind the concept of market efficiency. The prices of common stocks are constantly adjusting to the differences in investors' required returns, k, and the investors' expected return, K. The expected return is the return that is expected to be earned each period on a given asset over an infinite time horizon. If the expected return is less than the required return, investors will sell the asset since the return is not sufficient for the amount of risk that is involved. This will drive the price down to the point where the required return equals the expected return. The opposite is true for an asset that has an expected return greater than its required return. Investors will buy the asset, driving its price up to the point where the expected return equals the required return.

The basic stock valuation equation

The value of common stock is equal to the present value of all future dividends it is expected to provide over an infinite time horizon. From a valuation viewpoint, capital gains are not considered, only dividends are taken into account. The basic stock valuation equation is as follows:

$$P_0 = \frac{D_1}{(1+r_s)^1} + \frac{D_2}{(1+r_s)^2} + \cdots + \frac{D_\infty}{(1+r_s)^\infty}$$

where:

P_0 = value of common stock

D_t = per-share dividend expected at the end of year t

r_s = required return on common stock

The equation can be simplified by redefining each year's anticipated dividend growth. For stocks that have dividends with zero growth, the following zero growth model can be used.

$$P_0 = \frac{D_1}{r_s}$$

The constant growth model assumes that dividends will grow at a constant rate, g, which is less than the required return. To find the growth rate of a stock's dividend, simply apply the technique described in Chapter 4 for finding growth rates. In its simplified state, the constant growth model can be written as follows:

$$P_0 = \frac{D_1}{r_s - g}$$

where: g = constant growth rate

The variable growth model assumes a shift in the growth rate, g, after n years. To use the model, one must find the dividends at the end of each year during the initial growth period. Next, find the present value of dividends occurring within the initial growth period and sum these values to obtain the net present value of the dividends during the initial growth period. Next find the value of the stock at the end of the initial growth period by multiplying the dividend of the last year of initial growth by the new growth rate. Plug the new dividend into the constant growth model to find the stock's value. Finally, find the present value of the stock in the new growth period and add it to the present value of its dividends in the initial growth period to determine the stock's value.

Example

Determine the value of a stock which had a recent dividend payment of $1.00 in 2007. The dividend is expected to grow at a 10% rate for the next 2 years. After 2 years, the growth rate is expected to drop to 5%. The firm has a 12% required return.

t	End of Year	Dividend in Year 0	$FVIF_{10\%,t}$	Dividend at the End of Year t	$PVIF_{12\%,t}$	Present Value of Dividends
1	2008	$1.00	1.100	$1.10	0.893	0.98
2	2009	$1.00	1.210	$1.21	0.797	0.96

Sum of present value of dividends = $1.94

$$D_{2010} = D_{2009} \times 1.05 = \$1.21 \times 1.05 = \$1.27$$

$$P_{2009} = \frac{D_{2010}}{r_s - g_2} = \frac{\$1.27}{0.12 - 0.05} = \$18.14$$

$$\$18.14 \times PVIF_{12\%,2} = \$18.14 \times 0.797 = \$14.46$$

$$P_{2007} = \$1.94 + \$14.46 = \$16.40$$

Other approaches to common stock valuation

The book value per share is the amount per share of common stock to be received if all of the firm's assets are sold for their exact book value and if the proceeds remaining, after all liabilities are paid, are distributed among the common stockholders. This method is not often used because it ignores the firm's earning potential.

The liquidation value per share is the actual amount per share of common stock to be received if all of the firm's assets are sold, all liabilities are paid, and any remaining money is divided among the shareholders. The liquidation value per share is more accurate than the book value approach but it still fails to recognize future earnings.

The price/earnings multiple approach is calculated by multiplying the firm's expected earnings per share (EPS) by the average price/earnings (*P/E*) ratio for the industry. The price/earnings multiple approach should be used before the book value or liquidation value approach because it takes into account the expected earnings of the firm.

Decision making and common stock value

Stock valuation is based on expected returns and risk. Changes in these variables can have a substantial impact on the valuation process.

Assuming that economic conditions remain constant, an increase in stockholders' dividend expectations should raise the value of the firm. If a financial manager can increase the level of expected returns without increasing risk, the value of the firm will increase.

Any action taken by the financial manager that increases risk will also increase the required return. An increase in the required return will lower the share value, P_0, of a firm. Any decision made by the financial manager that increases risk will reduce the share value of a firm. The same holds true of any reduction in risk. With reduced risk, share value will increase.

Any decision made by the financial manager rarely affects return and risk independently. Keep in mind that the net result of the financial manager's decision should be an increase in shareholder wealth.

■ Sample Problems and Solutions

Example 1.   Stock Valuation

Assume the current dividend is $3.00 per year. The firm has grown at a constant rate of 5% for the last 10 years, and this growth rate is expected to continue. If the appropriate discount rate is 14%, what is the value of the stock?

Solution

Use the Gordon growth model, $P = (D_0(1 + g))/(r_s - g)$, where P = price of the stock, D_0 = the current dividend, r = discount rate, and g = growth rate.

$$\text{price stock} = \frac{\$3.00(1.05)}{0.14 - 0.05} = \$35$$

Example 2

Assume that *next period's* dividend is expected to be $3.15. If a growth rate of 5% is assumed and the appropriate discount rate is 14%, what is the value of the stock?

Solution

The usual error that students make using the Gordon growth model is getting confused with what goes in the numerator. If next period's dividend is given in the problem, then the formula is

$$P = D_1/(r_s - g)$$

where D_1 = *next period's* dividend.

$$\text{price stock} = \frac{\$3.15}{0.14 - 0.05} = \$35$$

Example 3.   Zero Growth Model

What is the price of a share of stock for a firm that pays a $2.00 dividend? The dividend has never changed and is not expected to in the future. The appropriate discount rate is 12%.

Solution

If the dividends are expected to stay the same forever, then the zero growth model can be used. After reviewing the Gordon growth model, what would you expect the zero growth model to be? If the growth rate is zero, then the Gordon growth model becomes the formula for a perpetuity, which is what we would expect.

$$\text{price stock} = \$2/0.12 = \$16.67$$

Example 4.   Mixing It Up

A more realistic example than the constant growth or zero growth model is what might be called an uneven growth. Suppose that you are evaluating the stock of a relatively new firm. For the first several years you expect high growth, say 20%. Then a more moderate level of growth may be observed. Finally, the dividends may be constant when the firm has matured. The principles used to work out the value of this stock are the same as used in the other examples. That is, find the present value of the cash flows. Begin by drawing a time line, then compute the present value of each cash flow and, finally, add them all together.

A firm is expected to grow at an annual rate of 20% for the next 2 years. The growth is expected to decrease to 8% for the following 2 years and to be 4% thereafter. Assuming the current dividend is $2.00/yr and that the appropriate discount rate is 15%, what would be the value of the stock?

Solution

First draw a time line that shows what the dividends are going to be each year.

2   2.4   2.88   3.11   3.36   3.49   ... constant growth at 4%

0   1   2   3   4   5   6   7

Next compute the present value of the first 4 dividends.

$$PV = 2.4/1.15 + 2.88/1.15^2 + 3.11/1.15^3 + 3.36/1.15^4 = \$8.23$$

Now find the present value of the constant growth portion of the cash flow.

$$PV = 3.49/(0.15 - 0.04) = \$38.78/(1.15^4) = \$22.17$$

Finally, add the two parts together.

$$\text{Price of stock} = \$8.23 + \$22.17 = \$30.40$$

Note: The most common mistake in these types of problems is to not discount the growth portion of the cash flow for the right number of periods. Recognize that the Gordon growth model finds the value one period before the dividend in the numerator is received. This is at the end of period 4. That means that the $38.78 must be discounted back 4 periods to find its value at time 0.

■ Stock Valuation Quick Drill Problems

These problems are quick and easy practice to see how well you have understood the concepts in this chapter. The answers follow.

1. What is the price of a share of preferred stock that has a dividend of $3 if the cost of preferred (r_p) is 15%?

2. What is the value of a share of preferred stock if the dividend is $3 and the price is $30?

3. What would you pay for a share of common stock if you expect the next dividend to be $2 and you expect to sell it in one year for $20, assuming the cost of equity (r_e) is 10%?

4. What would you pay for a share of common stock if you expect the next dividend to be $2 and you expect to sell it in one year for $20, assuming the cost of equity (r_e) is 15%?

5. What would you pay for a share of stock if the next dividend was $2, the one after that was $2.5 and after two years you expected to sell the stock for $15, assuming a cost of equity of 15%?

6. What would you pay for a share of common stock with a $3 dividend that was not expected to grow in the future, assuming a 15% cost of equity?

7. What would you pay for a share of common stock where the last dividend was $3 and that was expected to grow at 5% per year indefinitely, assuming a 15% cost of equity?

8. What would you pay for a share of common stock where the last dividend was $3 and that was expected to grow at 8% per year indefinitely, assuming a 15% cost of equity?

9. What would you pay for a share of common stock where the last dividend was $3 and that was expected to grow at 5% per year indefinitely, assuming a 25% cost of equity?

10. What would you pay for a share of common stock where the last dividend was $3 and that was expected to grow at –5% per year indefinitely, assuming a 25% cost of equity?

11. You do not expect there to be a dividend paid next year. After that, however, you expect a $2 dividend that will grow at a constant 6% thereafter. How much would you pay for the stock assuming a cost of equity of 10%?

12. What will be the price of the stock discussed in Problem 11 one year from now?

13. What is the percentage increase in price between now and one year from now using the results found in Problems 11 and 12?

14. A stock currently sells for $25 and pays a $3 dividend. What is the current yield?

15. Suppose the current yield on a stock was 3% and the cost of equity was 15%. What would you expect the appreciation in the stock's price to be?

16. The beta of a stock is 1.5. The required return on the market is 12% and the risk free rate is 5%. What is the cost of equity?

17. What is the price of a share of stock if the beta is 2, its next dividend is projected to be $3 and its growth rate is expected to be a constant 7%, assuming the market return is 15% and the risk free rate is 6%?

18. The PE ratio for a firm is 20. Expected earnings per share are $1.5. What is the current price of the firm's stock?

19. You wish to estimate the value of a company that has not yet issued stock. The PE ratios of similar firms is 16. You expect earnings to be $200,000. What is the total value of the firm?

20. Given the data in Problem 19, what would be the price per share if you issue 100,000 shares?

Answers

1. $20

2. 10%

3. $20.00

4. $19.13

5. $14.97

6. $20.00

7. $31.50

8. $46.29

9. $15.75

10. $9.50

11. $45.45

12. $50.00

13. 10%

14. 12%

15. 12%

16. 15.5%

17. 17.65

18. $30.00

19. $3,200,000

20. $32

■ Study Tips

1. The Gordon growth model is really a fairly simple equation to use; however, students tend to make errors using it by being sloppy about counting time periods. The Gordon growth model finds the value of stock with constant growth one period before the time when the dividend in the numerator occurs. For example, if the dividend used in the numerator is received at the end of period 5, the Gordon growth model provides the value of the stock at the end of period 4. Review the examples above and make sure that you understand this point.

2. The mathematics of solving for the price of stock with odd growth at the beginning followed by constant growth is about as difficult as you will encounter in this course. Spend the time it takes to fully understand how to do these problems. This is where your work on time value of money begins to pay off.

3. If your calculator has the ability to handle multiple cash flows you should learn how to apply this to solving theses problems.

■ Sample Exam—Chapter 7

True/False

T F 1. It is easier to value stock than it is to find the value of bonds.

T F 2. The value of a share of stock depends on the cash flows investors can expect to receive by owning that stock.

T F 3. The dividend valuation model assumes that dividends continue being paid forever.

T F 4. When valuing common stock, capital gains (as opposed to dividends) determine a majority of the stock's current value.

T F 5. When using the constant growth model for the valuation of common stock, the constant growth rate, g, has to be greater than the required return, r_s, in order for the model to be useful.

T F   6. The book value of an asset is simply the amount paid for the asset minus its accumulated depreciation.

T F   7. Any action that increases the risk of an asset will also increase that asset's required return.

T F   8. Under the efficient market hypothesis, when the expected return of a common stock is less than its required return, investors will buy the stock and drive the price upward.

T F   9. The Gordon growth model requires that required return exceed long term expected growth.

T F   0. The most accurate approach to common stock valuation is the book value per share method.

T F 11. The numerator in the Gordon growth model is NEXT period's expected dividend.

T F 12. The price earnings approach to stock valuation relies on the market accurately setting PEs that reflect firm value.

T F 13. The variable growth model used in the valuation of common stock can be used to find the value of preferred stock.

T F 14. The price/earnings multiple approach to common stock valuation takes a firm's expected earnings per share and multiples it by the firm's *P/E* ratio to find the value of the firm's stock.

T F 15. Stock market efficiency says that the price of a security accurately reflects all available information about that firm.

Multiple Choice

1. _____ is the process that links risk and return in order to determine the worth of an asset.
    a. Depreciation
    b. Valuation
    c. Evaluation
    d. Discounting

2. The value of an asset is the _____ of all future cash flows it is expected to provide over a relevant time period.
    a. required return
    b. future value
    c. present value
    d. sum

3. Risk is generally incorporated into the _____ in the present value model.
    a. discount rate
    b. cash flows
    c. timing
    d. total value

4. Stocks are difficult to value because the following information is difficult to accurately obtain.
   a.   future dividends
   b.   required returns
   c.   future growth rate
   d.   all of the above

5. The present value of a stock's _____ determines the value of the stock.
   a.   dividends
   b.   coupon payment
   c.   maturity value
   d.   coupon payment and maturity value

6. Stock represents _____
   a.   debt
   b.   Retained earnings
   c.   equity
   d.   interest

7. The Gordon growth model requires that analysts determine
   a.   a growth rate.
   b.   a required return.
   c.   next period's dividend.
   d.   all of the above.

8. If next period's dividend is $3.00, the required return is 12% and the growth rate is 7%, what is the firm's stock price?
   a. $25.00
   b. $60
   c. $64.20
   d. $120.00

9. The _____ model is used when valuing preferred stock.
   a.   constant growth
   b.   zero growth version of Gordon model
   c.   Gordon model
   d.   book value

10. Hightech Inc. has an expected dividend next year of $3.20 per share, a growth rate for dividends of 8%, and a required return of 15%. What is the value of a share of Hightech's common stock?
    a. $45.71
    b. $40.00
    c. $21.33
    d. $27.83

11. What is the value of the firm in the event that all assets are sold for their exact accounting value and the proceeds remaining after paying all liabilities are divided among the common stockholders?
    a. Liquidation value
    b. Book value
    c. *P/E* multiple
    d. Sell-off value

12. The concept that relies on investors buying or selling any security that they identify as mis-priced and thereby causing it price to adjust is known as the
    a. efficient markets theory.
    b. Gordon growth model.
    c. dividend valuation model
    d. market model.

13. The CURRENT dividend is $2, the growth rate is 5% and the required return is 10%. What is the value of the stock?
    a. $2.00
    b. $20.00
    c. $40.00
    d. $42.00

14. The financial manager should be concerned about increasing _____ since it will cause the value of the firm's stock to rise.
    a. firm growth.
    b. required return.
    c. risk.
    d. profit.

15. The use of the _____ approach to common stock valuation is superior since it takes into consideration the firm's expected earnings.
    a. book value
    b. present value of interest
    c. liquidation value
    d. *P/E* multiple

16. The key inputs to the valuation process include cash flows (returns), the required return (risk), and
    a. discount rates.
    b. present value.
    c. timing.
    d. expected return.

17. Venture capitalists are responsible for
    a. selling stock to the public.
    b. the IPO.
    c. marketing firm stock.
    d. providing start up capital.

18. Investment bankers are responsible for
    a. providing start up capital.
    b. marketing the firm's stock to the public.
    c. minimizing risk to investors.
    d. providing the firm a fair return.

19. According to the efficient market theory, whenever investors find that the required return of stock is less than the expected return of the stock, the investor will buy the stock. This will
    a. drive the price up.
    b. cause the market to crash.
    c. not affect the price.
    d. drive the price down.

20. The required return for Par Four Inc.'s stock is assumed to be 12%, and Par Four has paid the following dividends. What is the value of Par Four's stock under the constant growth model of common stock valuation?

Year	Dividend per Share ($)
2004	1.32
2003	1.21
2001	1.16
2000	1.12

    a. $11
    b. $15.11
    c. $19.80
    d. $21.82

21. American depository shares:
    a. are backed by American depository receipts.
    b. are held in the vaults of banks in the company's home countries.
    c. permit foreign investors to buy U.S. companies.
    d. trade primarily in the bond markets.

22. Mattel's *Wall Street Journal* quote included a closing value of $26.82 and a net price change of –$0.22. Based on this information, we know that _____ was Mattel's closing price on the prior day.
    a. $26.60
    b. $26.82
    c. $27.04
    d. $27.26

23. A U.S. investor can buy:
    a. American depository receipts (ADRs).
    b. American depository shares (ADSs).
    c. ADRs and ADSs.
    d. Neither ADRs or ADSs.

Essay

1. Distinguish between venture capitalists and investment bankers.

2. What are the sources of error in estimating the value of a share of stock? Which is most likely to be accurate: the computed price of a share of stock or the computed price of a bond?

■ Chapter 7 Answer Sheet

True/False

1. F
2. T
3. T
4. F
5. F
6. T
7. T
8. F
9. T
10. F
11. T
12. T
13. F
14. T
15. T

Multiple Choice

1. B
2. C
3. A
4. D
5. A
6. C
7. D
8. B
9. B
10. A
11. B
12. A
13. D
14. A
15. D
16. C
17. D
18. B
19. A
20. D
21. A
22. C
23. B

$$P_0 = \frac{\$3.20}{0.15 - 0.08} = \$45.71$$

$$PV = FV(PVIF), 1.12 =$$
$$1.32(PVIF_{3,g})g = 5.63\%$$
$$P_0 = \frac{1.39}{0.12 - 0.0563} = \$21.82$$

Essay

1. Investment bankers help the firm go public and to market its stock to the public. They operate in the primary market. Venture capitalists provide startup capital to firms that show a promising future.

2. An analyst must estimate the future dividends, the future growth rate and the riskiness of a firm before applying the Gordon growth model. All of these factors are subject to estimation error and make the estimated price of the stock little more than an educated guess. On the other hand, the inputs to the valuation of a bond are known with some degree of confidence.

Chapter 8
Capital Budgeting Cash Flows

■ Chapter Summary

This chapter provides the tools needed to analyze an investment opportunity. An investment will involve putting out money today with the expectation that more money will be received in the future. These cash flows must be estimated as precisely as possible before they are evaluated using the evaluation tools that will be introduced in the next chapter.

 Understand the motives for key capital expenditure and the steps in the capital budgeting process. There are five steps to capital budgeting: (1) Proposal generation, (2) Review and analysis, (3) Decision making, (4) Implementation, and (5) Follow-up. This chapter focuses on steps 2 and 3.

 Define *basic capital budgeting terminology.* Be able to distinguish between independent versus mutually exclusive cash flows, unlimited funds versus capital rationing, accept-reject versus ranking approaches, conventional versus nonconventional cash flow patterns, and annuity versus mixed stream cash flows.

 Discuss relevant cash flows, expansion versus replacement decisions, sunk costs and opportunity costs, and international capital budgeting. The relevant cash flows can be divided into three main areas. First there are the initial cash flows. These occur at the beginning of the project and represent the initial outlay required to enter into the project. The operating cash flows are the annual cash flows that occur each year while the project is under way. The terminal cash flow occurs at the end of the project and includes the cost of closing the project down.

 Calculate the initial investment associated with a proposed capital expenditure. The initial cash flow includes the installed cost of the new asset, any after-tax proceeds from selling old assets, and any changes in the net working capital that result from beginning the project.

 Find the relevant operating cash inflows associated with a proposed capital expenditure. You can compute the operating cash flows using a format that looks much like a conventional income statement. One unique feature of the operating cash flow is that the depreciation must be added back in at the end because it is a non-cash expense.

 Determine the terminal cash flow associated with a proposed capital expenditure. The terminal cash flow will include the proceeds of selling the equipment or assets used in the project. The taxes on the sale of the asset must be included. Any net working capital will be recovered.

■ Chapter Notes

The capital budgeting decision process

 Capital budgeting is the process of evaluating and selecting long-term investments that are most likely to increase shareholder wealth. The most common long-term investment is the fixed asset. These assets are often termed earning assets because they provide the basis for the firm's earning power and value.

Capital expenditure motive

A capital expenditure is an outlay of funds by the firm that is expected to produce benefits over a period of time greater than one year. The motives for capital expenditures vary; the following table describes the key motives for making capital expenditures.

Motive	Description
Expansion	The most common motive for capital expenditure. By expanding the level of operations for a growing firm, the firm finds it necessary to acquire fixed assets.
Replacement	As a firm's growth reaches maturity, a majority of its capital expenditures will be for the replacement of worn-out assets.
Renewal	Instead of replacing an obsolete asset, sometimes it may be more cost effective to overhaul or repair the old asset.
Other Purposes	Some capital expenditures do not clearly fall into one of the previous categories. Often firms outlay capital for intangible investments such as advertising, research and development, and management consulting.

Steps in the process

The capital budgeting process is made up of five steps. The process begins with proposal generation followed by review and analysis, decision making, implementation, and follow-up. The steps in the capital budgeting process are summarized in the following table.

Steps	Description
Proposal Generation	Proposals for capital expenditures are made at all levels within an organization. Proposals often travel from an originator at a lower level in the organization to a reviewer at a higher level in the organization.
Review and Analysis	Capital expenditure proposals are reviewed on the basis of two criteria: (1) to assess their appropriateness in light of the firm's overall objectives and plans, and (2) to evaluate their economic validity. When the analysis is completed, a summary and recommendation is submitted to the decision maker.
Decision Making	The final decision on proposed capital expenditures is often made on the basis of dollar amount. Clearly, the most expensive capital expenditures will be left to the board of directors while inexpensive items, such as a $5 trash can, will be handled by the lowest levels of management.
Implementation	Once a proposal has been approved and funds have been made available, the implementation phase begins. The implementation of minor outlays often begins immediately while the implementation of major outlays may occur in phases.
Follow-up	Follow-up involves monitoring the results of the capital expenditure during the operating phase of the project. When actual costs deviate from projected costs, action may be needed to improve efficiency and cut costs.

Basic terminology

Independent *projects* are projects where cash flows are unrelated or independent from one another. The acceptance of one project does not necessarily eliminate other projects.

Mutually exclusive projects are projects that are competing with one another. The acceptance of a mutually exclusive project automatically eliminates other mutually exclusive projects.

When a firm has unlimited funds, all independent projects that provide returns greater than the firm's hurdle rate will be accepted. However, most firms are not in this situation. Most firms use *capital rationing* which means that the firm must ration its funds by allocating them to projects that will maximize share value. Under capital rationing, numerous projects will compete for limited dollars.

There are two basic approaches to capital budgeting. The *accept-reject approach* allows firms to either accept or reject projects that are brought before them based on some minimum acceptance criteria. The *ranking approach* ranks projects on the basis of some predetermined measure such as the rate of return.

Conventional cash flow patterns consist of an initial outflow of cash in year 0 followed by a series of inflows. A nonconventional *cash flow* pattern is one in which an initial outflow is not followed by a series of inflows. For example, a machine is purchased in year 0 for $10,000. The machine provides $5,000 of cash inflows in years 1, 2, 3, and 4. In year 3 the machine must be overhauled at a cost of $6,000. The outflow of $6,000 in year 3 breaks the pattern of steady inflows.

An *annuity* is a stream of equal cash flows. A series of cash flows that exhibit any pattern different from an annuity is termed a *mixed stream* of cash flows.

The relevant cash flows

A project having the conventional pattern of cash flows will consist of three basic components: (1) the initial investment, (2) operating cash inflows, and (3) terminal cash flows. All projects will have the first two components; however some will not have a terminal cash flow.

Expansion versus replacement decisions.

The calculation of cash flows received from expansion is quite different from the calculation of cash flows received from replacement. In expansion, the initial investment, operating cash inflows, and terminal cash flows are simply the after-tax cash inflows and outflows provided by the project. Under replacement, the initial investment is the cost of acquiring the new asset plus the after-tax liquidation of the asset being replaced. The operation cash flows are the difference between the cash flows provided by the new asset and the cash flows that would have been provided by the old asset. The terminal cash flow can be found by taking the difference between the after-tax cash flows expected upon termination of the new and old assets.

International capital budgeting and long term investments.

When referring to international budgeting, two things must be remembered. Cash inflows and outflows are occurring in a foreign currency so there is some exchange rate risk. Also, some foreign investments may face significant political risk.

Finding the initial investment

The initial investment in the capital budgeting procedure is found by subtracting all cash inflows occurring at time 0 from all cash outflows occurring at time 0. There are three basic variables that make up the initial investment. They are (1) the installation cost of the new asset, (2) the after-tax proceeds from the sale of the old asset, and (3) the change in net working capital.

The installed cost of the new asset is found by adding the cost of the new asset to its installation cost. Installation costs are any additional costs that are necessary to place an asset into operation.

The after-tax proceeds from the sale of an old asset decrease the firm's initial investment in the new asset. These proceeds are found by subtracting applicable taxes from the old asset's sale price and should be net of any removal or cleanup costs.

To understand the tax consequences for the sale of the old asset, the concept of book value must be understood. Book value is simply the installed cost of an asset minus its accumulated depreciation. With the concept of book value in mind, it is recognized that there are several tax situations that result from the sale of an old asset. These situations are summarized in the following table.

Situation	Consequence
The sale of the asset is for more than its initial purchase price.	Two components: (1) capital gains, and (2) recaptured depreciation. Both are taxed as ordinary income.
The sale of the asset is for more than its book value but less than its initial purchase price.	No capital gain but firm still experiences recaptured depreciation which is taxed as ordinary income.
The sale of the asset is for its book value.	The firm breaks even and there are no tax consequences.
The sale of the asset is for less than its book value.	This will result in a loss, and the tax effect of the loss can be used to offset ordinary income.

When calculating the initial investment, the change in net working capital must be included. If current assets increase more than current liabilities, an increased investment in net working capital would occur and an initial *outflow* associated with the project would result. The opposite is true for a decrease in net working capital. A decrease in net working capital will result in an initial *inflow.*

Finding the operating cash inflows

Operating cash inflows are the relevant cash inflows that are provided by a long-term investment. Three things need to be considered when measuring the cash flows provided by a project. The cash flows that are provided by a project are (1) *incremental,* (2) *after-tax,* and (3) *cash inflows.*

The incremental cash flows represent the additional cash flows that are expected to result from a proposed project. Incremental cash flows are important because the financial manager is only concerned with how much more or less operating cash flows a new project is providing.

The cash flows provided by a proposed project must be measured on an after-tax basis to ensure fairness when evaluating competing projects.

Benefits that are provided by a proposed project must be measured on a cash flow basis and not by "accounting profits." Accounting profits do not pay the firm's obligations; only cash pays the firm's liabilities.

Finding the terminal cash flow

The terminal cash flow is the relevant cash flow that is provided by the liquidation of a long-term investment at the end of its useful life. The terminal cash flow is the after-tax cash flow, separate from the operating cash inflows that occur in the final year of a project. For replacement projects, the proceeds from the sale of both the new and old assets must be considered. For expansion, renewal, and other types of projects, the proceeds from the old asset will be zero. The components of the terminal cash flow are described in the following table.

After-tax proceeds from the sale of new asset =
Proceeds from sale of new asset
  ±Tax on sale of new asset
After-tax proceeds from sale of old asset =
Proceeds from sale of old asset
  ±Tax on sale of old asset
  ± Change in net working capital
Terminal Cash Flow

■ Sample Problems and Solutions

Example 1.

A firm has the opportunity to replace its 5-year-old popcorn machine with a brand new one costing $10,000. The new machine will require $5,000 in freight and installation charges. An increase in net working capital of $2,000 is also required. The old machine was originally purchased for $8,000 and had an expected life of 10 years. The company uses straight line depreciation. The old machine can be sold today for $5,000. The new popcorn machine is not expected to increase revenues, but will decrease operating costs from $3,000 a year to $1,800 per year. The new machine has a life of 10 years and will be depreciated using the straight line method. The company has a cost of capital of 10%, and its tax rate is 40%. What is the net upfront cost and what are the annual after-tax cash flows in years 1 through 10?

Solution

Step 1: Calculate the book value of the old machine.

$$\$8,000/10 = \$800 \times 5 \text{ years old} = \$4,000$$
$$\$8,000 - \$4,000 = \$4,000$$

The old machine is being depreciated using straight line depreciation. To find the annual depreciation, divide the original book value by 10. Find the accumulated depreciation by multiplying by the number of years the asset has been on the books. Finally, the current book value will be the original book value minus the accumulated depreciation.

Step 2: Calculate the gain or loss on the old machine.

Sales price $,5000

−Book value $4,000

Gain on sale $1,000

Step 3: Calculate the tax paid on the gain, or taxes saved on the loss, from the sale of the old machine.

$$\$1,000 \times 0.40 = \$400$$

Since there was a gain on the sale of the old machine, taxes must be paid. The amount of the tax due is 40% of the gain. Had the book value been greater than the sales price, there would have been a tax savings.

Step 4: Calculate the installed cost of the new machine.

Cost $10,000

installation and shipping $ 5,000

                                            $15,000

Step 5: Calculate the increase in net working capital.

$2,000 is given in the problem.

Note: There is really no calculation needed for this problem; however, sometimes you may need to find the change in the difference between current assets and current liabilities.

Step 6: The net initial investment is the sum of Step 3, Step 4, and Step 5 minus the proceeds from the sale of the old machine. Remember that Step 3 will be negative if the old machine was sold at a loss.

+New Project Cost	−15,000
−Proceeds from old machine	+5,000
+Increase in NWC	− 2,000
(+ or −) Tax effects	− 400
Net Initial Investment	−12,400

Step 7: Calculate the net annual after-tax cash flows in years 1 through 10. Use the following format:

ΔR where: $\Delta R = Rev_{new} - Rev_{old}$

$-\Delta O$ $\Delta O = \text{Operating Cost}_{new} - \text{Operating Cost}_{old}$

$-\underline{\Delta D}$ $\Delta D = \text{Depreciation}_{new} - \text{Depreciation}_{old}$

EBT

$-\underline{tax}$

EAT

$+\underline{\Delta D}$

CFAT

	Years 1–5	Years 6–9	Year 10
ΔR	0	0	0
–Δ0	+1,200	+1,200	1,200
–ΔD	–700	–1,500	–1,500
EBT	+500	–300	–300
–tax	–200	+120	+120
EAT	300	–180	–180
+AD	+700	+1,500	+1500
CFAT	+1,000	+1,320	+1,320
Net working capital			+2,000
Terminal year cash flow			3,320

Note: The main area of confusion on this problem is the change in the depreciation. The new depreciation is $15,000/10 = $1,500 per year. The old depreciation was $800 per year. The change in depreciation is the new minus the old = $1,500 – $800 = $700 per year. After 5 years, the old machine will be fully depreciated, so in years 6–10 depreciation is $1,500 per year.

Example 2.   Expansion-type cash flow

A firm is considering expanding its line of soft drinks as a result of market share. The new production line will cost $250,000 plus $100,000 for a new building and installation. Net working capital is expected to increase by $50,000. The new line will be depreciated over its expected 7-year life using straight line depreciation. Revenues generated by the new line are expected to be $20,000 the first year and are expected to increase at a rate of $5000 per year thereafter. Operating costs are expected to be $10,000 in the first year and are expected to increase at a rate of $1500 per year thereafter. After 7 years, the project will have a salvage value of $10,000. The firm has a cost of capital of 12% and a tax rate of 40%. What are the net initial investment and annual cash flows associated with the project? *Hint*: The steps are very similar to Example 1 above.

Solution

Initial Investment	
Purchase price	$250,000
Installation	100,000
Initial cost	350,000
Increase in Working Capital	50,000
Net investment	$400,000

The initial cost of $350,000 is the amount that will be depreciated over the life of the project. Since the machine will have a $10,000 residual value, the annual depreciation will be ($350,000 – $10,000)/7 = **$48,571**.

Annual Cash Flows

	Year 1	Year 2	Year 3	Year 4	Year 5	Year 6	Year 7
Rev	$20,000	25,000	30,000	35,000	40,000	45,000	50,000
–Oper Costs	10,000	11,500	13,000	14,500	16,000	17,500	19,000
–Deprec	48,571	48,571	48,571	48,571	48,571	48,571	48,571
EBT	–38,571	–35,071	–31,571	–28,071	–24,571	–21,071	–17,571
–/+Tax	+15,429	+14,028	+12,628	+11,228	+9,828	+8,428	+7,028
EAT	–23,142	–21,043	–18,943	–16,843	–14,743	–12,643	–10,543
+Deprec	48,571	48,571	48,571	48,571	48,571	48,571	48,571
Working Capital	0	0	0	0	0	0	50,000
Salvage	0	0	0	0	0	0	10,000
Net Cash Flow	+25,429	27,528	29,628	31,728	33,828	35,928	98,028

■ Capital Budgeting Cash Flow Quick Drill Problems

These problems are quick and easy practice to see how well you have understood the concepts in this chapter. The answers follow.

1. Your company has decided to purchase a new computer system for $150,000. Installation and training will cost an additional $40,000 and $25,000, respectively. What is the net purchase price?

2. From Question 1, what amount would you use as the basis for computing depreciation on the new computer system?

3. The computer system your company is currently using was purchased 3 years ago for $140,000 and has a MACRS depreciable life of 5 years. What is the book value of the old computer system?

4. Your company is selling the old computer system for $25,000. Using the information from Question 3, what is the taxable gain (loss) on the sale of the old computer system? Assuming a 40% tax rate, what is the tax on the sale? Is this amount added to or subtracted from the net purchase price when computing the initial investment?

5. Using the information from Questions 1 through 4, what is the initial cash flow, assuming the computer system will reduce net working capital by $32,000?

6. Using the straight-line depreciation method, what is the annual depreciation of commercial property that cost $2.5 million? Assume a 39-year depreciable life.

7. Suppose you owned a sporting goods store and decided to expand your operations by opening a new store. You project that revenue will reach $250,000 for the new store in the first year and increase by 20 percent over the next 3 years. Expenses are estimated at 75% of sales, the initial cost of the expansion was $400,000 (depreciable over 39 years using the straight-line method), and your tax rate is 40%. What are the annual cash flows from 2001 to 2004?

8. As the manager of a printing company, you were impressed at a local trade show with a next-generation printing machine. It occupies less space, is more efficient, and provides a better quality product. This machine costs $260,000 with annual operating costs of $15,000. However, 2 years ago you purchased a printing machine for $190,000 with annual operating costs of $29,000. You are depreciating the old printing machine over 3 years using MACRS, as you would for the new printing machine. Revenues will increase from $760,000 to $790,000 with the replacement of the old printing machine. Note that the change in operating cost is $15,000 – $29,000. Assume a 40% tax rate and compute the annual cash flows for the next 4 years.

9. Using the information from Question 8, you plan to sell the new printing machine after 4 years for $60,000. What is the terminal cash flow?

10. The initial cash flow for a project is –$250 million. Cash flows are projected to be –$150 million in 2001, $300 million in 2002, $450 million in 2003, and $500 million in 2004. If the cost of capital is 12 percent and additional costs in 2004 are –$250 million what is the NPV?

11. Suppose the initial cash flow for a project is –$500 million. Cash flows are projected to be –$300 million and 2001, –$200 million in 2002, $250 million in 2003, $500 million in 2004, $600 million in 2005, and $850 million in 2006. If the cost of capital is 14% and additional costs for terminating the project in 2006 are –$175 million, what is the NPV?

12. Suppose the cash inflow in the last year of a project is $22 million. The new asset is to be sold for $5 million, resulting in a tax of $450,000. If net working capital was initially decreased by $400,000, what is the terminal cash flow?

13. As a top manager, you must decide which of the proposed projects should be accepted for the upcoming year since only $6 million is available for the next year's capital budget. What is the total NPV of the projects that should be accepted?

Project	Cost (millions)	NPV (millions)	PI
A	3.25	0.80	1.25
B	1.75	0.52	1.30
C	4.50	0.69	1.15
D	3.75	0.95	1.25
E	1.25	0.25	1.20
F	0.50	0.25	1.50

14. Suppose that you are evaluating a project with a cost of $15,000 and 5 annual cash inflows in $6,500 each. The return on the market is 12%, the risk-free rate of interest is 6%, and the firm's beta is 1.2. The project you are evaluating is very different from those usually undertaken by the firm. Another firm, which is exclusively in the business of doing projects like the one under consideration, has a beta of 2.0. Should you recommend that the firm accept the project? Assume the firm is all equity financed.

15. Your company must decide between two positive *NPV* projects with unequal lives. The three-year project has an initial cash flow of –$2 million, with cash inflows of $4 million per year. The six-year project has an initial cash flow of –$6 million, with cash inflows of $3 million per year. Assume a cost of capital of 12% and that neither project has additional end of project costs. What is the NPV for each project using the replacement chain approach? Which project should your company accept?

16. Refer to the information from Question 15 and give your accept/reject decision using the equal annual annuity method.

17. Use the replacement chain approach to evaluate the following projects. Project A has a 2-year life, an initial cost of $2.25 million, and cash inflows of $1.5 million per year. Project B has a 4-year life, an initial cost of $5 million, and cash inflows of $2 million per year. What is the NPV for each project and which should you accept? Assume a 15% cost of capital.

18. Refer to the information from Question 17 and give your accept/reject decision using the equal annual annuity method.

Answers

1. –$215,000

2. –$215,000

3. $40,600

4. –$15,600 (loss); –$6,240; added

5. –$151,760

6. $64,103

7. $41,603; $49,103; $58,103; $68,903

8. $49,320, $67,880, $42,000, $33,680

9. $69,680

10. $334,410,223

11. –$166,873,735

12. $26,150,000

13. F, B & D; total cost = $6 million; total NPV = $1.72 million

14. $r_i = 0.18$; yes, *NPV* of $5,327

15. 3-year = $13,022,069; 6-year = $6,334,222; accept 3-year

16. 3-year = $26,394,184; 6-year = $12,838,714; accept 3-year

17. A = $331,144; B = $709,957; accept B

18. A = $773,256; B = $1,657,822; accept B

Long Sample Problem

The calculation of cash flows for capital budgeting is one of the more complex activities you will face in this course. These problems are often very long and complex. The following is a long problem and its cash flow solution as solved using Excel.

■ Cash Flow Analysis

Prepare your answer using an Excel spreadsheet.

You have decided that your town needs a new Mexican restaurant. It will feature live musicians, appetizers, and a well stocked bar. You are trying to decide whether you should invest in this venture. Your first step is to prepare a complete capital budgeting analysis for the 5 years the restaurant will operate before you sell it.

After talking with local vendors, restaurant owners, bankers, and builders you collect the following data.

You will need to make tenant improvements to the property. These will include cooking equipment, a stage, seating, and interior décor. The construction is estimated to cost $1,500,000. An additional $275,000 will be spent on chairs, tables, bar equipment, and decorations. Depreciation will be over 7 years using MACRS. You determine that you will require an average cash balance of $15,000 and inventory of $20,000. Accounts payable should average $10,000. You learn that you can borrow the money to pay for these expenses at a 15% interest rate.

You feel that your chances of success will increase if you have a market study performed by a group of ECU faculty. The charge for this report will be $100,000.

The site you have selected for the lounge is in a building currently owned by your family. Your parents have said that you can use the retail space in any way you wish for free. After checking on local lease rates you determine this space would lease for $75,000 per year. Your family also owns another restaurant downtown. You predict that your new one will decrease its revenues by $15,000/year. Your parents tell you that this sum will be taken from your annual family stipend.

Revenues are estimated to be $500,000 the first year. Revenues are expected to increase by 20% the second year, 15% the third year and to continue increasing at 10% thereafter. Fixed annual operating costs are estimated to be as follows. Employee salaries = $110,000, heat, electric, water, janitorial = $75,000. The food and liquor bill is expected to be 15% of revenues. Total taxes are estimated to be 40% of net revenues.

Your plan is to run the bar for 5 years, then to sell it to an investor for $2,000,000.

Prepare a cash flow analysis that includes the initial investment, the annual cash flows and the terminal cash flow.

Solution

Initial cash flow		**Mexican Restaurant**
Purchase price		
Construction	(1,500,000)	
Appointments	(275,000)	
	(1,775,000)	
NWC	(25,000)	
Net Cost	(1,800,000)	

	Growth rate of revenue	20%	15%	10%	10%
			Annual Cash Flows		
		Year 1	**Year 2**	**Year 3**	**Year 4**	**Year 5**
Revenues		500,000	600,000	690,000	759,000	834,900
Expenses						
Salaries		110,000	110,000	110,000	110,000	110,000
Utilities		75,000	75,000	75,000	75,000	75,000
Food and Liquor		75,000	90,000	103,500	113,850	125,235
Rent (opportunity cost)		75,000	75,000	75,000	75,000	5,000
Indirect expense		15,000	15,000	15,000	15,000	15,000
Total Operating Expenses		350,000	365,000	378,500	388,850	400,235
Depreciation 7 year		(248,500)	(443,750)	(301,750)	(230,750)	(159,750)
Total depreciation		(248,500)	(443,750)	(301,750)	(230,750)	(159,750)
Earnings before tax		(98,500)	(208,750)	9,750	139,400	274,915
Tax (40%)		39,400	83,500	(3,900)	(55,760)	(109,966)
Earnings after-tax		(59,100)	(125,250)	5,850	83,640	164,949
Depreciation		248,500	443,750	301,750	230,750	159,750
Sale of lounge						2,000,000
Tax on sale						(643,800)
NWC	Initial Invest					25,000
Net Cash Flow	(1,800,000)	189,400	318,500	307,600	314,390	1,705,899

Tax calculation

The calculation of the tax on the sale of the assets in the terminal year can be confusing.

Accumulated Depreciation = Sum of depreciation	(1,384,500)
Book Value = Initial cost – Accumulated depreciation	390,500
Taxable gain = Sales price – Book value	1,609,500
Tax on gain = 0.4	$1,609,500

■ Study Tips

1. Building cash flow estimates is a job ideally suited to the spreadsheet. Try to use Excel or Lotus to work out your homework assignments. The copy command and summation commands make the process go quickly. You will find it much easier to correct your mistakes as well.

2. Review, if necessary, finding book value. You will need this ability when working any replacement-type cash flow problem. Determine the accumulated depreciation, then subtract this figure from the original book value.

3. An easy check you can perform is to make sure that the earnings before tax (EBT) and the tax figure always have different signs. For example, if earnings before tax is –$17,571, the tax will be a *positive* amount. Likewise, if the EBT is positive, the tax will be negative.

4. Some students wonder why they need to subtract out depreciation when computing EBT, since depreciation is added back in at the bottom. The reason is that by subtracting out depreciation, an accurate EBT can be found for estimating taxes.

5. Keep in mind that financial managers focus on actual cash flows. Any operating cash flows that arise from depreciation write-offs that would have supposedly occurred if an asset had not been sold is not directly included in the analysis. The taxable portion of the gain arising from an earlier asset sale is lower because the it has a larger non-depreciated basis.

■ Student Notes

■ Sample Exam—Chapter 8

True/False

T F   1.   An outlay for advertising and management consulting is considered a current expenditure.

T F   2.   A firm's fixed asset investments provide the basis for the firm's earning power and value.

T F   3.   If a firm has unlimited funds to invest, then all the mutually exclusive projects that meet its minimum investment criteria will be implemented.

T F   4.   The purchase of additional machinery or a new factory is an example of the renewal type of capital expenditure.

T F   5.   Mutually exclusive projects have the same function and compete with one another.

T F   6.   The book value of an asset is equal to the asset's after-tax proceeds that are provided after the asset has been sold.

T F   7.   Projects should be evaluated on the basis of accounting profits, since these profits actually cover the company's obligations.

T F   8.   The relevant cash flows for a proposed project are the incremental after-tax cash outflows and the resulting cash inflows.

T F   9.   All projects will have an initial investment, cash inflows, and a terminal cash flow.

T F 10.   When considering international projects, it is important to consider exchange rate risk and political risk.

T F 11.   Net working capital is the amount by which a firm's current assets exceed its current liabilities.

T F 12.   When the sale of an asset is equal to its book value, a firm will have to pay taxes on recaptured depreciation.

T F 13.   The salvage value of an asset should be net of any removal or cleanup costs associated with the termination of a project.

T F 14.   Most firms practice capital rationing, which means that projects will be competing for limited dollars.

T F 15.   A capital expenditure is a short-term outlay of funds that is expected to produce cash flows usually in less than one year.

Multiple Choice

1. The most common motive for adding fixed assets to a firm is
   a. replacement.
   b. expansion.
   c. renewal.
   d. government regulation.

2. The first step in the capital budgeting process is
   a. proposal generation.
   b. analysis.
   c. review.
   d. decision making.

3. A firm that has limited dollars available for capital expenditures often practices
   a. capital dependency.
   b. net working capital constraints.
   c. capital rationing.
   d. bond financing.

4. A series of equal annual cash flows is termed
   a. a mixed stream.
   b. nonconventional.
   c. conventional.
   d. an annuity.

5. A project having the conventional pattern of cash flows exhibits all of the following EXCEPT
   a. operating cash inflows.
   b. a terminal cash flow.
   c. operating cash outflows.
   d. initial investment.

6. A firm has unlimited funds in which to evaluate the following five projects.

Project	Status	Return(%)
1	Independent	13
2	Independent	12
3	Independent	15
4	Mutually Exclusive	14
5	Mutually Exclusive	16

What will the ranking of the projects be on the basis of their returns, from the best to the worst?
a.   5, 3, 1, and 2
b.   3, 2, 1, 5 and 4
c.   3, 2, 1, and 5
d.   5, 3, 4, 1, and 2

7.   The relevant cash flows of a project are best described as
a.   accounting cash flows.
b.   incremental cash flows.
c.   incidental cash flows.
d.   accounting profits.

8.   An important cash inflow associated with a replacement project is
a.   the cost of the new asset.
b.   installation costs.
c.   the sale of the old asset.
d.   the tax savings.

9.   The change in net working capital must be considered a part of the _____ when evaluating a capital budgeting project.
a.   initial cash outflow
b.   initial investment
c.   operating cash inflow
d.   terminal cash flow

10. The sale of an ordinary asset for its book value results in
a.   no tax benefit.
b.   recaptured depreciation.
c.   an ordinary tax benefit.
d.   a capital gain.

11. One of the basic techniques used to evaluate after-tax operating cash flows is to
a.   add cash expenses to net income.
b.   subtract depreciation from net income.
c.   add noncash charges to net income.
d.   subtract retained earnings from net income.

12. A corporation has decided to replace an existing machine with a newer model. The old machine had an initial purchase price of $30,000 with $5,000 installation costs and has $20,000 in accumulated depreciation. If the 40% tax rate applies to the corporation and the old asset can be sold for $10,000, what will be the tax effect of the replacement?
a.   loss of $2,000
b.   no effect
c.   benefit of $2,000
d.   loss of $4,000

13. The cash flows in an expansion project are different from those in a replacement project in that the cash flows from the old asset in an expansion project
    a. will be evaluated on an after-tax basis.
    b. will always be zero.
    c. will always be negative.
    d. will always equal the terminal cash flow.

14. The book value of an asset is equal to the
    a. purchase price minus depr. expense.
    c. purchase price minus accumulated depr.
    b. purchase price minus recaptured depr.
    d. fair market value.

15. A conventional cash flow pattern associated with capital investment projects consists of an initial outflow followed by
    a. a broken series of outflows.
    b. a broken series of inflows.
    c. a series of outflows.
    d. a series of inflows.

16. The final step in the capital budgeting process is
    a. implementation.
    b. follow-up.
    c. review.
    d. analysis.

17. Using the following data, what is the change in net working capital for Upgrade Corporation?

Current Account	Change in Balance
Cash	+$12,000
Accounts Payable	+$21,000
Accruals	+$ 6,000
Depreciation	+$10,000
Inventories	+$24,000

    a. +$9,000
    b. −$1,000
    c. −$4,000
    d. +$19,000

18. The _____ evaluates capital expenditure projects to determine whether they meet a firm's minimum acceptance criterion.
    a. ranking approach
    b. book value
    c. P/E multiple approach
    d. accept-reject approach

19. The initial cash flows and operating cash inflows are referred to as the
    a. necessary cash flows.
    b. ordinary cash flows.
    c. relevant cash flows.
    d. consistent cash flows.

20. _____ projects do not compete with one another, so the acceptance of one will have no bearing on the other projects being considered by the corporation.
    a. Independent
    b. Mutually exclusive
    c. Capital
    d. Replacement

21. Individuals can approach the acquisition process much as corporations do, using a five-step process. In which step is the purchase made?
    a. Step 1
    b. Step 3
    c. Step 4
    d. Step 5

22. Giancarlo has received an inheritance from his rich uncle and is contemplating the purchase of a Suzuki XL7. In an attempt to make a rational decision, Giancarlo has identified the following cash flow estimates:

Negotiated price of new Suzuki XL7:	$24,675
Taxes and fees on new car purchase:	$ 1,732
Proceeds from the trade-in of old car:	$ 9,285
Estimated value of Suzuki XL7 in 5 years:	$ 7,285
Estimated value of old car in 5 years:	$ 3,572
Estimated annual repair cost on Suzuki XL7:	$ 350
Estimated annual repair cost on old car:	$ 925

What would be Giancarlo's initial investment in the Suzuki XL7?
    a. $13,370
    b. $15,390
    c. $17,122
    d. $26,406

23. What would be Gioncarlo's operating cash flow in Year 5
    a. ($575)
    b. $350
    c. $375
    d. $4,127

24. What would be Gioncarlo's terminal cash flow?
    a. $3,177
    b. $3,572
    c. $3,752
    d. $7,324

Essay

A firm is contemplating replacing its old copier with a new one which is faster and easier to operate. The old machine was being depreciated over 5 years using straight line depreciation. Its original installed cost was $12,000. The old machine has been in use 4 years. It can be traded in for $2,500. The new machine will cost $21,000. It will also be depreciated over 5 years using the straight line method. It is not expected to have a residual value. Net working capital will decrease because supply levels can be reduced by $1,000.

While the new machine is not expected to affect revenues, it will result in labor savings of $5,000 per year due to its greater speed. Reduced training expenses are expected to save an additional $1,500 per year. The firm is in the 40% tax bracket.

1.   What is the initial cash flow for the copier?

2.   What is the operating cash flow?

3.   What is the terminal cash flow?

■ Chapter 8 Answer Sheet

True/False	Multiple Choice
1. F	1. B
2. T	2. A
3. F	3. C
4. F	4. D
5. T	5. C
6. F	6. A
7. F	7. B
8. T	8. C
9. F	9. B
10. T	10. A
11. T	11. C
12. F	12. C $30,000 - 5,000 = 25,000$
13. T	$25,000 - 20,000 = 5,000$
14. T	$10,000 - 5,000 = 5,000$
15. F	$5,000 \times 0.40 = \$2,000$
	13. B
	14. C
	15. D
	16. B
	17. A $(\$12,000 + 24,000) - (\$21,000 + 6,000) = \$9,000$
	18. D
	19. C
	20. A
	21. C
	22. C
	23. A
	24. C

Essay

1.

Initial Cash Flow	
Purchase price	+21,000
Sale of old copier	−2,500
Tax on sale of old machine	+40
Decrease in net working capital	−1,000
Total	17,540

2. & 3.

	Operating Cash Flows				
	Year 1	Year 2	Year 3	Year 4	Year 5
Rev	0	0	0	0	0
Oper	6,500	6,500	6,500	6,500	6,500
Depr	1,800	4,200	4,200	4,200	4,200
EBT	4,700	2,300	2,300	2,300	2,300
Tax	1,880	920	920	920	920
EAT	2,820	1,380	1,380	1,380	1,380
Depr	1,800	4,200	4,200	4,200	4,200
Working Cap	0	0	0	0	(1,000)
Net Cash Flow	4,620	5,580	5,580	5,580	4,580

Chapter 9
Capital Budgeting Techniques

■ Chapter Summary

In this chapter, the tools that you have been developing since Chapter 5 come together to help evaluate projects. The main methods for evaluating projects are the net present value and the internal rate of return. You already know the mechanics necessary to compute both of these numbers. This chapter discusses the theory, advantages, and disadvantages of each method. The next chapter provides techniques for dealing with some of the problems that arise in their application. While you may not find this chapter as difficult as others, it is among the most valuable.

LG 1 *Understand the role of capital budgeting techniques in the capital budgeting process.* Capital budgeting is the process of evaluating and selecting investment opportunities. Capital budgeting techniques provide a method for using TVM to help select among competing investments.

LG 2 *Calculate, interpret, and evaluate the payback period.* The payback method is not a good way to evaluate projects. The problem is that it ignores risk and the time value of money. It is included in the text because it appeals to many managers who are not trained in finance, and therefore the method is still used by industry. Learn the method—it is easy—but be aware that it should never be relied on.

LG 3 *Calculate, interpret, and evaluate the net present value (NPV).* You will not find it difficult to learn to use NPV to evaluate projects because this method is just an extension of the time value of money principles learned in Chapter 5. Be sure to use time lines for evaluating projects with more complex cash flows. The higher the concentration of cash inflows in later periods the greater the importance of using a low discount rate to maximize NPV.

LG 4 *Calculate, interpret, and evaluate the internal rate of return (IRR).* The IRR is computed in the same way that you learned to compute the yield to maturity for bonds. The YTM provides the return to an investor for holding a bond to maturity, and the IRR provides the return to a firm for accepting a project. The number of IRRs equals the number of sign changes in its cash flows.

LG 5 *Use net present value profiles to compare net present value and internal rate of return techniques.* A net present value profile is a graph that shows the net present value at a variety of different costs of capital. The value of the NPV profile is that it shows the sensitivity of NPV to the selection of the discount rate. The IRR can be read directly off the NPV profile where the graph crosses the *x* axis, depicting NPV equal to zero.

LG 6 *Discuss NPV and IRR in terms of conflicting rankings and the theoretical and practical strengths of each approach.* NPV and IRR will always provide the same accept/reject decision. However, they will not always rank projects the same. This conflict becomes important when a firm cannot afford to accept both projects or when it is trying to select among mutually exclusive projects.

■ Chapter Notes

Capital budgeting techniques

Capital budgeting techniques are used by firms to evaluate projects that will increase shareholders' wealth. The preferred techniques combine time value procedures, risk and return considerations, and valuation concepts to select the projects that are most consistent with the firm's goals. The three most popular capital budgeting techniques are the payback period, net present value, and internal rate of return.

Payback period

The payback period is the exact amount of time required for a firm to recover its initial investment in a project as calculated from cash inflows. The payback period is popular because of its ease in calculation, but it is not often used because it fails to recognize the time value of money.

Net present value

Net present value is the preferred technique because it gives consideration to the time value of money. The net present value is found by subtracting the initial investment from the present value of the cash inflows discounted at a rate equal to the firm's cost of capital. The formula for NPV is shown in the following equation.

$$NPV = \sum_{t=1}^{n} \frac{CF_t}{(1+r)^t} - II$$

Where:

Ft = individual year's cash flow

r = firm's cost of capital

II = initial investment

If the NPV of a project is greater than $0, the project should be accepted, and if the NPV is less than $0, the project should be rejected.

Internal rate of return (IRR)

The internal rate of return (IRR) is probably the most widely used capital budgeting technique. The IRR is defined as the discount rate that equates the present value of cash inflows with the initial investment associated with a project. If the IRR of a project is greater than the firm's cost of capital, the project should be accepted, and if the IRR is less than the cost of capital, the projects should be rejected. The equation used to find a project's IRR is shown in the following formula.

$$\sum_{t=1}^{n} \frac{CF_t}{(1+IRR)^t} = II$$

Comparing NPV and IRR techniques

The NPV and IRR often rank projects differently. The NPV assumes the reinvestment of funds at the firm's cost of capital, while the IRR assumes the reinvestment of funds at a rate equal to the project's IRR.

The net present value profile can help you to understand why NPV and IRR can rank projects differently. In the following figure, the NPV of projects A and B have been computed at a variety of discount rates. At a 5% discount rate, project A is preferred since it has the higher NPV. At a 10% discount rate project B is preferred because it has the higher NPV. This example shows that the preference depends on the discount rate. If IRR were used to rank projects it would always rank B as best. This is because the project's IRR is where it crosses the x axis, and B crosses further out.

Theoretically, the NPV is the better approach to capital budgeting. The NPV's assumption of reinvestment at the firm's cost of capital is more realistic than the IRR's assumption of reinvestment at the project's IRR. But there is evidence that suggests some financial managers prefer the IRR technique. Most business people are more concerned with rates of return rather than actual dollar returns.

■ Sample Problems and Solutions

Example 1. Payback

Suppose that you want to invest in a $100,000 project that you expect to provide cash inflows of $50,000 in the first year, $25,000 the second, and $20,000 per year thereafter. What is the payback period?

Solution

The payback period is simply the number of years that it takes to recover your investment. Note that payback ignores the timing and riskiness of the cash flows, as well as any cash flows that are received after the payback period has passed. Compute payback by determining the cumulative cash flows received by year.

Year	Cash Flow	Cumulative Cash Flow
Year 1	$50,000	$50,000
Year 2	25,000	75,000
Year 3	20,000	95,000
Year 4	20,000	(1/4) 5,000

After 3-1/4 years, the investment of $100,000 will be received. Thus the payback is 3-1/4 years.

Example 2.   Net Present Value

How would you explain what a NPV of $10,000 meant to someone who had not taken any finance?

Solution

You would explain that the $10,000 was how much more was earned by this project, in today's dollars, than was necessary to compensate you for the risk of the project.

Example 3

If your company was not subject to capital rationing, would you accept a project that had a net present value of $1.00, even if the initial investment was $1 billion?

Solution

Yes. Refer to the answer to Example 2. An NPV of $1.00 says that you have received everything you needed to be adequately compensated for the risk of the project, plus $1.00 more. The problem does not say what the rate of return may have been. If the discount rate was 25%, then you will have earned 25% compounded every year, plus an extra dollar.

Example 4

You estimate the net initial investment of a project to be $250,000. Annual cash inflows of $50,000 per year for 8 years are expected to follow. The firm's cost of capital is 12%. Should you invest?

a.   Table Solution

Find the present value of the cash inflows and the present value of the cash outflows, then net the two together.

$$\text{NPV} = \$50,000(\text{PVIFA}_{8\text{yrs},12\%}) - \$250,000 = 50,000(4.9676) - 250,000 = -1,620$$

Since the net present value is less than 0, you should not invest in this project.

b.   Calculator Solution

Refer to the financial calculator section in the back of the study guide for detailed keystroke examples.

$$CF_0 = -250,000$$
$$C_{01} = 50,000$$
$$F_{01} = 8$$
$$I = 12$$
$$\text{NPV} = -\$1,618.01$$

Example 5

You estimate the relevant net cash inflows on an investment to be $20,000 per year for 6 years. The initial investment is $60,000 and the cost of capital is 10%. Should you invest?

a.   Table Solution

$$\text{NPV} = \$20,000(\text{PVIFA}_{6\text{yrs},10\%}) - \$60,000 = 20,000(4.3553) - 60,000 = 27,106$$

Since the NPV is positive, you should invest.

b.   **Calculator Solution**

$$CF_0 = -60,000$$
$$C_{01} = 20,000$$
$$F_{01} = 6$$
$$I = 10$$
$$NPV = \$27,105.21$$

Example 6

Assume that you are evaluating an investment that requires you to invest \$10,000 per year for 3 years. Following this you will not receive anything for two years, then you will receive \$20,000 for the next 3 years. If the cost of capital is 12%, should this project be accepted?

a.   **Table Solution**

If the initial cash flow is disbursed over a period spanning several years, find the present value of the cash outflows and subtract this amount from the present value of the cash inflows.

It is often best to draw a time line when the cash flows become complicated.

	−10,000	−10,000	−10,000	0	0	20,000	20,000	20,000
0	1	2	3	4	5	6	7	

First, find the *PV* of the cash outflows.

$$PV_{\text{initial cash flow}} = -\$10,000(\text{PVIFA}_{2\text{yrs},12\%}) - \$10,000 = -\$16,900 - 10,000 = -\$26,900$$

Next, find the PV of the cash inflows.

$$PV_{\text{cash inflows}} = \$20,000(\text{PVIFA}_{3\text{yrs},12\%})(\text{PVIF}_{4\text{yrs},12\%}) = \$20,000(2.402)(0.6355) = \$30,529$$

Finally, net the cash inflows against the cash outflows.

$$NPV = \$30,529 - \$26,900 = \$3,629$$

Since the NPV is positive, the investment should be accepted.

b.   **Calculator Solution**

$$CF_0 = -10,000$$
$$C_{01} = -10,000$$
$$F_{01} = 2$$
$$C_{02} = 0$$
$$F_{02} = 2$$
$$C_{03} = 20,000$$
$$F_{03} = 3$$
$$I = 12$$
$$NPV = \$3,627.63$$

Example 7

You are asked to evaluate two projects, X and Y. The cash flow for each is listed below. The firm's cost of capital is 12%. Using the NPV method, which project would you select? Why?

Year	X	Y
0	(10,000)	(10,000)
1	6,500	3,500
2	3,000	3,500
3	3,000	3,500
4	1,000	3,500

a. **Table Solution**

$$NPV_x = \$6,500/1.12 + \$3,000/1.12^2 + \$3,000/1.12^3 + \$1,000/1.12^4 - \$10,000 = \$966$$
$$NPV_y = \$3,500(PVIFA_{4yrs,12\%}) - \$10,000 = \$630$$

Since the NPV of project X is greater than the NPV of project Y, accept X.

b. **Calculator Solution**

X	Y
$CF_0 = -10,000$	$CF_0 = -10,000$
$C_{01} = 6,500$	$C_{01} = 3,500$
$F_{01} = 1$	$F_{01} = 4$
$C_{02} = 3,000$	$I = 12$
$F_{02} = 2$	$NPV_y = \$630.72$
$C_{03} = 1,000$	
$F_{03} = 1$	
$I = 12$	
$NPV_x = \$966.01$	

Example 8.   Internal Rate of Return

Compute the internal rate of return for project Y in example 7 above.

Solution

The internal rate of return is the interest rate that sets the present value of the cash inflows equal to the present value of the cash outflows.

$$\$10,000 = \$3,500(PVIFA_{4yrs, IRR})$$
$$\$10,000/\$3,500 = 2.857 = PVIFA_{4yrs, IRR}$$

Now, look up the PVIFA in the table across from 4 periods that is closest to 2.857. The factor under 15% is 2.855. Therefore, the IRR of project Y is about 15%. Since this is greater than the cost of capital of 12%, the project should be accepted. Note that the decision reached using the IRR method is the same as what was reached in example 7 using NPV. This will always be the case. If computed properly, IRR and NPV will always give the same accept/reject decision.

Example 9.   Net present value profile

Assume that you want to evaluate an investment that requires you to pay out $15,000 now and that promises to return $4,000 each year for 5 years. Compute the net present value profile for this project.

Solution

To compute a net present value profile you need to find the net present value at a variety of discounts rates, then plot the result. It is not too important which discount rates you choose to use. Since the calculation of NPV is very easy for 0% discount, be sure to begin there. You then want to choose discount rates that result in some positive and some negative NPVs.

Discount Rate	NPV
0.0%	$5,000
2.5%	$3,583
5.0%	$2,318
7.5%	$1,184
10.0%	$ 163
12.5%	–$ 758
15.0%	–$1,591
17.5%	–$2,348

Net Present Value Profile

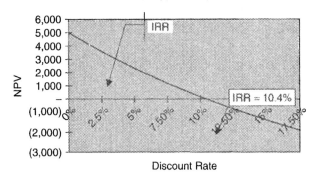

Once the NPVs and discount rates are plotted, it is easy to find the IRR. This is where the NPV is equal to zero. The steeper the NPV profile, the more sensitive the investment is to the discount rate assumption.

■ Capital Budgeting Quick Drill Problems

1. XYZ Company wants to know the payback period for a project with an initial investment of $4 million and annual cash flows of $800,000.

2. Suppose the annual cash flows listed for Question 1 start at $800,000 and then decrease by 15% each year. What is the payback period?

3. A firm is evaluating a project with an initial cost of $3.35 million and annual cash flows of $1.15 million for 4 years. If the cost of capital for the firm is 14%, what is the NPV? Should the firm accept or reject the project?

4. Suppose the cost of capital for the firm in Question 3 increases to 15%, what is the NPV? Should the firm accept or reject the project?

5. Evergreen Inc. is evaluating a project with an initial cost of $6 million. Cash flows would start at $1 million and increase by $750,000 annually for the next 3 years. If the cost of the capital for the firm is 12%, what is the NPV? Should the firm accept or reject the project?

6. A project has projected cash outflows of $2 million in the current time period. Additional cash outflows of $1 million, $1 million, and $2 million are projected during the next 3 years of operation. Cash inflows of $1.3 million are expected in years 4 through 13 (10 cash inflows). Should the project be accepted if the company has a cost of capital of 14%? (What is the NPV?)

7. Would the accept/reject decision change for the project described in Question 6 if the costs of capital fell to 12%?

8. Suppose that a $10,000 investment will yield 3 cash flows of $4,000 each. With a discount rate of 12%, what is the PI? What is the accept/reject decision?

9. Rank the following projects by PI.

Project	Net Investment	*PV* (Cash inflows)	NPV
A	$400	$480	$80
B	700	735	35
C	150	225	75
D	1,000	950	(50)
E	250	275	25

10. If the initial investment for a project is $500 and the cash inflows are $300 for 3 years, what is the IRR?

11. If the initial investment for a project is $500 and the cash inflows are $300 for year 1, $250 for year 2, and $150 for year 3, what is the IRR?

12. If the initial investment for a project is $1,500 and the cash inflows are $300 for 4 years, what is the IRR?

13. Suppose Project A has a NPV of $350 with an IRR of 12% and Project B has a NPV of $300 with an IRR of 20%. If these projects are mutually exclusive, which project should you accept? Why?

14. What is the NPV of a project with initial investments of $3 million at the beginning of years 1 and 2, and cash inflows of $1.5 million at the beginning of years 2 through 6? Assume the cost of capital is 10. Should the project be accepted? (Hint: at the beginning of year 2 the net cash flow is –1.5 million.)

Answers

1. 5 years

2. 9.6 years

3. $769; accept

4. –$66,775; reject

5. $132,831; accept

6. –$419,655; reject

7. $114,621; accept

8. 0.96; reject

9. C, A, E, B, D

10. 36.31%

11. 21.48%

12. –8.36%

13. Project A; The reinvestment rate assumption is a problem when you are attempting to rank mutually exclusive projects with IRR. Thus, NPV is more useful when attempting to select among mutually exclusive projects.

14. –$41,093; reject

Long Problem Continued

In the last chapter we looked at a long problem and used it to compute the initial, annual and terminal cash flows. Now that we know how to compute NPV and IRR let's complete this long problem. Refer to the data in the long problem in chapter 8 and answer the following.

1. Compute the NPV and IRR, assuming a cost of capital of 14%. Is the project acceptable?

2. Prepare an NPV profile. Locate the IRR and the 14% cost of capital on this graph. (To locate points on the graph go to View, Toolbars, and click on Drawing. Select Autoshapes)

3. Prepare a sensitivity profile looking at different assumed initial sales amounts. Use some estimates above the original estimate and some below.

4. What final sales price makes this project just acceptable using the assumptions provided used in question 2? (In Excel go to Tools, Goal Seek and input that you want the value of NPV to be zero by changing the final purchase price.)

Solution Prepared Using Excel

NPV	(109,028)					
IRR	0.1216					
PI	0.9394					
IRR	0.1216					
Discount Rate	0.14					
Growth Rate			0.10	0.07	0.05	0.05

Cost of Capital	NPV		Sales	NPV
0.00	1,035,789		450,000	(223,728)
0.03	716,453		500,000	(109,028)
0.05	530,252		550,000	5,671
0.08	284,708		600,000	120,371
0.10	140,471			
0.12	(5,741)			
0.14	(109,028)			

Sensitivity to the initial sales estimate is found by plugging in different values for sales and recording the resulting NPV. The project's sensitivity to the cost of capital and to sales is graphed below.

■ Study Tips

1. Learn the advantages and disadvantages of the NPV and IRR approaches. This question appears on virtually every exam given on this chapter.

2. Whatever the cashflow stream may be, the NPV will simply be the present value. Be careful to keep track of all of the cashflow signs.

3. Whenever analyzing complicated cash flows, draw a time line so that you will correctly count the periods back to time 0.

4. Remember not to use the IRR to rank projects. The reinvestment interest rate assumption may cause you to rank projects incorrectly. If you need to rank projects for firms experiencing capital rationing, use NPV.

■ Student Notes

_____

_____

_____

_____

_____

■ Sample Exam—Chapter 9

True/False

T F 1. The payback period is the amount of time, rounded to the nearest year, that is required for a firm to recover the cost of a new asset.

T F 2. Net present value is considered a sophisticated capital budgeting technique since it gives consideration to the time value of money.

T F 3. The internal rate of return is the discount rate that equates the present value of the cash inflows of a project with its initial investment.

T F 4. If the NPV of a project is zero, the IRR of that project will always be less than the firm's cost of capital.

T F 5. The goal of the firm should be to use its budget to generate the highest possible internal rate of return for its cash inflows.

T F 6. The NPV assumes that intermediate cash inflows are invested at a rate equal to the firm's cost of capital.

T F 7. The NPV profile shows how sensitive a project's NPV is to changes in the discount rate.

T F   8. The IRR can be read directly off an NPV profile as the point where the profile crosses the *x* axis.

T F   9. For conventional projects, the NPV and the IRR will always produce the same accept-reject decision.

T F 10. The internal rate of return assumes that the intermediate cash flows associated with a project will be reinvested at the project's IRR.

Multiple Choice

1. The _____ is the exact amount of time it takes the firm to recover its initial investment.
    a. internal rate of return
    b. net present value
    c. payback period
    d. certainty equivalent

2. A firm is evaluating a proposal which has an initial investment of $45,000 and has cash flows of $5,000 in year 1, $20,000 in year 2, $15,000 in year 3, and $10,000 in year 4. The payback period of the project is
    a. 3.5 years.
    b. 3 years.
    c. 4 years.
    d. 2.5 years.

3. All of the following are examples of sophisticated capital budgeting techniques EXCEPT
    a. net present value.
    b. annualized net present value.
    c. internal rate of return.
    d. payback period.

4. The _____ is the discount rate that equates the present value of the cash inflows with the initial investment.
    a. cost of capital
    b. internal rate of return
    c. average rate of return
    d. opportunity cost

5. A firm with a cost of capital of 11% is evaluating 4 capital projects. The internal rates of return are as follows:

Project	IRR
1	13%
2	10%
3	11%
4	15%

The firm should
a.   accept 4 and 1, and reject 2 and 3.
b.   accept 4,1, and 3, and reject 2.
c.   accept 4, and reject 1,2, and 3.
d.   accept 3, and reject 1,2, and 4.

6.   The _____ is the minimum amount of return that must be earned on a project in order to leave the firm's value unchanged.
a.   internal rate of return
b.   compound rate
c.   discount rate
d.   risk-free interest rate

For Questions 7 and 8, refer to the following information:

A firm must choose from 5 capital budgeting proposals outlined below. The firm is subject to capital rationing and has a capital budget of $500,000. The firm's cost of capital is 12%.

Project	Initial Investment	IRR	NPV
1	$100,000	17%	$50,000
2	200,000	15%	10,000
3	125,000	14%	30,000
4	100,000	11%	–2,500
5	75,000	19%	25,000

7.   Using the internal rate of return approach to ranking projects, which projects should the firm accept?
a.   1,2,3, and 5
b.   1,2, and 5
c.   1,2, and 3
d.   1,2,3,4, and 5

8.   Using the net present value approach to ranking projects, which projects should the firm accept?
a.   1,2,3,4, and 5
b.   1,2, and 3
c.   1,2,3, and 5
d.   1,2, and 5

9.   A firm is evaluating an investment proposal which has an initial investment of $8,000 and discounted cash flows valued at $6,000. The net present value of the investment is
a. $0.
b.   –$2,000.
c. $2,000.
d. $6,000.

10. Net present value and internal rate of return analyses
    a. always result in the same ranking of projects.
    b. always result in the same accept/reject decision.
    c. may result in differing rankings of projects.
    d. both b. and c. are correct.

11. Unlike the IRR criteria, the NPV approach assumes an interest rate equal to the
    a. market interest rate.
    b. project's internal rate of return.
    c. risk free rate of return.
    d. firm's cost of capital.

For Questions 12 and 13, refer to the following information:

A firm has undertaken a project with an initial investment of $100,000. The firm's cost of capital is 14%.

Year	Cash Inflow
1	$50,000
2	$65,000
3	$90,000

12. What is the NPV for the project?
    a. $50,000
    b. $32,486
    c. $54,622
    d. $76,549

13. What is the IRR for the project?
    a. 41%
    b. 46%
    c. 32%
    d. 22%

14. All of the following are weaknesses of the payback period EXCEPT
    a. a disregard for cash flows after the payback period.
    b. only an implicit consideration of the timing of cash flows.
    c. the difficulty of specifying the appropriate payback period.
    d. that it uses cash flows, not accounting profits.

15. In the context of capital budgeting, risk refers to:
    a. the degree of variability of the cash inflows.
    b. the degree of variability of the initial investment.
    c. the chance that the net present value will be greater than zero.
    d. the chance that the internal rate of return will exceed the cost of capital.

16. Sophisticated capital budgeting techniques do not
    a. examine the size of the initial outlay.
    b. use net profits as a measure of return.
    c. explicitly consider the time value of money.
    d. take into account an unconventional cash flow pattern.

17. The amount by which the required discount rate exceeds the risk-free rate is called
    a. the opportunity cost.
    b. the risk premium.
    c. the risk equivalent.
    d. the excess risk.

18. The minimum return that must be earned on a project in order to leave the firm's value unchanged is
    a. the internal rate of return.
    b. the interest rate.
    c. the discount rate.
    d. the compound rate.

19. The use of certainty equivalent method to evaluate cash flows is a variation of
    a. the internal rate of return method of analysis.
    b. the payback method of analysis.
    c. the net present value method of analysis.
    d. the sensitivity method of analysis.

20. A firm would accept a project with a net present value of zero because
    a. the project would maintain the wealth of the firm's owners.
    b. the project would enhance the wealth of the firm's owners.
    c. the return on the project would be positive.
    d. the return on the project would be zero.

21. The _____ technique is widely applied in personal finance to measure both actual and forecast returns.
    a. internal rate of return
    b. net present value
    c. payback
    d. profitability index

22. The discounted payback period method takes _____ into consideration.
    a. payments after the payback period
    b. time value of money
    c. both of the above
    d. neither of the above

23. Chris has been offered the chance to invest $120,000 in a partnership which is expected to return $25,000 per year. If Chris is in the thirty percent tax bracket and limits investments to those with a payback of 6 years, should Chris invest?
    a. Yes, because the payback period is 3.36 years.
    b. Yes, because the payback period is 4.80 years.
    c. No, because the payback period is 6.86 years.
    d. No, because the payback period is 16 years.

24. Jenna is considering an investment which has a price of $16,000. She expects to receive $1,000 for 3 years, followed by $1,400 for another 4 years. At the end of the 7th year, Jenna expects to sell the investment for $25,000. What is the investment's internal rate of return?
    a. 11.49%
    b. 12.85%
    c. 16.23%
    d. 30.00%

25. In the problem above, if Jenna can borrow money at a rate of 10%, what is the investment's net present value?
    a. $1,484
    b. $2,650
    c. $4,515
    d. $4,849

Essay

1. Which of the following mutually exclusive projects should be accepted using NPV?

	Project A	Project B
Cost of Capital	10%	10%
Initial Investment	$50,000	$75,000
Cash Flow Year 1	$25,000	$25,000
Cash Flow Year 2	$30,000	$25,000
Cash Flow Year 3	$10,000	$45,000

2. In the above example, which project(s) should be accepted if the projects are independent of one another and the IRR approach is used as the accept/reject criterion?

■ Chapter 9 Answer Sheet

True/False		Multiple Choice	
1.	F	1.	C
2.	T	2.	A
3.	T	3.	D
4.	F	4.	B
5.	F	5.	B
6.	T	6.	C
7.	T	7.	A
8.	T	8.	C
9.	T	9.	B (6,000 – 8,000)
10.	T	10.	D
		11.	D
		12.	C (*PV* of CF_1, CF_2, and CF_3 at 14% –$100,000)
		13.	A (must use a financial calculator)
		14.	D
		15.	A
		16.	B
		17.	B
		18.	C
		19.	C
		20.	A
		21.	A
		22.	B
		23.	C
		24.	B
		25.	B

Essay

1. Project A has an NPV of $5,034. Project B has an NPV of $2,198. Since the projects are mutually exclusive, only one of the projects may be chosen. The project that would increase shareholder wealth the most would be Project A.

2. Project A provides an IRR of 16.34%. Project B provides an IRR of 11.49%. Since the projects are independent of one another and they both provide an IRR greater than the firm's cost of capital, both should be accepted.

Chapter 10
Risk and Refinements
in Capital Budgeting

■ Chapter Summary

In this chapter, we learn a number of valuable techniques that increase our ability to accurately and appropriately evaluate investment opportunities. These methods include adjusting for project risk, performing scenario analysis, and evaluating projects under capital rationing and with different lives.

 Understand the importance of recognizing risk in the analysis of capital budgeting projects. If a project is more or less risky than the normal project taken on by the firm, the firm cannot use the cost of capital in its evaluation. Doing so would result it the firm's accepting projects it should reject or rejecting projects it should accept.

 Discuss break-even cash flow, scenario analyses, and simulation as behavioral approaches for dealing with risk, and the unique risks facing multinational companies. There are a number of methods that provide analysts with information about how a project will affect cash flows when assumptions change. These methods alert the firm to the significance of possible errors and help managers understand where they should focus attention.

 Discuss the Unique risks that multinational companies face. Firms that operate internationally face all of the risk domestic firms face, but must also deal with exchange rate risk and political risk.

 Describe the determination and use of risk-adjusted discount rates (RADRs) portfolio effects, and the practical aspects of RADRs. One way to adjust for risk is to increase the discount rate used in the capital budgeting process to compensate for the increased risk of a specific project compared to a firm's usual projects.

 Select the best of a group of unequal-lived mutually exclusive projects using annualized net present values (ANPVs). Longer lived projects will tend to have higher NPVs than shorter ones because there is more time for the NPV to accumulate. This may bias the financial manager into accepting long projects when a series of short projects may be more profitable.

 Explain the role of real options and the objective and procedures for selecting projects. The ability to abandon, change, or time a project has a value that should be recognized and included in the project evaluation.

■ Chapter Notes

 In the prior chapter we applied our capital budgeting techniques in a world we assumed to be certain. Unfortunately, there is a great deal of uncertainty the must be dealt with when making capital budgeting decisions. This chapter introduces a number of ways to handle this uncertainty.

Approaches for dealing with risk

 There are several approaches for dealing with risk in capital budgeting. Here we discuss three: risk and cash inflows, scenario analyses, and simulation.

Risk and cash inflows requires that the analyst reflect unusually high or low risk by either adjusting the discount rate used to compute the present value or by adjusting the cash flows to a level that is sure to be received. Both of these methods requires subjective estimates of either the discount rate or the cash flow. The discount rate may be adjusted to match that of a firm already doing business in a field similar what is being analyzed. Adjusting the cash flows is most appropriate if some portion of the projected revenue stream is guaranteed, say by a binding contract. When cash flows are adjusted in this manner, they should be discounted using a risk free interest rate.

Scenario analysis is a behavioral approach that uses a number of possible values for a given variable to assess its impact on a firm's return. One of the most common scenario approaches in capital budgeting is to estimate a project's NPV by using a pessimistic (worst), most likely (expected), and optimistic (best) cash flow. Behavioral approaches let the analyst get a "feel" for how the changing cash flows affect the project. Advanced scenario analyses evaluate the impact on returns of simultaneous changes in multiple variables.

Simulation is the process of applying predetermined probability distributions and random numbers to estimate risky outcomes. By combining the various cash flow components together in a mathematical model and repeating the process numerous times using random-number-generated probability distributions, the financial manager can simulate an NPV for projects of similar risk.

 International risk: As discussed in Chapter 8, firms doing business in foreign countries face two types of risk. The first is exchange rate risk, which is the risk associated with a movement in the exchange rate between the dollar and the currency in which an American company is contracting business. The other is political risk, which is the risk associated with the presence of a foreign government over which American companies have little or no control.

Risk adjustment techniques

 Sometimes it is necessary to adjust the risk of a project because the risk of the project may not be equal to the firm's cost of capital. The initial outflow of a project is certain and is not affected by the time value of money, so only risk-adjusting techniques for cash inflows are necessary. There are two approaches to risk adjustment: (1) adjust the cash inflows, or (2) adjust the discount rate, r.

Example

In year one, a certain project has projected cash flows of $8,000. If the financial manager is 95% sure that the $8,000 can be reached in year one, the project will have a certainty equivalent of ($8,000 × 0.95) = $7,600 in year one.

After the certainty equivalent has been determined, it is discounted at the risk-free rate, R_f. All of the discounted certainty equivalents are summed to find the NPV of the project.

Another common approach to risk adjustment is to adjust the discount rate to produce a risk-adjusted discount rate (RADR). The higher the risk of a project, the higher the RADR will be, and the NPV will consequently be lowered. One popular method for firms to determine the appropriate RADR is for the firm to develop some type of market risk-return function that bases discount rates on a project's coefficient of variation, a common measure of risk. By setting RADRs at different coefficients of variation, an appropriate RADR can be found for projects of varying risk.

Another approach for determining RADRs would be to place projects with similar risk into risk classes and assign an appropriate RADR for each class. For example, all projects with below average risk may be assigned an RADR of 6%. All projects with average risk may be assigned an RADR of 10%, and projects with the highest risk may be assigned an RADR of 15%.

Capital budgeting refinements

Sometimes it is necessary to make adjustments in the analysis of capital budgeting projects to accommodate special circumstances. There are two areas in which special forms of analysis are used: (1) comparing mutually exclusive projects having unequal lives, and (2) capital rationing by a firm.

Differing Lives

It is incorrect to compare projects with unequal lives using NPV. One popular remedy is to adjust the cash flows of each project until they are of equal length. For example, if 1 project was 2 years long and another was 4 years long, the short one could be doubled. This method is easy to understand but can become difficult if the projects are not multiples of each other.

A second solution to unequal lives is to convert the NPV of projects with unequal lives into equal amounts so that the projects can be compared fairly. The annualized net present value approach is a three-part process.

Step 1   Calculate the NPV of each project using the appropriate cost of capital.

Step 2   Divide the NPV of each project by the PVIFA at the given cost of capital and the project's life to get an annualized NPV for each project.

Step 3   The project with the highest ANPV should be selected.

Example.   Differing project lives

Your firm is considering the two projects detailed in the following table. Which project would you take? Note that since the projects have very different lives, either the replacement chain approach or the annualized net present value approach must be used in your analysis. Assume a 12% discount rate.

Year	Project 1	Project 2
Year 0	−10,000	−10,000
Year 1	3,750	2,500
Year 2	3,750	2,500
Year 3	3,750	2,500
Year 4	3,750	2,500
Year 5	3,750	2,500
Year 6		2,500
Year 7		2,500
Year 8		2,500
Year 9		2,500
Year 10		2,500

Solution

If the projects are compared ignoring the fact that they have very different lives, Project 2 is the best.

$$NPV_1 = \$3,750(PVIFA_{5yrs,\ 12\%}) - \$10,000 = \$3,518$$
$$NPV_2 = \$2,500(PVIFA_{10yrs,12\%}) - \$10,000 = \$4,125$$

Since the NPV_2 is greater than NPV_1 you might be tempted to say Project 2 is the better. This conclusion ignores the idea that if Project 1 is accepted, another project could be taken at the end of five years. We do not know if another project exactly like Project 1 will be available, but if this is a normal type project for the firm, it is reasonable to assume that another one like it could be located. To compare Project 1 to Project 2 then, we need to find the NPV of Project 1 assuming it is repeated one time. This will make the projects have equal length.

Year	Project 1
Year 0	−10,000
Year 1	3,750
Year 2	3,750
Year 3	3,750
Year 4	3,750
Year 5	3,750 − 10,000
Year 6	3,750
Year 7	3,750
Year 8	3,750
Year 9	3,750
Year 10	3,750

There are several ways to solve this problem. Probably the easiest is to recognize that there is a 10-period annuity of $3,750. You can find the present value of the annuity and subtract the present value of the cash outflows.

$$NPV = \$3,750(PVIFA_{10yrs,12\%}) - \$10,000(PVIF_{5yrs,\,12\%}) - \$10,000$$

$$NPV = \$21,188.25 - \$5,674 - \$10,000$$

$$NPV = \$5,514$$

Now we see that the first project is better.

The replacement chain approach shown above is not practical to use when it takes many iterations of one or the other project to make the two projects have equal lives. For example, suppose Project 1 had 8 periods and Project 2 had 14 periods. In this case you can use the equivalent annualized net present value approach. This method is shown below.

Step 1: Compute the NPV for each project—this was done above. $NPV_1 = \$3,518$ and $NPV_2 = \$4,125$.

Step 2: Compute the annualized net present value by dividing the NPV of each project by the present value interest factor for an annuity at the given cost of capital and the project's life.

$$ANPV_1 = \$3,518/PVIFA_{5yrs,12\%} = \$3,518/3.605 = \$975.87$$

$$ANPV_2 = \$4,125/PVIFA_{10yrs,12\%} = \$4,125/5.6502 = \$730.06$$

Project 1 is again selected because $ANPV_1$ is greater than $ANPV_2$.

Real Options

Real options refer to opportunities that are embedded in capital projects and that enable managers to alter their cash flows and risk in a way that affects project acceptability. These are sometimes referred to as strategic options.

Some of the more common types of real options include abandonment, flexibility, growth, and time. Many of these options are embedded in capital projects and explicit recognition of their value will cause the project's strategic NPV to differ from its traditional NPV.

$$NPV_{strategic} = NPV_{traditional} + \text{Value of real options}$$

It is important to realize that the attraction of real options when determining NPV could cause an otherwise unacceptable project to become acceptable.

Capital Rationing

Firms often find that they cannot accept all of the projects that have positive net present values because of limited funds. It may be because they have self-imposed limits on borrowing or because they wish to fund their growth through internally generated funds. There are two customary techniques for dealing with limited funds: the internal rate of return approach and the NPV approach.

The IRR approach requires that the analysts sort the available projects in order by decreasing IRR. The projects are then graphed, along with the cost of capital. Projects above the cost of capital line are accepted and those below are rejected. The following figure demonstrates this method.

The first two projects would be accepted and the third would be rejected. While the IRR approach is intuitive, there is no guarantee that the projects accepted will maximize total dollar returns and, therefore, owners' wealth.

The NPV approach can be more tedious to apply but is preferred. The NPV of each project is computed. Various feasible combinations of projects are evaluated until the set of projects is identified that maximizes the total NPV of all projects.

■ Study Tips

1. One of the most significant points made by this chapter is that you must adjust for risk when appropriate. Pay particular attention to when risk adjustment may be required.

2. The reason for discussing breakeven analysis in this chapter is that it highlights how increasing fixed costs increases risk by increasing breakeven sales.

3. Remember that the adjustment of the discount rate is preferred to the certainty equivalent method for adjusting for risk.

4. In the last chapter we noted that IRR leads to different rankings than does NPV. In this chapter IRR is shown as a ranking tool. Keep in mind that when IRR is used to rank, the results should be confirmed by using NPV.

■ Student Notes

_____

_____

_____

_____

_____

■ Sample Exam—Chapter 10

True/False

T   F   1.   It is appropriate to use the firm's cost of capital when evaluating any capital budgeting project.

T   F   2.   If a project is more risky than those the firm usually accepts, it will have to have a greater NPV to be acceptable.

T   F   3.   Behavior approaches to evaluating capital projects allow the analyst to get a feel for the level of project risk.

T   F   4.   Scenario analysis is an approach that evaluates the impact of simultaneous changes in a number of variables.

T   F   5.   A net present value profile is a graphical presentation of the NPV at various discount rates.

T   F   6.   Certainty equivalents determine the rate of return that must be earned on a given project to compensate the firm's owners adequately.

T   F   7.   In reference to capital budgeting, risk is the chance that a project has a high degree of variability in the initial investment.

T   F   8.   The break-even cash inflow is the minimum level of cash inflow necessary for a project to be acceptable.

T   F   9.   A higher risk adjusted discount rate (RADR) will result in a higher NPV.

T   F   10. When dealing with mutually exclusive, unequal-lived projects, the use of NPV to select the better project may result in an incorrect decision.

Multiple Choice

1.   A method for evaluating a project that uses a number of possible values for a given variable, such as cash inflows, to assess its impact on the firm's return is
   a.   sensitivity analysis.
   b.   scenario analysis.
   c.   certainty equivalent.
   d.   risk-adjusted cash flow.

2.   A statistically based behavioral approach to project analysis that applies predetermined probability distributions is the
   a.   simulation method.
   b.   scenario approach.
   c.   sensitivity approach.
   d.   certainty equivalent.

3.   Which of the following is not a normal risk consideration unique to multinational firms?
   a.   exchange rate risk
   b.   political risk
   c.   tax issues related to transfer pricing
   d.   market risk

4. The percent of estimated cash inflow that investors would be satisfied to receive for certain is known as the _____
    a. certainty equivalent.
    b. risk-adjusted cash flow.
    c. NPV.
    d. discounted cash flow.

5. When using the certainty equivalent cash-flow approach, cash flows are discounted back to the present using
    a. the IRR.
    b. the WACCAT.
    c. the risk-free rate.
    d. zero percent.

6. The rate of return that must be earned on a given project to compensate owners for projects with unusual risk levels is the
    a. WACCAT.
    b. risk-adjusted discount rate.
    c. IRR.
    d. risky interest rate.

7. From a practical standpoint it makes more sense to adjust for risk in capital budgeting using
    a. portfolio interest rates.
    b. certainty equivalents.
    c. WACCAT.
    d. risk-adjusted discount rates.

8. After adjusting the following cash flow for unequal lives using the replacement chain approach, the NPV of Project 1 is _____ and the NPV of Project 2 is _____.

	Project 1	Project 2
Year 0	–10,000	–10,000
Year 1	3750	2500
Year 2	3750	2500
Year 3	3750	2500
Year 4	3750	2500
Year 5	3750	2500
Year 6		2500
Year 7		2500
Year 8		2500
Year 9		2500
Year 10		2500

    a. 3518; 4125
    c. 5514; 4125
    b. 4125; 5514
    d. none of the above

9. Unlike the IRR criteria, the NPV approach assumes an interest rate equal to the_____ when not adjusting for risk.

   a. market interest rate
   b. project's internal rate of return
   c. risk-free rate of return
   d. firm's cost of capital

For Questions 10 and 11, refer to the following information:

A firm is considering investing in a capital project which has an initial investment of $75,000 and cash flows and certainty equivalents as outlined below. The firm has a cost of capital of 14% and the risk-free rate is 6%.

Year	Cash Inflow	Certainty Equivalent
1	$30,000	0.90
2	35,000	0.80
3	40,000	0.75

10. The certain cash inflow for year 1 is
    a. $31,800.
    b. $30,000.
    c. $0.
    d. $27,000.

11. Using the certainty equivalent method, the net present value for the project is
    a. $5,246.
    b. $581.
    c. $18,036.
    d. –$2,700.

12. The objective of _____ is to select the group of projects that provides the highest overall net present value and does not require more dollars than are budgeted.
    a. scenario analysis
    c. capital rationing
    b. simulation
    d. sensitivity analysis

13. The following 2 projects are mutually exclusive. Both have a cost of capital of 10%.

	Project A	Project B
Length of cash inflows	5	7
NPV	$12,000	$14,000

What is the annualized net present value of Project A and Project B?
a. $3,165 and $2,876
b. $2,378 and $1,850
c. $2,986 and $4,197
d. $4,174 and $3,915

14. A project that has a coefficient of variation of zero is considered
    a. slightly risky.
    b. a bad investment.
    c. very risky.
    d. risk-free.

15. An increase in the risk adjusted discount rate will result in
    a. no change to the NPV.
    b. a decrease in the NPV.
    c. an increase in the NPV.
    d. an increase in the IRR.

16. The amount by which the required discount rate exceeds the risk-free rate is called the
    a. risk equivalent.
    b. risk premium.
    c. excess risk.
    d. market risk function.

17. Vang Vu has carefully investigated investment in Mung Technologies. Purchasing 100 shares would cost $5,000. However, Mung Technologies is expected to offer an annual dividend of $60 and be sold at a price of $6,500 in 3 years. Although Vang normally requires a return of 10%, this company has a low beta, resulting in a required return of only 8.5%. Should Vang invest in Mung Technologies?
    a. No, because the net present value is $242.
    b. Yes, because the required rate of return is less than that normally required.
    c. Yes, because the net present value is $89.
    d. Yes, because the net present value is $242.

18. Risk classes and risk-adjusted discount rates are based upon
    a. the CAPM, but not risk-return behavior of past projects.
    b. government-dictated classifications and yields.
    c. risk-return behavior of past projects, but not the CAPM.
    d. risk-return behavior of past projects and the CAPM.

19. Tim Demmer, a rodeo clown, is evaluating the cost of a recreation vehicle, which costs $98,000. Tim plans on keeping the RV for 5 years, at which time he believes he will be able to sell it for $55,000. Using the RV will cut down on hotel and meal costs by about $16,000 per year, on an after-tax basis. Assuming a discount rate of 7% for projects of this relative low risk, what is the RV's ANPV?
    a. $1,037
    b. $1,119
    c. $1,663
    d. $6,817

20. Sarah Alain has to make a choice between two investments. Investment A has a net present value of $55,000, lasts 6 years, and requires a discount rate of 9%. Investment B has a net present value of $45,000, lasts 5 years, and has a discount rate of 13%. Project selection should be based upon:

   a. annualized net present value.
   b. discount rates.
   c. initial costs.
   d. net present value.

21. In the problem above, which investment should Sarah Alain select?

   a. Investment A, which has an annualized net present value of $9,167.
   b. Investment A, which has an annualized net present value of $12,261.
   c. Investment B, which has an annualized net present value of $9,000
   d. Investment B, which has an annualized net present value of $12,794.

■ Chapter 10 Answer Sheet

True/False	Multiple Choice	
1. F		1. B
2. F		2. A
3. T		3. D
4. T		4. A
5. T		5. C
6. F		6. B
7. F		7. D
8. T		8. C
9. F		9. D
10. T		10. D ($30,000 \times 0.9 = 27,000$)

For question 5:

$$NPV = \$3,750(PVIFA_{10yrs,12\%})$$
$$- \$10,000(PVIF_{5yrs,12\%}) - \$10,000$$
$$NPV = \$21,188.25 - \$5,674 - \$10,000$$
$$NPV = \$5,514$$

11. B ($27,000/1.06 + 28,000/1.06^2 + 30,000/1.06^3$
    $-75,000$)

12. C

13. A ($12,000/PVIFA_{5yrs,10\%}$),($14,000/PVIFA_{7yrs,10\%}$)

14. D

15. B

16. B

17. D

18. D

19. C

20. A

21. D

Chapter 11
The Cost of Capital

■ Chapter Summary

The last two chapters dealt with the problem of analyzing investment opportunities by introducing you to cash flows and capital budgeting methods. This chapter extends this topic by discussing how to find the rate used in net present value and internal rate of return calculations. The most difficult part of this chapter is learning how to account for changing discount rates that result from increasing the demand for funds by firms that have many investment opportunities. In this chapter it is assumed that the optimal or target mix of debt and equity is known. We conclude the long-term financing discussion in the next chapter by discussing the determinants of this mix.

 Understand the key assumptions, the basic concept, and the specific sources of capital associated with the cost of capital. The cost of capital is the rate of return a firm must earn on its project investments to maintain its market value. There are four main sources of capital discussed in this chapter. Debt is the lowest cost source of capital because interest paid to bondholders is tax deductible to the firm. Equity-either common or preferred stock-can be sold to raise capital. Additionally, equity from common stockholders can be raised from retaining earnings rather than paying dividends.

 Determine the cost of long-term debt and the cost of preferred stock. In Chapter 8 you learned to compute the yield to maturity for bonds. This method is used to compute the cost of debt. Because interest payments are tax deductible, only after-tax costs are used. The cost of preferred stock is the dividend that must be paid, which is not tax deductible.

 Calculate the cost of common stock equity and convert it into the cost of retained earnings and the cost of new issues of common stock. There are two models that were introduced in Chapters 7 and 8 that can be used to compute the cost of equity financing. The reason for using multiple models is that the inputs to each model are uncertain. By combining the results, a better estimate of cost can be achieved.

 Calculate the weighted average cost of capital (WACC) and discuss alternative weighting schemes and economic value added (EVA). Once all of the component costs are found, the weighted average cost of capital is computed where the weights are the proportion of each source of capital in the firm's target capital structure. This WACC is used as the discount rate in capital budgeting problems.

 Describe the procedures used to determine break points and the weighted marginal cost of capital (WMCC). As the amount of funds raised increases, the cost of those funds also increases. The breaking point refers to the point where the cost of a component rises.

Explain the weighted marginal cost of capital (WMCC) and its use with the investment opportunities schedule (IOS) to make financing/investment decisions. When the WMCC curve is plotted together with the investment opportunity schedule it is easy to visualize which projects should be accepted. Accept only those where the yield on the project is greater than the cost of funds. This method is especially valuable for firms with many investment opportunities.

■ Chapter Outline

An overview of the cost of capital

The cost of capital is the rate of return that a firm must earn on an investment to maintain the market value of its stock. The flip side is that the cost of capital is the average cost of all the sources of financing for the firm. The cost of capital plays a major role in the long-term investment decisions of the firm, and because it has a substantial part in determining the validity of a project (NPV > $0, IRR > r), it is an important concept to understand.

The basic concept

There are four basic sources of long-term funds that are available to the firm. These are long-term debt, preferred stock, retained earnings, and common stock. Long-term debt reflects money borrowed from creditors, whereas preferred stock, common stock, and retained earnings are classified as equity. The firm should try to maintain an optimal mix of debt and equity financing. This optimal mix is known as the target capital structure and will be discussed in the next chapter. In practice, firms attempt to keep financing within a target range, such as 40% to 50% debt.

The cost of long-term debt

The cost of long-term debt, r_i, is the after-tax cost today of raising long-term funds through borrowing. In most cases, long-term debt is borrowed in the form of bonds that pay interest semi-annually. For simplicity and ease of calculation, we will assume that the interest is paid annually. The net proceeds of these bonds consist of the selling price of the bond minus the flotation costs, which are the total costs of issuing and selling a bond.

Before-tax cost of debt

The before-tax cost of debt, r_d, for a bond can be found in one of three ways: (1) quotation, (2) calculation, and (3) approximation.

When the net proceeds from the sale of a bond are equal to its face value, the coupon interest rate can be used for the bond's before-tax cost. Also, when the yield to maturity (YTM) for other bonds of similar risk is available, the similar bond's YTM can be used for the firm's before-tax cost of long-term debt. This is termed a cost quotation.

When the net proceeds from the sale of the bond differ from the face value of the bond, it is necessary to either calculate the cost or approximate the cost. The calculation of the before-tax cost of debt for a bond involves finding the YTM for the bond either by the trial and error approach that was discussed in Chapter 8 or by using a hand-held business/financial calculator.

The equation used for approximating the before-tax cost of long-term debt for a bond is demonstrated in the following formula:

$$r_d = \frac{I + \frac{M - N_d}{n}}{\frac{N_d + M}{2}}$$

where:

   I = annual interest in dollars

   M = par value of bond

   N_d = net proceeds from the sale of debt (bond)

   n = number of years to the bond's maturity

After-tax cost of debt

As mentioned earlier, the cost of financing must be stated on an after-tax basis. The interest on debt is tax deductible, so it reduces the firm's taxable income by the amount of deductible interest. The equation used to find the after-tax cost of debt is demonstrated in the following formula:

$$r_i = r_d \times (1 - T)$$

where:

   r_i = after-tax cost of debt

   r_d = before-tax cost of debt

   T = corporate tax rate

Example

Velvet Corporation has a before-tax cost of debt of 8.4% and a corporate tax rate of 40%. What is the after-tax cost of debt for Velvet Corporation?

$r_i = 0.084 \times (1 - 0.40)$

$r_i = 5.04\%$

Since the interest on the debt is tax deductible, Velvet is paying only 5.04% for the debt and is receiving a 3.36% (or 8.4 × 0.4) tax deduction for every dollar spent on interest.

The cost of preferred stock

Preferred stock is a special form of ownership because its dividends must be distributed before any dividends are paid to the common stockholders. Most preferred stock dividends are stated as a dollar amount, but sometimes they are stated as a percentage of the stock's par value. In order to calculate the cost of preferred stock, it is necessary to convert the dividend of any preferred stock that is stated as a percentage into a dollar amount. Once the dividend is stated as a dollar amount, the cost of the preferred stock can be found by using the following equation:

$$r_p = \frac{D_p}{N_p}$$

where:

   r_p = cost of preferred stock

   D_p = annual dollar dividend

   N_p = net proceeds from the sale of the stock

Preferred stock dividends are paid out of the firm's after-tax cash flows, so no tax adjustment is necessary.

The cost of common stock

There are two forms of common stock financing: retained earnings and new issues of common stock. Before finding each of these costs, the cost of common stock equity must be estimated. The cost of common stock equity, k_s, is the rate at which investors discount the expected dividends of the firm to determine its share value. There are two techniques that are used to estimate r_s. The constant-growth valuation model was discussed in Chapter 8 and is presented in the following equation:

$$P_0 = \frac{D_1}{r_s - g}$$

where:

P_0 = value of common stock

D_1 = per-share dividend expected at the end of year 1

r_s = required return on common stock

g = constant rate of growth in dividends

To find the cost of common stock equity, simply solve the equation for k_s.

$$r_s = \frac{D_1}{P_0} + g$$

Example

Velvet Corporation wishes to estimate its cost of common stock equity, k_s. The firm expects to pay a dividend, D_1, of $2.87 at the end of 2009. The current market price, P_0, of its common stock is $35, and the dividends paid on its common stock over the past 5 years are presented in the following table:

Year	Dividend
2008	$2.70
2007	2.56
2006	2.42
2005	2.26
2004	2.14

Using a financial calculator, the growth rate has been determined to be 6%. (See Chapter 6 to review growth rates.) Substituting the information into the equation used to solve for k_s will result in:

$$r_s = \frac{\$2.87}{\$35} + 6\% = 8.2\% + 6\% = 14.2\%$$

The 14.2% represents the return required by *existing* shareholders on their investment.

The capital asset pricing model (CAPM) introduced in Chapter 7 can also be used to estimate the cost of common stock equity. The CAPM describes the relationship between the required return, or the cost of common equity in this case, and the nondiversifiable risk of the firm as measured by the beta coefficient, β. The following equation represents the basic CAPM:

$$r_s = R_F + [b \times (r_m - R_F)]$$

where:

R_F= risk-free rate of return

b = beta coefficient

r_m = market return; return on the market portfolio of assets

The cost of retained earnings

Earnings, after all expenses and preferred dividends are paid, belong to the common stockholders. The firm can pay out all earnings or pay only a portion of the earnings as dividends and retain the balance. The earnings that are retained represent an additional investment by the existing common stockholders. Viewing retained earnings as the equivalent of the issuance of additional common stock, the cost of retained earnings, r_r, can be set equal to the cost of common stock equity.

$$r_r = r_s$$

The cost of new issues of common stock

The cost of new issues of common stock is found by calculating the cost of common stock equity after the amount of underpricing and flotation costs are considered. To sell a new issue of common stock, it normally has to be underpriced, which means selling the stock at a price below the current market, P_0. In addition, flotation costs must be paid to the investment banker for selling the new shares. Both underpricing and flotation costs will reduce the proceeds from the sale of new common stock. The cost of new issues can be found by using the constant-growth valuation model used for finding the cost of existing common stock. Simply adjust the current market price of the stock, P_0, for any underpricing and flotation cost.

$$r_n = \frac{D_1}{N_n} + g$$

Where:

r_n = cost of new issues

N_n = net proceeds from the sale of new issues

The weighted average cost of capital

The weighted average cost of capital (WACC) is found by weighting the cost of each specific type of capital by its proportion in the firm's capital structure to find the average cost of funds over the long run. We previously discussed the procedure for finding the specific after-tax cost of each source of capital. To determine the weights to use, simply add the total dollar amount of long-term financed capital and divide each component by the total amount to find its proportion.

Example

Velvet Corporation has the following capital structure:

Source	Amount
Long-term debt	$200,000
Preferred stock	25,000
Common stock equity	275,000
Total	$500,000

The total dollar amount of financed capital is $500,000. To determine each component's weight, simply divide the amount of the financed capital being used by $500,000. For example, to get the weight of long-term debt, divide $200,000 by $500,000.

$$w_i = \frac{\$200,000}{\$500,000} = 0.40$$

$$w_p = \frac{\$25,000}{\$500,000} = 0.05$$

$$w_s = \frac{\$275,000}{\$500,000} = 0.55$$

Remember that these weights should total to 1. Once the weights have been determined, the cost of each component can be multiplied by its weight to determine the WACC.

Where:

w_i = proportion of long-term debt in capital structure

w_p = proportion of preferred stock in capital structure

w_s = proportion of common stock in capital structure

The marginal cost and investment decisions

The firm's weighted average cost of capital is a key input to the investment decision-making process, so it is important to understand that as new amounts of financing are introduced, the WACC changes. With increased amounts of financing, the cost of the various types of financing will increase due to the increased risk to the fund's suppliers. The weighted marginal cost of capital (WMCC) is the firm's WACC associated with its next dollar of new financing. In other words, the WMCC is simply the WACC at any point in time adjusted to reflect the new financing. To calculate the WMCC, *the breaking point* has to be calculated. The breaking point is the level of total new financing at which the cost of one of the financing components rises, thereby causing an upward shift in the WMCC. The breaking point can be calculated by using the following equation:

$$BP_j = \frac{AF_j}{w_j}$$

Where:

BP_j = breaking point for financing source j

AF_j = amount of funds available from financing source j at a given cost

w_j = capital structure weight for financing source j

Once the break points have been calculated, the WMCC over the various ranges must be determined. When these new ranges are grouped together, they can be used to prepare a WMCC schedule, which is a graph that relates the firm's WACC to the level of new financing.

The investment opportunities schedule (IOS)

The firm's investment opportunities schedule is simply a ranking of projects from the highest return to the lowest return. The IOS graphically presents the return on the different investment opportunities facing a firm. The WMCC is also plotted on the graph. If a project's return is above the WMCC, the project should be accepted. If the project falls below the WMCC, the project should be rejected.

Total Dollars Invested

In the above graph, the solid or darker line is the return on three different investments available to the firm. It is called the investment opportunity schedule. The dashed or lighter line is the WACC at various amounts of investment. This is the marginal cost of capital schedule. In the above example, projects A and B would be accepted, and project C would be rejected because its return is below the WMCC.

■ Sample Problems and Solutions

Example 1. Cost of debt

Find the cost of debt for a bond that is selling for $950, has 5 years to maturity, and has a coupon interest rate of 10%. Assume the tax rate is 40%.

a. Equation Solution

The cost of debt is found using the procedure shown earlier for computing the yield to maturity. The difference is that the market price is adjusted to reflect any discounts, fees, or costs that the firm must pay. In this problem, no costs are mentioned so we assume that there are not any. The YTM can be found easily on a financial calculator or by using the approximation equation.

$$\text{Approximate Yield (YTM)} = \frac{I + \dfrac{M - N_d}{n}}{\dfrac{N_d + M}{2}}$$

$$\text{YTM} = \frac{90 + \dfrac{(1000 - 950)}{5}}{\dfrac{1000 + 950}{2}} = 0.113$$

$$r_d = 0.113 \times (1 - 0.4) = 0.0678 = 6.78\%$$

b.   Calculator Solution

$N = 5$

$PV = 950$

$PMT = -100$

$FV = -1,000$

$CPT\ I = 11.37$

$r_d = 0.1137 \times (1 - 0.4) = 0.0682 = 6.82\%$

Example 2.   Cost of long-term debt

Laurie's Rose Distributors is contemplating expanding by selling bonds. Her investment banker advises that the bonds should sell for $1,100, less 3% for fees. If the bonds have a coupon rate of 10% and mature in 10 years, what is Laurie's cost of debt? Assume a 40% tax rate.

a.   Equation Solution

The above estimation equation can be used.

The market price will be $1,100 - (1,100 \times 0.03) = $1,067.

$$YTM = \frac{100 + \dfrac{(1000 - 1,067)}{10}}{\dfrac{1000 + 1,067}{2}} = 0.0903$$

$r_d = 0.0903 \times (1 - 0.4) = 0.0542 = 5.42\%$

b.   Calculator Solution

$N\quad = 10$

$PV\quad = 1,067$

$PMT\quad = -100$

$FV\quad = -1,000$

$CPT\ I = 8.96$

$r_d = 0.0896 \times (1 - 0.4) = 0.0538 = 5.38\%$

Example 3.   Cost of preferred stock

Compute the cost of preferred stock financing if the promised annual dividend is $2.00 and the current market price of the stock is $22.00.

Solution

Preferred stock pays a dividend in perpetuity, meaning forever. By rearranging the equation we learned for valuing a perpetuity, we can find the return. No tax adjustment is needed since preferred stock dividends are not tax deductible. Since this is not a new issue of preferred stock, there are no flotation costs to be considered.

$$r_p = \frac{D_p}{N_p}$$

so

$$r_p = D_P/N_p = \$2/\$22 = 0.0909 = 9.09\%$$

Example 4.   Cost of equity

Compute the cost of equity if the common stock is selling for $35, the growth rate is expected to be 5%, and next year's dividend is expected to be $3.

Solution

Given the available information, the only model that can be used is the Gordon growth model. By rearranging the terms, we find that:

$$r_s = D_1/P + g$$

so

$$r_s = \$3/\$35 + 0.05 = 0.136 = 13.6\%$$

Note: The most common mistake made when using this equation is to mix decimals and percentages. Do not say the $r_s = 3/35 + 5\% = 0.086 + 5 = 5.086\%$.

Example 5.   Cost of equity

Compute the cost of equity if the firm's beta is 1.12, the risk-free rate of interest is 7%, and the return on the market is 13%.

Solution

The only method to solve for the cost of equity that is possible, given the above information, is the CAPM.

$$r_s = 0.07 + 1.12(0.13 - 0.07) = 0.137 = 13.7\%$$

Example 6.   Cost of equity

Compute the cost of equity if new stock must be sold and the flotation costs are expected to be 5% of the current market price of the stock. The stock is selling for $35, the growth rate is expected to be 5%, and the next dividend is expected to be $3.

Solution

When flotation costs exist, the cost of common stock to the firm rises because the firm receives a lesser amount. In this example, when stock is sold, the public will pay $35 per share, but the firm will receive only $33.25 (or, $35 \times (1 - 0.05)$) of the proceeds.

$$r_s = \$3/\$33.25 + 0.05 = 0.1402 = 14.02\%$$

Note: Compare this result to Example 4. The only difference was that flotation costs are included here. As a result, the cost of equity increases.

Example 7.   Weighted average cost of capital

Compute the weighted average cost of capital for Bob's Crystal Pool Supply given that $r_d = 10\%$(after-tax), $r_p = 12\%$, and $r_s = 13.7\%$. The target capital structure is 60% common stock, 30% debt, and 10% preferred stock.

Solution

$$WACC = 0.60(0.137) + 0.30\ (0.10) + 0.1(0.12) = 0.1242 = 12.42\%$$

Example 8.   Marginal cost of capital schedule (simple)

Suppose that Richard's Pool Basketball Inc. had a target capital structure of 10% preferred, 30% debt, and 60% common. Its tax rate is 40%. The firm's dividend next period will be $2, and the growth rate is expected to be constant at 5%. The current price of that stock is $20. If new equity is sold, the firm expects to net $18 from the sale. The pretax cost of debt is 12%. The cost of preferred is 14%. The firm has $10 in retained earnings. What is the marginal cost of capital schedule?

Solution

These problems can seem difficult because a number of steps are involved. First, you must find the cost of each component. Second, you must find breakpoints where the costs change. Third, you must compute the weighted average cost at each of the breakpoints. Finally, you can graph the results.

Step 1: Compute the cost of common equity
   a.   retained earnings—$r_s = \$2/20 + 0.05 = 0.15$
   b.   new equity—$r_s = 2/18 + 0.05 = 0.161$

Step 2: Compute the breakpoint for common equity

$$\$10/0.6 = 16.67$$

Step 3: Compute the cost below and above the breakpoint
   a.   Cost of capital $0 to $16,667,000

$$WACC = 0.6(0.15) + 0.3(0.12)(1 - 0.4) + 0.1(0.14) = 0.126$$

   b.   Cost of capital above $16,667,000

$$WACC = 0.6(0.161) + 0.3(0.12)(0.6) + 0.1(0.14) = 0.132$$

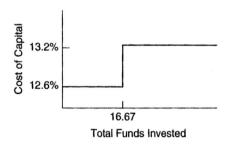

Example 9.   Marginal cost of capital schedule (complex)

Linda's Drive-Through Lumber Express has a target capital structure of 60% common stock, 30% debt, and 10% preferred stock. The cost for retained earnings is 15% and the cost of new or external equity is 16%. Linda's Lumber expects to have $20 million of retained earnings available. Linda can sell $15 million of first-mortgage bonds with an after-tax cost of 9%. The firm's bankers feel the company can sell $10 million of debentures with a cost of 9.5%. Additional debt would cost 10% after tax. The cost of preferred stock is 14%. Compute the marginal cost of capital schedule and breakpoints.

Solution

Step 1: Find the breakpoints

To find the breakpoints, divide the amount of money available at a particular cost by the proportion of the target capital structure made up by that component.

a.   retained earnings: $20 million/0.60 = $33.33 million

b.   first-mortgage bonds: $15 million/0.30 = $50 million

c.   debentures: $10 million/0.30 = $33.33 million

$20 million can be raised from retained earnings before the cost of common equity must go up due to flotation costs incurred by selling stocks publicly. $15 million in low-cost debt can be sold before more costly debt must be used. After the $10 million or 9.5% debt is gone, 10% debt must be used.

Step 2: Compute the WACC for each breakpoint

Look over the breakpoints and find the lowest one. There are 2 at $33 million, but the one for debt is after the $50 million breakpoint. Therefore the first actual breakpoint is at $33 million due to using up retained earnings. The WACC will be computed using the lowest cost of each component.

$$WACC_{\text{0 to \$33 million}} = 0.6(0.15) + 0.3(0.09) + 0.1(0.14) = 0.131 = 13.1\%$$

The next breakpoint occurs because Linda's runs out of first-mortgage bonds. A total of $50 million will be raised before this occurs. In the range between $33 million and $50 million, equity will cost more but all other components will stay the same as above.

$$WACC_{\text{\$33 million to \$50 million}} = 0.6(0.16) + 0.3(0.09) + 0.1(0.14) = 0.137 = 13.7\%$$

The next breakpoint occurs because Linda's runs out of 9.5% debentures. A total of $83 million will have been raised when this happens.

$$WACC_{\text{\$50 million to \$83 million}} = 0.6(0.16) + 0.3(0.095) + 0.1(0.14) = 0.139 = 13.9\%$$

The last breakpoint is when the firm must begin using 10% debt.

$$WACC_{\text{over \$83 million}} = 0.6(0.16) + 0.3(0.10) + 0.1(0.14) = 0.14 = 14\%$$

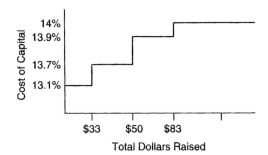

■ Quick Drill Self Test

1. The current market price of a $1,000 par bond is $925. Its semiannual coupon rate is 7% and it matures in 5 years. What is the pre-tax cost of debt (r_d)?

2. The current market price of a $1,000 par bond is $1,025. Its semiannual coupon rate is 7% and it matures in 5 years. What is the pre-tax cost of debt (r_d)?

3. What is the after-tax cost of debt using the data in Problem 1 and assuming a 40% marginal tax rate?

4. What is the after-tax cost of debt using the data in Problem 2 and assuming a 40% tax rate?

5. What is the cost of preferred stock financing if it pays a constant dividend of $3.00 and is currently selling for $35.00 per share?

6. What is the after-tax cost of preferred using the data from Problem 5?

7. Use CAPM to compute the cost of equity given that the firm's beta is 1.1, the risk-free rate is 6% and the return on the market is 13%.

8. Use the Gordon growth model to compute the cost of equity given that the next dividend is expected to be $2.00, the current price is $30.00 and the expected growth rate is 8%.

9. The LAST dividend paid was $1.50. What is the cost of equity using the Gordon growth model assuming current price of $25.00 and an expected growth rate of 7%?

10. Use the data from Problem 2 and assume the bond yield premium is 4% to compute the cost of equity.

11. Assume you have equal faith in each method used to compute the cost of equity. Use the results from Problems 7, 8, and 10 to compute the cost of equity.

12. Again using the solutions to Problems 7, 8, and 10, find the cost of equity assuming you are twice as confident in the CAPM approach as you are in either of the other 2 approaches to finding the cost of equity (weights are 50%, 25% and 25%).

13. A firm currently has long-term debt totaling $1,500,000, preferred stock totaling $250,000 and equity outstanding of $3,000,000. Using the answers to Problems 4, 5, 12 compute the weighted average cost of capital after-tax.

14. If the firm discussed in Problem 13 had outstanding current debt of $100,000 would the WACC change?

15. If the firm discussed in Problem 13 has $125,000 of retained earnings this year, what is the break point for equity?

16. If the firm discussed in Problem 13 can sell $100,000 in bonds before the cost of debt will rise, what is the breakpoint for debt?

17. If the firm discussed in Problem 13 can sell $50,000 of preferred before the cost of preferred stock rises, what is the breakpoint for preferred stock?

18. How much in total capital can be raised, using the assumptions discussed in Problems 15, 16, and 17, before the WACCAT will increase?

19. What is the WACC before the breakpoint using the results of Problems 13?

20. What is the WACC after the breakpoint using the results of Problem 13 and Problems 15–17 and assuming that new equity can be sold at a cost of 15%?

Answers to Quick Drill Self Test

1. 8.89%

2. 6.41%

3. 5.33%

4. 3.85%

5. 8.57%

6. 8.57%

7. 13.70%

8. 14.67%

9. 13.42%

10. 10.41%

11. 12.93%

12. 13.12%

13. 9.95%

14. No

15. $197,910.07

16. $316,656.11

17. $950,570.07

18. $197,910.07

19. 9.95%

20. 11.14%

■ Study Tips

1. Recognize that there is only one generally accepted method to find the cost of debt. This is because you can be confident of the inputs to this model. There is also only one method for finding the cost of preferred stock. There are multiple methods for finding the cost of common equity because of the uncertainty of the inputs. Be sure to know the alternative methods.

2. When computing the cost of debt, be sure to multiply by (1-tax) to get the after-tax cost. The after-tax cost will be given in some problems. Be alert to the wording of the problem.

3. There are two steps to the calculation of the weighted average cost of capital. First, compute the cost of each component, then find the weighted average.

4. Students often have trouble computing the marginal cost of capital schedule. Study the two examples given in the last section carefully. The breakpoints represent the *total* amount of money raised before there is an increase in cost. So if debt occupies 10% of the capital structure and if there is $10,000 of debt available at one price, then a total of $100,000 can be raised before there will be an increase. This is because 10% of $100,000 is $10,000.

■ Student Notes

_____

_____

_____

_____

_____

■ Sample Exam—Chapter 11

True/False

T F 1. The cost of capital is the rate of return a firm must earn on investments in order to leave share price unchanged.

T F 2. If risk is unchanged, the undertaking of projects with a rate of return above the cost of capital will decrease the value of the firm.

T F 3. The specific cost of each source of financing is viewed on a before-tax basis.

T F 4. The net proceeds used in calculating the cost of long-term debt are funds actually received from the sale after paying for flotation costs.

T F 5. When the net proceeds from the sale of a bond equal its par value, the coupon interest rate will be the bond's before-tax cost of capital.

T F 6. The cost of preferred stock is typically lower than the cost of long-term debt because dividends paid on preferred stock are tax deductible.

T   F   7.   The cost of common stock equity may be measured using either the zero-growth valuation model or the CAPM.

T   F   8.   Due to the absence of flotation costs, the cost of retained earnings is always lower than the cost of a new issue of common stock.

T   F   9.   The CAPM describes the relationship between the required return and the nonsystematic risk of the firm as measured by the beta coefficient.

T   F   10.   Larger volumes of new financing are associated with greater risk and lead to higher financing costs.

T   F   11.   Since preferred stock is a form of ownership, the stock will never mature.

T   F   12.   The weighted marginal cost of capital is the firm's weighted average cost of capital associated with its next dollar of total financing.

T   F   13.   A firm's investment opportunities schedule is a ranking of investment possibilities from best (highest returns) to worst (lowest return).

T   F   14.   As the cumulative amount of money invested in a firm's capital projects increases, its returns on the projects will increase.

T   F   15.   According to the firm's owner wealth maximization goal, the firm should accept projects up to the point where the marginal return on its investment equals its weighted marginal cost of capital.

Multiple Choice

1.   The _____ is the rate of return a firm must earn on its investment in order to maintain the market value of its stock.
   a.   gross profit margin
   b.   internal rate of return
   c.   net present value
   d.   cost of capital

2.   The WACC represents the average _____ for the firm.
   a.   cost of equity
   b.   return on fixed assets
   c.   cost of financing
   d.   return on investment

3.   The cost of capital reflects the cost of funds
   a.   over the short run.
   b.   at current book values.
   c.   set by the federal government.
   d.   over the long run.

4. The firm's optimal mix of debt and equity is called its
   a. target capital structure.
   b. maximum wealth ratio.
   c. optimal mix.
   d. debt-to-equity ratio.

5. The specific cost of each source of long-term financing is based on _____ and _____ costs.
   a. before-tax; current
   b. after-tax; historical
   c. after-tax; current
   d. before-tax; historical

6. A tax adjustment must be made in determining the cost of
   a. common stock.
   b. long-term debt.
   c. retained earnings.
   d. preferred stock.

7. A firm has issued 8% preferred stock, which sold for $100 per share par value. The flotation costs of the stock equaled $3 and the firm's marginal tax rate is 40%. The cost of the preferred stock is
   a. 8.25%.
   b. 7.50%.
   c. 7.35%.
   d. 9.85%.

8. The approximate before-tax cost of debt for a 20-year, 9%, $1,000 par value bond selling at $950 is
   a. 10.63%.
   c. 7.45%.
   b. 11.39%.
   d. 9.49%.

9. The cost of common stock equity may be estimated by using the
   a. IRR.
   b. NPV.
   c. Constant-growth valuation model.
   d. MIRR model.

10. The cost of retained earnings is equal to
    a. the cost of long-term debt.
    b. the cost of common stock equity.
    c. zero.
    d. the marginal cost of capital.

11. A firm has a beta of 0.90. The market return equals 12% and the risk-free rate of return equals 4%. The estimated cost of common stock equity is
    a. 11.2%.
    b. 9.8%.
    c. 10.4%.
    d. 12.6%.

12. One major expense associated with issuing new shares of common stock is
    a. legal fees.
    b. selling fees.
    c. registration fees.
    d. overpricing.

13. A firm has common stock with a market price of $45 per share and an expected dividend of $3 per share at the end of the coming year. The growth rate in dividends has been 4%. The cost of the firm's common stock equity is
    a. 9.75%.
    b. 10.67%.
    c. 8.42%.
    d. 11.25%.

14. Generally the least expensive form of long-term capital is
    a. short-term debt.
    b. retained earnings.
    c. long-term debt.
    d. common stock.

15. A firm has determined its cost of each source of capital and optimal capital structure, which is composed of the following sources:

Source of Capital	Proportion	After-Tax Cost
Long-term debt	45%	7%
Preferred stock	15%	10%
Common stock equity	40%	14%

The weighted average cost of capital is
    a. 0.25%.
    b. 11.45%.
    c. 9.75%.
    d. 8.35%.

16. A firm's before-tax cost of long-term debt 10.45%. What is the firm's after-tax cost of long-term debt if the firm has a 40% corporate tax rate?
    a. 8.48%
    b. 6.27%
    c. 5.32%
    d. 9.75%

17. For which source of funds does the firm not incur flotation costs?
    a. common stock
    b. preferred stock
    c. long-term debt
    d. retained earnings

18. A firm has discovered that its retained earnings of $400,000 will soon be exhausted. What is the point at which the firm will no longer be able to sustain the retained earnings cost of 6% if they have a historical weight of 40% in the firm's WACC?
    a. $750,000
    b. $160,000
    c. $1,000,000
    d. $100,000

19. When determining the after-tax cost of a bond, the face value of the bond must be adjusted to the net proceeds amounts by considering
    a. risk.
    b. flotation cost.
    c. taxes.
    d. returns.

20. When the face value of a bond equals its selling price, the firm's cost of the bond will be equal to
    a. the coupon interest rate.
    b. the firm's WACC.
    c. the risk-free rate.
    d. the firm's WMCC.

21. An individual's average cost of borrowing can be referred to as their:
    a. internal rate of return.
    b. payback period.
    c. personal cost of capital.
    d. risk-adjusted required rate of return.

22. In the process of buying a motorcycle, Joshua Brent is comparing the interest rate offered by the motorcycle shop with a second mortgage on his home. The motorcycle shop is offering 7.0%, while the interest rate on his second mortgage would be 8.0%. Given that Joshua is in the 25% tax bracket, which financing source should be used?
    a. the motorcycle shop, because the interest rate is 1.0% lower
    b. the motorcycle shop, which would result in a cost of 5.25% after-taxes
    c. the motorcycle shop, which would result in a cost of 8.75% after-taxes
    d. a second mortgage on his house, which would have a cost of 6.0% after-taxes

23. Philip Munson currently has two outstanding loans. One is an 8.2% loan with an outstanding balance of $15,000. The other is a 9.6% loan with an outstanding balance of $35,000. Philip's banker has allowed him to combine these loans into one with an interest rate of 9%. What should Philip do?
    a. Keep the current loans, which have a weighted average cost of 8.62%.
    b. Keep the current loans, which have a weighted average cost of 8.90%.
    c. Keep the current loans, which have a weighted average cost of 9.18%.
    d. Accept the bank's offer of money at 9.0%.

24. Which of the following statements about economic value added (EVA®) is false?
    a. EVA requires the use of the weighted average cost of capital.
    b. EVA is a dynamic approach to decision making.
    c. EVA is a popular measure that firms can use to determine whether an investment contributed to owner wealth.
    d. EVA can be used with both proposed and existing projects.

Essay

1. How can the weighted average marginal cost of capital be used with the investment opportunities schedule to make the firm's financing/investment decisions?

2. Explain why the cost of retained earnings is lower than the cost of external equity.

■ Chapter 11 Answer Sheet

True/False

1. T
2. F
3. F
4. T
5. T
6. F
7. F
8. T
9. F
10. T
11. T
12. T
13. T
14. F
15. T

Multiple Choice

1. D
2. C
3. D
4. A
5. C
6. B
7. A
8. D
9. C
10. B
11. A $0.04 + [0.90 \times (0.12 - 0.04)] = 11.20\%$
12. B
13. B
14. C
15. A
16. B $10.45 \times 0.60 = 6.27\%$
17. D
18. C
19. B
20. A
21. C
22. D
23. D
24. B

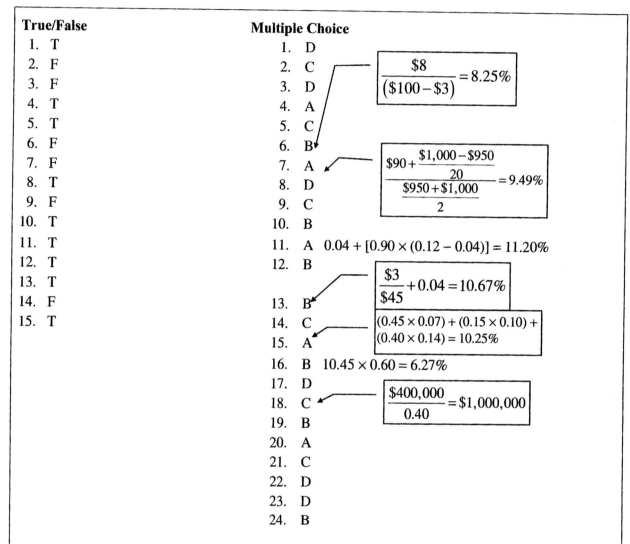

$$\frac{\$8}{(\$100 - \$3)} = 8.25\%$$

$$\frac{\$90 + \dfrac{\$1,000 - \$950}{20}}{\dfrac{\$950 + \$1,000}{2}} = 9.49\%$$

$$\frac{\$3}{\$45} + 0.04 = 10.67\%$$

$$(0.45 \times 0.07) + (0.15 \times 0.10) + (0.40 \times 0.14) = 10.25\%$$

$$\frac{\$400,000}{0.40} = \$1,000,000$$

Essay

1.   The investment opportunity schedule ranks available investments by return. This is used with the marginal cost of capital schedule to find the level of financing that maximizes owners' wealth. Firms accept those investments up to the point at which the marginal return on the investment equals the firm's weighted average cost of capital.

2.   External equity is more costly because the firm will incur flotation costs in selling stock in the market. These costs include selling fees and underpricing.

Chapter 12
Leverage and Capital Structure

■ Chapter Summary

The chapter discusses how a firm manager may decide between debt or equity financing. The term "capital structure" refers to how much long-term financing comes from debt and equity. Increasing debt increases fixed-cost financing or financial leverage. Increasing the amount of long-term assets or fixed costs increases operating leverage. No definitive methods are presented that will lead the manager to choose a particular capital structure because finance has simply not found any model that gives us a reliable answer. This chapter does discuss the issues that must be considered, however. It also provides some tools to use when deciding how to finance a particular project. A key to understanding this chapter is that fixed costs are stated in terms of dollars per period, while variable costs are in dollars per unit terms.

 Discuss leverage, capital structure, break-even analysis, the operating break-even point, and the effect of changing cost on it. Break-even analysis is useful for determining both the level of sales necessary to cover all operating costs and the profitability at different sales levels. Break-even analysis can also be used to look at the impact on profits from varying the different cost components.

 Understand operating, financial, and total leverage and the relationships among them. Operating leverage refers to leverage due to the use of fixed-cost assets. Financial leverage is the use of fixed-cost financing such as debt and preferred stock. Total leverage relates the level of earnings to the use of fixed operating costs and fixed financing costs. Total leverage is a combination of operating leverage and financial leverage. Financial leverage is multiplied by operating leverage to compute total leverage.

 Describe the basic types of capital, external assessment of capital structure, capital structure of non-U.S. firms, and capital structure theory. Capital structure refers to how the firm is financed through the combination of debt and equity. Ratios such as the debt ratio and the times-interest-earned ratio are used to assess the ability of the firm to manage fixed cost financing. Early capital structure theories focused on the tax deductibility of debt to conclude that firms should be 100% debt financed. More recent theories note that bankruptcy costs and agency costs mitigate the value of the tax deductibility of interest expense.

 Explain the optimal capital structure using a graphical view of the firm's cost of capital functions and a zero-growth valuation model. The optimal capital structure is that combination of debt and equity that maximizes the value of the firm. This will occur at the point where the tax benefit of the debt just equals the cost of potential bankruptcy and agency cost.

 Discuss the EBIT-EPS approach to capital structure. The higher the debt, the faster EPS rises when EBIT rises. At low EBIT, low leverage is preferred. At higher EBIT, more leverage is preferred. EBIT-EPS analysis locates the indifference point where EPS is the same regardless of financing. If EBIT is expected to be above this indifference point, debt financing should be used. If it is below this point, equity financing is preferred.

Review the return and risk of alternative capital structures, their linkage to market value and other important considerations related to capital structure. Keep focused on the idea that the optimal capital structure is one that optimizes firm value. The optimal capital structure will balance return and risk in a way that maximizes market value.

■ Chapter Outline

Leverage

Leverage results from the use of fixed-cost assets or fixed-cost funds to magnify returns to the firm's stockholders. With an increase in leverage, the risk and return to the firm usually increases. There are three basic types of leverage:

> *Operating leverage*—the relationship between the firm's sales revenue and its earnings before interest and taxes (EBIT).

> *Financial leverage*—the relationship between the firm's EBIT and its common stock earnings per share (EPS).

> *Total leverage*—the relationship between the firm's sales revenues and its EPS.

Break-even analysis

Before examining the different types of leverage, it is important to understand the effects of fixed costs on the firm's operations. Break-even analysis is used to determine the level of operations necessary to cover all operating costs and to evaluate the profitability associated with various levels of sales. To determine the operating break-even point (the level of sales necessary to cover all operating costs), the EBIT must be set equal to zero. In other words, what level of sales must be achieved to just cover all costs and therefore have an EBIT of 0?

The following formula is used to calculate EBIT:

$$EBIT = (P \times Q) - FC - (VC \times Q)$$

where:

P = sales price per unit

Q = sales quantity in units

FC = fixed operating costs per period

VC = variable operating costs per period

By setting the EBIT equal to zero, the break-even point in units can be determined. By rearranging and solving for Q, the following break-even equation is derived:

$$Q = \frac{FC}{P - VC}$$

The break-even point can be represented graphically as follows:

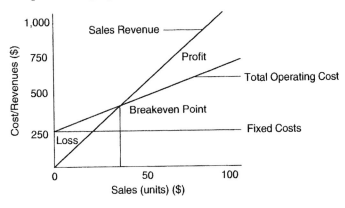

The point where total operating cost equals sales revenue is where EBIT equals zero. This point is the firm's operating break-even point. If fixed costs increased, total operating costs would also increase, and therefore the level of sales necessary to break even would increase.

Operating leverage

Operating leverage reflects the use of a firm's fixed operating costs to generate changes in the firm's EBIT through increased sales. Since fixed costs by their very nature do not fluctuate with sales, when sales increase, total operating costs would increase but only by the increase in variable costs. Therefore, firms that choose to use more fixed costs relative to variable costs can magnify their earnings. To measure the degree of operating leverage (DOL), the following equation should be used:

$$DOL = \frac{\% \text{ change in EBIT}}{\% \text{ change in sales}}$$

Financial leverage

Financial leverage reflects the use of fixed financial costs to magnify the effects of changes in EBIT on the firm's EPS. Fixed financial costs are those associated with the use of debt and preferred stock, since interest and preferred dividends are fixed and must be paid. The degree of financial leverage (DFL) can be measured by using the following formula:

$$DFL = \frac{\% \text{ change in EPS}}{\% \text{ change in EBIT}}$$

Total leverage

Total leverage reflects the use of a firm's fixed costs, both operating and financial, to magnify the effect of changes in sales on the firm's EPS. The degree of total leverage (DTL) can be measured by using the following formula:

$$DTL = \frac{\% \text{ change in EPS}}{\% \text{ change in sales}}$$

or

$$DTL = DOL \times DFL$$

High operating leverage and high financial leverage will cause total leverage to be high. The opposite is also true, but the relationship between operating leverage and financial leverage is multiplicative instead of additive.

Example

A firm has a DOL of 1.4 and a DFL of 4.5. What is the firm's DTL?

$$DTL = DOL \times DFL$$
$$DTL = 1.4 \times 4.5 = 6.3$$

The firm's capital structure

The term "capital" refers to the long-term funds of the firm. There are two types of capital: (1) debt, and (2) equity.

Debt capital includes all the long-term borrowing of the firm. Debt is cheaper than the other forms of financing due to three risk-reduction factors:

1. a higher priority claim against earnings or assets available for payment
2. stronger legal pressure against the company to make payment over preferred or common stockholders
3. the significantly lower debt costs to the firm due to the tax deductibility of interest payments.

Equity capital includes all long-term funds provided by the firm's owners, the stockholders. There are two forms of equity capital: (1) preferred stock, and (2) common stock equity, which includes common stock and retained earnings. The order of cost for equity, from most expensive to least expensive, is common stock, retained earnings, and preferred stock.

Often by examining a selection of financial ratios, a firm's financial leverage can be assessed. The debt ratio measures the degree of indebtedness of the firm. The higher this ratio, the higher the firm's financial leverage. The times-interest-earned-ratio measures the firm's ability to meet interest payments as they come due. In general, a poor times-interest-earned-ratio is associated with a high degree of financial leverage.

Capital structure theory

At this point in time there is not a specific methodology that can be used to determine a firm's optimal capital structure. However, there is theoretical and empirical research that suggests, by assuming perfect markets for securities (equity), that there is a theoretical optimal capital structure based on balancing the benefits and costs of debt financing. The cost of debt financing is based on the following factors:

Tax benefits—The interest paid on debt is tax deductible, thus reducing the firm's cost of debt.

Increased probability of bankruptcy—The probability that a firm will go bankrupt is based on both business risk and financial risk. Business risk varies from firm to firm and is not affected by capital structure decisions. The firm's capital structure directly affects its financial risk. The more fixed-cost financing—debt and preferred stock—a firm has in its capital structure, the greater its financial leverage and risk, and the greater chance of bankruptcy.

Agency cost—This is the cost of the lender's monitoring and controlling the firm's actions that are centered on the debt capital.

Asymmetric information—This situation arises when managers of a firm have more information about operations and future prospects than do investors.

The optimal capital structure is the point at which the weighted average cost of capital is minimized, thereby maximizing the firm's value. This can be represented by the following equation in which EBIT is held constant and the WACC, r_a, is minimized to provide the highest possible firm value, V.

$$V = \frac{\text{EBIT} \times (1-T)}{r_a}$$

The EBIT-EPS approach to capital structure

The EBIT-EPS approach to capital structure involves selecting the capital structure that maximizes earnings per share over the expected range of earnings before interest and taxes (EBIT). The EBIT-EPS approach can best be presented graphically and involves plotting the EPS for various expected EBITs of different capital structures.

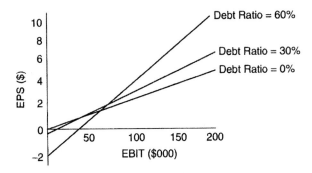

The graphical representation of the EBIT-EPS approach reveals that over certain ranges of expected EBIT, an optimal capital structure exists that maximizes EPS. The graph also reveals that the steeper the slope of the capital structure line, the greater the financial risk of that capital structure. The increased risk is caused by increased leverage.

The basic shortcoming of the EBIT-EPS approach to capital structure is that it concentrates on earnings rather than owners' wealth maximization. The EBIT-EPS approach generally ignores risk, which plays a major role in determining owners' wealth.

Choosing the optimal capital structure

An optimal capital structure is one that balances risk and return in a way that maximizes owners' wealth. To link these two factors, the risk associated with each capital structure should be included in the required rate of return for that structure. This can be done by estimating the beta for each alternative capital structure and using the CAPM to calculate the required return, r_s.

Another approach would involve linking the financial risk associated with each capital structure directly to the required return. An example of this would involve estimating the required return for different levels of risk as measured by the coefficient of variation of EPS. Once a capital structure has been set and an EPS has been determined, the per-share value of the firm can be found by using the zero-growth valuation model. We can use this model with the simplifying assumption that all earnings are paid out as dividends.

$$P_o = \frac{EPS}{r_s}$$

There is one important point to remember when evaluating various capital structures. The maximization of profit does not necessarily mean owners' wealth maximization. The financial manager should only implement capital structures that increase the wealth of the firm's shareholders.

■ Sample Problems and Solutions

Example 1. Degree of operating leverage

Given the data below, compute the degree of operating leverage.

	2009	2008
Sales (dollars)	$5,000	$10,000
Less variable operating cost	2,500	5,000
Less fixed operating cost	2,500	2,500
EBIT	$0	$2,500

Solution

The formula for the degree of operating leverage is:

$$DOL = \frac{\% \text{ change in EBIT}}{\% \text{ change in sales}}$$

so

$$\% \Delta EBIT = \frac{0 - 2,500}{2,500} = -100\%$$

$$\% \Delta SALES = \frac{5,000 - 10,000}{10,000} = -50\%$$

so

$$DOL = \frac{-100\%}{-50\%} = 2$$

Example 2.   Degree of financial leverage

Using the data in the following table, compute the degree of financial leverage.

	2009	2008
EBIT	$6,000	$10,000
Less interest	2,000	2,000
Earnings before tax	4,000	8,000
Less tax	1,600	3,200
Earnings after-tax	2,400	4,800
Less preferred dividend	2,400	2,400
Earnings for shareholders	0	2,400
Earnings per share (EPS)	$0	$2,40

Solution

The degree of financial leverage is found using the following equation:

$$DFL = \frac{\% \text{ change in EPS}}{\% \text{ change in EBIT}}$$

so

$$\% \Delta EPS = \frac{0 - 2.4}{2.4} = -100\%$$

$$\% \Delta EBIT = \frac{6,000 - 10,000}{10,000} = -40\%$$

and

$$DFL = \frac{-100\%}{-40\%} = 2.5$$

Example 3.   Degree of total leverage

Use the data presented in Examples 1 and 2 to compute the degree of total leverage (DTL).

Solution

The degree of total leverage is computed as the product of DOL and DFL.

$$DTL = DOL \times DFL$$

Using the values for DOL and DFL already computed,

$$DTL = 2 \times 2.5$$
$$DTL = 5$$

Example 4.   Break-even analysis

Debbie's Deli Delight is a New York-style delicatessen that specializes in massive roast beef sandwiches and spicy hot dogs. Her average sale is $5.00. She has fixed costs of $2,500 per month, which includes her rent, utilities, and payments on her equipment. Her variable costs are $1.75 per sandwich for the food and labor. She is open 6 days per week. Compute her break-even sales per month.

Solution

The formula for computing the break-even is:

$$Q = \frac{FC}{P - VC}$$

where Q is the quantity of goods needed to break-even, FC is the fixed costs, VC is the variable cost/unit, and P is the average selling price/unit.

$$Q = \frac{\$2,500}{\$5 - \$1.75}$$

$$Q = \frac{\$2,500}{\$3.25} = 769.23 \text{ sandwiches}$$

The break-even point in sales is found by multiplying the number of sandwiches that must be sold times the price per sandwich.

$$BE \text{ sales} = 769.23 \times \$5 = \$3,846.15$$

Example 5.   Break-even analysis

Mary's Meatballs by Mail Inc. distributes authentic Italian meatballs by mail order. Her only fixed costs are a telephone line and the printing and mailing of a catalog. These costs total $300 per month. Her average order is $5. The variable cost per sale is $2.50, which includes postage. What are Mary's break-even sales per month?

Solution

Using the same method as above, the quantity break-even point is:

$$Q = \$300/(\$5 - \$2.50) = 120 \text{ meatball orders.}$$

The break-even point in dollars is $5 \times 120 = \$600$.

Note that Mary's Meatballs has much lower fixed costs than Debbie's Deli; Mary's also enjoys lower risk because of a much lower break-even point. On the other hand, if sales were to skyrocket, Debbie's stands to earn more because her variable costs are lower.

■ Study Tips

1.   Recognize that there is no one solution to the capital structure question. Since different firms have different bankruptcy and agency costs, different levels of debt will serve to maximize firm value in different industries.

2.   One more time, the goal of optimizing capital structure is to maximize the value of the firm.

3. There are three ways to measure the leverage of your firm. The DOL measures your use of fixed-cost assets. Break-even analysis demonstrates how risk increases as the use of fixed assets increase. DFL increases as the use of debt increases. EBIT-EPS analysis can help choose between financing options that have different levels of debt. Finally, DTL is the product of DOL and DFL. Firms are believed to want to try to keep DTL from getting too high. So if one type of leverage is high, the firm will keep the other low. For example, if a firm must have many fixed assets to produce its product, it will try to keep its debt level low.

■ Student Notes

_____

_____

_____

_____

_____

■ Sample Exam—Chapter 12

True/False

T F 1. The firm's operating break-even point is the level of sales necessary to cover all of the firm's fixed costs.

T F 2. The amount of leverage in the firm's capital structure can significantly affect its value by affecting return and risk.

T F 3. An increase in the sales price per unit will generally reduce the firm's break-even point.

T F 4. Leverage results from the use of fixed-cost assets or funds to magnify returns to the firm's owners.

T F 5. Operating leverage is concerned with the relationship between the firm's sales revenue and its operating expenses.

T F 6. Financial leverage is concerned with the relationship between the firm's earnings after interest and taxes and its common stock earnings per share.

T F 7. In theory, there is an optimal capital structure.

T F 8. Total leverage is determined by adding the firm's operating leverage to its financial leverage.

T F 9. Whenever the percentage change in EBIT resulting from a given percentage change in sales is greater than the percentage change in sales, financial leverage exists.

T F 10. A shift toward less fixed cost decreases business risk, which in turn causes EBIT to increase by more for a given increase in sales.

T F 11. The probability that a firm will go bankrupt is largely dependent on its business risk and financial risk.

T F 12. Assuming that EBIT is held constant, the value of the firm is maximized when the WACC is maximized.

T F 13. The EBIT-EPS approach tends to concentrate on maximization of owners' wealth rather than earnings maximization.

T F 14. The steeper the slope of the line relating EBIT to EPS, the greater the financial risk.

T F 15. If expected EBIT is less than the EBIT-EPS indifferent point computed for two financing plans, the plan with greater debt should be chosen.

Multiple Choice

1. _____ analysis is a technique used to assess the returns associated with various cost structures and levels of sales.
    a. Risk
    b. Break-even
    c. Ratio
    d. Return

2. Fixed costs are a function of _____, not sales, and are typically contractual.
    a. EBIT
    b. variable cost
    c. time
    d. marginal cost

3. At the operating break-even point, _____ equals zero.
    a. fixed cost
    b. sales revenue
    c. variable cost
    d. EBIT

4. If a firm's fixed operating costs increase, the firm's operating break-even point will
    a. increase.
    b. not be affected.
    c. decrease.
    d. remain unchanged.

5. A firm has fixed operating costs of $4,500, the sale price per unit of its product is $12, and its variable cost per unit is $7. The firm's break-even point in units is
    a. 375.
    b. 6,000.
    c. 643.
    d. 900.

6. _____ results from the use of fixed-cost assets or funds to magnify returns to the firm's owners.
   a. Debt
   b. Equity
   c. Leverage
   d. Operating margin

7. Through the effects of financial leverage, when EBIT decreases, earnings per share will
   a. decrease.
   b. increase.
   c. remain unchanged.
   d. not be effected.

8. A decrease in fixed operating costs will result in _____ in the degree of operating leverage.
   a. a decrease
   b. no change
   c. an increase
   d. an undetermined change

9. The basic sources of capital for a firm include all of the following EXCEPT
   a. preferred stock.
   b. dividends.
   c. long-term debt.
   d. retained earnings.

10. _____ risk is the risk of being unable to cover operating costs.
   a. Total
   b. Leverage
   c. Financial
   d. Business

11. _____ leverage is concerned with the relationship between sales revenues and earnings before interest and taxes.
   a. Financial
   b. Total
   c. Operating
   d. Fixed

12. The inexpensive nature of long-term debt in a firm's capital structure is due to the fact that
   a. interest payments are tax deductible.
   b. it is riskier than other forms of capital.
   c. debt is based on the risk-free rate.
   d. equity capital has a fixed return.

13. The probability of bankruptcy is determined by
   a. total risk.
   b. market risk.
   c. financial risk.
   d. operating risk.

14. Fixed financing costs include
    a. interest expense.
    b. interest and depreciation expense.
    c. interest expense and preferred stock dividends.
    d. interest expense, preferred dividends, and common stock dividends.

15. The key differences between debt and equity capital include all of the following EXCEPT
    a. maturity.
    b. tax treatment.
    c. voice in management.
    d. effect on operating leverage.

16. _____ leverage is concerned with the relationship between earnings before interest and taxes and earnings per share.
    a. Total
    b. Financial
    c. Operating
    d. Fixed

17. A firm has fixed operating costs of $200,000, a sales price per unit of $75, and a variable cost per unit of $50. The firm's operating break-even point in dollars is
    a. $600,000.
    b. $750,000.
    c. $8,000.
    d. $45,000.

18. The firm's degree of total leverage is found by _____ the firm's degree of financial leverage _____ its operating leverage.
    a. adding; to
    b. subtracting; from
    c. dividing; by
    d. multiplying; by

19. The basic shortcoming of the EBIT-EPS approach to capital structure is
    a. that it is difficult to compute.
    b. its disregard for the firm's dividend payout ratio.
    c. that it concentrates on EPS maximization instead of owner's wealth maximization.
    d. its disregard for the firm's retained earnings.

20. In theory, the firm should maintain financial leverage consistent with a capital structure that
    a. maximizes EPS.
    b. maximizes owner's wealth.
    c. minimizes EPS.
    d. minimizes taxes.

21. Continuing with the example in Chapter 12 where Rick Polo analyzed the benefits of a fuel savings device. Let's assume that the demand for the fuel savings devices push their installment cost up to $300 and monthly fees to $17 per month. Given that the benefit of having these devices stays at $28, what is the breakeven point (in months)?

    a.   10.7 months

    b.   17.6 months

    c.   27.3 months

    d.   Trick question, Rick would never break even

22. Les Peila currently owns a vehicle used to transport his son's Little League team to games around the state. He currently has disposable income of $3,000, of which $500 goes to the bank in payment of the loan obtained to purchase the vehicle. When working overtime in the winter, to build up a savings account for payment of gasoline and food expenses when the team plays away from home, Les can increase his disposable income to $3,750. What is Les's degree of financial leverage?

    a.   1.20

    b.   1.25

    c.   1.30

    d.   6.00

23. The Rossins are applying for a mortgage loan. The family's monthly gross income is $5,750 and they currently have monthly installment loan obligations of $160. The $250,000 mortgage loan they are applying for will require monthly payments of $1900. The lender requires (1) the monthly mortgage payment to be less than 27% of monthly gross income and (2) total monthly installment payments (including the mortgage payment) to be less than 36% of monthly gross income. Will the Rossins get the home loan?

    a.   No, they fail to qualify based on both ratios.

    b.   No, because their monthly mortgage will be 33.0% of gross income.

    c.   No, because their monthly installment loan obligation will be 35.8% of gross income.

    d.   Yes, the Rossins qualify on the basis of both ratios.

Essay

1. What is the general relationship between the operating leverage, financial leverage, and total leverage of the firm?

2. What are some of the factors that influence the use of debt in the capital structure?

■ Chapter 12 Answer Sheet

True/False

1. F
2. T
3. T
4. T
5. F
6. F
7. T
8. F
9. F
10. F
11. T
12. F
13. F
14. T
15. F

Multiple Choice

1. B
2. C
3. D
4. A
5. D
6. C
7. A
8. A
9. B
10. D
11. C
12. A
13. A
14. C
15. D
16. B
17. A
18. D
19. C
20. B
21. C
22. A
23. A

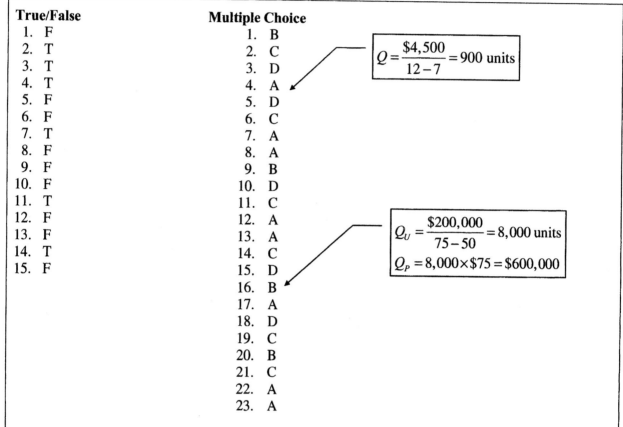

$$Q = \frac{\$4,500}{12-7} = 900 \text{ units}$$

$$Q_U = \frac{\$200,000}{75-50} = 8,000 \text{ units}$$

$$Q_P = 8,000 \times \$75 = \$600,000$$

Essay

1. Operating leverage deals with the use of fixed assets. Financial leverage deals with the use of fixed-cost funds. Total leverage is the product of the two. Another way of looking at DOL is that it represents the leverage from the top of the income statement to EBIT. DFL is the leverage from EBIT to the bottom of the income statement. DTL is the leverage from the top to the bottom of the income statement.

2. Using debt as a source of some portion of the firm's long-term funds is influenced by the tax deductibility of the interest expense. But the use of debt also increases the risk that the firm will be unable to pay its fixed financial costs. Also, lenders impose restrictions on the firm and the costs of monitoring these constraints are called agency costs. Asymmetric information may also influence the use of debt, according to research.

Chapter 13
Dividend Policy

■ Chapter Summary

This chapter describes dividends and dividend policies. Dividends are basically a source of cash for shareholders and provide them with information about the firm's current and future expectations. This chapter is mostly descriptive in nature. Carefully review the types of dividends and the related policies.

LG 1 *Understand cash dividend payment procedures, the tax treatment of dividends, and the role of dividend reinvestment plans.* Dividends are normally declared each quarter by the board of directors. Dividends are usually paid either in cash or by offering additional shares of stock. For most individuals, the dividend tax rate is the same as that on capital gains.

LG 2 *Describe the residual theory of dividends and the key arguments with regard to dividend irrelevance and relevance.* Residual theory states that dividends are the residual earnings left after undertaking all acceptable investment opportunities. There is substantial debate about whether dividend policies really affect the firm's value.

LG 3 *Discuss the key factors involved in establishing a dividend policy.* Legal, contractual, and internal constraints affect a firm's dividend policy by placing restrictions on the amount of cash that is available to be paid. Growth prospects, owner considerations, and market considerations also can affect dividend policy.

LG 4 *Review and evaluate the three basic types of dividend policy.* A constant-payout ratio requires that the firm pay out a fixed percentage of its earnings as dividends every year. This will result in fluctuating income to stockholders. A regular dividend policy fixes the amount of the dividend at a constant amount that is not changed from year to year unless earnings warrant a change. This provides a level payment to stockholders but may put a burden on the firm in lean years.

LG 5 *Evaluate stock dividends from accounting, shareholder, and company points of view.* The use of stock dividends merely shifts funds between equity accounts. The shareholders really receive nothing of value since the percentage ownership of the firm does not change. In reality, stock dividends are more costly for the firm, but they satisfy shareholders without spending cash.

LG 6 *Explain stock splits and stock repurchases as well as the firm's motivation for undertaking each of them.* Stock dividends do not cost the firm any cash yet tend to be popular with shareholders. Stock splits keep the price of the stock where management wants it. Stock repurchases may be the best investment available for a firm if its stock is underpriced.

■ Chapter Notes

Dividend Fundamentals

Because retained earnings—earnings that are not distributed as a form of dividends—are a form of internal financing, the dividend decision can affect the firm's external financing requirements.

Every person, whose name is recorded as a stockholder on the *date of record*, will at a specified future time receive a declared dividend. Because of the time needed to make bookkeeping entries, the stock will begin selling without the right to receive the current dividend four days prior to the date of record. During this time, the stock is said to be selling *ex dividend*.

The *payment date* is the actual date on which the firm will mail the dividend payment to the holder of record. The payment date is generally set a few weeks after the record date. For example:

Declaration date	Ex-date	Record date	Payment date
June 10	June 25	July 1	August 1

If the board of directors declares a dividend on June 10 with a record date of July 1 and a payment date of August 1, the ex-date will be June 25. This is 4 days plus a 2-day weekend before the record date. Purchasers of the stock on June 24 will receive the dividend. Investors who purchase the stock on June 25 or later will not receive the dividend.

Dividend reinvestment plans (DRPs) enable stockholders to use dividends received on the firm's stock to acquire additional shares, even fractional shares, at little or no transaction cost.

Relevance of Dividend Policy

Residual theory of dividends: This theory that states the dividend paid by a firm should be the amount left over after all acceptable investment opportunities have been undertaken. The residual theory implies that retained earnings should be used to finance all acceptable investments. If the amount of financing needed is in excess of retained earnings, new forms of financing should be used. If retained earnings are in excess of the firm's financing needs, the residual funds should be distributed to the owners of the firm in the form of dividends. This view of dividends tends to suggest that the required return of investors, k_s, is not influenced by the firm's dividend policy, a premise that suggests that dividend policy is irrelevant.

Dividend irrelevance theory: This theory put forth by Miller and Modigliani, states that in a perfect world the value of a firm is unaffected by the distribution of dividends and is determined solely by the earning power and risk of its assets. Miller and Modigliani argue that dividends act as a signal to investors about the future of a firm. An increase in dividends would be viewed as a positive signal that would cause investors to bid up the share price.

Dividend relevance theory: Gordon and Lintner theorize that stockholders prefer current dividends and that there is a direct relationship between the dividend policy of the firm and its market value.

Factors affecting dividend policy

Legal constraints: Most states prohibit corporations from paying out as cash dividends any portion of the firm's legal capital. Certain states measure legal capital by the par value of outstanding common stock, while others include any paid-in capital in excess of par.

Contractual constraints: Often a firm's ability to pay cash dividends is constrained by certain restrictive provisions in a loan agreement.

Internal constraints: A firm's ability to pay dividends is generally constrained by the amount of excess cash available to pay the dividends.

Growth prospects: Firms that are in a growth stage generally need all the funds that they can get to finance capital expenditures and usually pay little or no dividends.

Owner considerations: Firms must establish a policy that has a favorable effect on the wealth of the majority of the owners.

Market considerations: Firms must be aware of the market's expected response to types of dividend policies.

Types of dividend policies

A firm's dividend policy must be formulated with two objectives in mind: maximizing the wealth of the firm's owners and providing for sufficient financing. Three of the more commonly used dividend policies are the constant-payout ratio, regular, and low-regular-and-extra dividend policy.

- *Constant-payout ratio*: A firm's dividend payout ratio is calculated by dividing the firm's cash dividend per share by its earnings per share, which indicates the percentage of each dollar earned that is distributed to the owners in the form of cash. With a constant-payout ratio, the firm pays this percentage out of earnings to the owners in the form of a dividend each period.
- *Regular dividend policy*: Firms using a regular dividend policy pay out a fixed-dollar dividend in each period. The regular dividend does not fluctuate with earnings and dividends rarely decrease. A regular dividend policy removes owner uncertainty and reduces the risk of the stock.
- *Low-regular-and-extra dividend policy*: Some firms pay a low regular dividend and supplement this low dividend when earnings warrant it. The dividend that is paid in addition to the regular dividend is called an extra dividend. The use of an extra dividend is especially common in firms that experience cyclical shifts in earnings.

Other forms of dividends

Stock dividends: A stock dividend is the payment to existing owners of a dividend in the form of stock instead of cash. Therefore, the payment of a stock dividend is a shifting of funds between capital accounts rather than a use of funds. The shareholder receiving a stock dividend receives nothing of value. After the dividend is paid, the per-share value of the shareholder's stock will decrease in proportion to the dividend in such a way that the market value of their holdings in the firm will remain unchanged.

Stock splits: Stock splits are not a form of dividends, but they have the same effect on a firm's share price as that of a stock dividend. A stock split is used to lower the market price of a firm's stock by increasing the number of shares belonging to each shareholder. Most splits are in the form of a 2-for-1 split, in which 2 new shares are exchanged for each old share, or a 3-for-2 split, in which 3 new shares are exchanged for 2 old shares. A stock split has no effect on the firm's capital structure, but simply lowers the stock's market price to enhance trading activity. Theoretically, a stock split has no impact on investor wealth and is typically nontaxable.

Stock repurchases: Motives for stock repurchases include obtaining shares to be used in acquisitions, having shares available for employee stock option plans, or retiring shares. Recently, stock repurchases have been used to enhance shareholder value. The enhancement of shareholder value through a stock repurchase can be achieved by (1) reducing the number of shares outstanding and thereby raising earnings per share (EPS), (2) sending a positive signal to investors in the marketplace that management believes that the stock is undervalued, and (3) providing a temporary floor for the stock price, which may have been declining.

■ Sample Problems and Solutions

Example 1.   Dividend Policy

Starjump's Coffee has had the following earnings per share over the 2001–2009 period:

Year	Earnings per Share
2001	1.50
2002	1.00
2003	0.80
2004	1.20
2005	1.30
2006	1.60
2007	1.10
2008	0.90
2009	1.60

a.   If the firm's dividend policy is based on a constant payout ratio of 50% for all years with positive earnings, determine the annual dividend paid in each year.

b.   If the firm has a regular dividend policy of paying $0.60 per share per year, regardless of the per-share earnings, until the per-share earnings remain above $1.20 for 2 periods, at which time the dividend would be increased to $0.80 per share, determine the annual dividend paid in each year.

c.   If the firm's policy is to pay out $0.20 per share each period, except in those periods when earnings are above $1.00, when they pay out an extra dividend equal to 30% of the earnings above $1.00, determine the amount of regular and extra dividends paid each year.

Solution

a. If the firm paid out 50% of each year's earnings in years with positive earnings, the dividends paid per share (DPS) would be as follows:

Year	2001	2002	2003	2004	2005	2006	2007	2008	2009
DPS	$0.75	$0.50	$0.40	$0.60	$0.65	$0.80	$0.55	$0.45	$0.80

b. If the firm paid out a fixed $0.60 per share until earnings were above $1.20 for 2 years, at which time they raised the dividend to $0.80 per share, the dividend paid would be as follows:

Year	2001	2002	2003	2004	2005	2006	2007	2008	2009
DPS	$0.60	$0.60	$0.60	$0.60	$0.60	$0.80	$0.80	$0.80	$0.80

c. If the firm pays a regular dividend plus an extra dividend the payout would be as follows:

Year	2001	2002	2003	2004	2005	2006	2007	2008	2009
RDPS	$0.20	$0.20	$0.20	$0.20	$0.20	$0.20	$0.20	$0.20	$0.20
EDPS	$0.15	$0.00	$0.00	$0.06	$0.09	$0.18	$0.03	$0.00	$0.18
TDPS	$0.35	$0.20	$0.20	$0.26	$0.29	$0.38	$0.23	$0.20	$0.38

Note (RDPS = regular dividend per share, EDPS = extra DPS, and TDPS = total DPS)

■ Study Tips

1. This is another low-math, high-memorization chapter. On separate paper, see if you can list the different types of dividend policies, the dividend theories, and the factors that affect dividend policy.

2. Study the advantages and disadvantages of the different dividend policies carefully. This material makes good essay questions on exams.

■ Student Notes

_____

_____

_____

_____

_____

■ Sample Exam—Chapter 13

True/False

T   F   1.   Dividend reinvestment plans (DRPs) are used by firms to allow existing shareholders to purchase additional shares of stock with their dividends.

T   F   2.   A stock split commonly increases the number of shares outstanding and the stock's per share par value.

T   F   3.   The date of record for dividends is the actual date on which the company will mail the dividend payment to the holders of record.

T   F   4.   The ex dividend date period begins four business days prior to the record date.

T   F   5.   The dividend decision can significantly affect the firm's share price and external financing requirements.

T   F   6.   The residual theory of dividends is based on the argument that the required return of investors is not influenced by the firm's dividend policy and, thus, dividend policy is irrelevant.

T   F   7.   The payment of a stock dividend is a use of funds rather than a shifting of funds between capital accounts.

T   F   8.   Paying a fixed or increasing dividend increases owners' wealth since it eliminates uncertainty about the frequency and magnitude of dividends.

T   F   9.   Firms have no restrictions on the amount that can be paid to shareholders as dividends.

T   F   10. The constant-payout ratio is the preferred method for calculating dividends.

Multiple Choice

1.   A dividend reinvestment plan
     a.   invests dividends in the money markets.
     b.   reinvests the dividends in the firm's debt.
     c.   reinvests in retained earnings.
     d.   reinvests in the firm's stock.

2.   A firm has after-tax earnings of $2,000,000 and has declared a cash dividend of $600,000. The firm's dividend payout ratio is
     a.   70%.
     b.   12%.
     c.   30%.
     d.   0.70%.

3.   The payment of cash dividends to corporate stockholders is decided by the
     a.   board of directors.
     b.   stockholders.
     c.   top management.
     d.   SEC.

4. The residual theory of dividends suggests that dividends are _____ to the value of the firm.
   a. relevant
   b. positively correlated
   c. residual
   d. irrelevant

5. Dividend policy is a form of
   a. financing policy.
   b. working capital policy.
   c. capital budgeting policy.
   d. dividend reinvestment policy.

6. Modigliani and Miller argue that when the firm has no acceptable investment opportunities, it should
   a. raise its cost of capital.
   b. keep the unneeded funds.
   c. distribute the unneeded funds to the owners.
   d. lower its cost of capital.

7. The most commonly used dividend policies are all of the following EXCEPT
   a. low-regular-and-extra.
   b. high-low.
   c. regular.
   d. constant-payout-ratio.

8. The purpose of a stock split is to
   a. lower the market price of the stock.
   b. change the firm's capital structure.
   c. raise the market price of the stock.
   d. increase dividends.

9. When common stock is repurchased and retired, the underlying motive is to
   a. reduce the stock's dividends.
   b. raise the market price of the stock.
   c. delay taxes.
   d. distribute the excess cash to the owners.

10. _____ policy is when the firm pays out a fixed dollar dividend each period.
    a. Regular dividend
    b. Constant-payout-ratio dividend
    c. Extra dividend
    d. Steady dividend

11. A _____ lowers the market price of a firm's stock by increasing the number of shares outstanding.
     a.   stock dividend
     b.   stock split
     c.   stock repurchase
     d.   dividend reinvestment policy

12. Which of the following is not a reason for a firm to repurchase stock?
     a.   enhance shareholder value
     b.   discourage a takeover
     c.   retire shares
     d.   decrease market value of the shares

13. The Board of Directors of VICEM Industries on Monday, February 4 declared a dividend payable to all holders on record on Monday, February 11, with payment on Tuesday, February 19. In order to receive a dividend from VICEM, investors would have to own the shares as of the close of trading on:
     a.   Monday, February 4.
     b.   Wednesday, February 6.
     c.   Monday, February 11.
     d.   Tuesday, February 19.

14. Tyler Weinrich, a single investor in the 15% federal tax bracket owns 150 shares of Newmont Exploration. The stock has risen from its purchase price of $40 to $75 dollars per share. Because the Board of Directors believes the Newmont Exploration will be more actively traded in the $40 to $60 range, it has just announced a 3-for-2 stock split. Assuming no other information came out about Newmont Exploration, how many shares would Tyler have and what would be their price after the stock split?
     a.   100 shares, at $40 per share
     b.   100 shares, at $50 per share
     c.   225 shares, at $50 per share
     d.   225 shares, at $60 per share

15. As a result of the Tax Increase Prevention and Reconciliation Act of 2005, the maximum tax rate on dividends was:
     a.   5%, or 10% below the maximum tax rate on capital gains.
     b.   5%, which is equal to the maximum tax rate on capital gains.
     c.   15%, which is 10% above the maximum tax rate on capital gains.
     d.   15%, which is equal to the maximum tax rate on capital gains.

Essay

1.   What are dividend reinvestment plans and how do they work?

2.   Explain why the residual theory of dividends leads Miller and Modigliani to theorize the irrelevance of dividends.

■ Chapter 13 Answer Sheet

True/False		Multiple Choice	
1.	T	1.	D
2.	F	2.	C
3.	F	3.	A
4.	T	4.	D
5.	T	5.	A
6.	T	6.	C
7.	F	7.	B
8.	T	8.	A
9.	F	9.	D
10.	F	10.	A
		11.	B
		12.	D
		13.	B
		14.	C
		15.	D

$$\frac{\$600,000}{\$2,000,000} = 30\%$$

Essay

1. Dividend reinvestment plans allow shareholders to use the dividends they received to purchase additional shares or fractional shares of stock at little or no transaction cost. A third-party trustee can purchase the outstanding shares on the open market and then sell them to the shareholders. Another method allows the shareholders to purchase newly issued shares from the firm, usually for slightly less than the going market price.

2. According to the residual theory of dividends, dividends will be paid only when the need for additional funds is less than the earnings of the firm. The argument supporting this approach is that only sound management will ensure that the company has the money to compete effectively and this will increase share price. This tends to suggest that the required return of investors, k_s, is not influenced by the firm's dividend policy. Miller and Modigliani's argument is consistent with this and they theorize that the value of the firm is determined solely by the earning power and risk of its assets and that dividend policy has no effect on the value of the firm.

Chapter 14
Working Capital and Current Assets Management

■ Chapter Summary

In the last two chapters we studied leverage and capital structure and dividend policy. These topics related to long-term capital. This chapter moves our discussion to the management of the firm's working capital or current assets. There is a trade-off between the risk of having too little working capital on hand and the reduced profitability that results from having excess working capital.

In addition to discussing the issues related to determining the optimal level of working capital, this chapter also investigates the management of inventory and accounts receivable.

 Understand short-term financial management, net working capital and the related tradeoff between profitability and risks. Net working capital is defined as the difference between the firm's current assets and its current liabilities, or as the portion of current assets financed with long-term funds. Firm's with inadequate working capital run the risk of not being able to meet their current obligations. On the other hand, excess working capital will reduce profits.

 Describe the cash conversion cycle, its funding requirements, and the key strategies for managing it. Cash and near-cash balances are held to satisfy the transaction motive, which is to make planned payments, to satisfy the safety motive, and to maintain the ability to quickly take advantage of unexpected opportunities.

 Discuss inventory management: differing views, common techniques, and international concerns. The three types of inventory are the raw materials, work-in-process, and finished goods inventory. Different company officials will view the inventory in different ways. For example, the marketing manager will prefer a larger inventory than will the financial manager. We discuss three inventory management methods: the ABC system, the basic economic order quantity model, the reorder point, the materials requirement planning system, and the just-in-time system. The models listed above provide techniques to managing inventory levels. The ABC system puts focus on those inventories that are most costly. The EOQ model can be used to determine the optimal order quantity. The JIT system is used to minimize inventory cost.

 Explain the credit selection process and the quantitative procedure for evaluating changes in credit standards. A firm's credit terms specify the repayment terms required of all its credit customers. The basic components include the cash discount, the cash discount period, and the credit period. The firm's collection policy is the set of procedures for collecting accounts receivable when they are due. The level of bad debt expense will be a function of both the credit standards and the collection policy. Aging of accounts receivable is a technique that indicates the proportion of the accounts receivable balance that has been outstanding for a specified period of time.

Review the procedures for quantitatively considering cash discounts, other aspects of credit terms, and credit monitoring. Some firms that routinely give up supplier discounts may find that taking these discounts could be a major source of additional income. Other firms may not be able to take the discounts because they lack alternative sources of funds.

Understand the management of receipts and disbursements, including float, speeding collections, slowing payments, cash concentration, zero-balance accounts, and investing in marketable securities. Collections are frequently speeded up by using lockboxes, where payments are mailed directly to the bank, direct sends, where large checks are presented directly to the paying bank, and other techniques. Marketable securities are highly liquid substitutes for holding cash. These securities can be quickly converted into cash but have the advantage of earning interest. Among the more popular marketable securities are government issues. These are easily converted to cash but earn low interest because they are very low risk.

■ Chapter Outline

Net working capital fundamentals

The goal of short-term financial management is to manage each of the firm's current assets and current liabilities to achieve a balance between profitability and risk that maximizes the value of the owners' investment in the firm.

Current assets—Commonly called working capital, current assets represent the portion of investment that is transformed from cash to inventories to receivables and back to cash in the recurring operating cycle of the firm. Current assets are expected to be turned into cash within a year.

Current liabilities—Current liabilities represent the firm's short-term financing. They include all debts of the firm that come due in one year or less.

Net working capital—Net working capital is the difference between the firm's current assets and its current liabilities.

The tradeoff between profit and risk

Profitability is the relationship between revenues and costs generated by using the firm's assets, both current and fixed, in productive activities.

Risk is the probability that a firm will be unable to pay its bills as they come due. A firm that cannot pay its bills as they come due is said to be technically insolvent.

The effects of changes in the current assets and current liabilities on profits and risk can be demonstrated in the following chart.

Ratio	Change in Ratio	Effect on Profit	Effect on Risk
Current assets / Total assets	Increase	Decrease	Decrease
	Decrease	Increase	Increase
Current liabilities / Total assets	Increase	Increase	Increase
	Decrease	Decrease	Decrease

The *operating cycle* of a firm is the amount of time that elapses from the point when the firm inputs material and labor into the production process to the point when cash is collected from the sale of the finished product that contains these production inputs. The operating cycle is made up of two components: (1) the average age of inventory (AAI) and (2) the average collection period of sales (ACP).

$$OC = AAI + ACP$$

The *cash conversion cycle* represents the amount of time the firm's cash is tied up between payment for production inputs and receipt of payment from the sale of the resulting finished product and can be determined by the following equation:

$$CCC = OC - APP = AAI + ACP - APP$$

where:

  CCC = cash conversion cycle

  OC = operating cycle

  APP = average payment period (the time it takes a firm to pay for production inputs such as raw materials and labor)

Ideally, a firm would like to have a negative cash conversion cycle, but more realistically firms often have a positive cash conversion cycle which means that the firm must use nonspontaneous forms of financing to support the cash conversion cycle. When a positive cash conversion cycle is present, there are three basic strategies that a firm can employ to manage the cycle:

1. Increase inventory turnover,
2. Accelerate the collection of accounts receivable, or
3. Stretch accounts payable, as was discussed in the last chapter.

Permanent versus seasonal funding needs

The firm's financing requirements can be separated into permanent and seasonal needs. Permanent needs are the financing requirements for the firm's fixed assets plus the permanent portion of the firm's current assets. These requirements remain unchanged over the year.

The seasonal need consists of the financing requirements for the temporary current assets, which vary from time to time over the year.

Aggressive financing strategy: This strategy results in the firms' financing all of its seasonal needs and possibly some of its permanent needs with short-term funds. Financing with short-term funds is less expensive than using long-term funds. However, an increase in risk associated with the aggressive strategy results from the fact that the firm has only a limited amount of short-term borrowing capacity. If it draws too heavily on this capacity, unexpected needs for funds may become difficult to satisfy.

Conservative financing strategy: This strategy has the firm financing all projected fund requirements with long-term funds and using short-term financing only for emergencies or unexpected outflows.

Inventory management

The three basic types of inventory are raw materials, work-in-process, and finished goods.

Raw materials—Items purchased by the firm for use in the manufacture of a finished product

Work-in-process—Inventory that consists of all items that are currently in production

Finished goods inventory—Items that have been produced but not yet sold

Inventory should be viewed as an investment since it requires that the firm tie up its money and forgo certain other earnings opportunities. In general, the higher a firm's average inventories, the larger the dollar investment and cost required; the lower its average inventories, the smaller the dollar investment and cost required.

Techniques for managing inventory

Techniques that are commonly used in managing inventory are (1) The ABC system, (2) the basic economic order quantity (*EOQ*) model, (3) the reorder point, (4) the materials requirement planning (MRP) system, and (5) the just-in-time (JIT) system.

The ABC system: The ABC system divides inventory into three groups. The A group includes the items that require the largest dollar investment. The B group consists of the items accounting for the next largest investment. The C group typically consists of a large number of items accounting for a relatively small dollar investment. Control of the A items should be most intensive and control of the C group should be the least intensive.

EOQ model: This inventory management technique determines an item's optimal order quantity, which is the one that minimizes the total of its order and carrying costs.

$$EOQ = \sqrt{\frac{2 \times S \times O}{C}}$$

Where:

S = usage in units per period

O = order cost per order

C = carrying cost per unit per period

The reorder point: Once the firm has determined its economic order quantity, it must determine when to place orders. Assuming a constant usage rate for inventory, the reorder point can be determined by the following equation:

Reorder point = lead time in days × daily usage

Because of the difficulty in precisely predicting lead times and daily usage rates, many firms typically maintain safety stocks, which are extra inventories that can be drawn down when actual outcomes are greater than expected. Note that in the absence of a reorder point, carrying costs will equal ordering costs for firms managing inventory using the *EOQ* model.

MRP system: This inventory management system uses *EOQ* concepts and a computer to compare production needs to available inventory balances and determine when orders should be placed for various items on a product's bill of materials.

JIT system: Inventory management system minimizes inventory investment by having material inputs arrive at exactly the time they are needed for production.

Accounts Receivable Management

A firm's credit selection activity focuses on determining whether to extend credit to a customer and how much credit to extend. To begin the credit selection process, appropriate sources of credit information and methods of credit analysis must be developed. The five C's of credit are the traditional focus of credit investigation.

Five C's of Credit:

1. *Character*: The applicant's record of meeting past obligations
2. *Capacity*: The applicant's ability to repay the requested credit
3. *Capital*: The applicant's debt relative to equity
4. *Collateral*: The amount of assets the applicant has available for use in securing the credit
5. *Conditions*: The current economic and business climate, as well as any unique circumstances affecting either party to the credit transaction

Obtaining credit information

The major external sources of credit information are as follows:

Financial statements: The firm can analyze the applicant firm's liquidity, activity, debt, and profitability through the firm's past financial statements.

Dun & Bradstreet (D&B): The largest mercantile credit-reporting agency in the United States is D&B. D&B subscribers are provided with credit ratings and key estimates of overall financial strength for millions of U.S. and international firms.

Credit interchange bureaus: The National Credit Interchange System is a national network of local credit bureaus that exchange information.

Direct credit information exchanges: Often firms can obtain credit information through local, regional, or national credit associations.

Bank checking: Occasionally it will be possible to obtain credit information from the applicant's bank.

Credit scoring

Credit scoring is a procedure resulting in a score reflecting an applicant's overall credit strength, derived as a weighted average of scores on key financial and credit characteristics.

Example

Credit Scoring of Wildwood Inc.			
Financial and Credit Characteristics	**Score (0 to 100)**	**Predetermined Weight**	**Weighted Score**
Credit references	75	0.20	15.00
Home ownership	100	0.10	10.00
Income range	85	0.25	21.25
Payment history	80	0.25	20.00
Years at address	85	0.15	12.75
Years on job	90	0.15	13.50
		Total 1.0	Credit score 92.50

Credit Score	**Action**
Greater than 80	Extend credit terms
60 to 79	Extend limited credit
Less than 59	Reject application

Managing international credit: Credit management is usually more difficult for firms that operate internationally because international operations typically expose a firm to exchange rate risk and because there are dangers and delays involved with shipping goods long distances.

Changing credit standards

The firm's credit standards are the minimum requirements for extending credit to a customer. When evaluating proposed changes in credit standards, the three major variables that should be considered are (1) sales volume, (2) the investment in accounts receivable, and (3) bad debt expenses.

The basic changes and effects on profits expected to result from the relaxation of credit standards are tabulated as follows:

Variable	Direction of Change	Effect on Profits
Sales volume	Increase	Positive
Investment in accounts receivable	Increase	Negative
Bad debt expenses	Increase	Negative

Determining the value of key variables

Profit contribution from additional sales: Fixed costs are not affected by a change in the sales level of the firm, so the additional contribution from increased sales will simply be the sales price per unit minus the variable cost per unit. The additional profit contribution per unit is multiplied by the increase in sales to determine the effect on net profits. For example, Zach's Inc. is expecting a 5%, or 2,000 units, increase in sales as a result of a relaxation of its credit terms. Zach's product has a selling price of $20 and a variable cost per unit of $12. The total additional profit contribution from the increase in sales will be $16,000 [($20 – $12) × 2,000 units].

Cost of the marginal investment in accounts receivable: The cost of the marginal investment in accounts receivable can be calculated by finding the difference between the cost of carrying receivables before and after the introduction of the relaxed credit standards. When changing the credit standards, only out-of-pocket costs are examined. Fixed costs are ignored because they are sunk and are not affected by this decision. The average investment in accounts receivable can be calculated by the following formula:

$$\text{Average investment in accounts receivable} = \frac{\text{total cost of annual sales}}{\text{turnover of accounts receivable}}$$

where:

$$\text{Turnover of accounts receivable} = \frac{360}{\text{average collection period}}$$

Cost of marginal bad debts: The cost of marginal bad debts is found by taking the difference between the level of bad debts before and after the relaxation of credit standards.

Once the values of three variables have been determined, the additional profit contribution from sales must be compared to the sum of the cost of the marginal investment in accounts receivable and the cost of marginal bad debts. If the additional profit contribution is greater than marginal cost, the credit standards should be relaxed.

Credit terms: The supplier's credit terms state the credit period and the date the credit period ends. The supplier's credit terms are often stated on the supplier's invoice in such shorthand expressions as "3/10 net 30." The credit term would read as "3% discount if paid within 10 days; full payment must be made within 30 days from the beginning of the credit period."

Changing credit terms

A firm's credit terms specify the repayment requirements that it places on all of its credit customers. Often a type of shorthand is used. For example, credit terms may be stated as 3/10 net 30, which reads as, "3% discount if paid in cash within 10 days after the beginning of the credit period, otherwise full payment must be received within 30 days after the beginning of the credit period." Credit terms cover three things: (1) the cash discount (in this example 3%), (2) the cash discount period (10 days), and (3) the credit period (30 days).

Cash discount: When a firm increases the cash discount provided in its credit terms, the following results can be expected.

Variable	Direction of Change	Effect on Profits
Sales volume	Increase	Positive
Investments in accounts receivable due to nondiscount takers paying early	Decrease	Positive
Investment in accounts receivable due to new customers	Increase	Negative
Bad debt expense	Decrease	Positive
Profit per unit	Decrease	Negative

Cash discount period: When a firm increases the cash discount period provided in its credit terms, the following results can be expected.

Variable	Direction of Change	Effect on Profits
Sales volume	Increase	Positive
Investments in accounts receivable due to nondiscount takers paying early	Decrease	Positive
Investment in accounts receivable due to discount takers still getting cash discount but paying later	Increase	Negative
Investment in accounts receivable due to new customers	Increase	Negative
Bad debt expense	Decrease	Positive
Profit per unit	Decrease	Negative

Credit period: When a firm increases the length of the credit period provided in its credit terms, the following results can be expected.

Variable	Direction of Change	Effect on Profits
Sales volume	Increase	Positive
Investment in accounts receivable	Increase	Negative
Bad debt expenses	Increase	Negative

Collection policy

The firm's collection policy includes the procedures used to collect accounts receivable once they are due. The effectiveness of this policy can be partly evaluated by looking at the level of bad debt expenses.

A number of collection techniques are used by the firm. The basic techniques are listed in the order typically followed in the collection process: letters, telephone calls, personal visits, collection agencies, and legal action.

Cash management techniques

 Financial managers have a variety of cash techniques that can provide additional savings to the firm. These techniques provide savings by taking advantage of certain imperfections in the collection and payment systems.

Float

Float refers to funds that have been dispatched by a payer but are not yet in a form that can be spent by the payee. Float has three basic components:

1. *Mail float*—The delay between the time when a payer places payment in the mail and the time when it is received by the payee

2. *Processing float*—The delay between the receipt of a check by the payee and the deposit of it in the firm's account

3. *Clearing float*—The delay between the deposit of a check by the payee and the actual availability of the funds

Speeding up collections

A variety of techniques are available for speeding up the collection process and thereby reducing the collection float.

Concentration banking: Concentration banking is a collection procedure in which payments are made to regionally dispersed collection centers, and then deposited in local banks for quick clearing, thus reducing collection float by shortening mail and clearing float.

Lockboxes: The lockbox system is a collection procedure in which payers send their payments to a nearby post office box that is emptied by the firm's bank several times daily. The bank deposits the payment checks in the firm's account and reduces collection float by shortening processing float as well as mail and clearing float.

Direct sends: Direct send is a collection procedure in which the payee presents payment checks directly to the banks on which they are drawn, thus reducing clearing float.

Slowing down disbursements

Controlled disbursing: Controlled disbursing is the strategic use of mailing points and bank accounts to lengthen mail float and clearing float, respectively.

Playing the float: Playing the float is a method of consciously anticipating the resulting float associated with the payment process and using it to keep funds in an interest-earning form for as long as possible.

Firms that aggressively manage cash disbursements will often require some type of safety device that is utilized in the event of a shortage of funds.

In an *overdraft system*, if the firm's checking account balance is insufficient to cover all checks presented against the account, the bank will automatically lend the firm enough money to cover the amount of the overdraft.

A *zero-balance account* is a checking account in which a zero balance is maintained and the firm is required to deposit funds to cover checks drawn on the account only as they are presented for payment.

Investing in marketable securities

Marketable securities are short-term, interest earning, money market instruments that can easily be converted into cash. To be truly marketable, a security must have two basic characteristics:

1. *Ready market*: The market for a security should have both breadth and depth to minimize the amount of time required to convert it to cash. The breadth of a market is determined by the number of buyers, and the depth of the market is determined by its ability to absorb the purchase or sale of a large dollar amount of a particular security.

2. *Safety of principal*: There should be little or no loss in the value of a marketable security over time.

Government issues

Government issues have relatively low yields due to their low risk and the fact that the interest income on all Treasury issues and most federal agency issues is exempt from state and local taxes.

Treasury bills—U.S. Treasury obligations issued weekly on an auction basis, having varying maturities, generally under a year, and virtually no risk. The smallest denomination treasury bill is $10,000.

Treasury notes—U.S. Treasury obligations with initial maturities of between one and ten years, paying interest at a stated rate semiannually, and having virtually no risk. Treasury notes have denominations of either $1,000 or $5,000.

Federal agency issues—Low-risk securities issued by government agencies but not guaranteed by the U.S. Treasury, having generally short maturities, and offering slightly higher yields than comparable U.S. Treasury issues. These securities have denominations of $1,000 or more.

Non-government issues

Non-government issues of marketable securities typically have slightly higher yields than government issues with similar maturities due to the slightly higher risks associated with them and the fact that their interest income is taxable on all levels.

Negotiable certificates of deposit (CDs)—Negotiable instruments representing specific cash deposits in commercial banks, having varying maturities and yields based on size, maturity, and prevailing money market conditions.

Commercial paper—A short-term, unsecured promissory note issued by a corporation that has a very high credit standing. These securities are generally issued in multiples of $100,000.

Banker's acceptance—Short-term, low-risk marketable securities arising from bank guarantees of business transactions that are sold by banks at a discount from their maturity value.

Eurodollar deposits—Deposits of currency not native to the country in which the bank is located. The deposits are negotiable, usually pay interest at maturity, and are typically denominated in units of $1 million.

Money market mutual funds—Professionally managed portfolios of various popular marketable securities, having instant liquidity, competitive yields, and low transaction costs.

Repurchase agreement—An agreement whereby a bank or securities dealer sells a firm specific securities and agrees to repurchase them at a specific price and time.

■ Sample Problems and Solutions

Example 1.   Permanent versus seasonal funds requirements

Whirlybird Parachute Stuffers, Inc. has the following distribution of current and fixed assets. Divide the firm's monthly total funds requirement into a permanent and a seasonal component. What are the monthly average permanent and seasonal funds requirements?

Month	Current Assets	Fixed Assets	Total Assets
January	$2100	$6000	$8100
February	2300	6000	8300
March	2400	6000	8400
April	2400	6000	8400
May	2600	6000	8600
June	5000	6000	11000
July	6000	6000	12000
August	6000	6000	12000
September	3000	6000	9000
October	2500	6000	8500
November	2000	6000	8000
December	1500	6000	7500

Put your answer below:

Month	Total Funds Requirement	Permanent Requirement	Seasonal Requirement
January			
February			
March			
April			
May			
June			
July			
August			
September			
October			
November			
December			

Solution

To solve this problem you must determine the minimum long-term funds needed so that the firm does not have to rely on short-term funds for at least one month. The permanent requirement is the base level of total assets that remain on the books throughout the year. Total assets are always $7,500 or more. Therefore, the permanent requirement is $7,500. The seasonal is the difference between the total funds and the permanent funds. The monthly funds requirements are shown below.

Month	Total Funds Requirement	Permanent Requirement	Seasonal Requirement
January	$8100	$7500	$600
February	8300	7500	800
March	8400	7500	900
April	8400	7500	900
May	8600	7500	1100
June	11000	7500	3500
July	12000	7500	4500
August	12000	7500	4500
September	9000	7500	1500
October	8500	7500	1000
November	8000	7500	500
December	7500	7500	0

From this table we see that the permanent monthly average is $7500. The monthly seasonal average is $1,650. This is found by summing up the seasonal requirement and dividing by 12 ($19,800/12). Many bank loans require that short-term loans and lines of credit be completely retired for at least one month of the year. This is to assure that the short-term funds have not become part of the long-term financing of the firm.

Example 2. Aggressive versus conservative financing strategy

Whirlybird Parachute Stuffers, Inc. (see Example 1) is debating whether to follow a conservative or an aggressive financing strategy. Use the answer to Example 1 to recommend a strategy, assuming that short-term funds cost 10% and long-term funds cost 14%.

Solution

Aggressive: Remember that the aggressive strategy finances the permanent with long-term funds and the seasonal with short-term funds. The cost of financing under an aggressive strategy is found by multiplying the short-term interest rate times the average seasonal borrowing and adding the cost of long-term borrowing.

$$(10\% \times \$1,650) + (14\% \times \$7,500) = \$1,215$$

Conservative: Remember the conservative strategy uses long-term funds for all financing requirements. The maximum amount required is borrowed, and in months when the entire amount is not needed, it is invested on a short-term basis. The cost of a conservative strategy is found by multiplying the long-run rate by the maximum funds needed.

$$(0.14 \times \$12,000) = \$1,680.$$

Example 3.   Payment dates

If Whirlybird Parachute Stuffers, Inc. sends a bill to Harvey Field Charters dated June 25, determine, under each of the following credit terms, when the payment must be made.

a.   net 30

b.   net 30 EOM

c.   net 45 date of invoice

Solution

a.   July 25

b.   July 30

c.   August 9

Example 4.   Cash Conversion Cycle

Cascade Bilge Pumps has an average inventory age of 80 days, an average collection period of 70 days, and an average payment period of 60 days. Compute the firm's cash cycle and cash turnover, (frequency of its cash cycle), assuming a 360-day year.

Solution

a.   The cash cycle can be found by adding the average age of inventory to the average collection period and subtracting the average payment period.

$$\text{Cash cycle} = 80 \text{ days} + 70 \text{ days} - 60 \text{ days} = 90 \text{ days}$$

b.   Cash turnover is found by dividing the cash cycle into the number of days in the year.

$$\text{Cash turnover} = 360 \text{ days} \div 90 \text{ days} = 4 \text{ times}$$

Example 5.   Direct sends

Tumbleweed Development has just received four checks from the sale of properties to investors. The checks, however, are drawn on a distant bank. The following table summarizes the checks.

Check From	Amount	Number of Days Float Expected
Tardy Hardy	$30,000	5 days
Bogus Bob	160,000	6 days
Fly by Night	10,000	3 days
Flaky Jake	50,000	7 days

The firm has an opportunity cost of 11%. They can contract with Burgess Air to have a jet fly to each city and present the checks for payment, having the funds wired directly to Tumbleweed's home office. This would result in collection in 1 day rather than the number of days above. The cost for Burgess Air's service is $125 per check or $400 for all four checks. Should Tumbleweed use the direct send?

Solution

To determine whether direct send is a good idea, compute the total benefit from having the funds available for investment sooner. Do this by computing the opportunity cost/day multiplied by the number of days saved.

Check From	Amount	Times Opportunity Cost/Day	Times Number of Days	Benefit
Tardy Hardy	$30,000	0.0003055	4 days	$ 36.67
Bogus Bob	160,000	0.0003055	5 days	244.44
Fly by Night	10,000	0.0003055	2 days	6.11
Flaky Jake	50,000	0.0003055	6 days	91.67
		Total Benefit		$378.89

This is the number of days from the table above, minus 1

The opportunity cost per day is the annual interest rate divided by 360 [(0.11/360)]. Since the benefit from a direct send of Bogus Bob's check is greater than $125, it should be flown. However, the total benefit is less than $400, so the rest should be collected in the usual way.

Example 6. Accounts Receivable and Cost

Heidi's Dog Frisbees sold 100,000 frisbees last year, but, based on proposed changes in credit terms, the firm anticipates that sales will increase by 10%, to 110,000 units, in the coming year. The firm's total fixed cost is $120,000, its variable cost per unit is $1.60, and the sale price per frisbee is $4.00. The firm expects the costs and the sales price to remain unchanged in the coming year.

a. Calculate the average cost per unit under both the present and the proposed plans.

b. Calculate the additional profit contribution from sales expected to result from implementation of the proposed plan.

Solution

a. The average cost per Frisbee under each plan can be found by dividing the total cost, based upon the expected sales, by the unit level of sales.

Present plan:
Total cost = $120,000 + ($1.60) × (100,000)
= $120,000 + $160,000 = $280,000

Average cost/unit = $280,000/100,000 = $2.80

Proposed plan
Total cost = $120,000 + ($1.60) × (110,000) = $296,000

Average cost/unit = $296,000/110,000 = $2.69

b. The additional profit contribution from sales expected to result from implementation of the proposal is most easily calculated by multiplying the added units of sales by their per-unit profit contribution, which can be found by subtracting the variable cost per unit from the sale price per unit.

Additional profit = (110,000 − 100,000) × ($4.00 − $1.60) = $24,000

Example 7.   Accounts receivable

Assume that under both the current and proposed plans in Example 1, Heidi's makes all sales on credit. Under the present plan, the average collection period is 36 days; under the proposed plan, it would be 72 days. The firm's required return on investment is 20%.

a.   Calculate the firm's average investment in accounts receivable under both the present and proposed plans.

b.   Determine the firm's cost of the marginal investment in accounts receivable, based on the required return of 20%.

c.   If bad debts are unaffected by the proposal, would you recommend the proposed plan?

Solution

a.   To find the average investment in accounts receivable, divide the total cost of the firm's annual sales by the turnover of accounts receivable.

Present plan

Cost of sales = 100,000 units × $2.80/unit = $280,000

Turnover of accounts receivable = 360/36 = 10

Average investment in A/R = $280,000/10 = $28,000

Proposed plan

Cost of sales = 110,000 units × $2.69/unit = $296,000

Turnover of A/R = 360/72 days = 5

Average investment in A/R = $296,000/5 = $59,200

b.   The cost of the marginal investment in accounts receivable is found by multiplying the marginal investment in accounts receivable by the firm's required return on investment.

Marginal investment = $59,200 − $28,000 = $31,200

Cost of the marginal investment in A/R = 0.20($31,200) = $6,240

c.   The proposal would be highly acceptable because the additional profit contribution from sales of $24,000 exceeds the cost of the marginal investment in accounts receivable of $6,240.

Example 8.   Bad debt expense

Assume that, under the present and proposed plans, Heidi's has bad debt expenses of 1% and 3%, respectively. Calculate the cost of the marginal bad debts associated with implementation of the proposed plan. Would this added information change the decision reached in Example 2?

Solution

The cost of the marginal bad debts is found by calculating the cost of bad debts under each plan and then taking their difference.

Proposed plan: (0.03)(110,000)($4.00) = $13,200

Present plan: (0.01)(100,000)($4.00) = $ 4,000

$ 9,200

Adding the cost of the marginal bad debts, $9,200, to the cost of the marginal investment in accounts receivable, $6,240, results in a total cost of the proposed plan equaling $15,440. Comparing this cost to the $24,000 additional profit contribution from marginal sales indicates that the proposed plan would still be acceptable. The marginal profit would be $8,560 [$24,000 – $15,440].

Example 9.   ABC Inventory

Alena's Health Foods has only ten different items in its inventory. The average number of these items in inventory and their associated unit costs are given below. If the firm wishes to apply an ABC inventory control system, indicate a suggested breakdown of these items into A, B, C classifications.

Item Number	Average Number of Units in Inventory	Average Cost per Unit
1	60	$1.00
2	150	9.00
3	400	0.90
4	1,000	25.00
5	3,000	4.00
6	620	10.00
7	30	200.00
8	25,000	0.02
9	100	10.00
10	20,000	0.08

Solution

There is no one correct answer to this problem. A reasonable classification can be made by first determining the average dollar investment in each item by multiplying the average number of units by their average unit cost.

Item Number	Average Dollar Investment
1	$ 60
2	1,350
3	360
4	25,000
5	12,000
6	6,200
7	6,000
8	500
9	1,000
10	1,600

From a subjective evaluation of the average dollar investments, the following classification can be made.

Class	Item Number
A	4, 5
B	6, 7
C	1, 2, 3, 8, 9, 10

The class A items are in the range of $12,000 to $25,000 average dollar investment; the B items are in the range of $6,000 to $6,200 average dollar investment; and the C items are $1,600 or less in average dollar investment.

Example 10.   EOQ

Chad's Lakeside Marina sells 100,000 gallons of fuel each year. Due to the near perfect weather in Florida, fuel sales are constant throughout the year. Fuel can be purchased and received within 15 days. Chad's has sufficient storage capacity for up to 50,000 gallons. The firm has analyzed its inventory costs and has found that its order cost is $250 per order and its carrying cost is $2 per gallon per year.

a.   Calculate the *EOQ* for the company's gas.

b.   Calculate the total cost of the plan suggested by the *EOQ*.

c.   Calculate the firm's reorder point in terms of gallons.

Solution

a.   In order to calculate the *EOQ*, the values of *S* (100,000 gallons), *O* ($250), and *C* (2), are substituted into the *EOQ* formula.

$$EOQ = \sqrt{\frac{2SO}{C}} = \sqrt{\frac{(2)(100,000)(\$250)}{\$2}} = 5,000 \text{ gallons}$$

b.   Each component of the total inventory cost can be estimated separately. It is best to determine the order cost first because we must round off for an even number of orders.

Order cost: Dividing the annual usage by the *EOQ* results in the number of orders.

Number of orders = 100,000/5,000 gallons = 20 orders

Annual order cost = $20 \times \$250 = \$5,000$

Carrying cost: Multiply the average inventory by the carrying cost per unit.

Average inventory = 5,000 gallons/2 = 2,500 gallons

Annual carrying cost = $2,500 \times \$2 = \$5,000$

Annual inventory cost = ordering cost + carrying cost

$$= \$5,000 + \$5,000 = \$10,000$$

We know that *EOQ* and total cost were correctly calculated because annual ordering cost equals annual carrying cost.

c.   The reorder point can be calculated by multiplying daily usage by the lead time, given as 15 days. Daily usage is annual usage of 100,000 gallons divided by 360 days in a year.

Daily usage = 100,000 gallons/360 days = 277.78 gals/day

Reorder point = $277.78 \times 15 = 4166.67$ gallons

Rounding to the next higher number, we determine that 4,167 gallons is the reorder point.

■ Study Tips

1. Short-term financial management is one of the most important and time-consuming tasks for the financial manager.

2. Recognize that there is a tradeoff between the profitability and the risk associated with various liquidity strategies.

3. Reducing inventory will cause the current ratio to fall. While we often think of high current ratios as good, effective inventory management will actually reduce it.

4. Credit management balances the risk of credit losses against losing business by being too restrictive. The goal is not to have zero credit loss. It is to maximize profit. If there are no credit losses the credit policy is probably too restrictive.

■ Student Notes

_____

_____

_____

_____

_____

■ Sample Exam—Chapter 14

True/False

T   F   1. Short-term financial management is concerned with management of the firm's current assets and current liabilities.

T   F   2. The more predictable its cash inflows, the more net working capital a firm needs.

T   F   3. The net working capital can be defined as the portion of the firm's current assets financed with long-term funds.

T   F   4. An increase in current assets increases net working capital, thereby reducing the risk of technical insolvency.

T   F   5. The aggressive financing strategy operates with minimum net working capital since only the permanent portion of the firm's current assets is being financed with long-term funds.

T   F   6. The conservative strategy is less profitable than the aggressive approach because it requires the firm to pay interest on unneeded funds.

T   F   7. Generally, as the firm's sales increase, accounts payable and accruals also increase.

T   F   8.   In credit terms, EOM (end of month) indicates that the accounts payable must be paid by the end of the month in which the merchandise has been purchased.

T   F   9.   If a firm anticipates stretching accounts payable, its cost of forgoing a cash discount is reduced.

T   F   10. The effective interest rate for a discount loan is greater than the loan's stated interest rate.

T   F   11. If levels of cash or marketable securities are too high, the profitability of the firm will be lower than if more optimal balances were maintained.

T   F   12. The firm's operating cycle is simply the sum of the average age of inventory and average payment period.

T   F   13. A positive cash conversion cycle means that the firm must obtain financing to support the cash conversion cycle.

T   F   14. Collection float is experienced by the payer and is a delay in the receipt of funds.

T   F   15. Concentration banking is used to reduce disbursement float by lengthening the mail and clearing float components.

T   F   16. The lockbox system is used to reduce collection float by shortening all three basic float components (mail, clearing, and processing).

T   F   17. A zero-balance account is a checking account in which a zero balance is maintained and the bank automatically covers all checks presented against the firm's account.

T   F   18. A broad market is one that can absorb the purchase or sale of a large number of securities.

T   F   19. To be truly marketable, a security must have two basic characteristics: a ready market, and safety of principal.

T   F   20. Federal agency issues are obligations of the U.S. Treasury and are readily accepted as low-risk securities.

T   F   21. Since treasury bills are guaranteed by the U.S. Treasury, they are considered virtually risk-free.

T   F   22. Commercial paper is a short-term fund on deposit at commercial banks having variable yields based on size, maturity, and prevailing money market conditions.

T   F   23. The yields of negotiable certificates of deposit are typically above those on U.S. Treasury issues and comparable to the yields on commercial paper with similar maturities.

T   F   24. The cash management techniques are aimed at minimizing the firm's financing requirements by taking advantage of certain imperfections in the collection and payment system.

T   F   25. Firms tend to use excess bank balances to purchase marketable securities because the rate of interest applied by banks to checking accounts is relatively low.

T   F   26. The *EOQ* occurs at the point where order costs are equal to carrying costs.

Multiple Choice

1. The portion of a firm's current assets financed with long-term funds may be called
   a. inventory.
   b. working capital.
   c. net working capital.
   d. accounts receivable.

2. The conversion of current assets from inventory to receivables to cash provides the cash used to pay the current liabilities, which represents a(n) _____ of cash.
   a. use, source
   b. outflow, inflow
   c. source, use
   d. inflow, outflow

3. The most difficult set of accounts to predict is
   a. current assets.
   b. fixed assets.
   c. long-term debt.
   d. current liabilities.

4. An increase in the current asset to total asset ratio has the effects of _____ on profits and _____ on risk.
   a. a decrease, an increase
   b. an increase, an increase
   c. a decrease, a decrease
   d. an increase, a decrease

For Questions 5, 6, and 7, refer to the following information.

Encore Inc.

Assets		Liabilities and Equity	
Current assets	$ 30,000	Current liabilities	$ 25,000
Fixed assets	75,000	Long-term debt	35,000
		Equity	45,000
Total	$105,000	Total	$105,000

The company earns 7% on current assets and 20% on fixed assets.

5. The firm's current ratio is
   a. 0.2857.
   b. 0.375.
   c. 1.2.
   d. 2.5.

6. The firm's net working capital is
   a. $10,000.
   b. –$5,000.
   c. $5,000.
   d. –$10,000.

7. The firm's annual profits on total assets is
   a. $4,100.
   b. $17,100.
   c. $18,900.
   d. $3,000.

8. In economic conditions characterized by a scarcity of short-term funds, a firm would best choose the _____ financing strategy.
   a. permanent
   b. conservative
   c. aggressive
   d. seasonal

9. _____ are the major source of unsecured short-term financing for business firms.
   a. Accruals
   b. Notes payable
   c. Accounts receivable
   d. Accounts payable

10. _____ are liabilities for services received for which payment has yet to be made. The most common accounts are taxes and wages.
    a. Accounts payable
    b. Accruals
    c. Notes payable
    d. Accounts receivable

11. Financing that arises from the normal operations of the firm is said to be
    a. accrued.
    b. payable.
    c. spontaneous.
    d. expected.

12. One of the most common designations for the beginning of the credit period is
    a. the end of the month.
    b. the date of invoice.
    c. the transaction date.
    d. both a. and b. are true

13. Cash and _____ are the firm's most liquid assets.
    a. marketable securities
    b. accounts payable
    c. inventory
    d. accruals

14. A _____ is a future debit written against a customer's checking account for an amount agreed upon by the firm to which it is payable.
    a. float
    b. wire transfer
    c. direct send
    d. preauthorized check

15. One way to improve the cash conversion cycle is to
    a. speed up collections.
    b. borrow funds.
    c. reduce inventory turnover.
    d. speed up disbursements.

16. _____ refer to the cost to the firm of forgone returns due to the failure to make short-term investments.
    a. Carrying costs
    b. Opportunity costs
    c. Flotation costs
    d. Administrative costs

17. A firm has an average age of inventory of 65 days, an average collection period of 30 days, and an average payment period of 20 days. The firm's operating cycle is
    a. 95 days.
    b. 115 days.
    c. 50 days.
    d. 85 days.

18. The _____ is the time period that elapses from the point when the firm sells a finished good on account to the point when the receivable is collected.
    a. average payment period
    b. average collection period
    c. average age of inventory
    d. cash conversion cycle

19. An increase in the average collection period will result in _____ in the operating cycle.
    a. a decrease
    b. no change
    c. an undetermined change
    d. an increase

20. A firm anticipates $1,000,000 in cash outlays during the coming year. If it costs $30 to convert marketable securities to cash and the marketable securities portfolio can earn an annual 9% rate of return, the economic conversion quantity of cash is
    a. $666,666.
    b. $18,257.
    c. $25,820.
    d. $32,489.

21. A decrease in the production time to manufacture a finished good will result in _____ in the cash conversion cycle.
    a. no change
    b. a decrease
    c. an increase
    d. an undetermined change

22. _____ refers to funds that have been dispatched by a payer but are not in a form that can be spent by the payee.
    a. A direct send
    b. Float
    c. The operating cycle
    d. The cash conversion cycle

23. Balances held to satisfy the safety motive are generally held as
    a. cash.
    b. accounts receivable.
    c. bonds.
    d. marketable securities.

24. A firm with an average age of inventory of 80 days, an average collection period of 60 days, and an average payment period of 50 days has a cash conversion cycle of
    a. 1.6 times.
    b. 140 days.
    c. 2.8 times.
    d. 90 days.

25. Samantha pays her bills immediately upon receipt. Careful analysis of her payments indicates that she pays her average bill 11 days before the due date. She makes about $4,500 per month and has average monthly bills of $2,400, plus another $850 in cash payments at the grocery story, gasoline station, and similar establishments. Marketable securities are earning 5.3%, which is 4% more than the current yield on her savings interest-bearing checking account of 1.3%. How much money could she save by slowing down her payments?
    a. $3.83
    b. $34.72
    c. $46.01
    d. $86.25

26. Cell phone service providers offer a variety of text messaging service options. One provider's standard add-on is 300 messages for $5, or approximately 1 2/3 cents per call. Alternatively, one can pay $10 for 1000 messages. In both cases there is a $0.20 charge per additional text message. During the past month, you sent 320 text messages. Which of the services would have been the best for you?

   a. The 300-message option, at a total cost of $4.33
   b. The 300-message option, at a total cost of $5.00
   c. The 300-message option, at a total cost of $9.00
   d. The 1000-message option, at a total cost of $10.00

Essay

1. Discuss the tradeoff between risk and profitability that results from choosing an aggressive financing policy over a conservative one.

2. Discuss the methods available to a firm to speed up collections.

■ Chapter 14 Answer Sheet

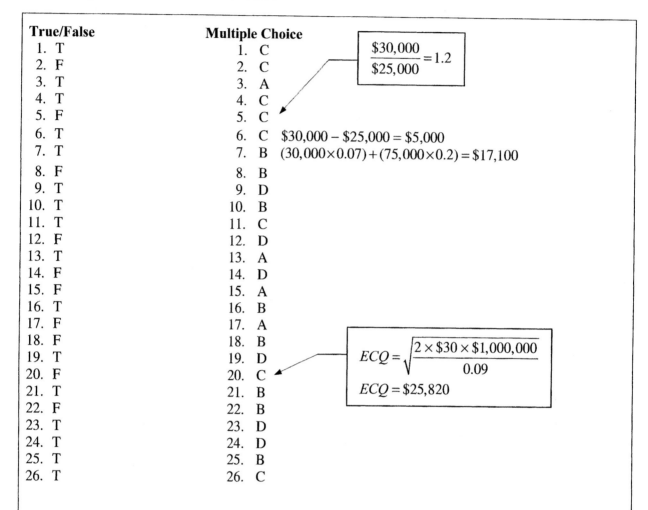

True/False	Multiple Choice	
1. T	1. C	
2. F	2. C	
3. T	3. A	
4. T	4. C	
5. F	5. C	
6. T	6. C	$\$30,000 - \$25,000 = \$5,000$
7. T	7. B	$(30,000 \times 0.07) + (75,000 \times 0.2) = \$17,100$
8. F	8. B	
9. T	9. D	
10. T	10. B	
11. T	11. C	
12. F	12. D	
13. T	13. A	
14. F	14. D	
15. F	15. A	
16. T	16. B	
17. F	17. A	
18. F	18. B	
19. T	19. D	
20. F	20. C	
21. T	21. B	
22. F	22. B	
23. T	23. D	
24. T	24. D	
25. T	25. B	
26. T	26. C	

$$\frac{\$30,000}{\$25,000} = 1.2$$

$$ECQ = \sqrt{\frac{2 \times \$30 \times \$1,000,000}{0.09}}$$

$$ECQ = \$25,820$$

Essay

1. The conservative strategy requires that the firm pay interest on unused funds. It is safer, since the funds are on hand when needed, but more costly. The alternative saves interest cost, but is riskier since short-term funds may not be available when they are needed for emergencies and other unexpected situations.

2. Collections can be sped up by using several different management options. Concentration banking reduces float by having banks in regions where there are many collections. Lockboxes can reduce float by having a bank pick up and process collections from a post office box. Direct sends are used to collect on large checks. A firm can also use preauthorized checks, depository transfer checks, and wire transfers.

Chapter 15
Current Liabilities Management

■ Chapter Summary

In the last chapter we studied net working capital and current asset management. We now move to the other side of the balance sheet and study current liability management. Current liabilities are short-term sources of funds and include account payable and short-term loans.

Some short-term financing is usually available spontaneously from increases in accounts payable and accruals that normally accompany increased sales volume. Various types of bank loans, commercial paper, and international loans are also available sources of short-term money.

LG 1   *Review accounts payable, the key components of credit terms, and the procedures for analyzing them.* Credit terms often allow a firm to delay payments to its suppliers for a specified number of days. There is usually a cost to this delay that must be considered.

LG 2   *Understand the effects of stretching accounts payable on their cost and on the use of accruals.* Spontaneous financing arises from the normal operation of the firm and is the increase in account—payable and accruals that accompany increased sales volume. Accounts payable often represent a low cost form of short-term financing. Accruals are liabilities for services received for which payment has yet to be made. These are usually wages and taxes.

LG 3   *Describe interest rates and the basic types of unsecured bank sources of short-term loans.* Some firms that routinely give up supplier discounts may find that taking these discounts could be a major source of additional income. Other firms may not be able to take the discounts because they lack alternative sources of funds.

LG 4   *Discuss the basic features of commercial paper and the key aspects of international short-term loans.* Commercial paper is short-term debt raised from the public that provides a very inexpensive source of funds. Banks make unsecured loans in the form of single-payment notes, lines of credit, and revolving credit agreements.

LG 5   *Explain the characteristics of secured short-term loans and the use of accounts receivable as short-term loan collateral.* Firms usually turn to secured sources of financing only after exhausting their unsecured options. Short-term loans are secured with collateral that is often in the form of accounts receivable or inventory. An alternative is factoring, which is the outright sale of accounts receivable to a financial institution.

LG 6   *Describe the various ways in which inventory can be used as short-term loan collateral.* Inventory is an asset and as such can be used pledged to a lender a security for debt.

■ Chapter Notes

Spontaneous sources of short-term financing

The two major spontaneous sources of short-term financing are accounts payable and accruals. Accounts payable, a major source of unsecured short-term financing, often allows the firm to take a cash discount and pay a reduced amount if payment is made by an earlier date than otherwise required.

Accounts payable

Credit terms: The supplier's credit terms state the credit period and the date the credit period begins. The supplier's credit terms are often stated on the supplier's invoice in such shorthand expressions as "3/10 net 30 EOM." The credit term would read as, "3% discount if paid within 10 days; full payment must be made within 30 days from the beginning of the credit period, which is the end of the month (EOM)."

The cost of giving up a cash discount can be found by using the following equation:

$$\text{Cost of giving up cash discount} = \frac{CD}{100\% - CD} \times \frac{365}{N}$$

Where:

CD = the stated cash discount in percentage terms

N = the number of days payment can be delayed by giving up the cash discount

Stretching accounts payable: Firms often stretch accounts payable by paying bills as late as possible without damaging their credit ratings. Such a strategy can reduce the cost of giving up a cash discount. For example, a firm that is given the credit terms of 2/10 net 30 EOM has a cost of giving up the cash discount of 36%. If the firm can stretch its accounts payable to 70 days without damaging its credit rating, the cost of giving up the cash discount would be reduced to 12%.

Accruals

Accruals are liabilities for services received for which payment has yet to be made. The most common accruals are wages and taxes. Taxes cannot be manipulated by the firm, but payment to employees can. The firm manipulates the payment of wages by changing the frequency of payment.

Unsecured sources of short-term loans

Business can obtain unsecured short-term loans from two major sources—banks and commercial paper.

Bank loans: The interest rate on a bank loan is typically based upon the prime rate of interest and can be a fixed or a floating rate. On a fixed-rate loan, the rate of interest is determined as a set increment above the prime rate on the date of the loan and remains unvarying at that fixed rate until maturity. On a floating rate loan, the increment above the prime rate is initially established, and the rate of interest is allowed to "float," or vary, above prime as the prime rate varies until maturity.

Banks lend unsecured short-term funds in three basic ways. *Single payment notes* are short-term, one-time loans that are payable as a single amount at their maturity. A *line of credit* is an agreement between a commercial bank and a business specifying the amount of unsecured short-term borrowing the bank will make available to the firm over a given period of time. A *revolving credit agreement* is a line of credit guaranteed to the borrower by the bank for a stated time period, regardless of the scarcity of money.

Commercial paper: Commercial paper is a form of financing that consists of short-term, unsecured promissory notes issued by firms with high credit standing. The interest paid by the issuer of commercial paper is determined by the size of the discount and the length of time to maturity.

Example

Whitmore Corporation has just issued $500,000 of commercial paper that has a 90 day maturity and sells for $485,000. At the end of the 90 days the purchaser of the paper will receive $500,000 for its $485,000 investment. The interest paid on the financing is therefore 12.54% [($15,000 ÷ $485,000) × (365 days ÷ 90 days)].

Secured sources of short-term loans

Once a firm has exhausted its unsecured sources of short-term financing, it may be able to obtain additional short-term loans on a secured basis. Secured short-term financing has specific assets pledged as collateral.

Characteristics of secured short-term loans

Collateral: Lenders of secured short-term funds prefer collateral that has a life, or duration, that is closely matched to the term of the loan. This assures the lender that the collateral can be used to satisfy the loan in the event of default.

Terms: Under the terms of the secured loan, the lender determines the desirable percentage advance to make against the collateral. This percentage advance is the percent of the book value of the collateral that constitutes the principal of a secured loan.

The use of accounts receivable as collateral

Two commonly used means of obtaining short-term financing with accounts receivable are pledging accounts receivable and factoring accounts receivable.

Pledging accounts receivable: A pledge of accounts receivable is the use of a firm's accounts receivable as security, or collateral, to obtain a short-term loan. Accounts receivable are normally quite liquid and they are an attractive form of short-term collateral.

Factoring accounts receivable: Factoring accounts receivable involves the sale of the receivable, at a discount, to a factor or other financial institution. A factor is a financial institution that purchases accounts receivable from businesses.

The use of inventory as collateral

 LG 6

There are three ways in which a firm may use inventory as a form of collateral.

A *floating inventory lien* is a lender's claim on the borrower's general inventory as collateral for a secured loan. A *trust inventory loan* is an agreement under which the lender advances 80% to 100% of the cost of the borrower's relatively expensive inventory items in exchange for the borrower's promise to immediately repay the loan, with accrued interest, upon the sale of each item. A *warehouse receipt* is an arrangement in which the lender receives control of the pledged inventory collateral, which is warehoused by a designated agent on the lender's behalf.

■ Sample Problems and Solutions

Example 1.   Loss of Loan Discounts

Determine the cost of giving up the cash discount under each of the following terms of sale.

a.   2/10 net 30

b.   3/10 net 30

c.   1/10 net 60

Solution

Solve this problem by using the equation for calculating the cost of forgoing cash discounts.

$$\text{Cost of giving up cash discount} = \frac{CD}{100\% - CD} \times \frac{365}{N}$$

Where:

CD = the stated cash discount in percent terms

N = the number of days payment can be delayed by giving up the cash discount

a.   (0.02/0.98)(365/20) = 37.24%

b.   (0.03/0.97)(365/20) = 56.44%

c.   (0.01/0.99)(365/50) = 7.37%

Example 2.   Compensating Balance

Calculate the effective interest cost on a $300,000 line of credit with a 14% stated interest rate and a 15% compensating balance.

Solution

If the firm borrows the full amount of the loan, it actually will receive only 85% of the funds, since 15% of the money must be held in a compensating balance. The annual interest in dollars on the loan would be $42,000 (i.e., 0.14 × $300,000) for a year. The effective interest cost can be found by dividing the interest paid by the amount of money the firm actually receives.

Effective interest rate = $42,000/(0.85 × 300,000) = $42,000/$255,000 = 16.47%

Example 3. Commitment fees

A firm is charged a 0.4% commitment fee on the average unused portion of a revolving credit agreement. If the agreement is for $2,000,000 and the firm's average borrowing is $1,400,000, calculate the dollar amount of the commitment fee.

Solution

Applying the 0.4% commitment fee to the average unused balance of $600,000 yields a commitment cost of $2,400 (i.e., $0.004 \times (\$2,000,000 - \$1,400,000)$).

Example 4. Accounts Receivable as Collateral

Hole in the Wall Bank is considering making a loan secured by accounts receivable to BC and SDK Group, Inc., who wish to borrow as much as possible. The bank's policy is to accept as collateral the accounts of customers that pay within 15 days of the end of the 45-day credit period and have an average account age that is no more than 8 days beyond the customer's average payment period. The BC and SDK Group's accounts receivable balances, ages and average payment period for each credit customer are given below. The BC and SDK Group extends net 45-day credit terms.

Customer	Accounts Receivable	Average Age of Account	Average Payment Period of Customer
A	$10,000	65	70
B	25,000	40	50
C	40,000	50	60
D	20,000	20	45
E	30,000	10	55
F	15,000	60	50
G	20,000	50	65
H	25,000	12	50

a. Calculate the dollar amount of acceptable accounts receivable collateral held by the BC and SDK Group.

b. If the bank reduces acceptable collateral by 5% for returns and allowances, how much acceptable collateral does the firm have?

c. If the bank will advance 70% against the adjusted acceptable collateral, how much can the firm borrow?

Solution

a. The acceptable accounts are those that are paid within 15 days of the end of the credit period, which would be within 60 days, and that on the average, are not more than 8 days beyond the customer's average payment period. For each customer, the account balance, if acceptable, and its disposition are given next page.

Customer	Disposition	Account Balance
A	age > 60 days	0
B	OK	$25,000
C	OK	40,000
D	OK	20,000
E	OK	30,000
F	10 days beyond average pay period	0
G	Age > 60 days	0
H	OK	25,000
	Total Acceptable Accounts	$140,000

b. The acceptable collateral would be 95% of the amount of acceptable accounts because a 5% reserve is maintained.

Acceptable collateral = (0.95) × ($140,000) = $133,000

c. The firm can borrow 70% of the acceptable collateral.

Borrowing = (0.70) × ($133,000) = $93,100.

■ Study Tips

1. Spontaneous sources of unsecured short-term financing can result from the normal business operation.

2. The decision to give up the cash discount should be the result of analysis of the cost of not taking the discount.

3. Commercial banks are the principals providers of unsecured short-term loans to business.

4. A firm may exhaust its unsecured short-term borrowing capacity. That is, beyond some level of borrowing, lenders consider a firm too risky to be given an unsecured short-term loan. The next step is to arrange for secured short-term financing.

■ Student Notes

_____

_____

_____

_____

_____

■ Sample Exam—Chapter 15

True/False

T   F   1.   Commercial paper is short-term public debt secured by accounts receivable.

T   F   2.   Generally, as the firm's sales increase, accounts payable and accruals also increase.

T   F   3.   In credit terms, EOM (end of month) indicates that the accounts payable must be paid by the end of the month in which the merchandise has been purchased.

T   F   4.   If a firm anticipates stretching accounts payable, its cost of forgoing a cash discount is reduced.

T   F   5.   The effective interest rate for a discount loan is greater than the loan's stated interest rate.

T   F   6.   The interest rate on a line of credit is normally stated as a fixed rate—the prime rate—plus a percent.

T   F   7.   Firms are able to raise finds through the sale of commercial paper more cheaply than by borrowing from a commercial bank.

T   F   8.   Self-liquidating loans are mainly invested in productive assets, which provide the mechanism through which the loan is repaid.

T   F   9.   Secured short-term financing has specific assets pledged as collateral and appears on the balance sheet as current liabilities.

T   F   10.   Commercial banks and other institutions do not normally consider secured loans less risky than unsecured loans and, therefore require higher interest rates on them.

Multiple Choice

1.   A firm purchased goods with a purchase price of $2,500 and credit terms of 2/10 net 30. The firm paid for these goods on the 5th day after the date of sale. The firm must pay _____ for the goods.
   a. $2,450
   b. $2,475
   c. $2,500
   d. $1,250

2.   The cost of forgoing a cash discount under the terms of sale 2/10 net 30 (assume a 360-day year) is
   a.   12.44%.
   b.   8.35%.
   c.   24.49%.
   d.   36.73%.

3. The _____ is the lowest rate of interest charged on business loans to the best business borrowers by the nation's leading banks.
    a. prime rate
    b. commercial paper rate
    c. treasury bill rate
    d. federal funds rate

4. Much of the commercial paper is issued by
    a. commercial finance companies.
    b. small businesses.
    c. venture capitalists.
    d. small manufacturing firms.

5. Loans on which the interest is paid in advance are often called
    a. reduced-principle loans.
    b. premium loans.
    c. called loans.
    d. discount loans.

6. Collateral is typically required for a
    a. secured short-term loan.
    b. line of credit.
    c. single payment note.
    d. called loan.

7. The interest rate charged on a secured short-term loan to a corporation is typically _____ the interest rate on an unsecured loan.
    a. unrelated to
    b. the same as
    c. lower than
    d. higher than

8. _____ involves the sale of accounts receivable.
    a. A field warehouse arrangement
    b. Factoring
    c. Pledging of accounts receivable
    d. A lien

9. A loan that is made for a specific purpose for a short time (usually less than one year) and usually has its interest rate tied to prime is called a
    a. discount loan.
    b. factor.
    c. pledge.
    d. single payment note.

10. An agreement between a commercial bank and a business specifying the amount of unsecured short-term borrowing the bank will make available to the firm over a given period of time is a
    a. discount loan.
    b. factor.
    c. line of credit.
    d. single payment note.

11. Current liabilities for an individual include all of the following except
    a. outstanding home mortgage balance.
    b. student loan payments due next June.
    c. unpaid bills from your local electric company.
    d. VISA credit card balances.

12. A local automobile dealership gives Megan the choice of a low interest rate or cash discount on the purchase of a popular sports car for $14,000. Specifically, Megan will receive a $600 cash discount if she pays 4.9% over the next 4 years. If she forgoes the cash discount, the dealership will offer her a car at a 4-year interest rate of 2.9%. In order to get the good rate, Megan will have to pay $500 up front. Ignoring time-value-of-money, which of these 2 choices should Megan except?
    a. The 2.9% loan, with total payments of $15,566
    b. The 2.9% loan, with total payments of $16,182
    c. The 4.9% loan, with total payments of $16,026
    d. The 4.9% loan, with total payments of $16,144

13. Austin Lynd is considering borrowing $10,000 over the next 9 months (270 days) using a variable rate loan. He will be charged 1.25% above the prime rate, which is now 8.5%. Approximately what interest expense will Austin incur if interest rates fall from this level by 0.5 percent in 60 days and then rise by 1.0% after 150 days for the remainder of the period?
    a. $638
    b. $688
    c. $725
    d. $858

Essay

1. Discuss the trade-off between risk and profitability that results from choosing an aggressive financing policy over a conservative one.

2. Explain why banks do not consider secured lending to be less risky than unsecured loans.

■ Chapter 15 Answer Sheet

True/False

1. F
2. T
3. F
4. T
5. T
6. F
7. T
8. T
9. T
10. T

Multiple Choice

1. A $\$2,500 \times (1 - 0.02) = \$2,450$
2. C
3. A
4. A
5. D
6. A
7. D
8. B
9. D
10. C
11. A
12. C
13. C

$$\frac{2\%}{100\% - 2\%} \times \frac{360}{20} = 36.73\%$$

Essay

1. The conservative strategy requires that the firm pay interest on unused funds. It is safer, since the funds are on hand when needed, but more costly. The alternative saves interest cost, but is riskier since short-term funds may not be available when they are needed.

2. Having an interest in collateral reduces the amount of loss a lender will suffer in the event of a default, but the collateral does not reduce the probability of a default. What lenders want is to be repaid on schedule. The cost of administering a secured loan is greater than the cost of administering an unsecured loan, so interest rates are usually higher.

Chapter 16
Hybrid and Derivative Securities

■ Chapter Summary

This chapter examines a number of alternatives to financing other than using bonds or common stock. The securities discussed here are very commonly used by a variety of corporations. Leasing has become a favored method of financing capital assets. For example, many airlines lease the aircraft they use rather than purchasing them outright.

This chapter also discusses convertibles, warrants and options. Convertibility and warrants are features that are added to securities to make them more attractive to investors and to thereby lower their cost to the issuer. Options are a type of derivative security that allows the investor to take advantage of expected security price changes with lower initial investment.

Hybrid securities blend the characteristics of both debt and equity. Preferred stock, leases, convertible securities, and stock purchase warrants are examples of hybrid securities.

Derivative securities are neither debt nor equity but derive their value from an underlying asset that is often another security. Options are derivative securities.

LG 1 *Differentiate between hybrid and derivative securities and their roles in the corporation.* Preferred stock features fixed dividends that must be paid before common stockholders can be paid dividends. Preferred stockholders can not usually vote on directors. Preferred is often more costly than debt to a firm because the cash flows are less certain and because the dividends are not tax deductible.

LG 2 *Review the types of leases, leasing arrangements, the lease-versus-purchase decision, the effects of leasing on future financing, and the advantages and disadvantages of leasing.* Operating leases are typically short term and cancelable. An example of an operating lease may be where a firm leases a copy machine for two years. Financial leases are longer term and are not cancelable. An example of a financial lease is where an airline leases aircraft.

LG 3 *Describe the types of convertible securities, their general features, and financing with convertibles.* Convertible securities are offered by firms to lower the cost of acquiring funds. Investors will pay more for a convertible security than for one without the conversion feature because it gives them an opportunity to share in any gains enjoyed by stockholders without taking the risk of loss. The purchase of a convertible security is like buying a nonconvertible security plus a stock option.

LG 4 *Demonstrate the procedures for determining the straight bond value, conversion (or stock) value, and market value of a convertible bond.* The straight bond value is the price the security would sell for without the conversion feature. The conversion value is the value of the convertible measured in terms of the market price of the common stock into which the security can be converted. The actual market value of the convertible security is likely to be greater than its straight value or its conversion value.

Explain the key characteristics of stock-purchase warrants, the implied price of an attached warrant, and the values of warrants. Stock-purchase warrants are another feature that firms may add to a security to make the security more attractive to investors. The warrant lets the holder buy stock at a specified price in the future. Warrants are like long-term stock options that are attached to some underlying security.

Define options and discuss calls and puts, options markets, options trading, the role of call and put options in fund raising, and hedging foreign currency exposures with options. A call option gives the holder the right to buy a security at a specified price within a specified length of time. A put option gives the holder the right to sell the security at the specified price.

■ Chapter Notes

Hybrid versus Derivative Securities

Preferred stock has characteristics of debt because it has a stated dividend that is given priority over common stock dividends. It also has characteristics of equity because it is a form of ownership with no maturity date. Because it combines characteristics of both types of securities it is called a hybrid security. Other popular hybrid securities include financial leases, convertible securities, and stock-purchase warrants.

Derivative securities derive their value from some other underlying security. The most popular derivatives are options. Options are not used by firms to raise money; rather they can help manage risk.

Leasing

Leasing allows the firm to obtain the use of certain fixed assets for which it must make a series of contractual, periodic, tax-deductible payments. The lessee is the receiver of the assets under the lease contract, and the lessor is the owner of the assets.

Types of leases

Operating leases: An operating lease is a contractual arrangement whereby the lessee agrees to make periodic payments to the lessor, often for five or fewer years, to obtain an asset's services. Operating leases are usually cancelable at the option of the lessee, who may be required to pay a predetermined penalty for cancellation.

Financial (or capital) leases: A financial lease is a longer-term lease than an operating lease. Financial leases are noncancelable and therefore obligate the lessee to make contractual payments for the use of an asset over a predefined period of time. The noncancelable feature of the financial lease makes it similar to certain types of long-term debt, in that the lease payment becomes a fixed, tax deductible expenditure that must be paid at predefined dates over a definite period.

Leasing arrangements

Lessors use three primary techniques for obtaining assets to be leased.

A *direct lease* results when a lessor owns or acquires the assets that are leased to a given lessee. In a direct lease, the lessor did not previously own the assets that are being leased. A *sale-leaseback* arrangement allows lessors to purchase assets already owned by a firm and then lease them back to the firm. A sale-leaseback arrangement is used by firms that are in need of funds for operations. Finally, a *leveraged lease* is a lease under which the lessor acts as an equity participant, supplying about 20% of the cost of the asset, while a lender supplies the balance. Leveraged lease usage is common when expensive assets are being leased.

The lease-versus-purchase decision

There are three alternatives that firms consider when evaluating the lease-versus-purchase decision. The alternatives are (1) lease the assets, (2) borrow funds to purchase the assets, or (3) purchase the assets using available liquid resources. Alternatives 2 and 3 are analyzed in a similar fashion.

The lease-versus-purchase decision is made by using basic present value techniques and consists of the following four steps:

Step 1. Find the after-tax cash outflow for each year under the lease alternative.

Step 2. Find the after-tax cash outflow for each year under the purchase alternative.

Step 3. Calculate the present value of the cash outflows associated with the lease (from Step 1) and purchase (from Step 2) alternatives using the after-tax cost of debt at the appropriate discount rate.

Step 4. Choose the alternative with the lower present value of cash outflows from Step 3.

Advantages and disadvantages of leasing

A few of the most commonly cited advantages and disadvantages of leasing are as follows:

Advantages

1. The use of sale-leaseback arrangements may permit the firm to increase its liquidity by converting an existing asset into cash, which can then be used as working capital.

2. When a firm becomes bankrupt or is reorganized, the maximum claim of lessors against the corporation is three years of lease payments and the return of the asset.

3. A lessee avoids many of the restrictive covenants that are normally included as part of a long-term loan.

4. Leasing provides for 100% of the financing needed to obtain the use of an asset.

Disadvantages

1. A lease does not have a stated interest cost.

2. At the end of the term of the lease agreement, the terminal value of an asset is realized by the lessor.

3.   Under a lease, the lessee is generally prohibited from making improvements on the leased property or asset without the approval of the lessor.

4.   If a lessee leases an asset that subsequently becomes obsolete, it still must make lease payments over the remaining term of the lease.

Convertible securities

A conversion feature is an option which is included as part of a bond or a preferred stock issue that allows its holder to change the security into a stated number of shares of common stock.

Convertible bonds: A convertible bond is almost always a debenture—an unsecured bond—with a call feature. Since convertible bonds provide their holders with the opportunity to convert the bonds into shares of common stock, the expense of convertible bonds is generally less than that of nonconvertible or *straight bonds*.

Convertible preferred stock: Convertible preferred stock can be sold with a lower stated dividend than a nonconvertible or *straight preferred stock*. The convertible preferred holder is assured of the fixed dividend payment associated with a preferred stock and also may receive the appreciation resulting from increases in the market price of the underlying common stock.

General features of convertibles

Conversion ratio: The conversion ratio is the ratio at which a convertible security can be exchanged for common stock. The conversion ratio can be stated in one of two ways:

1.   The conversion ratio may state the number of shares of common stock into which the security can be converted. To find the *conversion price*, which is the per-share price that is effectively paid for common stock as the result of conversion, the par value of the convertible security must be divided by the conversion ratio.

2.   Instead of the conversion ratio, the conversion price may be given. The conversion ratio can be found by dividing the par value of the convertible by the conversion price.

Conversion period: Convertible securities are almost always convertible anytime during the life of the security.

Conversion (or stock) value: The conversion (or stock) value is the value of the convertible measured in terms of the market price of the common stock into which it can be converted. The conversion value can be found simply by multiplying the conversion ratio by the current market price of the firm's common stock.

Financing with convertibles

Convertibles are used for several different reasons. The most commonly cited reasons are to obtain deferred common stock financing, to "sweeten" bond issues, to minimize restrictive covenants, and to raise cheap funds temporarily.

Virtually all convertible securities will have a call feature that has a call price equal to the par value of the security plus one year's stated interest on the security. The call feature can be used to force a conversion. If the convertible has been called in by the issuing firm and the market price of the firm's common stock does not reach a level sufficient to stimulate the conversion of the associated convertibles, an *overhanging issue* will exist.

Determining the value of a convertible bond

Straight bond value: The straight bond value of a convertible bond is the price at which it would sell in the market without the conversion feature. This value is found by determining the value of a nonconvertible bond with similar payments issued by a firm having the same risk.

Conversion (or stock) value: The conversion (or stock) value of a convertible security was defined earlier as the value of the convertible measured in terms of the market price of the common stock into which the security can be converted. When the market price of the common stock exceeds the conversion price, the conversion (or stock) value exceeds the par value.

Market value: The market value of a convertible is likely to be greater than its straight value or its conversion value. The amount by which the market value exceeds its straight or conversion value is often called the market premium.

Refer to the above graph. The horizontal line is the value of a straight (or conversion free) bond. Note that the value of the straight bond is not dependent on the value of the common stock. The conversion value goes up as the stock price rises. The market value of the convertible bond is above the conversion value because the holder of the convertible bond recognizes that the price of the stock may go even higher. This market premium is essentially the value the option convertibility gives the bondholder.

Stock-purchase warrants

Stock-purchase warrants give the holder the right to purchase a certain number of shares of common stock at a specified price over a certain period of time and are often attached as an enhancement to a debt issue.

Key characteristics of a warrant

Warrants as "sweeteners": Warrants are often attached to debt issues as "sweeteners" or added benefits. The attachment of a warrant will increase the marketability of the debt and will lower the required interest rate on the debt.

Exercise prices: The price at which holders of warrants can purchase a specified number of shares of common stock is normally referred to as the exercise (or option) price. This price is normally set at 10% to 20% above the market price of the firm's stock at the time of issuance.

Life of a warrant: The life of a warrant varies. Often a warrant will have a life of no more than ten years, while other warrants will have infinite lives.

Warrant trading: A warrant is usually detachable, which means that the bondholder may sell the warrant without selling the security to which it is attached. Warrants trade in both broker and dealer markets.

Value of an attached warrant

Implied price: The implied price of a warrant is the price that is effectively paid for each warrant attached to a bond and can be found by using the following equation:

Implied price of *all* warrants = price of bond with warrants attached − straight bond value

Theoretical value of a warrant: The theoretical value of a stock-purchase warrant is the amount for which one would expect the warrant to sell in the marketplace and can be found by using the following equation:

$$TVW = (P_0 - E) \times N$$

Where:

TVW = theoretical value of a warrant
P_0 = current market price of a share of common stock
E = exercise price of the warrant
N = number of shares of common stock obtainable with one warrant

Market value of a warrant: The market value of a stock-purchase warrant is generally above the theoretical value of the warrant. This is due to investor expectations about the common stock of the issuing firm.

Warrant premium: The warrant premium is the amount by which the market value of a stock-purchase warrant exceeds the theoretical value of the stock-purchase warrant.

Options

Options can be purchased by investors to obtain the right to buy or sell a specific number of shares of common stock on or before some future date at a stated price. The two most common types of options are calls and puts. Standardized options trade on many markets, however the dominant exchange is the Chicago Board Options Exchange.

A *call option* is an option to purchase a specified number of shares of a stock (typically 100) on or before a specified date at a specified price. The *striking price* is the price at which the holder of the option can buy the stock at any time prior to the option's expiration date.

A *put option* is an option to sell a given number of shares of a stock (typically 100) on or before the expiration date at a stated striking price.

The motive for purchasing call options is the expectation that the market price of the underlying stock will rise by more than enough to cover the cost of the option and thereby allow the purchaser of the call to profit.

Put options are purchased with the expectation that the share price of a given security will decline over the life of the option.

■ Sample Problems and Solutions

Example 1.   Preferred stock

Linda's Drive-through Lumber Express, Inc. has 10%, $80 preferred stock outstanding.

a.   How much is the annual preferred stock dividend?

b.   If the preferred stock is noncumulative and the dividends have been passed for the past two years, how much would have to be paid prior to payment of the common stockholders' dividend?

c.   If the preferred stock is cumulative and the situation in part **b** occurs, how much would have to be paid to the preferred shareholders prior to payment of dividends to the common stockholders?

Solution

a.   The annual preferred dividend is found by multiplying the dividend percentage by the stated value of the preferred. This gives a preferred dividend per share of $8 [$80 × 0.10].

b.   If the preferred stock is noncumulative, only the current dividend of $8 per share is paid prior to payment of dividends to common stockholders.

c.   If the preferred stock is cumulative, all dividends in arrears plus the current dividend must be paid to the preferred shareholders before the common stockholders can receive dividends. Because 2 past dividends plus the current dividend must be paid, the firm must pay 3 years of preferred stock dividends, which at $8 per year is $24 per share.

Example 2.   Convertible bonds

Porsche Refinements Inc. has convertible bonds outstanding that have a face value of $1,000. Each bond is convertible into 25 shares of common stock for the next 5 years, and 22 shares thereafter until the maturity of the bonds.

a.   Calculate the conversion price per share for each bond for (1) the first five years, and (2) the period beyond the fifth year.

b.   If the stock is currently selling for $35 per share, calculate the conversion premium for each bond as a percentage of the firm's current stock price.

c.   Calculate the conversion value of a bond at Porsche Refinements' current stock price, and also calculate the conversion value at a price of $40, $45, and $50 for the firm's stock.

Solution

a.   The conversion price per share for the bond can be found by dividing its face value by the number of shares into which it is convertible:

$$\frac{\$1,000}{25 \text{ shares}} = \$40 \text{ per share}$$

The conversion price beyond the 5th year is:

$$\frac{\$1,000}{22\ shares} = \$45.45 \ per \ share$$

b.   When the stock is currently selling for $35 per share and the convertible bond can be converted at a price of $40 per share, the conversion premium is $5 per share (i.e., $40 – $35). Stated as a percentage of the market price:

$$Conversion \ Premium = \frac{\$5 \ conversion \ premium}{\$35 \ share \ price} = 14.3\%$$

c.   When the stock is selling for a given price, the conversion value of the bond is found by multiplying the number of shares of stock into which the bond is converted by the market price of the common stock. In this case, the bond is converted into 25 shares of common stock. The conversion values are calculated as follows:

Market Price of Common Stock	Conversion Ratio	Conversion Value of Bond
$35	25 shares	$875
40	25 shares	1,000
45	25 shares	1,125
50	25 shares	1,250

Example 3.   Stock Warrants

Joe Student has an opportunity to invest $8,000 in either the stock or the warrants of the Carolina Panthers Football Franchise. The company's stock is currently selling for $40 per share, while its warrants, which provide for the purchase of 3 shares of common stock at $46 per share, are currently selling for $4 each.

a.   If Joe buys the stock today, holds it for one year, and sells it for $50, how much would he earn on his investment? Ignore brokerage fees.

b.   If Joe buys the warrants today, holds them for one year, and sells them for $15, how much would he earn on his investment?

Solution

a.   If Joe sells the stock for $50 per share, he will have earned $10 per share because the stock would have been purchased originally for $40 per share. Because Joe had $8,000 to invest, he would have purchased 200 shares (i.e., $8,000 ÷ $40 per share). Because he realizes a return equal to $10 per share, his total profit would be $2,000 (i.e., $10 × 200).

b.   If Joe spends his $8,000 purchasing the warrants at $4 each, he would purchase 2,000 warrants (i.e., $8000 ÷ $4 per warrant). If he is able to sell the warrants for $15 each, he would make $11 per warrant (i.e. $15 – $4). On the 2,000 warrants, his total earnings would be $22,000.

Example 4. Lease-versus-purchase analysis

Terry's Tires can purchase a $3,000 tire balancer with a useful life of 5 years. It is expected that the machine will be sold after 5 years for $200, and depreciation for tax purposes is to be on a straight-line basis. (Ignore terminal value for this example: $3,000/5 = $600.) Operating expenses will rise by $1,000 per year. The purchase will be financed with a 10% loan amortized over the 5 years.
Alternatively, Terry's could lease the balancer for a yearly rental of $700. Yearly expenses will increase by $900 with the lease.

Assuming a tax rate of 40%, a pre-tax cost of debt of 10% and that the firm will exercise its option to purchase the equipment at the terminal value, which financing alternative should Terry's choose?

Solution

End of Year	Loan Payment	Maintenance Cost	Depreciation	Interest	Total Deductions	Tax Shields	After-Tax Cash Outflows
1	$791.39	$1,000	$600	300.00	1,900.00	760.00	1,031.39
2	791.39	$1,000	$600	250.86	1,850.86	740.34	1,051.05
3	791.39	$1,000	$600	196.81	1,796.81	718.72	1,072.67
4	791.39	$1,000	$600	137.35	1,737.35	694.94	1,096.45
5	791.39	$1,000	$600	71.94	1,671.94	668.78	1,122.61

End of Year	Leasing			Purchasing		
	After-Tax Cash Outflows	Present Value Factors	Present Value of Outflows	After-Tax Cash Outflows	Present Value Factors	Present Value of Outflows
1	$960	0.943	$ 905.28	$1,031.39	0.943	$ 972.60
2	960	0.890	854.40	1,051.05	0.890	935.43
3	960	0.840	806.40	1,072.67	0.840	901.04
4	960	0.792	760.32	1096.45	0.792	868.39
5	960	0.747	717.12	1,122.61	0.747	838.59
	PV of Outflows		$4,043.52	PV of Outflows		$4,516.05

The after-tax cash outflow for leasing is computed as the lease cost plus the additional expenses multiplied by 1 minus the tax rate (i.e., ($700 + $900) × (1 − 0.4) = 960).

The after-tax cost of debt is used to find the present value of the cash outflow because the analysis is dealing only with the choice of financing methods where the cash flows can be predicted with near certainty (0.10 · (1 − 0.4) = 0.06).

The result is that Terry's should *lease* the machine because the present value of the cash outflows is lower for the lease option than for the purchase option. Note that this is different from the usual net present value calculation where you choose the option with highest NPV. Here we have computed the PV of the *outflows*, not the *inflows*.

■ Study Tips

1. You can remember how warrants and conversion features affect the required yield on securities by understanding the motivation behind offering these enhancements. A firm will only offer a convertible bond if it believes it will get something in return. The firm gets a lower cost of borrowing because investors will accept a lower return since they have the possibility of a big payoff if the stock price rises.

2. The big attraction of options, such as puts and calls, is that they let the investor capitalize on stock price movements with lower initial investments. Instead of buying the security, the investor only needs to buy the option. If the stock goes up, the investor can gain. Remember that the use of options is usually to take advantage of some short-run inefficiency in the market price of a security. If the markets are truly efficient, you cannot consistently earn gains with options. As a result, financial advisors suggest that options be left to the speculators and not be used by the small investor.

3. When making the lease-versus-purchase-decision, the important thing is to include in your analysis only those costs which differ between the alternatives. By omitting all common costs, the calculation can be kept manageable.

■ Student Notes

_____

_____

_____

_____

■ Sample Exam—Chapter 16

True/False

T　F　1.　Preferred stock is often considered a quasi-debt since it yields a fixed periodic payment.

T　F　2.　Leasing is considered a source of financing provided by the lessee to the lessor.

T　F　3.　The lease arrangement has more restrictive covenants than are normally included as part of a long-term loan.

T   F   4.   Convertibles can be used as a form of deferred common stock financing.

T   F   5.   The conversion value is the value of a convertible security as measured by the market price of the common stock into which it can be converted.

T   F   6.   In the case of an overhanging issue, if the firm were to call the issue, the bondholders would accept the call price rather than convert the bonds.

T   F   7.   The conversion value of a bond is the minimum price at which a convertible bond would be traded.

T   F   8.   A call option is an option to sell a specified number of shares of a stock on or before some future date at a stated price.

T   F   9.   A direct lease is a lease under which the lessee sells an asset for cash to a prospective lessor and then leases back the same asset, making periodic payments for its use.

T   F   10.   When the market price of the common stock exceeds the conversion price, the conversion value exceeds the par value of the convertible security.

T   F   11.   The amount of the claim of preferred stockholders in liquidation is normally equal to the market value of the preferred stock.

T   F   12.   An operating lease need not be capitalized, but its basic features must be disclosed in a footnote to the financial statements.

Multiple Choice

1.   Which of the following is considered a hybrid security?
   a.   preferred stock.
   b.   a put option.
   c.   common stock.
   d.   a call option.

2.   Which of the following is a derivative security?
   a.   preferred stock.
   b.   a lease.
   c.   an option.
   d.   convertible stock.

3.   From the corporation's point of view, the advantages of issuing preferred stock include all of the following EXCEPT
   a.   its increased financial leverage.
   b.   its difficulty to retire.
   c   its security from merger.
   d.   its flexible dividend policy.

4. A lease that is a contractual arrangement whereby the lessee agrees to make periodic payments to the lessor, often for 5 or fewer years and is cancellable (though with a penalty) is a
   a. financial lease.
   b. capital lease.
   c. hybrid lease.
   d. operating lease.

5. Assets leased under _____ leases generally have a useable life longer than the term of the lease.
   a. secured
   b. fixed
   c. capital
   d. operating

6. The consequences of missing a financial lease payment are _____ those of missing an interest or principal payment on debt.
   a. more severe than
   b. less severe than
   c. the same as
   d. unrelated to

7. A_____ is an option included as part of a bond or preferred stock that permits the holder to convert the security into a specified number of shares of common stock.
   a. call option
   c. stock-purchase warrant
   b. conversion feature
   d. put option

8. Convertible preferred stock is normally converted into
   a. debt.
   b. options.
   c. warrants.
   d. shares of common stock.

9. A_____ allows the firm to force conversion.
   a. call feature
   c. conversion feature
   b. put
   d. warrant

10. The call price of the security generally _____ the security's par value.
    a. is equal to
    b. is half
    c. is greater than
    d. is less than

11. A firm has outstanding convertible preferred stock with a $60 par value which is convertible into 4 shares of common stock. The conversion value is $40. The current market price of a share of common stock is
   a. $15.
   b. $10.
   c. $5.
   d. $20.

12. The _____ value is the price the bond would sell for in the market without the conversion feature.
   a. call
   b. striking price
   c. cumulative bond
   d. straight bond

13. A _____ gives the holder an option to purchase a certain number of shares of common stock at a specified price over a certain period of time.
   a. stock-purchase warrant
   b. put option
   c. conversion feature
   d. lease agreement

14. The effect of exercising a warrant on the firm's capital structure reduces leverage _____ converting a convertible security.
   a. less than
   b. without relationship to
   c. more than
   d. as much as

15. A firm has outstanding warrants that are exercisable at $47 per share and entitle holders to purchase 4 shares of common stock. The common stock is currently selling for $50 per share. The theoretical value of the warrant is
   a. $3.
   b. $4.
   c. $12.
   d. $12.25.

16. The option buyer that expects a stock price to rise will purchase a
   a. put.
   b. right.
   c. warrant.
   d. call.

17. For puts and calls, the exercise price is called the
    a. conversion price.
    b. striking price.
    c. option price.
    d. placed price.

18. The dominant organized options exchange is the
    a. Chicago Board Options Exchange.
    b. NYSE.
    c. over-the-counter exchange.
    d. AMEX.

19. An investor has $500 which he is interested in investing in XYZ stock, which is currently selling for $12 per share. XYZ's warrants are selling for $8 per warrant. Each warrant entitles the holder to purchase 5 shares of XYZ's common stock for $10 per share. The warrant premium is
    a. $4.
    b. $1.
    c. $2.
    d. $3.

20. The market value of a warrant is generally _____ the theoretical value of the warrant.
    a. unrelated to
    b. below
    c. equal to
    d. above

21. LeaseCompare.com (a real web-based buyers agent and lease facilitator) is offering to find and sell to you a 2008 Chevy Silverado. The terms are $1,000 down, plus a $400 security deposit paid up front, and you pay $423 for 48 months. You can drive the vehicle 48,000 miles, with a $0.18/mile fee for additional mileage. What is the cost of the lease assuming you drive under 48,000 miles during the lease period (for simplicity, ignore time-value-of-money)?
    a. $21,304
    b. $21,424
    c. $21,472
    d. $30,112

22. In comparison to LeaseCompare's offer above, Lithia Motors (an actual, publicly-held auto dealership network with over 100 outlets) is offering the same Chevy Silverado for $27,831. The financing package is $99 down and $30.54 per $1000 over 60 months (which equates to a 7.75% annualized percentage rate). According to LeaseCompare.com, the forecast value of the 2008 Silverado will be $12,607 in 48 months. Assuming you can earn 3% annual interest on savings and pay a 5.5% sales tax on purchases, what is the cost of purchasing the Silverado and selling it after 48 months (ignoring time-value-of-money for simplicity)?
    a. $28,189
    b. $29,720
    c. $29,819
    d. $29,831

23. Stock options do not trade on the:
    a. American Stock Exchange.
    b. Chicago Board Options Exchange.
    c. International Stock Exchange.
    d. New York Stock Exchange.

Essay

1. Discuss the advantages and disadvantages of leasing versus purchasing an asset.

2. Discuss why an issuer of bonds might choose to include warrants or a conversion feature with bonds.

■ Chapter 16 Answer Sheet

True/False

1. T
2. F
3. F
4. T
5. T
6. T
7. F
8. F
9. F
10. T
11. F
12. T

Multiple Choice

1. A
2. C
3. B
4. D
5. D
6. C
7. B
8. D
9. A
10. C
11. B $\$40 \div 4 = 10$
12. D
13. A
14. A
15. C $\$12 = (\$50 - \$47) \times 4$
16. D
17. B
18. A
19. C
20. D
21. C
22. D
23. D

$$TVW = (\$12 - \$10) \times 5$$
$$TVW = \$10$$
$$WP = \$10 - \$8 = \$2$$

Essay

1. There are many advantages to leasing, but the most important would be the conservation of working capital since there is usually no down payment required. Other advantages include the ability to depreciate land, avoidance of restrictive covenants, financing flexibility, and limited liability in the case of bankruptcy.

2. Warrants and convertibility are sweeteners that enhance the appeal of a security. Investors may perceive that they are getting something for nothing when one of these features is bundled with the bond. In fact, investors do pay for the features by reducing the required return. This reduction in required return is what motivates the issuer to include the enhancements.

Chapter 17
Mergers, LBOs, Divestitures, and Business Failure

■ Chapter Summary

This last section of the text includes a chapter on mergers, divestitures, and failure, and a chapter on international finance. These topics are included because of their general importance to businesses. Many of the very largest transactions in the world have involved one firm buying another. These transactions have tremendous impact on employees, competitors, and managers. The news sources regularly report even rumors that a merger may occur. You will find this chapter to be both interesting and an important part of your financial education.

LG 1 *Understand merger fundamentals, including terminology, motives for merging, and types of mergers.* A whole vocabulary has developed around mergers and acquisitions. There are acquirers, targets, white knights, strategic mergers, greenmail, and other terms that are regularly used to discuss the topic. This chapter begins with a review of these terms.

LG 2 *Describe the objectives and procedures used in leveraged buyouts (LBOs) and divestitures.* A leveraged buyout occurs when a large amount of debt is used to finance a takeover. Many LBOs are led by management. The heavy debt burden the new company must service makes these types of mergers very risky. A divestiture occurs when a division or subsidiary is sold.

LG 3 *Demonstrate the procedures used to value the target company and discuss the effect of stock swap transactions on earnings per share.* The value of a target can be estimated using valuation techniques. Capital budgeting methods can be applied to the cash flows. As always, positive *NPV* acquisitions would be acceptable. The problem is with accurately estimating the cash flows and the risk. Historically, many very costly errors have been made.

LG 4 *Discuss the merger negotiation process, holding companies, and international mergers.* Investment bankers are usually hired to identify a suitable target and to assist in the negotiations. Some mergers are friendly, and target management negotiates with the acquirer. Others are hostile and the acquirer must deal directly with the shareholders.

LG 5 *Understand the types and major causes of business failure and the use of voluntary settlements to sustain or liquidate the failed firm.* Firms fail because they have negative returns or because they are insolvent. The three major causes of failure are mismanagement, downturns in the economy, and corporate maturity.

LG 6 *Explain bankruptcy legislation and the procedures involved in reorganizing or liquidating a bankrupt firm.* The two most common forms of bankruptcy are Chapter 7 and Chapter 11 of the Bankruptcy Reform Act of 1978. A Chapter 7 bankruptcy requires that all of the assets of the firm be liquidated and distributed to the creditors. A Chapter 11 bankruptcy allows the troubled firm to reorganize under the protection of the bankruptcy court.

■ Chapter Notes

Merger fundamentals

Mergers are a form of external expansion that should be undertaken only when they are expected to enhance share value. Before reviewing the motives for merger, a few key definitions need to be considered.

Corporate restructuring—The activities involving expansion or contraction of a firm's operation or changes in its asset or financial (ownership) structure.

Merger—A merger occurs when two or more firms are combined and the resulting firm maintains the identity of one of the firms. Usually, the assets and liabilities of the smaller firm are merged into those of the larger firm.

Consolidation—Involves the combination of two or more firms to form a completely new corporation.

Holding company—A corporation that has voting control over one or more other corporations.

Acquiring versus target companies—The firm in a merger transaction that attempts to acquire another firm is commonly called the acquiring company. The firm that the acquiring company is pursuing is referred to as the target company.

Friendly versus hostile takeover—A friendly merger is a merger transaction endorsed by the target firm's management, approved by its stockholders, and easily consummated. A hostile merger is a merger transaction that is not supported by the target firm's management, forcing the acquiring company to try to gain control of the firm by buying shares in the marketplace.

Strategic versus financial mergers—Strategic mergers involve merging firms to achieve various economies of scale by eliminating redundant functions, increasing market share, and improving raw material sourcing and finished product distribution. Financial mergers are based on the acquisition of companies that can be restructured to improve their cash flow.

Motives for merging

Growth or diversification: Companies that desire rapid growth in size or market share or diversification in the range of their products may find that a merger can be used to fulfill this objective instead of going through the time-consuming process of internal growth or diversification.

Synergy: Synergy is the economies of scale resulting from the merged firms' lower overhead.

Fund raising: A firm may be unable to obtain funds for its own internal expansion but may be able to obtain funds for external business combinations.

Increased managerial skill or technology: If the firm cannot hire the management or develop the technology it needs, it might combine with a compatible firm that has the needed managerial personnel or technical expertise.

Tax considerations: In a merger, the tax benefit generally stems from the fact that one of the firms has a tax loss carryforward. This means that the company's tax loss can be applied against a limited amount of future income of the merged firm either over 15 years or until the total tax loss has been fully recovered, whichever is shorter.

Increased ownership liquidity: Increased owner liquidity results from the increased marketability associated with the shares of larger firms.

Defense against takeover: Often, when a firm becomes the target of an unfriendly takeover, it will, as a defense, acquire another company. The original target firm takes on additional debt to finance its defensive acquisition. Because of the debt load, the target firm becomes too large and too highly leveraged financially to be of any further interest to its suitor.

Types of mergers

There are four types of mergers: (1) horizontal merger, (2) vertical merger, (3) congeneric merger, and (4) conglomerate merger.

Horizontal merger—A merger of two firms in the same line of business.

Vertical merger—A merger in which a firm acquires a supplier or a customer.

Congeneric merger—A merger in which one firm acquires another firm that is in the same general industry but neither in the same line of business nor a supplier or customer.

Conglomerate merger—A merger combining firms in unrelated businesses.

LBOs and divestitures

A leveraged buyout (LBO) is an acquisition technique involving the use of a large amount of debt to purchase a firm. LBOs are an example of a financial merger undertaken to create a high-debt private corporation with improved cash flow and value. Junk bonds have been routinely used to raise the large amounts of debt needed to finance LBO transactions.

Divestiture is the selling of a firm's assets for various strategic motives. The motive for divestiture is to generate cash for expansion of other product lines, to get rid of a poorly performing operation, to streamline the corporation, or to restructure the corporation's business consistent with its strategic goals.

Analyzing and negotiating mergers

The value of the target firm can be used, along with a proposed financing scheme, to negotiate the transaction on a friendly or hostile basis. The value of the target firm could be estimated by using the valuation techniques presented in Chapter 7 and applied to long-term investment decisions in Chapters 8 and 9.

Once the value of the target company is determined, the acquirer must develop a proposed financing package. Often stock swap transactions are utilized. A stock swap transaction is an acquisition method in which the acquiring firm exchanges its shares for shares of the target company according to a predetermined ratio. The *ratio of exchange* is the ratio of the amount paid per share of the target company to the market price of the acquiring firm.

The merger negotiation process

Mergers are often handled by investment bankers—financial intermediaries hired by acquirers to find suitable target companies and assist in negotiations. A firm seeking a potential acquisition can hire an investment banker to find firms meeting its requirements.

Management negotiations: To initiate the negotiation process, the acquiring firm must make an offer either in cash or based on a stock swap with a specified ratio of exchange. The target company must then review the offer and, in light of alternative offers, accept or reject the terms presented.

Tender offers: When management negotiations for an acquisition break down, tender offers may then be used to negotiate a "hostile merger" directly with the firm's stockholders. A tender offer is a formal offer to purchase a given number of shares of a firm's stock at a specified price. Occasionally, the acquirer will make a two-tiered offer in which the terms offered are more attractive to those who tender shares early.

Fighting hostile takeovers

White knight—A takeover defense in which the target firm finds an acquirer more to its liking than the initial hostile acquirer and prompts the two to compete to take over the firm.

Poison pill—A takeover defense in which a firm issues securities that give their holders certain rights that become effective when a takeover is attempted; these rights make the target firm less desirable to a hostile acquirer. For example, a typical poison pill may give target stockholders the right to buy shares in any newly formed firm at a substantial discount below market price.

Greenmail—A takeover defense under which a target firm repurchases, through private negotiation, a large block of stock at a premium from one or more shareholders to end a hostile takeover attempt by those shareholders.

Leveraged recapitalization—A takeover defense in which the target firm pays a large debt-financed cash dividend, increasing the firm's financial leverage and deterring the takeover attempt.

Golden parachutes—Provisions in the employment contracts of key executives that provide them with sizable compensation if the firm is taken over; deters hostile takeovers to the extent that the cash outflows required are large enough to make the takeover unattractive.

Shark repellents—Anti-takeover amendments to a corporate charter that constrain the firm's ability to transfer managerial control of the firm as a result of a merger.

Holding companies

Advantages: The primary advantage of the holding company arrangement is the leveraged effect that permits the firm to control a large amount of assets with a relatively small dollar investment. Often, a pyramiding of holding companies occurs when one holding company controls other holding companies, thereby causing an even greater magnification of earnings and losses. The greater the leverage, the greater the risk involved.

Another advantage of the holding company arrangement is the risk protection resulting from the fact that the failure of one of the companies does not result in the failure of the entire holding company.

Disadvantages: The major disadvantages of the holding company arrangement are: (1) the increased risk resulting from the leverage effect, (2) double taxation, (3) difficulty to analyze, and (4) the high cost of administration.

Business failure fundamentals

Firms fail for one of three reason: (1) negative or low returns, (2) technical insolvency, and (3) bankruptcy.

Negative or low returns—If the firm fails to earn a return that is greater than its cost of capital, it can be viewed as having failed.

Technical insolvency—Business failure that occurs when a firm is unable to pay its liabilities as they come due.

Bankruptcy—Business failure that occurs when a firm's liabilities exceed the fair market value of its assets.

The major cause of business failure is mismanagement, which accounts for more than 50% of all cases. Other causes of business failure include changes in the economy and corporate maturity.

Reorganization and liquidation in bankruptcy

When a firm declares bankruptcy, the firm may either be reorganized or liquidated.

Reorganization—There are two types of reorganization petitions: voluntary and involuntary. *Voluntary reorganization* is a petition filed by a failed firm on its own behalf for reorganizing its structure and paying its creditors. An *involuntary reorganization* is a petition initiated by an outside party, usually a creditor, for the reorganization and payment of creditors of a failed firm.

Liquidation—The liquidation of a bankrupt firm usually occurs once the courts have determined that reorganization is not feasible. Liquidation consists of three important elements: (1) procedures, (2) priority of claims, and (3) final accounting. Under the procedures of liquidation, a judge may appoint a trustee to perform the many routine duties required in administering the bankruptcy. Once the trustee has overseen the payment of creditors according to the priority of claims, as outlined in Chapter 7 of the Bankruptcy Reform Act, he or she makes a final accounting to the bankruptcy court and creditors. Once the court approves the final accounting, the liquidation is complete.

Chapters 7 and 13 of the U.S. bankruptcy code also apply to individuals. Chapter 13's Wage Earner Plan lowers the debt obligations and establishes a debt-repayment schedule that is workable in light of the individual's income. In Chapter 7 personal bankruptcy the individual is able to erase virtually off of their debt obligations.

■ Sample Problems and Solutions

Example 1.   Tax effects of acquisitions

Campus Hot Dog Express is contemplating acquisition of Sidewalk Pretzels which currently has a tax loss carryforward of $8,000. The tax loss is broken into the following components.

Years Remaining to Carryforward	Amount
1	$2,000
2	2,000
3	800
4	1,200
5	800
Total Loss	$6,800

The firm expects that its earnings before taxes in the five years following the acquisition will be as follows:

Years after Acquisition	Earnings before Taxes
1	$1,800
2	2,000
3	1,000
4	1,000
5	2,000

Campus Hot Dogs is in the 40% tax bracket. Assume the tax loss carryforward is within the limits of the Tax Reform Act of 1986 and that the firm's cost of capital is 15%.

a.   Calculate the firm's tax payments without the acquisition.

b.   Calculate the firm's tax payments for each year with the proposed acquisition.

c.   What is the most Campus Hot Dogs should pay for Sidewalk Pretzels if its only value was the tax loss?

Solution

a.   Without the acquisition, the tax payments would be 40% of the before-tax earnings as follows:

Years	Tax Payment
1	$720
2	800
3	400
4	400
5	800

b.   If the firm were to make the acquisition, it would use the tax losses to lower its liabilities. The required calculations are given in tabular form as follows:

Year	Earnings before Taxes	Application of Tax Loss	Taxable Income	Tax Payment
1	$1,800	$1,800	0	0
2	2,000	2,000	0	0
3	1,000	1,000	0	0
4	1,000	1,000	0	0
5	2,000	1,000	1,000	400

c.   Campus Hot Dogs should not pay more than the present value of the net tax benefit. The net tax benefit of the proposed acquisition can be found by calculating the difference in tax payments without and with the acquisition, from parts **a**. and **b**.

Years	Net Tax Benefit
1	$720
2	800
3	400
4	400
5	400

The present value of the net tax benefit at 15% is $1,921.58 (by calculator).

Example 2.   Asset acquisition decision

Tar River Water Skis is contemplating acquisition of the Stay-Float Life Vest company for a cash price of $275,000. The Tar River Water Ski company is very highly leveraged and therefore has a cost of capital of 13%. As a result of acquiring Stay-Float, which is entirely financed with equity, Tar River expects its cost of capital to drop to 11%. Acquisition of Stay-Float is expected to increase Tar River's cash inflows by $40,000 per year for the next 15 years. Determine whether or not the proposed cash acquisition is desirable.

Solution

This is a standard capital budgeting problem. Find the present value of the $40,000 cash inflows at 11% and compare this present value to the purchase price.

$$\text{Net present value} = [7.191 \times \$40,000] - \$275,000 = \$12,640$$

Since the net present value is positive, Tar River Skis should go ahead with the acquisition. Keep in mind that in reality the decision should be based on your confidence in the accuracy of the forecasted cash flows and discount rate. The fact that many mergers turn out to be failures indicates that managers have trouble accurately forecasting these future numbers.

Example 3.   Earnings per share

Executive Dog Kennels wishes to evaluate the effect of a proposed merger on its long-run earnings per share. The firm's 2008 earnings were $600,000, and the firm has 200,000 shares of common stock outstanding. The firm is considering acquiring Pooper Scooper Limited, which has 50,000 shares of common stock outstanding on which it earned $250,000. The earnings of Pooper Scooper are expected to grow at a rate of 4% each year, while Executive Dog Kennel's earnings are expected to grow at an annual rate of 10%. The proposed ratio of exchange is 2.0.

a.   Calculate Executive's earnings per share for each year in the 2008–2015 period, assuming that it does not merge.

b.   Calculate Executive's earnings per share for each year in the 2008–2015 period, assuming that it does merge.

c.   What recommendation would you make?

Solution

a. In 2008, Executive earned $600,000 on its 200,000 outstanding shares, giving it earnings per share of $3($600,000/200,000). Applying an annual growth rate of 4% yields the following earnings per share for the 2008–2015 period.

Year	Earnings per Share
2008	$3.00
2009	3.12
2010	3.24
2011	3.37
2012	3.51
2013	3.60
2014	3.80
2015	3.95

b. If Executive Dog Kennels and Pooper Scooper merge, using a 2.0 ratio of exchange, an additional 100,000 shares would be issued (2.0 × 50,000 shares of Pooper), resulting in a total of 300,000 shares outstanding after the merger (200,000 shares + 100,000 shares). To find the earnings per share after the merger, the differing growth rates must be applied to the earnings streams, and then these earnings must be summed to get total earnings. Dividing the total earnings by the 300,000 shares then outstanding would give the postmerger earnings per share, calculated in tabular form as follows:

Year	Executive Dog Kennels Earnings (4% growth)	Pooper Scooper Earnings (10% growth)	Total Earnings	Postmerger Earnings per Share
2008	$600,000	$250,000	$850,000	$2.83
2009	624,000	275,000	899,000	3.00
2010	648,960	302,500	951,460	3.17
2011	674,918	332,750	1,007,668	3.36
2012	701,925	366,025	1,067,940	3.56
2013	729,992	402,628	1,132,620	3.78
2014	759,192	442,891	1,202,083	4.01
2015	789,560	487,180	1,276,740	4.26

$850,000/300,000

c. This would be a difficult call. It can be seen that, although the earnings per share are largest initially without the merger, after 2012 the merged firm would be expected to have greater earnings per share. The decision should be based on management's confidence in the accuracy of the forecasts, competitive pressures, and the value of other investment opportunities.

■ Study Tips

1. Corporate restructuring includes *both* expansion and contraction of a firm's operations.

2. Leveraged buyouts (LBOs) are an acquisition technique involving a large amount of debt. In the past, the funds were often raised by issuing junk bonds.

3. Mergers can be negotiated with the target's management (a friendly takeover) or with shareholders (a hostile takeover).

4. Review the three basic types of business failure. Note the most common causes of business failure.

5. Bankruptcy law allows firms to reorganize while being protected from claims by creditors. The threat of declaring a Chapter 11 bankruptcy can often be used to force creditors to cooperate when a firm is struggling.

■ Student Notes

_____

_____

_____

_____

_____

■ Sample Exam—Chapter 17

True/False

T F 1. Consolidation involves the combination of two or more firms, and the resulting firm maintains the identity of one of the firms.

T F 2. Vertical merger is a merger of two firms in the same line of business.

T F 3. The synergy of merger is the economies of scale resulting from the merged firms' lower overhead.

T F 4. LBOs are an example of a financial merger undertaken to create a high-debt private corporation with improved cash flow and value.

T F 5. Congeneric merger is a merger in which a firm acquires a supplier or a customer.

T F 6. The motive for divestiture is often to get rid of a product line in order to generate cash for expansion of other product lines.

T F 7. A stock swap transaction is an acquisition method in which the acquiring firm exchanges its shares for shares of the target company according to a predetermined ratio.

T   F   8.   A two-tier offer is a tender offer in which the terms offered are more attractive to those who tender shares early.

T   F   9.   Horizontal merger is a merger in which one firm acquires another firm in the same general industry but neither in the same line of business nor a supplier or a customer.

T   F   10. Poison pill is a takeover defense in which the target firm finds an acquirer more to its liking than the initial hostile acquirer and prompts the two to compete to take over the firm.

T   F   11. Pyramiding is an arrangement among holding companies wherein one company controls others, thereby causing an even greater magnification of earnings and losses.

T   F   12. Technical insolvency occurs when a firm's liabilities exceed the fair market value of its assets.

T   F   13. Under recapitalization, debts are generally exchanged for equity, or the maturities of existing debts are extended.

T   F   14. Mergers are often handled by investment bankers that find suitable target companies and assist in negotiations.

T   F   15. The tax loss carryforward benefits can be used in mergers but cannot be used in the formation of holding companies.

Multiple Choice

1. The combination of two or more companies to form a completely new corporation is a
    a.   merger.
    b.   consolidation.
    c.   congeneric formation.
    d.   holding company.

2. The firm in a merger transaction that attempts to merge or take over another company is called the
    a.   conglomerate.
    b.   target company.
    c.   acquiring company.
    d.   holding company.

3. The combination of two or more companies which results in one of the corporations having a voting control of one or more of the other companies is a
    a.   merger.
    b.   congeneric formation.
    c.   consolidation.
    d.   holding company.

4. _____ involves the combination of firms in unrelated businesses.
    a.   Conglomerate merger
    b.   Horizontal merger
    c.   Vertical merger
    d.   Congeneric merger

5. Typically, reasons for undertaking mergers are
   a. in conflict with wealth maximization.
   b. only strategic.
   c. only financial.
   d. strategic or financial.

6. A hostile merger is typically accomplished through
   a. an exchange of the acquirer's stock.
   b. a cash purchase.
   c. a tender offer.
   d. an exchange of the acquirer's bonds.

7. A _____ is undertaken with the goal of restructuring the acquired company in order to improve its cash flow and unlock its hidden value.
   a. financial merger
   b. strategic merger
   c. hostile takeover
   d. friendly takeover

8. The sale of a unit of a firm to existing management is often achieved through
   a. a cash exchange.
   b. a leveraged buyout.
   c. a limited partnership.
   d. an employee stock option.

9. The selling of some of a firm's assets is called
   a. reverse merger.
   b. vertical segmentation.
   c. business failure.
   d. divestiture.

10. Leveraged buyouts are clear examples of
    a. congeneric mergers.
    b. vertical mergers.
    c. financial mergers.
    d. strategic mergers.

11. A formal proposal to purchase a given number of shares of a firm's stock at a specified price is a
    a. tender offer.
    b. warrant.
    c. stock purchase option.
    d. right.

12. The stakeholders in targeted takeover companies include the
    a. stockholders.
    b. employees.
    c. creditors.
    d. all the above.

13. In defending against a hostile takeover, the strategy that involves the target firm creating securities that give their holders certain rights that become effective when a takeover is attempted is called the _____ strategy.
    a. golden parachute
    b. greenmail
    c. poison pill
    d. shark repellent

14. Business failure may be caused by all of the following EXCEPT
    a. economic downturns.
    b. increasing liquidity.
    c. mismanagement.
    d. corporate maturity.

15. _____ is an arrangement whereby the firm's creditors receive full payment, although not immediately.
    a. A liquidation
    b. A composition
    c. An extension
    d. A creditor control agreement

16. _____ may replace the operating management with a selected creditor.
    a. A credit control agreement
    b. A liquidation
    c. A composition
    d. An extension

17. When the ratio of exchange in a merger is equal to one and both the acquiring and the target companies have the same premerger earnings per share, the merged firm's earnings per share will initially
    a. increase.
    b. remain constant.
    c. drop to zero.
    d. decline.

18. All of the following are disadvantages of the holding company arrangement EXCEPT
    a. increased risk.
    b. double taxation.
    c. the high cost of administration.
    d. increased leverage.

19. Mergers are often handled by _____ that help find suitable target companies and assist in negotiations.
    a. management consultants
    b. brokerage houses
    c. investment bankers
    d. merger analysts

20. A(n) _____ is a form of divestiture in which an operating unit becomes an independent company.
    a. spin-off
    b. vertical merger
    c. leveraged buyout
    d. internal acquisition

21. The Van Dalsems' one son is now 2 years old and Shane and Jodi are evaluating the economic impact if Jodi reentered the workforce. If Jodi returned to her prior employer, she could earn $1,900 per month; however income and other payroll taxes would be approximately $500 per month. Her employer offers a variety of insurance and pension contribution benefits worth an estimated $475 per month. The cost of child care will be $520 per month. Other transportation, meal, clothing and related expenses would be $260 per month. Based on economic grounds, what would be the net gain from Jodi returning to the workforce?
    a. $1,095
    b. $1,355
    c. $1,615
    d. $1,825

22. The Wage Earner Plan, defined under Chapter 13 of the U.S. Bankruptcy Code:
    a. is similar to reorganization under corporate bankruptcy.
    b. results in late fees during the repayment period.
    c. requires forfeiture of home, auto, and most assets.
    d. wipes the slate clean, so the individual can start anew.

23. Which of the following is a false statement with regards to Chapter 7 of the U.S. Bankruptcy Code?
    a. Chapter 7 applies to both corporations and individuals.
    b. Chapter 7 bankruptcy requires individuals to continue making alimony and child support payments.
    c. Chapter 7 does not prohibit subsequent payments from Social Security, disability, and retirement programs.
    d. Chapter 7 requires individuals to make payment to the court, which then pays off creditors.

Essay

1. What are the usual reasons for mergers?

2. Distinguish between Chapter 7 and Chapter 11 bankruptcy.

■ Chapter 17 Answer Sheet

True/False

1. F
2. F
3. T
4. T
5. F
6. T
7. T
8. T
9. F
10. F
11. T
12. F
13. T
14. T
15. T

Multiple Choice

1. B
2. C
3. D
4. A
5. D
6. C
7. A
8. B
9. D
10. C
11. A
12. D
13. C
14. B
15. C
16. A
17. B
18. D
19. C
20. A
21. A
22. A
23. D

Essay

1. Firms merge for a large number of reasons. One important motivation is for rapid growth. There may also be synergies that can be captured by reducing overhead and duplicate costs. Often firms combine to increase their fund raising ability. There may be deficiencies in management ability or tax consequences. Finally, a merger may be motivated by an unsolicited takeover attempt.

2. Firms file Chapter 7 when they feel recovery from their problems is unlikely. Chapter 7 spells out how to liquidate the firm. Chapter 11 bankruptcy outlines how a firm can reorganize its business. It provides some breathing room from creditors while management initiates a new business plan.

Chapter 18
International Financial Management

■ Chapter Summary

This chapter provides a brief introduction to international finance. Of course, whole courses and even degree programs are offered on this topic. The reason for its inclusion here is the growing importance of international business and the globalization of product markets. This chapter introduces some of the issues confronting multinational firms and the additional risk these firms take by venturing into other countries.

LG 1 *Understand the major factors influencing the financial operations of multinational companies (MNCs).* Multinational firms must be concerned with different taxes in foreign countries. Accounting rules may differ from their country of origin, requiring multiple sets of books. The North American Free Trade Agreement (NAFTA), the European Community (EC), and the Mercorsur group have been developed to allow more efficient cross-boundary business. Multinationals may use the Euromarkets for raising both long-term and short-term funds.

LG 2 *Describe the key differences between purely domestic and international financial statements— consolidation, translation of individual accounts, and international profits.* U.S. companies must consolidate their financial statements to reflect subsidiaries. The amount of reporting depends on the percentage of ownership in the subsidiary. International companies must translate all items back into U.S. dollars.

LG 3 *Discuss exchange rate risk and political risk and explain how MNCs manage them.* Exchange rate risk is caused by varying exchange rates between two currencies. In the time between when a contract is negotiated and when it is concluded, exchange rate movements can adversely affect the profits on a business transaction. Many firms hedge exchange rates to reduce this risk. Political risk refers to the chance that a foreign government may enact rules and regulations that adversely affect the operations of a firm.

LG 4 *Describe foreign direct investment cash flows and decisions, the MNC's capital structure, and the international debt and equity instruments available to MNCs.* Foreign direct investment involves transfer of monetary and managerial assets to a foreign country. The local cost of equity capital is the starting point for estimating the discount rate used in project evaluation. Capital structures of multinational firms differ from those of domestic firms due to access to international capital markets, international diversification, and country factors.

LG 5 *Discuss the role of the Eurocurrency market in short-term borrowing and investing (lending) and the basics of international cash, credit, and inventory management.* In addition to the normal domestic sources of short-term financing, multinational firms can take advantage of Eurocurrency markets. Effective interest rates depend upon the nominal interest rates and an adjustment for changes in currency values.

LG 6 *Review recent trends in international mergers and joint ventures. International mergers are motivated by many of the same considerations that motivate domestic mergers.* Diversification, synergy, fund raising, increased managerial skill or technology, tax considerations, and defense against takeovers are reasons for international mergers.

■ Chapter Notes

The multinational company and its environment

Multinational companies (MNCs) are firms that have international assets and operations in foreign markets and draw part of their total revenue and profits from such markets. MNC activities are fostered through trading blocs and trade agreements.

Several important trading blocs have emerged, centered in North America, South America and Western Europe. The *North American Free Trade Agreement* (NAFTA) was signed by the presidents of the United States and Mexico and by the prime minister of Canada and it established free trade and open markets between Canada, Mexico, and the United States. In Europe, the *European Union* (EU) has been in existence since 1957. This single market has overall gross national income that is comparable to the United States and a much larger population.

The Maastricht Treaty of 1991 joined eleven nations with a single currency, the Euro. In the year 2002, the national currencies of all eleven countries participating in the monetary union disappeared, replaced by the Euro. Currently, over a dozen of its 27 members use the Euro as their national currency.

The third trading bloc is the Mercorsur Group of countries in South America. Brazil, Argentina, Paraguay and Uruguay removed barriers to intra-regional trade. An even larger trading bloc is ASEAN (Association of South East Asian Nations), which will include China in 2010 and encompass 1.8 billion people. Individual countries and trading blocs also sign trade agreements with other nations.

Taxes

Multinational companies have financial obligations in foreign countries in the form of taxes. This is often a complex issue because national governments follow a variety of tax policies. When examining taxation for a multinational firm, several factors need to be taken into account. First, foreign tax rates need to be examined. Second, *taxable income* in the foreign country needs to be defined. Third, the tax rules of the foreign country need to be examined. The U.S. government claims jurisdiction over all MNC income. However, the MNC may receive a credit for the foreign taxes paid.

Financial Markets

The *Euromarket* is the international financial market that provides for borrowing and lending currencies outside their country of origin. The Euromarket has experienced rapid growth and one reason for this is that it provides multinational companies with an "external" opportunity to borrow or lend funds with the additional feature of less government regulation. The Euromarket is dominated by the U.S. dollar and Euro.

One aspect of the Euromarket is the offshore centers which are certain cities or states (including London, Singapore, Bahrain, Nassau, Hong Kong, and Luxembourg) that have achieved prominence as major centers for Euromarket business. Although national governments have slowed their borrowing, MNCs continue to acquire vast sums in international markets.

Financial Statements

Several features distinguish domestically oriented financial statements and internationally based financial reports. Among these are the issues of consolidation, translation of individual accounts within the financial statements, and overall reporting of international profits.

Translation of individual accounts: International items in the firm's financial statements must be translated back into U.S. dollars.

International profits: Only certain transactional gains or losses—as defined in FASB No. 52—that are the result of exchange fluctuations are required to be reported in the firm's income statement. In the case of a self-sustaining foreign entity, the current-rate method is used. In the current-rate method foreign currency is translated into the currency in which the subsidiary normally does business. Gains and losses are charged to net income. In the next step, functional currency-dominated statements are translated to the parent company's currency. Translation gains and losses are charged to the MNC stockholder's equity accounts. The temporal method is employed when there is excessive inflation–historic exchange rates are used.

Risk

Two risks requiring special consideration by the multinational firm involve exchange rates and political factors relating to the policies and actions of host governments.

Relationships among currencies

The foreign exchange rate is defined as the value of two currencies with respect to each other. This exchange rate can be based on a floating relationship or a fixed relationship. A *floating relationship* means that the value of any two currencies with respect to each other is allowed to fluctuate on a daily basis. A *fixed (or semi-fixed) relationship* is the constant relationship of a currency to one of the major currencies, a combination (basket) of major currencies, or some type of international foreign exchange standard.

On any given day the relationship between any two of the major currencies will contain two sets of figures, one reflecting the *spot exchange rate*—the rate on that day—and the other indicating the *forward exchange rate*— the rate at some specified future date.

As a result of the fluctuations in exchange rates, two different types of risk can be encountered. *Accounting exposure* is the risk resulting from the effects of changes in foreign exchange rates on the translated value of a firm's financial statement accounts denominated in a given foreign currency. *Economic exposure* is the risk resulting from the effect of changes in foreign exchange rates on the firm's value.

Political risks

Political risk refers to the implementation by a host government of specific rules and regulations that can result in the discontinuity or seizure of the operations of a foreign company in that country. Political risks can be broken down into either macro or micro risk. *Macro political risk* refers to the subjection of all foreign firms to political risk (takeover) by a host country because of political change, revolution, or the adoption of new policies. *Micro political risk* refers to the subjection of an individual firm, a specific industry, or companies from a particular foreign country to political risk (takeover) by the host country.

Long-term investment and financing decisions

Multinational firms make long-term investments by transferring money and other assets from their home country to a host country and obtain long-term financing by issuing debt and equity in the international capital markets. Important long-term aspects of international manager/finance include foreign direct investment, investment cash flows and decisions, capital structure, long-term debt, and equity capital.

Foreign direct investment (FDI): FDI is the transfer by a multinational firm of capital, managerial, and technical assets from its home country to a host country. Estimating the amount of FDI should be based on the market value of the assets, which in turn is based on circumstances in the host country. In order to identify the appropriate discount rate, one should begin with the local cost of equity capital, augmented by exchange and political risks, and reduced by the benefit of being able to use the parent company's lower cost of capital. While most FDI enters the United States through the mergers and acquisitions process, FDI in emerging countries is primarily through establishment of new operations.

Several options are readily available to the MNCs in respect to long-term debt financing. The most popular is the *international bond*, which is a bond that is initially sold outside the country of the borrower and is often distributed in several countries. When the international bond is sold primarily in the country of the currency of the issue, it is called a *foreign bond*. When the international bond is sold primarily in countries other than the country of the currency in which the issue is denominated, it is called a *Eurobond*. MNCs use interest rate and currency swaps to hedge liabilities and assets.

MNCs can raise equity capital by (1) selling their shares of stock in international capital markets, or (2) utilizing joint ventures.

Short-term financial decisions

The *Eurocurrency market* offers nondomestic short-term borrowing and investing (lending) opportunities to the subsidiaries of MNCs.

MNCs can use hedging techniques to protect themselves against certain cash and marketable securities exposures. *Hedging techniques* in the international context include borrowing or lending in different currencies, undertaking contracts in the forward, futures, and/or options markets, and also swapping assets/liabilities with other parties.

Mergers and joint ventures

International mergers and joint ventures are formed for reasons similar to those motivating domestic mergers. Among these motives are growth or diversification, synergy, fund raising, increased managerial skill or technology, tax considerations, increased ownership liquidity, and defense against takeover.

■ Sample Problems and Solutions

Example 1.   Exchange rates

Cappuccino Distributors Inc. has a subsidiary in Mexico. The present exchange rate is U.S. $.1641/Peso or 16.41 cents per peso. Cappuccino makes cash outlays of 20 million pesos per year to Mexican suppliers. The subsidiary has an average collection period of 60 days, an average inventory age of 40 days, and an average payment period of 30 days. Cappuccino can adjust operations to change any of the 3 periods by 10 days (longer or shorter).

a.   What is the present peso minimum cash balance and dollar equivalent?

b.   If the peso is expected to appreciate to U.S $ 0.20/Peso, what adjustments should be made in the time periods?

c.   Calculate the foreign exchange gain in U.S. dollars for both the present cash cycle and the cycle indicated in part **b**, ignoring financing costs.

Solution

a.   The cash cycle is $60 + 40 - 30 = 70$ days.

The annual cash turnover is $(360 \text{ days} \div 70) = 5.14$ times.

In pesos, the minimum cash balance is $20,000,000 \div 5.14 = 3,891,051$ pesos.

In U.S. dollars, the minimum cash balance is

$3,891,051$ pesos $\times$ U.S. $0.1641 = $ U.S. $638,521.30$.

b. If the currency is expected to appreciate, the firm should increase assets and decrease liabilities. Here, the subsidiary should increase the collection period to 70 days, increase the average age of inventory to 50 days, and reduce payables to 20 days.

The new cash cycle is $70 + 50 - 20 = 100$ days.

The annual cash turnover is $(360 \text{ days} \div 100) = 3.6$ times.

In pesos, the minimum cash balance is $20,000,000 \div 3.6 = 5,555,556$ pesos.

In U.S. dollars, the minimum cash balance is

$5,555,556$ pesos $\times$ U.S. $\$0.20 = $ U.S. $\$1,111,111.20$.

c. Compare the foreign exchange gain that would have been received in part **a** with the gain that would have been received in part **b**. In both cases, the gain is $U.S. 0.0328 (0.20-0.1641) per peso times the minimum cash balance.

Present (part **a**): $3,891,050 \times$ U.S. $\$0.0328 = $ U.S.$\$127,626.44$

Change (part **b**): $5,555,556 \times$ U.S. $\$0.0328 = $ U.S.$\$182,222.23$

The net gain on adjustment is $\$182,222.23 - \$127,626.44 = \$54,595.79$.

The trick here is to accurately predict the relative change in exchange rates. Had the change gone the other way, losses would have occurred.

Example 2.   Translation of financial statement

A U.S. based multinational company, Chocolate Goodies, has a subsidiary in Switzerland. The balance sheet and income statement of the subsidiary are shown below. On 12/31/08, the exchange rate is SFr1.50/U.S.$. Assume that the local (Swiss franc, Sfr) figures remain the same on 12/31/09. The average Sfr$ rate of 2008 is Sfr1.50/US$ and Sfr1.55/U.S.$ in 2009. Assume all profits are paid out (repatriated) as dividends.

a. Complete the US$ translated figures for 12/31/08.

b. Complete the US$ translated figures for 12/31/09, assuming the U.S. dollar appreciates to Sfr1.60/U.S.$. Use the figure below to prepare your answers.

	12/31/08 Sfr	12/31/08 U.S. $	12/31/09 U.S. $
Cash	50		
Inventory	250		
Plant and Equipment	350		
Total	650		
Debt	300		
Paid-in Capital	150		
Retained Earnings	200		
Total	600		
Sales	4000		
Cost of Goods Sold	3200		
Operating Profits	800		

Solution

	12/31/08 Sfr	12/31/08 U.S. $	12/31/09 U.S. $
Cash	50	33.33	31.25
Inventory	250	166.67	156.25
Plant and Equipment	350	233.33	218.75
Total	650	433.33	406.25
Debt	300	200.00	187.50
Paid-in Capital	150	100.00	93.75
Retained Earnings	200	133.33	125.00
Total	600	433.33	406.25
Sales	4000	2666.67	2580.65
Cost of Goods Sold	3200	2133.33	2064.52
Operating Profits	800	533.33	516.13

■ Study Tips

1. Multinational companies (MNCs) can be defined as firms headquartered anywhere that generate a portion of their total revenue from operations in markets foreign to the location of their home office.

2. Special features of MNC financial statements include subsidiary characterization, functional currency, translation of foreign amounts to U.S. dollars, and techniques of reporting international profits.

3. Foreign exchange rate risk and political risk are two special risks affecting MNCs.

4. In addition to the normal domestic sources of short-term financing, multinational firms can take advantage of Eurocurrency markets.

5. Domestic and multinational firms merge for the same reasons.

■ Student Notes

_____

_____

_____

_____

_____

■ Sample Exam—Chapter 18

True/False

T F   1. A joint venture is a partnership under which the participants have contractually agreed to contribute specified amounts of money and expertise in exchange for stated proportions of ownership and profit.

T F   2. Functional currency is the currency of the economic environment in which a business entity primarily generates and expends cash, and in which its accounts are maintained.

T F   3. Multinational companies only face foreign exchange risks under the fixed currency arrangement.

T F   4. The three basic types of risk associated with international cash flows are (1) business and financial risks, (2) inflation and foreign exchange risks, and (3) political risks.

T F   5. The Euromarket is dominated by the Deutsche mark.

T F   6. The interest rates offered in the Euromarket on the U.S. dollar are greatly affected by the prime rate inside the United States.

T F   7. In the international context, the effective interest rate equals the nominal rate plus (or minus) any forecast appreciation (or depreciation) of a foreign currency relative to the currency of the MNC parent.

T F   8. Accounting exposure is the risk resulting from the effects of changes in foreign exchange rates on the translated value of a firm's financial statement accounts denominated in a given foreign currency.

T F   9. The Euromarket is the international financial market that provides for borrowing and lending currencies in Europe.

T F 10. In the case of short-term financing, the forces of supply and demand are among the main factors determining exchange rates in Eurocurrency markets.

T F 11. Economic exposure is the risk resulting from the effects of changes in foreign exchange rates on the firm's value.

T F 12. National entry controls systems are aimed at regulating the Eurocurrency market.

T F 13. The nominal interest rate, in the international context, is the stated interest rate charged on financing when only the MNC parent's currency is involved.

T F 14. Adjustments in the MNC's operations can be used to hedge against exchange rate fluctuations.

T F 15. The motives for domestic mergers differ greatly from the motives for international mergers.

Multiple Choice

1. The General Agreement on Tariffs and Trade (GATT) treaty has established the _____ to police trading practices and to mediate disputes between member countries.
   a. Aktiengesllschaft (GmbH)
   b. International Crime Police (Interpol)
   c. Societe Anonyme (S.A.)
   d. World Trade Organization (WTO)

2. All of the following are considered offshore centers EXCEPT
   a. Costa Rica.
   b. Singapore.
   c. Hong Kong.
   d. London.

3. The Euromarket is dominated by the
   a. Mexican peso.
   b. Japanese yen.
   c. French franc.
   d. U.S. dollar.

4. When fewer units of a foreign currency are required to buy one dollar, the currency is said to have _____ with respect to the dollar.
   a. consolidated
   b. appreciated
   c. depreciated
   d. remained fixed

5. The risk resulting from the effects of changes in foreign exchange rates on the translated value of a firm's accounts denominated in a given foreign currency is
   a. micro political risk.
   b. economic exposure.
   c. accounting exposure.
   d. macro political risk.

6. All of the following are considered to be major or "hard" currencies EXCEPT
   a. the Mexican peso.
   b. the Japanese yen.
   c. the U.S. dollar.
   d. the British pound.

7. Between two major currencies, the spot exchange rate is the rate _____ and the forward exchange rate is the rate
   a. today; on that date.
   b. on that date; today.
   c. at some specified future date; today.
   d. on that date; at some specified future date.

8. The transfer by a multinational firm of capital, managerial, and technical assets from its home country to a host country is termed
   a. an RDO.
   b. an FDI.
   c. an SDI.
   d. an ADR.

9. The center of the Euro-equity market, which deals in international equity issues is
   a. Hong Kong.
   b. Tokyo.
   c. London.
   d. New York.

10. Foreign bonds are sold primarily in
    a. the United States.
    b. Europe.
    c. Japan.
    d. the country of the currency of issue.

11. The _____ offers nondomestic short-term borrowing and investing opportunities to the multinational firm.
    a. Eurocurrency market
    b. Euro-equity market
    c. international bond market
    d. foreign direct investment bank

12. _____ are used to offset or protect against risk.
    a. FDIs
    b. Hedging strategies
    c. Joint ventures
    d. Share-issue privatizations

13. All of the following must be examined when evaluating the tax policies of multinational firms EXCEPT
    a. foreign tax rates.
    b. foreign definition of taxable income.
    c. foreign country's tax base.
    d. foreign tax rules.

14. The _____ refers to the transformation of the European Community into a single market.
    a. Euromarket
    b. European Open Market
    c. Euro-equity market
    d. Eurocurrency market

15. A(n) _____ is a partnership under which the participants have contractually agreed to contribute specified amounts of money and expertise in exchange for stated proportions of ownership and profit.
    a. limited partnership
    b. proprietorship
    c. S corporation
    d. joint venture

16. The _____ is the European Community's denomination of currency.
    a. Euro
    b. British Pound
    c. Deutsche Mark
    d. EC

17. The usual exchange rate quotation in international markets is given as _____ where the unit of the account is the Euro and the unit of currency being priced is 1 U.S. dollar.
    a. €1.00 = C$1.34
    b. US$1.83/€
    c. €1.83/US$
    d. US$ 3:1€

18. A _____ is an international bond that is sold primarily in countries other than the country of the currency in which the issue is denominated.
    a. foreign bond
    b. Eurobond
    c. hedge bond
    d. capitalization bond

19. NAFTA was signed by the leaders of all of the following countries EXCEPT
    a. United States.
    b. Mexico.
    c. Canada.
    d. Chile.

20. All of the following are used as exchange rate risk hedging tools EXCEPT
    a. FDIs.
    b. currency swaps.
    c. options contracts.
    d. futures contracts.

21. Which of the following countries has the highest corporate tax rate and yet is among the largest recipients of foreign direct investment?
    a. Australia
    b. Ireland
    c. United Kingdom
    d. United States

22. Kathy Anderson, a sports fanatic living in Chicago, is making plans to attend the 2010 Winter Olympics in Vancouver, British Columbia. Looking at a variety of web sites has revealed that travel aboard United Airlines will cost US$ 601, and staying at the Vancouver Holiday Inn will cost CAN$400 per night. Event tickets will range from CAN$50 to CAN$500 for popular events such as hockey, figure skating, and the Olympics' opening ceremony. Consequently, over her weeklong stay, Kathy is expecting to spend CAN$2000 on tickets. Meals over her seven-day/six-night stay will cost about CAN$75 per day. In addition, Kathy expects to spend another US$400 on gifts and souvenirs. If Kathy can lock in an exchange rate of US$0.88/CAN$, using foreign currency futures, what is the US$ cost of her trip?
   a. $5,251
   b. $5,335
   c. $5,696
   d. $6,338

23. Reasons for individuals to invest abroad include:
   a. benefiting from the devaluation of the US$.
   b. capitalizing on foreign direct investment.
   c. earning a higher return with less risk when foreign stocks account for 30% of one's stock portfolio.
   d. all of the above

24. The _____ is the preferred currency of central banks, although there is a greater circulation of the _____, which is also the dominant currency in international bond market trading.
   a. Euro; British pound
   b. Euro, U.S. dollar
   c. U.S. dollar; Euro
   d. U.S. dollar; Japanese yen

Essay

1. What special risks do multinational companies face?

2. What additional sources of financing are available to multinational companies?

■ Chapter 18 Answer Sheet

True/False		Multiple Choice	
1.	T	1.	D
2.	T	2.	A
3.	F	3.	D
4.	T	4.	B
5.	F	5.	C
6.	T	6.	A
7.	T	7.	D
8.	T	8.	B
9.	F	9.	C
10.	T	10.	D
11.	T	11.	A
12.	F	12.	B
13.	T	13.	C
14.	T	14.	B
15.	F	15.	D
		16.	A
		17.	C
		18.	B
		19.	D
		20.	A
		21.	D
		22.	B
		23.	D
		24.	C

Essay

1. MNCs face exchange rate and political risk. Exchange rate risk occurs due to the changing exchange rates between two countries doing business. Political risk stems mainly from political instability in a number of countries and from the associated implication for the assets and operations of MNCs with subsidiaries located in such countries.

2. MNCs have access to Eurocurrency markets in addition to their domestic sources of funds. The Eurocurrency markets allow multinationals to take advantage of unregulated financial markets to invest and raise short-term funds in a variety of currencies and to protect themselves against foreign exchange risk exposures.

Using the Financial Calculator

The majority of business and financial calculators offer a wide range of powerful functions. Students in the introductory finance course generally do not need to utilize all of these functions and most often find them confusing. The purpose of this appendix is to provide you with an easy and quick reference guide for some of the most commonly used financial functions.

The appendix discusses the basic functions of two of the most commonly used financial calculators, the Texas Instruments TIBAII Plus and the Hewlett Packard HP10B. After every example, the step-by-step process for the TIBAII Plus is outlined with the appropriate keystrokes, the display that will be shown on the calculator, and a description of the logic behind each step. Due to space constraints, the guide for the HP10B is not accompanied by a description section. For an explanation of the logic for the HP10B, simply refer to the step in the TIBAII Plus guide that corresponds with the step in the HP10B guide. The HP10B guide is utilized by following the steps in the left hand column and then proceeding with the steps in the right hand column.

TIBAII Plus

The TIBAII Plus is capable of performing four sets of functions. For the purpose of this appendix, only two sets are of importance. The first set of functions are the ones that are written on the face of the keys. The second set of functions are initiated by pressing the white "second function" key, which is located in the second row from the top of the keypad.

The second function key will be represented by 2nd in this appendix.

HP10B

The HP10B performs two sets of functions. Pressing the shift key invokes the function written at the top of any key. The shift key is situated on the lower left hand side of the calculator key pad and is yellow in color.

The shift key will be denoted as SHIFT in this appendix.

Calculating the present value of a lump sum amount

Example: Todd estimates that it will cost his son $55,000 to attend college in 4 years. How much should he invest today, at an annual interest rate of 12% (compounded monthly), to be able to send his son to college in 4 years?

TIBAII Plus

Keystrokes				Display	Description
2nd	CLRTVM			0.00	Clears the time-value-of-money worksheet
2nd	P/Y	12	ENTER	P/Y = 12.00	Sets the number of periods per year to 12
2nd	Quit			0.00	Brings the calculator to standard mode
55000	FV			FV = 55,000.00	Records the future cash flow of $55,000
12	I/Y			I/Y = 12.00	Records the periodic rate of interest as 12%
4	2nd		×P/Y	48.00	Calculates the number of time periods as 48
N				N = 48.00	Stores the number of time periods
CPT	PV			PV = −4,114.32	Calculates the present value of $55,000 in 4 years discounted at a monthly rate of 1%

Note: The display in the last step has a negative sign because it represents a cash outflow (investment) today.

HP10B

Keystrokes			Display		Keystrokes		Display
55000	FV		55,000.00	4	×P/YR		48
12	SHIFT	P/YR	12.00		PV		−34,114.32
12	I/YR		12.00				

Common error: When an incorrect answer is computed by the calculator, the usual mistake is a mismatch between the number of periods per year and the periodic interest rate. For example, make sure that you are not using a monthly interest rate with annual compounding.

Calculating the future value of a lump sum amount

Example: If Jack invests $5,000 today in an asset earning an 8% rate of return (compounded annually), how much will he have after 3 years?

TIBAII Plus

Keystrokes				Display	Description
2nd	CLRTVM			0.00	Clears the time-value-of-money worksheet
2nd	P/Y	1	ENTER	P/Y = 1.00	Sets the number of periods per year to 1
2nd	Quit			0.00	Brings the calculator to standard mode
5000	+/−		PV	PV = −5,000.00	Records the present cash outflow of $5,000
8	I/Y			I/Y = 8.00	Records the periodic rate of interest as 8%
3	N			N = 3.00	Stores the number of time periods
CPT	FV			FV = 6,298.56	Calculates the future value of $5,000 after 3 years compounded at 8%

HP10B

Keystrokes			Display	Keystrokes		Display
5000	+/−	PV	−5,000.00	3	N	3
1	SHIFT	P/YR	2.00	FV		6,298.56
8	I/YR		8.00			

Calculating the present value of an annuity

Example: How much should you invest today so that, starting 2 years from today, you can receive $4,000 per year for the next 4 years? Assume the discount rate is 14%.

TIBAII Plus

Keystrokes				Display	Description
2nd	CLRTVM			0.00	Clears the time-value-of-money worksheet
2nd	P/Y	1	ENTER	P/Y = 1.00	Sets the number of periods per year to 1
2nd	Quit			0.00	Brings the calculator to standard mode
4000	PMT			PMT = 4,000.00	Records the amount of the periodic payment
14	I/Y			I/Y = 14.00	Records the annual rate of interest as 14%
4	N			N = 4.00	Stores the number of time periods
CPT	PV			PV = −11,654.85	Calculates the present value of the annuity

HP10B

Keystrokes			Display	Keystrokes		Display
4000	PMT		4,000.00	4	N	4
11	SHIFT	P/YR	1.00	PV		−11,654.85
14	I/YR		14.00			

Calculating the present value of an annuity due

Example: In this case, instead of receiving payments at the end of the year, you will receive the payments at the beginning of each year. Therefore, your first payment will be received immediately.

There are two ways to calculate the present value of an annuity due:

1.   You can calculate the present value of an annuity as shown in the previous section, and multiply it by $(1 + r)$; or

2.   The **TIBAII Plus** allows you to set the timing of the payment. You have to set the payment mode at "Begin" and start from the first step. This method is shown below.

Keystrokes			Display	Description
2nd	CLRTVM		0.00	Clears the time-value-of-money worksheet
2nd	P/Y	1 ENTER	P/Y = 1.00	Sets the number of periods per year to 1
2nd	BGN		END	Shows the default setting for the payment mode
2nd	SET		BGN	Sets the payment mode to the beginning of the period
2nd	QUIT		0.00	Brings the calculator to the standard mode
4000	PMT		PMT = 4,000.00	Records the amount of the periodic payments
14	I/Y		I/Y = 14.00	Records the periodic rate of interest as 14%
4	N		N = 4.00	Stores the number of time periods
CPT	PV		PV = –13,286.53	Calculates the present value of the annuity
2nd	BGN		BGN	Invokes the payment mode
2nd	SET		END	Sets the payment mode to the end of the period
2nd	QUIT		0.00	Brings the calculator to the standard mode

HP10B

There are two ways in which the HP10B will calculate the value of an annuity due.

1.   Calculate the present value of the annuity and multiply it by $(1 + r)$.

2.   The HP10B allows you to set the timing of the payment. You have to set the payment mode at "BEGIN" and start from the first step. This method is shown below.

Keystrokes			Display		Keystrokes		Display
SHIFT	BEG/END		BEGIN	14	I/YR		14.00
4000	PMT		4,000.00	4	N		4.00
1	SHIFT	P/YR	1.00		PV		−13,286.53
					SHIFT	BEG/END	

Calculating the net present value of an annuity

Example: Rob thinks if he invests $100,000 by buying property today, he can get $20,000 in rent from it for each of the next 20 years (the rent will be paid semiannually). If he wants a rate of return of 15% (with semiannual discounting) on his investment, what is the net present value of this project?

Notes: The annual rate of return will be divided by 2; the semiannual rate of return will be 7.5%. The number of time periods will be multiplied by 2; $20 \times 2 = 40$. The amount of annual rent will be divided by 2; $20,000/2 = \$10,000$

TIBAII Plus

Keystrokes					Display	Description
2nd	CLRWork				0.00	Clears the Cash Flow worksheet
2nd	Reset		ENTER		RST 0.00	Resets all variables to zero
CF	100000		+/−		CF_0 −100,000.00	Inputs initial cash outflow
ENTER					$CF_0 = -100,000.00$	Stores initial cash outflow
↓	20000		÷		$CO1 = 20,000.00$	Calculates periodic cash inflows
2	ENTER				$CO1 = 10,000.00$	Stores semiannual cash inflow amount
↓	20	×	2	ENTER	$FO1 = 40.00$	Stores the number of times the semiannual cash inflow occurs
NPV	15	÷	2	ENTER	$I = 7.50$	Stores the semiannual interest rate as 7.5%
↓	CPT				$NPV = 25,944.09$	Calculates the net present value of the investment

HP10B

Keystrokes			Display	Keystrokes		Display
100000	+/–	CF$_j$	–100,000.0	15	I/YR	15.00
20000	÷	2 CF	10,000.00	SHIFT NPV		25,944.09
20	×	2 P/YR	2_			
SHIFT	N$_j$		40.00			

Calculating the net present value of a series of uneven cash flows

Example: BlueSky Corp. is considering investing in a project with the following cash flows:

Year	Amount
0	–$2,000
1	300
2	300
3	1000
4	1100

If BlueSky has to pay an annual interest rate of 10%, should they invest in the project?

TIBAII Plus

Keystrokes			Display	Description
2nd	CLRWork		0.00	Clears the Cash Flow worksheet
2nd	Reset	ENTER	RST 0.00	Resets all variables to zero
CF	2000	+/−	CF_0 − 2,000.00	Inputs initial cash outflow
ENTER			CF_0 = −2,000.00	Stores initial cash outflow
↓	300	ENTER	CO1 = 300.00	Stores the first cash inflow
↓		ENTER	FO1 = 1.00	Records the first cash inflow of $300
↓	300	ENTER	CO2 = 300.00	Stores the second cash inflow of $300
↓			FO2 = 1.00	Records the second cash inflow
↓	1000	ENTER	CO3 = 1,000.00	Stores the third cash inflow
↓			FO3 = 1.00	Records that the cash inflow of $1,000 occurs once
↓	1100	ENTER	CO4 = 1,100.00	Stores the fourth cash inflow
↓			FO4 = 1	Records that the cash inflow of $1,100 occurs once
NPV	10	ENTER	I = 10.00	Stores the annual interest rate as 10%
↓	CPT		NPV = 23.29	Calculates the net present value of the Investment

HP10B

Keystrokes			Display	Keystrokes			Display
2000	+/−	CF_j	−2,000.00	1100	CF_j		1100.00
300	CF		300.00	1	SHIFT	P/YR	1.00
2	SHIFT	N_j	2.00	10	I/YR		10.0000
1000	CF_j		1000.00	SHIFT	NPV		23.29

Calculating the internal rate of return of an annuity

Example: CompuLease is planning to spend $45,000 on a computer system that will be leased to a local business. The new computer system is expected to provide after-tax cash flows of $12,000 (paid annually) per year over the next 5 years. What is the internal rate of return for the investment?

TIBAII Plus

Keystrokes		Display	Description
2nd | CLRWork		0.00	Clears the Cash Flow worksheet
2nd | Reset | ENTER		RST 0.00	Resets all variables to zero
CF | 45000 | +/−		CF_0 −45,000.00	Inputs initial cash outflow
↓ | 12000 | ENTER		CO1 = 12000.00	Stores the first cash inflow
↓ | 5		FO1 = 5.00	Stores the number of times that cash inflow of $12000 repeats
IRR | CPT		IRR = 10.42	Calculates the annual IRR of the Investment

HP10B

Keystrokes			Display
45000 | +/− | CF_j			−45,000.00
1200 | CF			1200.00
5 | SHIFT | N_j			5.00
SHIFT | IRR/YR			10.42

Calculating the IRR of a series of uneven cash flows

Example: Hometime Inc. has the opportunity to make an investment that requires an initial investment of $2,500,000. The estimated cash inflows from the project for the next 4 years are shown below. What is the IRR on this investment?

TIBAII Plus

Year	Cashflow
0	–$2,500,000
1	600,000
2	800,000
3	900,000
4	1,200,000

Keystrokes			Display	Description
2nd	CLRWork		0.00	Clears the Cash Flow worksheet
2nd	Reset	ENTER	RST 0.00	Resets all variables to zero
CF	2500000	+/–	CF_0 –2,500,000.00	Inputs initial cash outflow
ENTER			CF_0 = –2,500,000.00	Stores initial cash outflow
↓	600000	ENTER	CO1 = 600,000.00	Stores the first cash inflow
↓			FO1 = 1	Records that the cash inflow of $600,000 occurs once
↓	800000	ENTER	CO2 = 800,000.00	Stores the second cash inflow
↓			FO2 = 1.00	Records that the cash inflow of $800,000 occurs once
↓	900000	ENTER	CO3 = 900,000.00	Stores the third cash inflow
↓			FO3 = 1	Records that the cash inflow of $900,000 occurs once
↓	1200000	ENTER	CFO4 = 1,200,000.00	Stores the fourth cash inflow
↓			FO4 = 1	Records that the cash inflow of 1,200,000.00 occurs once
IRR	CPT		IRR = 13.30	Calculates the IRR of the project

HP10B

Keystrokes			Display	Keystrokes		Display
2500000	+/−	CF$_j$	−2,500,000.0	1200000	CF$_j$	1,200,000.00
600000	CF		600,000.00	SHIFT	IRR/YR	13.30
800000	CF$_j$		800,000.00			
900000	CF$_j$		900,000.00			

Bond valuation with interest compounded annually.

Example: How much would you be willing to pay for a bond today if it pays $100 in interest annually for 15 years (starting next year) and has a principal payment of $1,000? The yield to maturity is 12%.

Note: This question can be interpreted as that of finding the NPV of an uneven cash flow series, with the initial cash outflow equal to zero. Hence, we will follow the steps used for calculating NPV to compute the current price of the bond.

TIBAII Plus

Keystrokes			Display	Description
2nd	CLRWork		0.00	Clears the Cash Flow worksheet
2nd	Reset	ENTER	RST 0.00	Resets all variables to zero
CF	0	ENTER	CF$_0$ 0.00	Inputs initial cash outflow
↓	100	ENTER	CO1 = 100.00	Stores the first cash inflow
↓	14		FO1 = 14.00	Stores the number of times that cash inflow of $100 repeats
↓	1100	ENTER	CO2 = 1,100.00	Stores the final cash inflow of $100 plus repayment of the $1,000 principal
NPV	12	ENTER	I = 12.00	Stores the annual discount rate as 12%
↓	CPT		NPV = 863.78	Calculates the initial price of the bond

HP10B

	Keystrokes		Display		Keystrokes		Display
0	CF$_j$		0.00	1	SHIFT	P/YR	1.00
100	CF		100.00	SHIFT	NPV		863.78
14	SHIFT	N$_j$	14.00				
1100	CF$_j$		1,100.00				

Bond valuation with interest compounded semiannually

Note: Most bonds pay interest semiannually. The following example will show the conversion required to calculate the current value of such bonds.

Example: If the bond described in the previous section pays interest semiannually, the calculations will be as follows:

TIBAII Plus

Keystrokes			Display	Description
2nd	CLRWork		0.00	Clears the Cash Flow worksheet
2nd	Reset	ENTER	RST 0.00	Resets all variables to zero
CF	0	ENTER	CF$_0$ 0.00	Inputs initial cash outflow
↓	100	÷	CO1 = 100.00	Calculates the semiannual interest payment
2	ENTER		CO1 = 50.00	Stores the semiannual interest payment of $50
↓	15	×	FO1 = 15.00	Calculates the number of periods when cash inflow of $50 will occur
2	− 1	ENTER	FO1 = 29	Stores the number of interest periods
↓	1050	ENTER	CO2 = 1,050.00	Stores the final cash inflow
NPV	12	÷	I = 12.00	Calculates the semiannual discount rate
2	ENTER		I = 6.00	Stores the semiannual discount rate as 6%
↓	CPT		NPV = 862.35	Calculates the initial price of the bond

HP10B

Keystrokes				Display	Keystrokes			Display
0	CF$_j$			0.00	1050	CF$_j$		1,050.00
100	÷	2	CF$_j$	50.00	2	SHIFT	P/YR	2.00
15	×	2	− 1	1_	12	I/YR		12.00
SHIFT	N$_j$			29.00	SHIFT	NPV		862.35

Tables

Table 1

Future Value of $1 at the End of *n* Periods

$$FVIF_{r,n} = (1 + r)^n$$

Period	1%	2%	3%	4%	5%	6%	7%	8%	9%	10%
1	1.0100	1.0200	1.0300	1.0400	1.0500	1.0600	1.0700	1.0800	1.0900	1.1000
2	1.0201	1.0404	1.0609	1.0816	1.1025	1.1236	1.1449	1.1664	1.1881	1.2100
3	1.0303	1.0612	1.0927	1.1249	1.1576	1.1910	1.2250	1.2597	1.2950	1.3310
4	1.0406	1.0824	1.1255	1.1699	1.2155	1.2625	1.3108	1.3605	1.4116	1.4641
5	1.0510	1.1041	1.1593	1.2167	1.2763	1.3382	1.4026	1.4693	1.5386	1.6105
6	1.0615	1.1262	1.1941	1.2653	1.3401	1.4185	1.5007	1.5869	1.6771	1.7716
7	1.0721	1.1487	1.2299	1.3159	1.4071	1.5036	1.6058	1.7138	1.8280	1.9487
8	1.0829	1.1717	1.2668	1.3686	1.4775	1.5938	1.7182	1.8509	1.9926	2.1436
9	1.0937	1.1951	1.3048	1.4233	1.5513	1.6895	1.8385	1.9990	2.1719	2.3579
10	1.1046	1.2190	1.3439	1.4802	1.6289	1.7908	1.9672	2.1589	2.3674	2.5937
11	1.1157	1.2434	1.3842	1.5395	1.7103	1.8983	2.1049	2.3316	2.5804	2.8531
12	1.1268	1.2682	1.4258	1.6010	1.7959	2.0122	2.2522	2.5182	2.8127	3.1384
13	1.1381	1.2936	1.4685	1.6651	1.8856	2.1329	2.4098	2.7196	3.0658	3.4523
14	1.1495	1.3195	1.5126	1.7317	1.9799	2.2609	2.5785	2.9372	3.3417	3.7975
15	1.1610	1.3459	1.5580	1.8009	2.0789	2.3966	2.7590	3.1722	3.6425	4.1772
18	1.1961	1.4282	1.7024	2.0258	2.4066	2.8543	3.3799	3.9960	4.7171	5.5599
20	1.2202	1.4859	1.8061	2.1911	2.6533	3.2071	3.8697	4.6610	5.6044	6.7275
22	1.2447	1.5460	1.9161	2.3699	2.9253	3.6035	4.4304	5.4365	6.6586	8.1403
24	1.2697	1.6084	2.0328	2.5633	3.2251	4.0489	5.0724	6.3412	7.9111	9.8497
25	1.2824	1.6406	2.0938	2.6658	3.3864	4.2919	5.4274	6.8485	8.6231	10.835
28	1.3213	1.7410	2.2879	2.9987	3.9201	5.1117	6.6488	8.6271	11.167	14.421
30	1.3478	1.8114	2.4273	3.2434	4.3219	5.7435	7.6123	10.063	13.268	17.449
35	1.4166	1.9999	2.8139	3.9461	5.5160	7.6861	10.677	14.785	20.414	28.102
40	1.4889	2.2080	3.2620	4.8010	7.0400	10.286	14.974	21.725	31.409	45.259
45	1.5648	2.4379	3.7816	5.8412	8.9850	13.765	21.002	31.920	48.327	72.890
50	1.6446	2.6916	4.3839	7.1067	11.467	18.420	29.457	46.902	74.358	117.39
180	5.9958	35.321	204.50	1164.1	6517.4	35896.8	194571.8	1038188	5454684	28228209

Table 2

Future Value of $1 at the End of _n_ Periods

Period	11%	12%	13%	14%	15%	18%	20%	25%	30%	35%
1	1.1100	1.1200	1.1300	1.1400	1.1500	1.1800	1.2000	1.2500	1.3000	1.3500
2	1.2321	1.2544	1.2769	1.2996	1.3225	1.3924	1.4400	1.5625	1.6900	1.8225
3	1.3676	1.4049	1.4429	1.4815	1.5209	1.6430	1.7280	1.9531	2.1970	2.4604
4	1.5181	1.5735	1.6305	1.6890	1.7490	1.9388	2.0736	2.4414	2.8561	3.3215
5	1.6851	1.7623	1.8424	1.9254	2.0114	2.2878	2.4883	3.0518	3.7129	4.4840
6	1.8704	1.9738	2.0820	2.1950	2.3131	2.6996	2.9860	3.8147	4.8268	6.0534
7	2.0762	2.2107	2.3526	2.5023	2.6600	3.1855	3.5832	4.7684	6.2749	8.1722
8	2.3045	2.4760	2.6584	2.8526	3.0590	3.7589	4.2998	5.9605	8.1573	11.032
9	2.5580	2.7731	3.0040	3.2519	3.5179	4.4355	5.1598	7.4506	10.604	14.894
10	2.8394	3.1058	3.3946	3.7072	4.0456	5.2338	6.1917	9.3132	13.786	20.107
11	3.1518	3.4785	3.8359	4.2262	4.6524	6.1759	7.4301	11.642	17.922	27.144
12	3.4985	3.8960	4.3345	4.8179	5.3503	7.2876	8.9161	14.552	23.298	36.644
13	3.8833	4.3635	4.8980	5.4924	6.1528	8.5994	10.699	18.190	30.288	49.470
14	4.3104	4.8871	5.5348	6.2613	7.0757	10.1472	12.839	22.737	39.374	66.784
15	4.7846	5.4736	6.2543	7.1379	8.1371	11.9737	15.407	28.422	51.186	90.158
18	6.5436	7.6900	9.0243	10.575	12.375	19.673	26.623	55.511	112.46	221.82
20	8.0623	9.6463	11.523	13.743	16.367	27.393	38.338	86.736	190.05	404.27
22	9.9336	12.100	14.714	17.861	21.645	38.142	55.206	135.53	321.18	736.79
24	12.239	15.179	18.788	23.212	28.625	53.109	79.497	211.76	542.80	1342.8
25	13.585	17.000	21.231	26.462	32.919	62.669	95.396	264.70	705.64	1812.8
28	18.580	23.884	30.633	39.204	50.066	102.967	164.84	516.99	1550.3	4460.1
30	22.892	29.960	39.116	50.950	66.212	143.371	237.38	807.79	2620.0	8128.5
35	38.575	52.800	72.069	98.100	133.176	327.997	590.67	2465.2	9727.9	36448.7
40	65.001	93.051	132.78	188.88	267.86	750.38	1469.8	7523.2	36118.9	163437.1
45	109.53	163.99	244.64	363.68	538.77	1716.7	3657.3	22958.9	134106.8	732857.6
50	184.56	289.00	450.74	700.23	1083.7	3927.4	9100.4	70064.9	497929.2	3286158

Table 3

| | Future Value of an Annuity of $1 per Period for n Periods | | | | | $PVIFAr,n = (1/r) - (1/r(1 + r)^n)$ | | | | |
Period	0.01	0.02	0.03	0.04	0.05	0.06	0.07	0.08	0.09	0.10
1.00	1.00	1.00	1.00	1.00	1.00	1.00	1.00	1.00	1.00	1.00
2.00	2.01	2.02	2.03	2.04	2.05	2.06	2.07	2.08	2.09	2.10
3.00	3.03	3.06	3.09	3.12	3.15	3.18	3.21	3.25	3.28	3.31
4.00	4.06	4.12	4.18	4.25	4.31	4.37	4.44	4.51	4.57	4.64
5.00	5.10	5.20	5.31	5.42	5.53	5.64	5.75	5.87	5.98	6.11
6.00	6.15	6.31	6.47	6.63	6.80	6.98	7.15	7.34	7.52	7.72
7.00	7.21	7.43	7.66	7.90	8.14	8.39	8.65	8.92	9.20	9.49
8.00	8.29	8.58	8.89	9.21	9.55	9.90	10.26	10.64	11.03	11.44
9.00	9.37	9.75	10.16	10.58	11.03	11.49	11.98	12.49	13.02	13.58
10.00	10.46	10.95	11.46	12.01	12.58	13.18	13.82	14.49	15.19	15.94
11.00	11.57	12.17	12.81	13.49	14.21	14.97	15.78	16.65	17.56	18.53
12.00	12.68	13.41	14.19	15.03	15.92	16.87	17.89	18.98	20.14	21.38
13.00	13.81	14.68	15.62	16.63	17.71	18.88	20.14	21.50	22.95	24.52
14.00	14.95	15.97	17.09	18.29	19.60	21.02	22.55	24.21	26.02	27.97
15.00	16.10	17.29	18.60	20.02	21.58	23.28	25.13	27.15	29.36	31.77
18.00	19.61	21.41	23.41	25.65	28.13	30.91	34.00	37.45	41.30	45.60
20.00	22.02	24.30	26.87	29.78	33.07	36.79	41.00	45.76	51.16	57.27
25.00	28.24	32.03	36.46	41.65	47.73	54.86	63.25	73.11	84.70	98.35
28.00	32.13	37.05	42.93	49.97	58.40	68.53	80.70	95.34	112.97	134.21
30.00	34.78	40.57	47.58	56.08	66.44	79.06	94.46	113.28	136.31	164.49
35.00	41.66	49.99	60.46	73.65	90.32	111.43	138.24	172.32	215.71	271.02
40.00	48.89	60.40	75.40	95.03	120.80	154.76	199.64	259.06	337.88	442.59
45.00	56.48	71.89	92.72	121.03	159.70	212.74	285.75	386.51	525.86	718.90
50.00	64.46	84.58	112.80	152.67	209.35	290.34	406.53	573.77	815.08	1,163.91
180.00	499.58	1,716.04	6,783.45	29,078.22	130,327.84	598,263.35	N/A	N/A	N/A	N/A

Table 4

	Future Value of an Annuity if $1 per Period for n Periods								
Period	**0.11**	**0.12**	**0.13**	**0.14**	**0.15**	**0.18**	**0.20**
1.00	1.00	1.00	1.00	1.00	1.00	1.00	1.00
2.00	2.11	2.12	2.13	2.14	2.15	2.18	2.20
3.00	3.34	3.37	3.41	3.44	3.47	3.57	3.64
4.00	4.71	4.78	4.85	4.92	4.99	5.22	5.37
5.00	6.23	6.35	6.48	6.61	6.74	7.15	7.44
6.00	7.91	8.12	8.32	8.54	8.75	9.44	9.93
7.00	9.78	10.09	10.40	10.73	11.07	12.14	12.92
8.00	11.86	12.30	12.76	13.23	13.73	15.33	16.50
9.00	14.16	14.78	15.42	16.09	16.79	19.09	20.80
10.00	16.72	17.55	18.42	19.34	20.30	23.52	25.96
11.00	19.56	20.65	21.81	23.04	24.35	28.76	32.15
12.00	22.71	24.13	25.65	27.27	29.00	34.93	39.58
13.00	26.21	28.03	29.98	32.09	34.35	42.22	48.50
14.00	30.09	32.39	34.88	37.58	40.50	50.82	59.20
15.00	34.41	37.28	40.42	43.84	47.58	60.97	72.04
18.00	50.40	55.75	61.73	68.39	75.84	103.74	128.12
20.00	64.20	72.05	80.95	91.02	102.44	146.63	186.69
25.00	114.41	133.33	155.62	181.87	212.79	342.60	471.98
28.00	159.82	190.70	227.95	272.89	327.10	566.48	819.22
30.00	199.02	241.33	293.20	356.79	434.75	790.95	1,181.88
35.00	341.59	431.66	546.68	693.57	881.17	1,816.65	2,948.34
40.00	581.83	767.09	1,013.70	1,342.03	1,779.09	4,163.21	7,343.86
45.00	986.64	1,358.23	1,874.16	2,590.56	3,585.13	9,531.58	18,281.31
50.00	1,668.77	2,400.02	3,459.51	4,994.52	7,217.72	21,813.09	45,497.19
180.00	N/A	N/A	N/A	N/A	N/A	N/A	N/A

Table 5

Present Value of $1 Due at End of n Periods

$$PVIF_{r,n} = 1/(1+r)^n$$

Period	1%	2%	3%	4%	5%	6%	7%	8%	9%	10%
1	0.9901	0.9804	0.9709	0.9615	0.9524	0.9434	0.9346	0.9259	0.9174	0.9091
2	0.9803	0.9612	0.9426	0.9246	0.9070	0.8900	0.8734	0.8573	0.8417	0.8264
3	0.9706	0.9423	0.9151	0.8890	0.8638	0.8396	0.8163	0.7938	0.7722	0.7513
4	0.9610	0.9238	0.8885	0.8548	0.8227	0.7921	0.7629	0.7350	0.7084	0.6830
5	0.9515	0.9057	0.8626	0.8219	0.7835	0.7473	0.7130	0.6806	0.6499	0.6209
6	0.9420	0.8880	0.8375	0.7903	0.7462	0.7050	0.6663	0.6302	0.5963	0.5645
7	0.9327	0.8706	0.8131	0.7599	0.7107	0.6651	0.6227	0.5835	0.5470	0.5132
8	0.9235	0.8535	0.7894	0.7307	0.6768	0.6274	0.5820	0.5403	0.5019	0.4665
9	0.9143	0.8368	0.7664	0.7026	0.6446	0.5919	0.5439	0.5002	0.4604	0.4241
10	0.9053	0.8203	0.7441	0.6756	0.6139	0.5584	0.5083	0.4632	0.4224	0.3855
11	0.8963	0.8043	0.7224	0.6496	0.5847	0.5268	0.4751	0.4289	0.3875	0.3505
12	0.8874	0.7885	0.7014	0.6246	0.5568	0.4970	0.4440	0.3971	0.3555	0.3186
13	0.8787	0.7730	0.6810	0.6006	0.5303	0.4688	0.4150	0.3677	0.3262	0.2897
14	0.8700	0.7579	0.6611	0.5775	0.5051	0.4423	0.3878	0.3405	0.2992	0.2633
15	0.8613	0.7430	0.6419	0.5553	0.4810	0.4173	0.3624	0.3152	0.2745	0.2394
18	0.8360	0.7002	0.5874	0.4936	0.4155	0.3503	0.2959	0.2502	0.2120	0.1799
20	0.8195	0.6730	0.5537	0.4564	0.3769	0.3118	0.2584	0.2145	0.1784	0.1486
25	0.7798	0.6095	0.4776	0.3751	0.2953	0.2330	0.1842	0.1460	0.1160	0.0923
28	0.7568	0.5744	0.4371	0.3335	0.2551	0.1956	0.1504	0.1159	0.0895	0.0693
30	0.7419	0.5521	0.4120	0.3083	0.2314	0.1741	0.1314	0.0994	0.0754	0.0573
35	0.7059	0.5000	0.3554	0.2534	0.1813	0.1301	0.0937	0.0676	0.0490	0.0356
40	0.6717	0.4529	0.3066	0.2083	0.1420	0.0972	0.0668	0.0460	0.0318	0.0221
45	0.6391	0.4102	0.2644	0.1712	0.1113	0.0727	0.0476	0.0313	0.0207	0.0137
50	0.6080	0.3715	0.2281	0.1407	0.0872	0.0543	0.0339	0.0213	0.0134	0.0085
180	0.1668	0.0283	0.0049	0.0009	0.0002	0.0000	0.0000	0.0000	0.0000	0.0000
360	0.0278	0.0008	0.0000	0.0000	0.0000	0.0000	0.0000	0.0000	0.0000	0.0000

Table 6

Present Value of $1 at End of *n* Periods

Period	11%	12%	13%	14%	15%	18%	20%	25%	30%	35%
1	0.9009	0.8929	0.8850	0.8772	0.8696	0.8475	0.8333	0.8000	0.7692	0.7407
2	0.8116	0.7972	0.7831	0.7695	0.7561	0.7182	0.6944	0.6400	0.5917	0.5487
3	0.7312	0.7118	0.6931	0.6750	0.6575	0.6086	0.5787	0.5120	0.4552	0.4064
4	0.6587	0.6355	0.6133	0.5921	0.5718	0.5158	0.4823	0.4096	0.3501	0.3011
5	0.5935	0.5674	0.5428	0.5194	0.4972	0.4371	0.4019	0.3277	0.2693	0.2230
6	0.5346	0.5066	0.4803	0.4556	0.4323	0.3704	0.3349	0.2621	0.2072	0.1652
7	0.4817	0.4523	0.4251	0.3996	0.3759	0.3139	0.2791	0.2097	0.1594	0.1224
8	0.4339	0.4039	0.3762	0.3506	0.3269	0.2660	0.2326	0.1678	0.1226	0.0906
9	0.3909	0.3606	0.3329	0.3075	0.2843	0.2255	0.1938	0.1342	0.0943	0.0671
10	0.3522	0.3220	0.2946	0.2697	0.2472	0.1911	0.1615	0.1074	0.0725	0.0497
11	0.3173	0.2875	0.2607	0.2366	0.2149	0.1619	0.1346	0.0859	0.0558	0.0368
12	0.2858	0.2567	0.2307	0.2076	0.1869	0.1372	0.1122	0.0687	0.0429	0.0273
13	0.2575	0.2292	0.2042	0.1821	0.1625	0.1163	0.0935	0.0550	0.0330	0.0202
14	0.2320	0.2046	0.1807	0.1597	0.1413	0.0985	0.0779	0.0440	0.0254	0.0150
15	0.2090	0.1827	0.1599	0.1401	0.1229	0.0835	0.0649	0.0352	0.0195	0.0111
18	0.1528	0.1300	0.1108	0.0946	0.0808	0.0508	0.0376	0.0180	0.0089	0.0045
20	0.1240	0.1037	0.0868	0.0728	0.0611	0.0365	0.0261	0.0115	0.0053	0.0025
22	0.1007	0.0826	0.0680	0.0560	0.0462	0.0262	0.0181	0.0074	0.0031	0.0014
24	0.0817	0.0659	0.0532	0.0431	0.0349	0.0188	0.0126	0.0047	0.0018	0.0007
25	0.0736	0.0588	0.0471	0.0378	0.0304	0.0160	0.0105	0.0038	0.0014	0.0006
28	0.0538	0.0419	0.0326	0.0255	0.0200	0.0097	0.0061	0.0019	0.0006	0.0002
30	0.0437	0.0334	0.0256	0.0196	0.0151	0.0070	0.0042	0.0012	0.0004	0.0001
35	0.0259	0.0189	0.0139	0.0102	0.0075	0.0030	0.0017	0.0004	0.0001	0.0000
40	0.0154	0.0107	0.0075	0.0053	0.0037	0.0013	0.0007	0.0001	0.0000	0.0000
45	0.0091	0.0061	0.0041	0.0027	0.0019	0.0006	0.0003	0.0000	0.0000	0.0000
50	0.0054	0.0035	0.0022	0.0014	0.0009	0.0003	0.0001	0.0000	0.0000	0.0000
180	0.0000	0.0000	0.0000	0.0000	0.0000	0.0000	0.0000	0.0000	0.0000	0.0000
360	0.0000	0.0000	0.0000	0.0000	0.0000	0.0000	0.0000	0.0000	0.0000	0.0000

Table 7

Present Value of an Annuity of $1 per Period for n Periods $PVIFA\ r,n = (1 - 1/(1 + r)^n)/r$

Period	1%	2%	3%	4%	5%	6%	7%	8%	9%	10%
1	0.9901	0.9804	0.9709	0.9615	0.9524	0.9434	0.9346	0.9259	0.9174	0.9091
2	1.9704	1.9416	1.9135	1.8861	1.8594	1.8334	1.8080	1.7833	1.7591	1.7355
3	2.9410	2.8839	2.8286	2.7751	2.7232	2.6730	2.6243	2.5771	2.5313	2.4869
4	3.9020	3.8077	3.7171	3.6299	3.5460	3.4651	3.3872	3.3121	3.2397	3.1699
5	4.8534	4.7135	4.5797	4.4518	4.3295	4.2124	4.1002	3.9927	3.8897	3.7908
6	5.7955	5.6014	5.4172	5.2421	5.0757	4.9173	4.7665	4.6229	4.4859	4.3553
7	6.7282	6.4720	6.2303	6.0021	5.7864	5.5824	5.3893	5.2064	5.0330	4.8684
8	7.6517	7.3255	7.0197	6.7327	6.4632	6.2098	5.9713	5.7466	5.5348	5.3349
9	8.5660	8.1622	7.7861	7.4353	7.1078	6.8017	6.5152	6.2469	5.9952	5.7590
10	9.4713	8.9826	8.5302	8.1109	7.7217	7.3601	7.0236	6.7101	6.4177	6.1446
11	10.368	9.7868	9.2526	8.7605	8.3064	7.8869	7.4987	7.1390	6.8052	6.4951
12	11.255	10.575	9.9540	9.3851	8.8633	8.3838	7.9427	7.5361	7.1607	6.8137
13	12.134	11.348	10.635	9.9856	9.3936	8.8527	8.3577	7.9038	7.4869	7.1034
14	13.004	12.106	11.296	10.563	9.8986	9.2950	8.7455	8.2442	7.7862	7.3667
15	13.865	12.849	11.938	11.118	10.380	9.712	9.108	8.5595	8.0607	7.6061
18	16.398	14.992	13.754	12.659	11.690	10.828	10.059	9.3719	8.7556	8.2014
20	18.046	16.351	14.877	13.590	12.462	11.470	10.594	9.8181	9.1285	8.5136
22	19.660	17.658	15.937	14.451	13.163	12.042	11.061	10.201	9.4424	8.7715
24	21.243	18.914	16.936	15.247	13.799	12.550	11.469	10.529	9.7066	8.9847
25	22.023	19.523	17.413	15.622	14.094	12.783	11.654	10.675	9.8226	9.0770
28	24.316	21.281	18.764	16.663	14.898	13.406	12.137	11.051	10.116	9.3066
30	25.808	22.396	19.600	17.292	15.372	13.765	12.409	11.258	10.274	9.4269
35	29.409	24.999	21.487	18.665	16.374	14.498	12.948	11.655	10.567	9.6442
40	32.835	27.355	23.115	19.793	17.159	15.046	13.332	11.925	10.757	9.7791
45	36.095	29.490	24.519	20.720	17.774	15.456	13.606	12.108	10.881	9.8628
50	39.196	31.424	25.730	21.482	18.256	15.762	13.801	12.233	10.962	9.9148
180	83.322	48.584	33.170	24.979	19.997	16.666	14.286	12.500	11.111	10.000
360	97.218	49.960	33.333	25.000	20.000	16.667	14.286	12.500	11.111	10.000

Table 8

Present Value of an Annuity of $1 per Period for *n* Periods

Period	11%	12%	13%	14%	15%	18%	20%	25%	30%	35%
1	0.9009	0.8929	0.8850	0.8772	0.8696	0.8475	0.8333	0.8000	0.7692	0.7407
2	1.7125	1.6901	1.6681	1.6467	1.6257	1.5656	1.5278	1.4400	1.3609	1.2894
3	2.4437	2.4018	2.3612	2.3216	2.2832	2.1743	2.1065	1.9520	1.8161	1.6959
4	3.1024	3.0373	2.9745	2.9137	2.8550	2.6901	2.5887	2.3616	2.1662	1.9969
5	3.6959	3.6048	3.5172	3.4331	3.3522	3.1272	2.9906	2.6893	2.4356	2.2200
6	4.2305	4.1114	3.9975	3.8887	3.7845	3.4976	3.3255	2.9514	2.6427	2.3852
7	4.7122	4.5638	4.4226	4.2883	4.1604	3.8115	3.6046	3.1611	2.8021	2.5075
8	5.1461	4.9676	4.7988	4.6389	4.4873	4.0776	3.8372	3.3289	2.9247	2.5982
9	5.5370	5.3282	5.1317	4.9464	4.7716	4.3030	4.0310	3.4631	3.0190	2.6653
10	5.8892	5.6502	5.4262	5.2161	5.0188	4.4941	4.1925	3.5705	3.0915	2.7150
11	6.2065	5.9377	5.6869	5.4527	5.2337	4.6560	4.3271	3.6564	3.1473	2.7519
12	6.4924	6.1944	5.9176	5.6603	5.4206	4.7932	4.4392	3.7251	3.1903	2.7792
13	6.7499	6.4235	6.1218	5.8424	5.5831	4.9095	4.5327	3.7801	3.2233	2.7994
14	6.9819	6.6282	6.3025	6.0021	5.7245	5.0081	4.6106	3.8241	3.2487	2.8144
15	7.1909	6.8109	6.4624	6.1422	5.8474	5.0916	4.6755	3.8593	3.2682	2.8255
18	7.7016	7.2497	6.8399	6.4674	6.1280	5.2732	4.8122	3.9279	3.3037	2.8443
20	7.9633	7.4694	7.0248	6.6231	6.2593	5.3527	4.8696	3.9539	3.3158	2.8501
22	8.1757	7.6446	7.1695	6.7429	6.3587	5.4099	4.9094	3.9705	3.3230	2.8533
24	8.3481	7.7843	7.2829	6.8351	6.4338	5.4509	4.9371	3.9811	3.3272	2.8550
25	8.4217	7.8431	7.3300	6.8729	6.4641	5.4669	4.9476	3.9849	3.3286	2.8556
28	8.6016	7.9844	7.4412	6.9607	6.5335	5.5016	4.9697	3.9923	3.3312	2.8565
30	8.6938	8.0552	7.4957	7.0027	6.5660	5.5168	4.9789	3.9950	3.3321	2.8568
35	8.8552	8.1755	7.5856	7.0700	6.6166	5.5386	4.9915	3.9984	3.3330	2.8571
40	8.9511	8.2438	7.6344	7.1050	6.6418	5.5482	4.9966	3.9995	3.3332	2.8571
45	9.0079	8.2825	7.6609	7.1232	6.6543	5.5523	4.9986	3.9998	3.3333	2.8571
50	9.0417	8.3045	7.6752	7.1327	6.6605	5.5541	4.9995	3.9999	3.3333	2.8571
180	9.0909	8.3333	7.6923	7.1429	6.6667	5.5556	5.0000	4.0000	3.3333	2.8571
360	9.0909	8.3333	7.6923	7.1429	6.6667	5.5556	5.0000	4.0000	3.3333	2.8571

Financial Dictionary

ABC system: Inventory management technique that divides inventory into three categories of descending importance based on the dollar investment in each.

ability to service debts: The ability of a firm to make the contractual payments required on a scheduled basis over the life of a debt.

accept-reject approach: The evaluation of capital expenditure proposals to determine whether they meet the firm's minimum acceptance criterion.

accounting exposure: The risk resulting from the effects of changes in foreign exchange rates on the translated value of a firm's financial statement accounts denominated in a given foreign currency.

accrual method: Recognizes revenue at the point of sale and recognizes expenses when incurred.

accruals: Liabilities for services received for which payment has yet to be made.

ACH (automated clearinghouse) credits: Deposits of payroll directly into the payees' (employees') accounts. Sacrifices disbursement float but may generate goodwill for the employer.

ACH (automated clearinghouse) debits: Preauthorized electronic withdrawals from the payer's account that are then transferred to the payee's account via a settlement among banks by the automated clearinghouse. They clear in one day, thereby reducing mail, processing, and clearing float.

acquiring company: The firm in a merger transaction that attempts to acquire another firm.

activity ratios: Used to measure the speed with which various accounts are converted into sales or cash.

adjustable-rate (or floating-rate) preferred stock (ARPS): Preferred stock whose dividend rate is tied to interest rates on specific government securities.

After-tax proceeds from sale of old asset: Found by subtracting applicable taxes from the proceeds from the sale of an old asset.

agency costs: Costs borne by stockholders to prevent or minimize agency problems and to contribute to the maximization of the owners' wealth. They include monitoring and bonding expenditures, opportunity costs, and structuring expenditures.

agency problem: The likelihood that managers may place personal goals ahead of corporate goals.

aggressive financing strategy: Strategy by which the firm finances its seasonal needs, and possibly some of its permanent needs, with short-term funds and the balance of its permanent needs with long-term funds.

aging schedule: A technique used to evaluate credit and/or collection policies that indicates the proportion of the accounts receivable balance that has been outstanding for a specified period of time.

all-current-rate method: The method by which the *functional currency*—denominated financial statements of an MNC's subsidiary— is translated into the parent company's currency.

American depository receipts (ADRs): Dollar-denominated receipts for the stock of foreign companies that are held in the vaults of banks in the companies' home countries.

American depository shares (ADSs): Securities, backed by *American depository receipts (ADRs)*, that permit U.S. investors to hold shares of non-U.S. companies and trade them in U.S. markets.

annual cleanup: The requirement that for a certain number of days during the year, borrowers under a line of credit carry a zero loan balance (i.e., owe the bank nothing).

annual percentage rate (APR): In personal finance, the effective interest rate, which must by law be clearly stated to borrowers and depositors.

annualized net present value (ANPV) approach: An approach to evaluating unequal-lived projects that converts the net present value of unequal-lived, mutually exclusive projects into an equivalent (in NPV terms) annual amount.

annuity: A stream of equal annual cash flows. These cash flows can be *inflows* of returns earned on investments or *outflows* of funds invested to earn future returns.

annuity due: An annuity for which the payments occur at the beginning of each period.

articles of partnership: The written contract used to formally establish a business partnership.

ask price: The lowest price at which a security is offered for sale.

assignment: A voluntary liquidation procedure by which a firm's creditors pass the power to liquidate the firm's assets to an adjustment bureau, a trade association, or a third party, which is designated the *assignee.*

asymmetric information: The situation in which managers of a firm have more information about operations and future prospects than do investors.

authorized shares: The number of shares of common stock that a firm's corporate charter allows without further stockholder approval.

average age of inventory: Average length of time inventory is held by the firm.

average collection period: The average amount of time needed to collect accounts receivable.

average payment period: The average amount of time needed to pay accounts payable.

average tax rate: A firm's taxes divided by its taxable income.

balance sheet: Summary statement of the firm's financial position at a given point in time.

balloon payment: At the maturity of a loan, a large lump-sum payment representing the entire loan principal if the periodic payments represent only interest.

banker's acceptances: Short-term, low-risk marketable securities arising from bank guarantees of business transactions; are sold by banks at a discount from their maturity value and provide yields slightly below those on negotiable CDs and commercial paper, but higher than those on U.S. Treasury issues.

bankruptcy: Business failure that occurs when a firm's liabilities exceed the fair market value of its assets.

Bankruptcy Reform Act of 1978: The current governing bankruptcy legislation in the United States.

bar chart: The simplest type of probability distribution; shows only a limited number of outcomes and associated probabilities for a given event.

Baumol model: A model that provides for cost-efficient transactional cash balances; assumes that the demand for cash can be predicted with certainty and determines the *economic conversion quantity (ECQ).*

bearer bonds: Bonds for which payments are made to the bearer.

best efforts basis: A public offering in which the investment banker uses his or her resources to sell the security issue without taking on the risk of underwriting and is compensated on the basis of the number of securities sold.

beta coefficient: A measure of nondiversifiable risk. An *index* of the degree of movement of an asset's return in response to a change in the *market return.*

bid price: The highest price offered to purchase a security.

bird-in-the-hand argument: The belief, in support of dividend relevance theory, that current dividend payments ("a bird in the hand") reduce investor uncertainty and ultimately result in a higher value for the firm's stock.

blue sky laws: State laws aimed at regulating the sale of securities within the state and thereby protecting investors.

board of directors: Group elected by the firm's stockholders and having ultimate authority to guide corporate affairs and make general policy.

bond: Long-term debt instrument used by business and government to raise large sums of money, generally from a diverse group of lenders.

bond indenture: A complex and lengthy legal document stating the conditions under which a bond has been issued.

bond-refunding decision: The decision facing firms, when bond interest rates drop, whether to refund (refinance) existing bonds with new bonds at the lower interest rate.

book value: The strict accounting value of an asset, calculated by subtracting its accumulated depreciation from installed cost.

book value per share: The amount per share of common stock to be received if all of the firm's assets are sold for their book value and if the proceeds remaining after payment of all liabilities (including preferred stock) are divided among the common stockholders.

book value weights: Weights that use accounting values to measure the proportion of each type of capital in the firm's financial structure; used in calculating the weighted average cost of capital.

breadth of a market: A characteristic of a ready market, determined by the number of participants (buyers) in the market.

break-even analysis (cost-volume-profit analysis): Used (1) to determine the level of operations necessary to cover all operating costs and (2) to evaluate the profitability associated with various levels of sales.

break-even cash inflow: The minimum level of cash inflow necessary for a project to be acceptable (i.e., NPV > $0.)

breaking point: The level of *total* new financing at which the cost of one of the financing components rises, thereby causing an upward shift in the *weighted marginal cost of capital (WMCC)*.

broker market: The *securities exchanges* on which the two sides of a transaction, the buyer and seller, are brought together to trade securities.

business risk: The risk to the firm of being unable to cover operating costs.

call feature: A feature that is included in almost all corporate bond issues that gives the issuer the opportunity to repurchase bonds prior to maturity at a stated price.

call option: An option to *purchase* a specified number of shares of a stock (typically 100) on or before some future date at a stated price.

call premium: The amount by which a bond's call price exceeds its par value.

call price: The stated price at which a bond may be repurchased, by use of a *call feature*, prior to maturity.

capital: The long-term funds of the firm; all items on the right-hand side of the firm's balance sheet, excluding current liabilities.

capital asset pricing model (CAPM): Describes the relationship between the required return, or cost of common stock equity capital, and the nondiversifiable risk of the firm as measured by the beta coefficient.

capital budgeting: The process of evaluating and selecting long-term investments that are consistent with the firm's goal of owner wealth maximization.

capital budgeting process: Consists of five distinct but interrelated steps: proposal generation, review and analysis, decision making, implementation, and follow-up.

capital expenditure: An outlay of funds by the firm that is expected to produce benefits over a period of time *greater than* one year.

capital gain: The amount by which the price at which an asset was sold exceeds the asset's initial purchase price.

capital market: A financial relationship, created by institutions and arrangements, that allows suppliers and demanders of *long-term funds* to make transactions.

capital rationing: The financial situation in which a firm has only a fixed number of dollars for allocation among competing capital expenditures.

capital structure: The mix of long-term debt and equity maintained by the firm.

capitalized lease: A *financial (capital) lease* that has the present value of all its payments included as an asset and corresponding liability on the firm's balance sheet, as required by Financial Accounting Standards Board (FASB) Standard No. 13.

carrying costs: The variable costs per unit of holding an item in inventory for a specified time period.

cash: The ready currency to which all liquid assets can be reduced.

cash bonuses: Bonus money paid to management for achieving certain performance goals.

cash budget (cash forecast): A statement of the firm's planned inflows and outflows of cash that is used to estimate its short-term cash requirements.

cash conversion cycle (CCC): Represents the amount of time the firm's cash is tied up between payment for production inputs and receipt of payment from the sale of the resulting finished product; calculated as the number of days in the firm's operating cycle minus the average payment period for inputs to production.

cash disbursements: All cash outlays by the firm during a given financial period.

cash discount: A percentage deduction from the purchase price if the buyer pays within a specified time that is shorter than the credit period.

cash discount period: The number of days after the beginning of the credit period during which the cash discount is available.

cash method: Recognizes revenues and expenses only with respect to actual inflows and outflows of cash.

cash receipts: All items from which the firm receives cash inflows during a given financial period.

certainty equivalents (CEs): Risk-adjustment factors that represent the percent of estimated cash inflows that investors would be satisfied to receive *for certain,* rather than the cash inflows that are *possible* for each year.

change in net working capital: The difference between a change in current assets and a change in current liabilities.

Chapter 11: The portion of the *Bankruptcy Reform Act of 1978* that outlines the procedures for reorganizing a failed (or failing) firm, whether its petition is filed voluntarily or involuntarily.

Chapter 7: The portion of the *Bankruptcy Reform Act of 1978* that details the procedures to be followed in liquidating a failed firm.

clearing float: The delay between the deposit of a check by the payee and the actual availability of the funds.

Clearing House Interbank Payment System (CHIPS): The most important wire transfer service; operated by international banking consortia.

clientele effect: The theory that a firm will attract shareholders whose preferences with respect to the payment and stability of dividends correspond to the payment pattern and stability of the firm itself.

closely owned stock: All common stock of a firm owned by a small group of investors such as a family.

coefficient of variation (CV): A measure of relative dispersion used in comparing the risk of assets with differing expected returns.

collateral: The items used by a borrower to back up a loan; any assets against which a lender has a legal claim if the borrower defaults on some provision of the loan.

collateral trust bonds: Bonds secured by stock and (or) bonds that are owned by the issuer.

collection float: The delay between the time when a payer or customer deducts a payment from its checking account ledger and the time when the payee or vendor actually receives the funds in a spendable form.

collection policy: The procedures for collecting a firm's accounts receivable when they are due.

commercial finance companies: Lending institutions that make *only* secured loans—both short-term and long-term—to businesses.

commercial paper: A short-term, unsecured promissory note issued by a corporation that has a very high credit standing, having a yield above that paid on U.S. Treasury issues and comparable to that available on negotiable CDs with similar maturities.

commitment fee: The fee that is normally charged on a revolving credit agreement, often based on the average unused balance of the borrower's credit line.

common stock: Collectively, units of ownership interest, or equity, in a corporation.

common stock equivalents (CSEs): All contingent securities that derive a major portion of their value from their conversion privileges or common stock characteristics.

common-size income statement: An income statement in which each item is expressed as a percentage of sales.

compensating balance: A required checking account balance equal to a certain percentage of the borrower's short-term unsecured bank loan.

competitive bidding: A method of choosing an investment banker in which the banker or group of bankers that bids the highest price for a security issue is awarded the issue.

composition: A pro rata cash settlement of creditor claims by the debtor firm; a uniform percentage of each dollar owed is paid.

compounded interest: Interest earned on a given deposit that has become part of the principal at the end of a specified period.

concentration banking: A collection procedure in which payments are made to regionally dispersed collection centers, then deposited in local banks for quick clearing. Reduces collection float by shortening mail and clearing float.

conflicting rankings: Conflicts in the ranking of a given project by NPV and IRR that result from differences in the magnitude and timing of cash flows.

congeneric merger: A merger in which one firm acquires another firm that is in the same general industry but neither in the same line of business nor a supplier or customer.

conglomerate merger: A merger combining firms in unrelated businesses.

conservative financing strategy: Strategy by which the firm finances all projected fund requirements with long-term funds and uses short-term financing only for emergencies or unexpected outflows.

consolidation: The combination of two or more firms to form a completely new corporation.

constant growth model: A widely cited dividend valuation approach that assumes that dividends will grow at a constant rate that is less than the required return.

constant growth valuation (Gordon) model: Assumes that the value of a share of stock equals the present value of all future dividends (assumed to grow at a constant rate) that it is expected to provide over an infinite time horizon.

constant-payout-ratio dividend policy: A dividend policy based on the payment of a certain percentage of earnings to owners in each dividend policy.

contingent securities: Convertibles, warrants, and stock options. Their presence affects the reporting of a firm's earnings per share (EPS).

continuous compounding: Compounding of interest an infinite number of times per year at intervals of microseconds.

continuous probability distribution: A probability distribution showing all the possible outcomes and associated probabilities for a given event.

controlled disbursing: The strategic use of mailing points and bank accounts to lengthen mail float and clearing float, respectively.

controller: The officer responsible for the firm's accounting activities, such as tax management, data processing, and cost and financial accounting.

conventional cash flow pattern: An initial outflow followed by a series of inflows.

conversion feature: A feature of so-called *convertible bonds* that allows bondholders to change each bond into a specified number of shares of common stock.

conversion feature: An option that is included as part of a bond or a preferred stock issue that allows its holder to change the security into a stated number of shares of common stock.

conversion price: The per-share price that is effectively paid for common stock as the result of conversion of a convertible security.

conversion ratio: The ratio at which a convertible security can be exchanged for common stock.

conversion (or stock) value: The value of a convertible security measured in terms of the market price of the common stock into which it can be converted.

convertible bond: A bond that can be changed into a specified number of shares of common stock.

convertible preferred stock: Preferred stock that can be changed into a specified number of shares of common stock.

corporate bond: A certificate indicating that a corporation has borrowed a certain amount of money from an institution or an individual and promises to repay it in the future under clearly defined terms.

corporate restructuring: The activities involving expansion or contraction of a firm's operations or changes in its asset or financial (ownership) structure.

correlation: A statistical measure of the relationship, if any, between series of numbers representing data of any kind.

correlation coefficient: A measure of the degree of correlation between two series.

cost of a new issue of common stock: Determined by calculating the cost of common stock after considering both the amount of underpricing and the associated flotation costs.

cost of capital: The rate of return that a firm must earn on its project investments to maintain its market value and attract needed funds.

cost of common stock equity: The rate at which investors discount the expected dividends of the firm to determine its share value.

cost of giving up a cash discount: The implied rate of interest paid to delay payment of an account payable for an additional number of days.

cost of long-term debt: The after tax cost today of raising long-term funds through borrowing.

cost of new asset: The net outflow required to acquire a new asset.

cost of preferred stock: The annual preferred stock dividend, divided by the net proceeds from the sale of the preferred stock.

cost of retained earnings: The same as the cost of an equivalent fully subscribed issue of additional common stock, which is measured by the cost of common stock equity.

coverage ratios: Ratios that measure the firm's ability to pay certain fixed charges.

credit analysis: The evaluation of credit applicants.

credit period: The number of days until full payment of an account payable is required.

credit policy: The determination of credit selection, credit standards, and credit terms.

credit scoring: A procedure resulting in a score reflecting an applicant's overall credit strength, derived as a weighted average of scores on key financial and credit characteristics.

credit selection: The decision whether to extend credit to a customer and how much credit toextend.

credit standards: The minimum requirements for extending credit to a customer.

credit terms: Specify the repayment terms required of a firm's credit customers.

creditor control: An arrangement in which the creditor committee replaces the firm's operating management and operates the firm until all claims have been settled.

cross-sectional analysis: The comparison of different firms' financial ratios at the same point in time; involves comparing the firm's ratios to those of an industry leader or to industry averages.

cumulative preferred stock: Preferred stock for which all past (unpaid) dividends in arrears must be paid along with the current dividend before payment of dividends to common stockholders.

cumulative translation adjustment: Equity reserve account on parent company's books in which translation gains and losses are accumulated.

cumulative voting system: The system under which each share of common stock is allotted a number of votes equal to the total number of corporate directors to be elected and votes can be given to *any* director(s).

current assets: Short-term assets, expected to be converted into cash within one year or less.

current expenditure: An outlay of funds by the firm resulting in benefits received within one year.

current liabilities: Short-term liabilities, expected to be converted into cash within one year.

current rate (translation) method: Technique used by U.S.-based companies to translate their foreign-currency-denominated assets and liabilities into dollars (for consideration with the parent company's financial statements).

current ratio: A measure of liquidity calculated by dividing the firm's current assets by its current liabilities.

current yield: A measure of a bond's cash return for the year; calculated by dividing the bond's annual interest payment by its current price.

date of invoice: Indicates that the beginning of the credit period is the date on the invoice for the purchase.

date of record (dividends): The date, set by the firm's directors, on which every person whose name is recorded as a stockholder will, at a specified future time, receive a declared dividend.

date of record (rights): The last date on which the recipient of a right must be the legal owner indicated in the company's stock ledger.

dealer market: The market in which the buyer and seller are not brought together directly but instead have their orders executed by dealers that make markets in a given security.

debentures: Unsecured bonds that only creditworthy firms can issue.

debt capital: All long-term borrowing incurred by the firm.

debt ratio: Measures the proportion of total assets financed by the firm's creditors.

debt-equity ratio: Measures the ratio of long-term debt to stockholders' equity.

debtor in possession (DIP): The term assigned to a firm that files a reorganization petition under Chapter 11 and then develops, if feasible, a reorganization plan.

degree of financial leverage (DFL): The numerical measure of the firm's financial leverage.

degree of indebtedness: Measures amount of debt relative to other significant balance sheet amounts.

degree of operating leverage (DOL): The numerical measure of the firm's operating leverage.

degree of total leverage (DTL): The numerical measure of the firm's total leverage.

Depository Institutions Deregulation and Monetary Control Act of 1980 (DIDMCA): Signaled the beginning of the "financial services revolution" by eliminating interest-rate ceilings on all accounts and permitting certain institutions to offer new types of accounts and services.

depository transfer check (DTC): An unsigned check drawn on one of the firm's bank accounts and deposited into its account at a concentration or major disbursement bank, thereby speeding up the transfer of funds.

depreciable life: Time period over which an asset is depreciated.

depreciation: The systematic charging of a portion of the costs of fixed assets against annual revenues over time.

depth of a market: A characteristic of a ready market, determined by its ability to absorb the purchase or sale of a large dollar amount of a particular security.

dilution of ownership: Occurs when a new stock issue results in each present stockholder having a claim on a smaller part of the firm's earnings than previously.

direct lease: A lease under which a lessor owns or acquires the assets that are leased to a given lessee.

direct send: A collection procedure in which the payee presents payment checks directly to the banks on which they are drawn, thus reducing clearing float.

disbursement float: The lapse between the time when a firm deducts a payment from its checking account ledger (disburses it) and the time when funds are actually withdrawn from its account.

discount: The amount by which a bond sells at a value that is less than its par, or face, value.

discount loans: Loans on which interest is paid in advance by deducting it from the amount borrowed.

discounting cash flows: The process of finding present values; the inverse of compounding interest.

diversifiable risk: The portion of an asset's risk that is attributable to firm-specific, random causes; can be eliminated through diversification.

divestiture: The selling of some of a firm's assets for various strategic motives.

dividend irrelevance theory: A theory put forth by Miller and Modigliani that, in a perfect world, the value of a firm is unaffected by the distribution of dividends and is determined solely by the earning power and risk of its assets.

dividend payout ratio: Indicates the percentage of each dollar earned that is distributed to the owners in the form of cash; calculated by dividing the firm's cash dividend per share by its earnings per share.

dividend policy: The firm's plan of action to be followed whenever a decision concerning dividends must be made.

dividend reinvestment plans (DRPs): Plans that enable stockholders to use dividends received on the firm's stock to acquire additional full or fractional shares at little or no transaction (brokerage) cost.

dividend relevance theory: The theory, attributed to Gordon and Lintner, that stockholders prefer current dividends and that there is a direct relationship between a firm's dividend policy and its market value.

dividends: Periodic distributions of earnings to the owners of stock in a firm.

double taxation: Occurs when the already once-taxed earnings of a corporation are distributed as cash dividends to its stockholders, who are then taxed again on these dividends.

Dun & Bradstreet (D&B): The largest mercantile credit-reporting agency in the United States.

DuPont formula: Relates the firm's net profit margin and total asset turnover to its return on total assets (ROA). The ROA is the product of the net profit margin and the total asset turnover.

DuPont system of analysis: Used by management as a framework for dissecting the firm's financial statements and assessing its financial condition.

earnings per share (EPS): The amount earned during the period on each outstanding share of common stock, calculated by dividing the period's total earnings available for the firm's common stockholders by the number of shares of common stock outstanding.

EBIT-EPS approach: An approach for selecting the capital structure that maximizes earnings per share (EPS) over the expected range of earnings before interest and taxes (EBIT).

economic conversion quantity (ECQ): The cost-minimizing quantity in which to convert marketable securities to cash.

economic exposure: The risk resulting from the effects of changes in foreign exchange rates on the firm's value.

economic order quantity (EOQ) model: An inventory management technique for determining an item's optimal order quantity, which is the one that minimizes the total of its order and carrying costs.

economic value added (EVA®): A popular, but static, approach to investment decisions used by many firms to determine whether an investment contributes positively to the owners' wealth.

effective interest rate: In the international context, the rate equal to the nominal rate plus (or minus) any forecast appreciation (or depreciation) of a foreign currency relative to the currency of the MNC parent.

effective (true) interest rate: The rate of interest actually paid or earned; in personal finance, commonly called the *annual percentage rate (APR).*

efficient market hypothesis: Theory describing the behavior of an assumed "perfect" market in which securities are typically in equilibrium, security prices fully reflect all public information available and react swiftly to new information, and, since stocks are fairly prices, investors need not waste time looking for mispriced securities. A market that allocates funds to their most productive uses as a result of competition among wealth-maximizing investors that determines and publicizes prices that are believed to be close to their true value. An assumed "perfect" market in which there are many small investors, each having the same information and expectations with respect to securities; there are no restrictions on investment, no taxes, and no transaction costs; and all investors are rational, they view securities similarly, and they are risk-averse, preferring higher returns and lower risk.

efficient portfolio: A portfolio that maximizes return for a given level of risk or minimizes risk for a given level of return.

end of month (EOM): Indicates that the credit period for all purchases made within a given month begins on the first day of the month immediately following.

ending cash: The sum of the firm's beginning cash and its net cash flow for the period.

equipment trust certificates: Bonds used to finance "rolling stock" such as airplanes, trucks, and railroad cars.

equity capital: The long-term funds provided by the firm's owners, the stockholders.

ethics: Standards of conduct or moral judgment.

Eurobond: A bond issued by an international borrower and sold to investors in countries with currencies other than the currency in which the bond is denominated. An international bond that is sold primarily in countries other than the country of the currency in which the issue is denominated.

Eurocurrency loan market: A large number of international banks that make long-term, floating rate, hard-currency (typically U.S. dollar-denominated) loans in the form of lines of credit to international corporate and government borrowers.

Eurocurrency market: International equivalent of the domestic money market. The portion of the Euromarket that provides short-term foreign-currency financing to subsidiaries of MNCs.

Eurodollar deposits: Deposits of currency not native to the country in which the bank is located; negotiable, usually pay interest at maturity, and are typically denominated in units of $1 million. Provide yields above nearly all other marketable securities with similar maturities.

Euro-equity market: The capital market around the world that deals in international equity issues; London has become the center of Euro-equity activity.

Euromarket: The international financial market that provides for borrowing and lending currencies outside their country of origin.

European Open Market: The transformation of the European Economic Community (EC) into a single market at year-end 1992.

ex dividend: Period beginning four *business days* prior to the date of record during which a stock will be sold without the right to receive the current dividend.

ex rights: Period beginning four *business days* prior to the date of record during which a stock will be sold without announced rights being attached to it.

excess cash balance: The (excess) amount available for investment by the firm if the period's ending cash is greater than the desired minimum cash balance; assumed to be invested in marketable securities.

excess earnings accumulation tax: The tax levied by the IRS on retained earnings above $250,000, when it has determined that the firm has accumulated an excess of earnings to allow owners to delay paying ordinary income taxes.

exchange rate risk: The danger that an unexpected change in the exchange rate between the dollar and the currency in which a project's cash flows are denominated can reduce the market value of that project's cash flow.

exchange rate risk: The risk caused by varying exchange rates between two currencies.

exercise (or option) price: The price at which holders of warrants can purchase a specified number of shares of common stock.

expectations hypothesis: Theory suggesting that the yield curve reflects investor expectations about future interest rates; an increasing inflation expectation results in an upward-sloping yield curve and a decreasing inflation expectation results in a downward-sloping yield curve.

expected return: The return that is expected to be earned each period on a given asset over an infinite time horizon.

expected value of a return: The most likely return on a given asset.

extendable notes: Debt with a short-term maturity, typically 1 to 5 years, that can be renewed for a similar period at the option of the holders.

extension: An arrangement whereby the firm's creditors receive payment in full, although not immediately.

external forecast: A sales forecast based on the relationships observed between the firm's sales and certain key external economic indicators.

external funds required ("plug" figure): Under the judgmental approach for developing a pro forma balance sheet, the amount of external financing needed to bring the statement into balance.

extra dividend: An additional dividend optionally paid by the firm if earnings are higher than normal in a given period.

factor: A financial institution that specializes in purchasing accounts receivable from businesses.

factoring accounts receivable: The outright sale of accounts receivable at a discount to a *factor* or other financial institution to obtain funds.

FASB No. 52: Statement issued by the FASB requiring U.S. multinationals first to convert the financial statement accounts of foreign subsidiaries into their *functional currency* and then to translate the accounts into the parent firm's currency using the *all-current-rate method.*

federal agency issues: Low-risk securities issued by government agencies but not guaranteed by the U.S. Treasury, having generally short maturities, and offering slightly higher yields than comparable U.S. Treasury issues.

fidelity bond: A contract under which a bonding company agrees to reimburse a firm for up to a stated amount if a specified manager's dishonest act results in a financial loss to the firm.

finance: The art and science of managing money.

financial (or capital) lease: A longer-term lease than an operating lease that is noncancelable and obligates the lessee to make payments for the use of an asset over a predefined period of time; the total payments over the term of the lease are greater than the lessor's initial cost of the leased asset.

Financial Accounting Standards Board (FASB): The accounting profession's rule-setting body, which authorizes *generally accepted accounting principles (GAAP).*

Financial Accounting Standards Board (FASB) Standard No. 52: Ruling by FASB—the policysetting body of the U.S. accounting profession—that mandates that U.S.-based companies must translate their foreign-currency-denominated assets and liabilities into dollars using the *current rate (translation) method.*

financial break-even points: The level of EBIT necessary just to cover all fixed financial costs; the level of EBIT for which EPS = $0.

financial institution: An intermediary that channels the savings of individuals, businesses, and governments into loans or investments.

financial leverage: The magnification of risk and return introduced through the use of fixed-cost financing such as debt and preferred stock. The potential use of fixed financial costs to magnify the effects of changes in earning before interest and taxes (EBIT) on the firm's earnings per share (EPS).

financial leverage multiplier (FLM): The ratio of the firm's total assets to stockholders' equity.

financial manager: Actively manages the financial affairs of any type of business, whether financial or nonfinancial, private or public, large or small, profit-seeking or not-for-profit.

financial markets: Provide a forum in which suppliers of funds and demanders of loans and investments can transact business directly.

financial merger: A merger transaction undertaken with the goal of restructuring the acquired company to improve its cash flow and unlock its hidden value.

financial planning process: Planning that begins with long-term (strategic) financial plans that in turn guide the formulation of short-term (operating) plans and budgets.

financial risk: The risk to the firm of being unable to cover required financial obligations (interest, lease payments, preferred stock dividends).

financial services: The part of finance concerned with design and delivery of advice and financial products to individuals, business, and government.

financial supermarket: An institution at which the customer can obtain a full array of the financial services now allowed under DIDMCA.

financing flows: Cash flows that result from debt and equity-financing transactions; includes incurrence and repayment of debt, cash inflow from the sale of stock, and cash outflows to repurchase stock or pay cash dividends.

finished goods inventory: Items that have been produced but not yet sold.

five C's of credit: The five key dimensions—character, capacity, capital, collateral, and conditions—used by a firm's credit analysts in their analysis of an applicant's creditworthiness.

fixed asset turnover: Measures the efficiency with which the firm has been using its *fixed*, or earning, assets to generate sales.

fixed (or semi-fixed) relationship: The constant (or relatively constant) relationship of a currency to one of the major currencies, a combination (basket) of major currencies, or some type of international foreign exchange standard.

fixed-payment coverage ratio: Measures the firm's ability to meet all fixed-payment obligations.

fixed-rate loan: A loan whose rate of interest is determined at a set increment above the prime rate and remains unvarying at that fixed rate until maturity.

flat yield curve: A yield curve that reflects relatively similar borrowing costs for both short- and longer-term loans.

float: Funds dispatched by a payer that are not yet in a form that can be spent by the payee.

floating inventory lien: A lender's claim on the borrower's general inventory as collateral for a secured loan.

floating rate bonds: A bond where the stated interest rate is adjusted periodically within stated limits in response to changes in specified money market or capital market rates.

floating relationship: The fluctuating relationship of the values of two currencies with respect to each other.

floating-rate loan: A loan whose rate of interest is established at an increment above the prime rate and is allowed to "float," or vary, above prime as the prime rate varies until maturity.

flotation costs: The total costs of issuing and selling a security.

foreign bond: A bond issued in a host country's financial market, in the host country's currency, by a foreign borrower. An international bond that is sold primarily in the country of the currency of the issue.

foreign direct investment: The transfer of capital, managerial, and technical assets to a foreign country.

foreign direct investment (FDI): The transfer, by a multinational firm, of capital, managerial, and technical assets from its home country to a host country.

foreign exchange manager: The manager responsible for monitoring and managing the firm's exposure to loss from currency fluctuations.

foreign exchange rate: The value of two currencies with respect to each other.

forward exchange rate: The rate of exchange between two currencies at some specified future date.

friendly merger: A merger transaction endorsed by the target firm's management, approved by its stockholders, and easily consummated.

fully diluted EPS: Earnings per share (EPS) calculated under the assumption that all contingent securities are converted and exercised and are therefore common stock.

functional currency: The currency of the economic environment in which a business entity primarily generates and expends cash and in which its accounts are maintained.

future value: The value of a present amount at a future date found by applying compound interest over a specified period of time.

future-value interest factor: The multiplier used to calculate at a specified interest rate the future value of a present amount as of a given time.

future-value interest factor for an annuity: The multiplier used to calculate the future value of an *ordinary annuity* at a specified interest rate over a given period of time.

generally accepted accounting principles (GAAP): The practice and procedure guidelines used to prepare and maintain financial records and reports; authorized by the *Financial Accounting Standards Board (FASB).*

Giro system: System through which retail transactions are handled in association with a foreign country's national postal system.

golden parachutes: Provisions in the employment contracts of key executives that provide them with sizable compensation if the firm is taken over; deters hostile takeovers to the extent that the cash outflows required are large enough to make the takeover unattractive.

Gordon model: A common name for the *constant growth model* that is widely cited in dividend valuation.

government security dealer: An institution that purchases for resale various government securities and other money market instruments.

greenmail: A takeover defense under which a target firm repurchases through private negotiation a large block of stock at a premium from one or more shareholders to end a hostile takeover attempt by those shareholders.

gross profit margin: Measures the percentage of each sales dollar remaining after the firm has paid for its goods.

hedging strategies: Techniques used to offset or protect against risk; in the international context these include borrowing or lending in different currencies, undertaking contracts in the forward, futures, and/or options markets, and also swapping assets/liabilities with other parties.

historic weights: Either book or market value weights based on *actual* capital structure proportions; used in calculating the weighted average cost of capital.

holders of record: Owners of the firm's shares on the *date of record.*

holding company: A corporation that has voting control of one or more other corporations.

horizontal merger: A merger of two firms *in the same line of business.*

hostile merger: A merger transaction not supported by the target firm's management, forcing the acquiring company to try to gain control of the firm by buying shares in the marketplace.

hostile takeover: A maneuver in which an outside group, without management support, tries to gain voting control of a firm by buying its shares in the marketplace.

implied price of a warrant: The price effectively paid for each warrant attached to a bond.

incentive plans: Management compensation plans that tend to tie management compensation to share price; most popular incentive plan involves the grant of *stock options.*

income bonds: Payment of interest is required only when earnings are available.

income statement: Provides a financial summary of the firm's operating results during a specified period.

incremental cash flows: The *additional* cash flows—outflows or inflows—that are expected to result from a proposed capital expenditure.

independent projects: Projects whose cash flows are unrelated or independent of one another; the acceptance of one *does not eliminate* the others from further consideration.

informational content: The information provided by the dividends of a firm with respect to future earnings, which causes owners to bid up (or down) the price of the firm's stock.

initial investment: The relevant cash outflow for a proposed project at time zero.

installation costs: Any added costs that are necessary to place an asset into operation.

installed cost of new asset: The cost of the asset plus its installation costs; equals the asset's depreciable value.

interest rate: The compensation paid by the borrower of funds to the lender; from the borrower's point of view, the cost of borrowing funds.

intermediate cash inflows: Cash inflows received before the termination of a project.

internal forecast: A sales forecast based on a build-up, or consensus, of forecasts through the firm's own sales channels.

internal rate of return (IRR): The discount rate that equates the present value of cash inflows with the initial investment associated with a project, thereby causing NPV = $0.

internal rate of return approach: An approach to capital rationing that involves the graphic plotting of project IRRs in descending order against the total dollar investment.

international bond: A bond that is initially sold outside the country of the borrower and often distributed in several countries.

international equity market: A vibrant equity market that emerged during the past decade to allow corporations to sell large blocks of shares in several different countries simultaneously.

intracompany netting technique: A technique used by multinational firms to minimize their cash requirements by transferring across national boundaries only the net amount of payments owed between them. Sometimes bookkeeping entries are substituted for international payment.

inventory turnover: Measures the activity, or liquidity, of a firm's inventory.

inverted yield curve: A downward-sloping yield curve that indicates generally cheaper long-term borrowing costs than short-term borrowing costs.

investment banker: A financial intermediary that purchases securities from corporate and government issuers and resells them to the general public in the primary market.

investment flows: Cash flows associated with purchase and sale of both fixed assets and equity investments in other firms.

investment opportunities schedule (IOS): A ranking of investment possibilities from best (highest returns) to worst (lowest returns). The graph that plots project IRRs in descending order against total dollar investment.

involuntary reorganization: A petition initiated by an outside party, usually a creditor, for the reorganization and payment of creditors of a failed firm.

issued shares: The number of shares of common stock that have been put into circulation; they represent the sum of outstanding shares and treasury stock.

joint venture: A partnership under which the participants have contractually agreed to contribute specified amounts of money and expertise in exchange for stated proportions of ownership and profit.

judgmental approach: A method for developing the pro forma balance sheet in which the values of certain balance sheet accounts are estimated while others are calculated, using the firm's external financing as a balancing, or "plug," figure.

junk bonds: Debt rated Ba or lower by Moody's or BB or lower by Standard & Poor's.

just-in-time (JIT) system: Inventory management system that minimizes inventory investment by having material inputs arrive at exactly the time they are needed for production.

lease-versus-purchase (or lease-versus-buy) decision: The decision facing firms needing to acquire new fixed assets; whether to lease the assets or to purchase them, using borrowed funds or available liquid resources.

leasing: The process by which a firm can obtain the use of certain fixed assets for which it must make a series of contractual, periodic, tax-deductible payments.

lessee: The receiver of the services of the assets under a lease contract.

lessor: The owner of assets that are being leased.

letter of credit: A letter written by a company's bank to the company's foreign supplier, stating that the bank will guarantee payment of an invoiced amount if all the underlying agreements are met.

letter to stockholders: Typically the first element of the annual stockholders' report and the primary communication from management to the firm's owners.

leverage: Results from the use of fixed-cost assets or funds to magnify returns to the firm's owners.

leveraged buyout (LBO): An acquisition technique involving the use of a large amount of debt to purchase a firm; an example of a *financial merger.*

leveraged lease: A lease under which the lessor acts as an equity participant, supplying only about 20 percent of the cost of the asset, while a lender supplies the balance.

leveraged recapitalization: A takeover defense in which the target firm pays a large debt-financed cash dividend, increasing the firm's financial leverage and deterring the takeover attempt.

lien: A publicly disclosed legal claim on collateral.

limited partnership: A partnership corporation: An intangible business entity created by law (often called a "legal entity").

line of credit: An agreement between a commercial bank and a business specifying the amount of unsecured short-term borrowing the bank will make available to the firm over a given period of time.

liquidation value per share: The *actual* amount per share of common stock to be received if all of the firm's assets are sold, liabilities (including preferred stock) are paid, and any remaining money is divided among the common stockholders.

liquidity: A firm's ability to satisfy its short-term obligations as they come due.

liquidity preference theory: Theory suggesting that for any given issuer, long-term interest rates tend to be higher than short-term rates due to the lower liquidity and higher responsiveness to general interest rate movements of longer-term securities; causes the yield curve to be upward-sloping.

liquidity preferences: General preferences of investors for shorter-term securities.

loan amortization: The determination of the equal annual loan payments necessary to provide a lender with a specified interest return and to repay the loan principal over a specified period.

loan amortization schedule: A schedule of equal payments to repay a loan. It shows the allocation of each loan payment to interest and principal.

lockbox system: A collection procedure in which payers send their payments to a nearby post office box that is emptied by the firm's bank several times daily; the bank deposits the payment checks in the firm's account. Reduces collection float by shortening processing float as well as mail and clearing float.

long-term (strategic) financial plans: Planned long-term financial actions and the anticipated financial impact of those actions.

long-term financing: Financing with an initial maturity of more than one year.

low-regular-and-extra dividend policy: A dividend policy based on paying a low regular dividend, supplemented by an additional dividend when earnings warrant it.

macro political risk: The subjection of *all* foreign firms to political risk (takeover) by a host country because of political change, revolution, or the adoption of new policies.

mail float: The delay between the time when a payer mails a payment and the time when the payee receives it.

maintenance clauses: Provisions within an operating lease requiring the lessor to maintain the assets and to make insurance and tax payments.

majority voting system: The system whereby, in the election of the board of directors, each stockholder is entitled to one vote for each share of stock owned and he or she can vote all shares for each director.

managerial finance: Concerns the duties of the financial manager in the business firm.

marginal analysis: Economic principle that states that financial decisions should be made and actions taken only when the added benefits exceed the added costs.

marginal tax rate: The rate at which additional income is taxed.

market makers: *Securities dealers* that "make markets" by offering to buy or sell certain securities at stated prices.

market premium: The amount by which the market value exceeds the straight or conversion value of a convertible security.

market return: The return on the market portfolio of all traded securities.

market risk-return function: A graph of the discount rates associated with each level of project risk.

market segmentation theory: Theory suggesting that the market for loans is segmented on the basis of maturity and that the sources of supply and demand for loans within each segment determine its prevailing interest rate; the slope of the yield curve is determined by the general relationship between the prevailing rates in each segment.

market stabilization: The process in which an underwriting syndicate places orders to buy the security that it is attempting to sell to keep the demand for the issue, and therefore its price, at the desired level.

market value weights: Weights that use market values to measure the proportion of each type of capital in the firm's financial structure; used in calculating the weighted average cost of capital.

marketable securities: Short-term debt instruments, such as U.S. Treasury bills, commercial paper, and negotiable certificates of deposit issued by government, business, and financial institutions, respectively.

materials requirement planning (MRP) system: Inventory management system that uses EOQ concepts and a computer to compare production needs to available inventory balances and determine when orders should be placed for various items on a product's *bill of materials.*

merger: The combination of two or more firms, in which the resulting firm maintains the identity of one of the firms, usually the larger one.

micro political risk: The subjection of an individual firm, a specific industry, or companies from a particular foreign country to political risk (takeover) by the host country.

Miller-Orr model: A model that provides for cost-efficient transactional cash balances; assumes uncertain cash flows and determines an upper limit and return point for cash balances.

mixed stream: A series of cash flows exhibiting any pattern other than that of an annuity.

modified accelerated cost recovery system (MACRS): System used to determine the depreciation of assets for tax purposes.

modified DuPont formula: Relates the firm's return on total assets (ROA) to its return on equity (ROE) using the *financial leverage multiplier (FLM)*.

money market: A financial relationship created between suppliers and demanders of *short-term funds*.

money market mutual funds: Professionally managed portfolios of various popular marketable securities, having instant liquidity, competitive yields, and low transaction costs.

mortgage bonds: Bonds secured by real estate or buildings.

multinational companies (MNCs): Firms that have international assets and operations in foreign markets and draw part of their total revenue and profits from such markets.

mutually exclusive projects: Projects that compete with one another, so that the acceptance of one *eliminates* the others from further consideration.

Nasdaq: An all-electronic trading platform used to execute securities trades.

national entry control systems: Comprehensive rules, regulations, and incentives aimed at regulating inflows of *foreign direct investments* involving MNCs and at the same time extracting more benefits from their presence.

near-cash: Marketable securities, which are viewed the same as cash because of their high liquidity.

negatively correlated: Descriptive of two series that move in opposite directions.

negotiable certificates of deposit (CDs): Negotiable instruments representing specific cash deposits in commercial banks, having varying maturities and yields based on size, maturity, and prevailing money market conditions. Yields are generally above those on U.S. Treasury issues and comparable to those on commercial paper with similar maturities.

negotiated offering: A security issue for which the investment banker is merely hired rather than awarded the issue through competitive bidding.

net cash flow: The mathematical difference between the firm's cash receipts and its cash disbursements in each period.

net present value (NPV): A sophisticated capital budgeting technique; found by subtracting a project's initial investment from the present value of its cash inflows discounted at a rate equal to the firm's cost of capital.

net present value approach: An approach to capital rationing that is based on the use of present values to determine the group of projects that will maximize owners' wealth.

net present value profiles: Graphs that depict the net present value of a project for various discount rates.

net proceeds: Funds actually received from the sale of a security.

net profit margin: Measures the percentage of each sales dollar remaining after all expenses, including taxes, have been deducted.

net working capital: The difference between the firm's current assets and its current liabilities, or, alternatively, the portion of current assets financed with long-term funds; can be *positive* or *negative*.

no par value: Used to describe stock that is issued without a par value, in which case the stock may be assigned a value or placed on the firm's books at the price at which it is sold.

no-par preferred stock: Preferred stock that has a specified annual dollar dividend but no stated face value.

nominal (stated) interest rate: Contractual rate of interest charged by a lender or promised by a borrower.

nominal rate of interest: The actual rate of interest charged by the supplier of funds and paid by the demander. In the international context, the stated interest rate charged on financing when only the MNC parent's currency is involved.

Non-cash charges: Expenses deducted on the income statement that do not involve an actual outlay of cash during the period.

nonconventional cash flow pattern: A pattern in which an initial outflow is *not* followed by a series of inflows.

noncumulative preferred stock: Preferred stock for which passed (unpaid) dividends do not accumulate.

nondiversifiable risk: The relevant portion of an asset's risk attributable to market factors that affect all firms; cannot be eliminated through diversification.

non-notification basis: The basis on which a borrower, having pledged an account receivable, continues to collect the account payments without notifying the account customer.

nonparticipating preferred stock: Preferred stock whose stockholders receive only the specified dividend payments.

nonrecourse basis: The basis on which accounts receivable are sold to a factor with the understanding that the factor accept all credit risks on the purchased accounts.

nonvoting common stock: Common stock that carries no voting rights; issued when the firm wishes to raise capital through the sale of common stock but does not want to relinquish its voting control.

normal probability distribution: A symmetrical probability distribution whose shape resembles a bell-shaped curve.

normal yield curve: An upward-sloping yield curve that indicates generally cheaper short-term borrowing costs than long-term borrowing costs.

North American Free Trade Agreement (NAFTA): The treaty establishing free trade and open markets between Canada, Mexico, and the United States.

notification basis: The basis on which an account customer whose account has been pledged (or factored) is notified to remit payments directly to the lender (or factor) rather than to the borrower.

offshore centers: Certain cities or states (including London, Singapore, Bahrain, Nassau, Hong Kong, and Luxembourg) that have achieved prominence as major centers for Euromarket business.

operating break-even point: The level of sales necessary to cover all operating costs; the point at which EBIT = $0.

operating cash flow (OCF): The cash flow a firm generates from its normal operations; calculated as *net operating profits after taxes (NPOAT)* plus depreciation.

operating cash inflows: The incremental after-tax cash inflows resulting from use of a project during its life.

operating change restrictions: Contractual restrictions that a bank may impose on a firm as part of a line of credit agreement.

operating cycle (OC): The amount of time that elapses from the point at which the firm begins to build inventory to the point at which cash is collected from sale of the resulting finished product. The recurring transition of a firm's working capital from cash to inventories to receivables and back to cash.

operating flows: Cash flows directly related to production and sale of the firm's product and services.

operating lease: A cancelable contractual arrangement whereby the lessee agrees to make periodic payments to the lessor, often for five or fewer years, for an asset's services; generally, the total payments over the term of the lease are less than the lessor's initial cost of the leased asset.

operating leverage: The potential use of fixed operating costs to magnify the effects of changes in sales on the firm's earnings before interest and taxes (EBIT).

operating profit margin: Measures the percentage of profit earned on each sales dollar before interest and taxes.

operating unit: A part of a business, such as a plant, division, product line, or subsidiary that contributes to the actual operations of the firm.

optimal capital structure: The capital structure at which the weighted average cost of capital is minimized, thereby maximizing the firm's value.

option: An instrument that provides its holder with an opportunity to purchase or sell a specified asset at a stated price on or before a set expiration date.

order costs: The fixed clerical costs of placing and receiving an inventory order.

ordinary annuity: An annuity for which the payments occur at the end of each period.

ordinary income: Income earned through the sale of a firm's goods or services.

outstanding shares: The number of shares of common stock sold to the public.

over-the-counter (OTC) market: Where smaller or unlisted securities are traded.

overdraft system: Automatic coverage by the bank of all checks presented against the firm's account, regardless of the account balance.

overhanging issue: A convertible security that cannot be forced into conversion by using the call feature.

oversubscribed issue: A security issue that is sold out.

oversubscription privilege: Provides for distribution of shares for which rights were not exercised to interested shareholders on a pro rata basis at the stated subscription price.

paid-in capital in excess of par: The amount of proceeds in excess of the par value received from the original sale of common stock.

par value: Per-share value arbitrarily assigned to an issue of common stock primarily for accounting purposes.

par-value preferred stock: Preferred stock with a stated face value that is used with the specified dividend percentage to determine the annual dollar dividend.

participating preferred stock: Preferred stock that provides for dividend payments based on certain formulas allowing preferred stockholders to participate with common stockholders in the receipt of dividends beyond a specified amount.

partnership: A business owned by two or more people and operated for profit.

payable-through draft: A draft drawn on the payer's checking account, payable to a given payee but not payable on demand; approval of the draft by the payer is required before the bank pays the draft.

payback period: The exact amount of time required for a firm to recover its initial investment in a project as calculated from cash inflows.

payment date: The actual date on which the firm will mail the dividend payment to the holders of record.

payment-in-kind (PIK) preferred stock: Preferred stock that pays dividends in additional shares of preferred stock rather than cash.

pecking order: A hierarchy of financing beginning with retained earnings followed by debt financing, and finally external equity financing.

percent-of-sales method: A method for developing the pro forma income statement that expresses the cost of goods sold, operating expenses, and interest expense as a percentage of projected sales.

percentage advance: The percent of the book value of the collateral that constitutes the principal of a secured loan.

perfectly negatively correlated: Describes two negatively correlated series that have a *correlation coefficient* of +1.

perfectly positively correlated: Describes two positively correlated series that have a *correlation coefficient* of 1.

performance plans: Management compensation plans that compensate management on the basis of proven performance measured by EPS, growth in EPS, and other ratios of return. *Performance shares* and/or *cash bonuses* are used as compensation under these plans.

performance shares: Shares of stock given to management for meeting stated performance goals.

permanent need: Financing requirements for the firm's fixed assets plus the permanent portion of the firm's current assets; these requirements remain unchanged over the year.

perpetuity: An annuity with an infinite life, making continual annual payments.

playing the float: A method of consciously anticipating the resulting float, or delay, associated with the payment process and using it to keep funds in an interest-earning form for as long as possible.

pledge of accounts receivable: The use of a firm's accounts receivable as security, or collateral, to obtain a short-term loan.

poison pill: A takeover defense in which a firm issues securities that give their holders certain rights that become effective when a takeover is attempted; these rights make the target firm less desirable to a hostile takeover.

political risk: Risk that arises from the danger that a host government might take actions that are harmful to foreign investors or from the possibility that political turmoil in a country might endanger investments made in that country by foreign nationals. The potential discontinuity or seizure of an MNC's operations in a host country due to the host's implementation of specific rules and regulations (such as nationalization, expropriation, or confiscation).

portfolio: A collection, or group, of assets.

positively correlated: Descriptive of two series that move in the same direction.

preauthorized check (PAC): A check written by the payee against a customer's checking account for a previously agreed-upon amount. Because of prior legal authorization, the check does not require the customer's signature.

preemptive rights: Allow common stockholders to maintain their proportionate ownership in the corporation when new issues are made.

preferred stock: A special form of ownership having a fixed periodic dividend that must be paid before payment of any common stock dividends.

premium: The amount by which a bond sells at a value that is greater than its par, or face, value.

present value: The current dollar value of a future amount. The amount of money that would have to be invested today at a given interest rate over a specified period to equal the future amount.

present-value interest factor: The multiplier used to calculate at a specified discount rate the present value of an amount to be received in a future period.

present-value interest factor for an annuity: The multiplier used to calculate the present value of an annuity at a specified discount rate over a given period of time.

president or chief executive officer (CEO): Corporate official responsible for managing the firm's day-to-day operations and carrying out the policies established by the board of directors.

price/earnings multiple approach: A technique to estimate the firm's share value; calculated by multiplying the firm's expected earnings per share (EPS) by the average price/earnings (P/E) ratio for the industry.

price/earnings (P/E) ratio: Reflects the amount investors are willing to pay for each dollar of the firm's earnings; the higher the P/E ratio, the greater the investor confidence in the firm.

primary EPS: Earnings per share (EPS) calculated under the assumption that all contingent securities *that derive the major portion of their value from their conversion privileges or common stock characteristics* are converted and exercised, and are therefore common stock.

primary market: Financial market in which securities are initially issued; the only market in which the issuer is directly involved in the transaction.

prime rate of interest (prime rate): The lowest rate of interest charged by the nation's leading banks on business loans to their most important and reliable business borrowers.

principal: The amount of money on which interest is paid.

private placement: The sale of a new security issue, typically debt or preferred stock, directly to an investor or group of investors.

privately owned stock: All common stock of a firm owned by a single individual.

pro forma statements: Projected, or forecast, financial statements—income statements and balance sheets.

probability distribution: A model that relates probabilities to the associated outcomes.

probability: The chance that a given outcome will occur.

proceeds from sale of old asset: The cash inflows, net of any removal or cleanup costs, resulting from the sale of an existing asset.

processing float: The delay between receipt of a check by the payee and its deposit in the firm's account.

profitability: The relationship between revenues and costs generated by using the firm's assets—both current and fixed—in productive activities.

prospectus: A portion of a security registration statement filed with the SEC that details the firm's operating and financial position; it must be made available to all potential buyers.

proxy battle: The attempt by a nonmanagement group to gain control of the management of a firm through the solicitation of a sufficient number of proxy votes.

proxy statement: A statement giving the votes of a stockholder or stockholders to another party.

public offering: The nonexclusive sale of either bonds or stock to the general public.

publicly held corporations: Corporations whose stock is traded on either an organized securities exchange or the over-the-counter exchange and/or those with more than $5 million in assets and 500 or more stockholders.

publicly owned stock: Common stock of a firm owned by a broad group of unrelated individual and/or institutional investors.

purchase options: Provisions frequently included in both operating and financial leases that allow the lessee to purchase the leased asset at maturity, typically for a prespecified price.

put option: An option to sell a given number of shares of a stock (typically 100) on or before a specified future date at a stated striking price.

putable bonds: Bonds that can be redeemed at par at the option of the holder either at specific dates or when the firm takes specific actions, such as being acquired, acquiring another, or issuing a large amount of additional debt.

pyramiding: An arrangement among holding companies wherein one holding company controls other holding companies, thereby causing an even greater magnification of earnings and losses.

quarterly compounding: Compounding of interest over four periods within the year.

quick (acid-test) ratio: A measure of liquidity calculated by dividing the firm's current assets minus inventory by current liabilities.

range: A measure of an asset's risk, which is found by subtracting the return associated with the pessimistic (worst) outcome from the return associated with optimistic (best) outcome.

ranking approach: The ranking of capital expenditure projects on the basis of some predetermined measure such as the rate of return.

ratio analysis: Involves the methods of calculating and interpreting financial ratios to assess the firm's performance and status.

ratio of exchange: The ratio of the amount *paid* per share of the target company to the per-share market price of the acquiring firm.

ratio of exchange in market price: The ratio of the market price per share of the acquiring firm *paid* to each dollar of market price per share of the target firm.

raw materials inventory: Items purchased by the firm for use in the manufacture of a finished product.

real rate of interest: The rate that creates an equilibrium between the supply of savings and the demand for investment funds in a perfect world, without inflation, where funds suppliers and demanders are indifferent to the term of loans or investments because they have no *liquidity preference* and where all outcomes are certain.

recapitalization: The reorganization procedure under which a failed firm's debts are generally exchanged for equity or the maturities of existing debts are extended.

recaptured depreciation: The portion of the sale price that is above book value and below the initial purchase price.

recovery period: The appropriate depreciable life of a particular asset as determined by MACRS.

red herring: On a prospectus, a statement, printed in red ink, indicating the tentative nature of a security offer while it is being reviewed by the SEC.

red-line method: Unsophisticated inventory management technique in which a reorder is placed when sufficient use of inventory items from a bin exposes a red line drawn inside the bin.

regular dividend policy: A dividend policy based on the payment of a fixed-dollar dividend in each period.

relevant cash flows: The incremental after-tax cash outflow (investment) and resulting subsequent inflows associated with a proposed capital expenditure.

renewal options: Provisions especially common in operating leases that grant the lessee the option to re-lease assets at their expiration.

reorder point: The point at which to reorder inventory, expressed equationally as: lead time in days × daily usage.

repurchase agreement: An agreement whereby a bank of securities dealers sells a firm specific securities and agrees to repurchase them at a specific price and time.

required return: A specified return required each period by investors for a given level of risk. The cost of funds obtained by selling an ownership (or equity) interest; it reflects the funds supplier's level of expected return.

required total financing: Amount of funds needed by the firm if the ending cash for the period is less than the desired minimum cash balance; typically represented by notes payable.

residual theory of dividends: A theory that the dividend paid by a firm should be the amount left over after all acceptable investment opportunities have been undertaken.

restrictive covenants: Contractual clauses in long-term debt agreement that place certain operating and financial constraints on the borrower.

retained earnings: The cumulative total of all earnings, net of dividends, that have been retained and reinvested in the firm since its inception.

return: The total gain or loss experienced on behalf of the owner of an investment over a given period of time; calculated by dividing the asset's change in value plus any cash distributions during the period by its beginning-of-period investment value.

return on equity (ROE): Measures the return earned on the owners' (both preferred and common stockholders') investment in the firm.

return on total assets (ROA): Measures the overall effectiveness of management in generating profits with its available assets; also called *return on investment.*

reverse stock split: A method that is used to raise the market price of a firm's stock by exchanging a certain number of outstanding shares for one new share of stock.

revolving credit agreement: A line of credit guaranteed to the borrower by the bank for a stated time period and regardless of the scarcity of money.

risk: The chance of financial loss, or more formally, the variability of returns associated with a given asset. The chance that actual outcomes may differ from those expected.

The probability that a firm will be unable to pay its bills as they come due.

risk premium: The amount by which the required discount rate for a project exceeds the risk-free rate.

risk-adjusted discount rate (RADR): The rate of return that must be earned on a given project to compensate the firm's owners adequately, thereby resulting in the maintenance or improvement of share price.

risk-averse: The attitude toward risk in which an increased return would be required for an increase in risk.

risk-free rate of interest, R_F: The required return on a risk-free asset, typically a three-month U.S. Treasury bill.

risk-free rate: The rate of return that one would earn on a virtually riskless investment such as a *U.S. Treasury bill.*

risk-indifferent: The attitude toward risk in which no change in return would be required for an increase in risk.

risk-return tradeoff: The expectation that for accepting greater risk, investors must be compensated with greater returns.

risk-seeking: The attitude toward risk in which a decreased return would be accepted for an increase in risk.

S corporation: A tax-reporting entity whose earnings are taxed not as a corporation but as the incomes of its stockholders, thus avoiding the usual *double taxation* on corporate earnings.

safety motive: A motive for holding cash or near-cash—to protect the firm against being unable to satisfy unexpected demands for cash.

safety of principal: The ease of salability of a security for close to its initial value.

safety stocks: Extra inventories that can be drawn down when actual lead times and/or usage rates are greater than expected.

sale-leaseback arrangement: A lease under which the lessee sells an asset to a prospective lessor and then leases back the same asset, making fixed periodic payments for its use.

sales forecast: The prediction of the firm's sales over a given period, based on external and/or internal data, and used as the key input to the short-term financial planning process.

scenario analysis: A technique for assessing risk that uses possible alternative conditions (scenarios) to obtain a sense of the variability in a project's return.

seasonal need: Financing requirements for temporary current assets, which vary over the year.

secondary market: Financial market in which preowned securities (those that are not new issues) are traded.

secured creditors: Creditors who have specific assets pledged as collateral and in liquidation of the failed firm receive proceeds from the sale of those assets.

secured loan: A loan that has specific assets pledged as collateral.

secured short-term financing: Short-term financing (loans) obtained by pledging specific assets as collateral.

Securities and Exchange Commission (SEC): The federal regulatory body that governs the sale and listing of securities.

securities exchanges: Organizations that provide the marketplace in which firms can raise funds through the sale of new securities and purchasers can resell securities.

security agreement: The agreement between the borrower and the lender that specifies the collateral held against a secured loan.

security market line (SML): The depiction of the *capital asset pricing model (CAPM)* as a graph that reflects the required return for each level of nondiversifiable risk (beta).

selling group: A group of brokerage firms, each of which agrees to sell a portion of a security issue and expects to make a profit on the *spread* between the price at which they buy and sell the securities.

semi-annual compounding: Compounding of interest over two periods within the year.

serial bonds: An issue of bonds of which a certain proportion matures each year.

shark repellents: Anti-takeover amendments to a corporate charter that constrain the firm's ability to transfer managerial control of the firm as a result of a merger.

shelf registration: An SEC procedure that allows firms with more than $150 million in outstanding common stock to file a "master

registration statement" covering a two-year period and then, during that period, to sell securities that have already been approved under the master statement.

short-term financial management: Management of current assets and current liabilities.

short-term (operating) financial plans: Planned short-term financial actions and the anticipated financial impact of those actions.

short-term self-liquidating loan: An unsecured short-term loan in which the use to which the borrowed money is put provides the mechanism through which the loan is repaid.

signal: A financing action by management that is believed to reflect its view with respect to the firm's stock value; generally, debt financing is viewed as a *positive signal* that management believes that the stock is "undervalued," and a stock issue is viewed as a *negative signal* that management believes that the stock is "overvalued."

simulation: A statistically based behavioral approach used in capital budgeting to get a feel for risk by applying predetermined probability distributions and random numbers to estimate risky outcomes.

single-payment note: A short-term, one-time loan payable as a single amount at its maturity.

sinking-fund requirement: A restrictive provision that is often included in a bond indenture providing for the systematic retirement of bonds prior to their maturity.

small (ordinary) stock dividend: A stock dividend that represents less than 20 to 25 percent of the common stock outstanding at the time the dividend is declared.

sole proprietorship: A business owned by one person and operated for his or her own profit.

speculative motive: A motive for holding cash or near-cash—to put unneeded funds to work or to be able to quickly take advantage of unexpected opportunities that may arise.

spin-off: A form of divestiture in which an operating unit becomes an independent company by issuing shares in it on a pro rata basis to the parent company's shareholders.

sponsored ADR: An ADR for which the issuing (foreign) company absorbs the legal and financial costs of creating and trading a security.

spontaneous financing: Financing that arises from the normal operations of the firm, the two major short-term sources of which are accounts payable and accruals.

spot exchange rate: The rate of exchange between two currencies on any given day.

spread: The difference between the price paid for a security by the investment banker and the sale price.

staggered funding: A way to play the float by depositing a certain proportion of a payroll or payment into the firm's checking account on several successive days *following* the actual issuance of checks.

stakeholder: Groups such as employees, customers, suppliers, creditors, and others who have a direct economic link to the firm.

standard debt provisions: Provisions in long-term debt agreements specifying certain criteria of satisfactory record keeping and reporting, tax payment, and general business maintenance on the part of the borrowing firm; normally, they do not place a burden on the financially sound business.

standard deviation: The most common statistical indicator of an asset's risk; it measures the dispersion around the *expected* value.

standby arrangement: A formal guarantee that any shares that are not subscribed or sold publicly will be purchased by the investment banker.

statement of cash flows: Provides a summary of the firm's operating, investment, and financing cash flows and reconciles them with changes in its cash and marketable securities during the period of concern.

statement of retained earnings: Reconciles the net income earned during a given year and any cash dividends paid with the change in retained earnings between the start and end of that year.

stock dividend: The payment to existing owners of a dividend in the form of stock.

stock options: An incentive allowing management to purchase stock at the market price set at the time of the grant. Options, generally extended to management, that permit purchase of the firm's common stock at a specified price over a stated period of time.

stock repurchase: The repurchasing by the firm of outstanding shares of its common stock in the marketplace; desired effects of stock repurchases

are that they enhance shareholder value and/or help to discourage unfriendly takeovers.

stock rights: Provide stockholders with the privilege to purchase additional shares of stock in direct proportion to their number of owned shares.

stock split: A method that is commonly used to lower the market price of a firm's stock by increasing the number of shares belonging to each shareholder.

stock swap transaction: An acquisition method in which the acquiring firm exchanges its shares for shares of the target company according to a predetermined ratio.

stock-purchase plans: An employee fringe benefit that allows the purchase of a firm's stock at a discount or on a matching basis with a part of the cost absorbed by the firm.

stock-purchase warrant: An instrument that gives its holder the right to purchase a certain number of shares of common stock at a specified price over a certain period of time.

stockholders: The true owners of the firm by virtue of their equity in the form of preferred and common stock.

stockholders' report: Annual report required of publicly held corporations that summarizes and documents for stockholders the firm's financial activities during the past year.

straight bond value: The price at which a convertible bond would sell in the market without the conversion feature.

straight bond: A bond that is nonconvertible, having no conversion feature.

straight preferred stock: Preferred stock that is nonconvertible, having no conversion feature.

strategic merger: A merger transaction undertaken to achieve economies of scale.

stretching accounts payable: Paying bills as late as possible without damaging one's credit rating.

striking price: The price at which the holder of a call option can buy (or the holder of a put option can sell) a specified amount of stock at any time before the option's expiration date.

subordinated debentures: Claims of these bonds are not satisfied until those of the creditors holding certain (senior) debts have been fully satisfied.

subordination: In a long-term debt agreement, the stipulation that all subsequent or less important creditors agree to wait until all claims of the senior debt are satisfied before having their claims satisfied.

subscription price: The price at which stock rights are exercisable for a specified period of time; is set below the prevailing market price.

subsidiaries: The companies controlled by a holding company.

supervoting shares: Stock that carries with it more votes per share than a share of regular common stock.

takeover defenses: Strategies for fighting hostile takeovers.

target capital structure: The desired optimal mix of debt and equity financing that most firms attempt to achieve and maintain.

target company: The firm in a merger transaction that the acquiring company is pursuing.

target dividend-payout ratio: A policy under which the firm attempts to pay out a certain percentage of earnings as a stated dollar dividend, which it adjusts toward a target payout as proven earnings increases occur.

target weights: Either book or market value weights based on desired capital structure proportions; used in calculating the weighted average cost of capital.

tax loss carryback/carryforward: A tax benefit that allows corporations experiencing operating losses to carry tax losses back up to 3 years and forward for as many as 15 years. In a merger, the tax loss of one of the firms that can be applied against a limited amount of future income of the merged firm either over 15 years or until the total tax loss has been fully recovered, whichever is shorter.

tax on sale of old asset: Tax that depends upon the relationship between the old asset's sale price, initial purchase price, and *book value.*

technical insolvency: Business failure that occurs when a firm is unable to pay its liabilities as they come due.

temporal method: A method that requires specific assets and liabilities to be translated at historical exchange rates and that foreign-exchange translation gains or losses be reflected in the current-year's income.

tender offer: A formal offer to purchase a given number of shares of a firm's stock at a specified price.

term (long-term) loan: A loan made by a financial institution to a business and having an initial maturity of more than one year.

term loan agreement: A formal contract, ranging from a few to a few hundred pages, specifying the conditions under which a financial institution has made a long-term loan.

term structure of interest rates: The relationship between the interest rate and the time to maturity.

terminal cash flow: The after-tax nonoperating cash flow occurring in the final year of a project, usually attributable to liquidation of the project.

time line: A horizontal line on which time zero is at the leftmost end and future periods are shown as you move from left to right; can be used to depict investment cash flows.

time-series analysis: Evaluation of the firm's financial performance over time, utilizing financial ratio analysis.

times-interest-earned ratio: Measures the firm's ability to make contractual interest payments.

total asset turnover: Indicates the efficiency with which the firm uses all its assets to generate sales.

total cost: The sum of the order costs and carrying costs of inventory.

total leverage: The potential use of *fixed costs, both operating and financial,* to magnify the effect of changes in sales on the firm's earnings per share (EPS).

total quality management (TQM): The application of quality principles to all aspects of a company's operations.

total risk: The combination of a security's nondiversifiable and diversifiable risk.

transactions motive: A motive for holding cash or near-cash—to make planned payments for items such as materials and wages.

transfer prices: Prices that subsidiaries charge each other for the goods and services traded between them.

treasurer: The officer responsible for the firm's financial activities, such as financial planning and fund raising, making capital expenditure decisions, managing cash, managing credit activities, and managing the pension fund.

Treasury bills: U.S. Treasury obligations issued weekly on an auction basis, having varying maturities, generally under a year, and virtually no risk.

Treasury notes: U.S. Treasury obligations with initial maturities of between one and ten years, paying interest at a stated rate semi-annually, and having virtually no risk.

treasury stock: The number of shares of outstanding stock that have been repurchased and held by the firm; shown on the firm's balance sheet as a deduction from stockholders' equity.

trust receipt inventory loan: An agreement under which the lender advances 80 to 100 percent of the cost of the borrower's relatively expensive inventory items in exchange for the borrower's promise to immediately repay the loan, with accrued interest, upon the sale of each item.

trustee: A paid individual, corporation, or commercial bank trust department that acts as the third party to a bond indenture to ensure that the issuer does not default on its contractual responsibilities to the bondholders.

two-tier offer: A tender offer in which the terms offered are more attractive to those who tender shares early.

U.S. Treasury bills (T-bills): Short-term IOUs issued by the U.S. Treasury; considered the risk-free asset.

uncorrelated: Describes two series that lack any relationship or interaction and therefore have a *correlation coefficient* close to zero.

underpriced: Stock sold at a price below its current market price.

undersubscribed issue: A security issue whose shares are not immediately sold.

underwriting: The process in which an investment banker buys a security issue from the issuing firm at a lower price than that for which he or she plans to sell it, thereby guaranteeing the issuer a specified amount from the issue and assuming the risk of price changes between the time of purchase and the time of sale.

underwriting syndicate: A group of investment banking firms, each of which will underwrite a portion of a large security issue, thus lessening the risk of loss to any single firm.

unlimited funds: The financial situation in which a firm is able to accept all independent projects that provide an acceptable return.

unlimited liability: The condition imposed by a sole proprietorship (or general partnership) allowing the owner's total wealth to be taken to satisfy creditors.

unsecured loan: A loan that has no assets pledged as collateral.

unsecured, or general, creditors: Creditors who have a general claim against all the firm's assets other than those specifically pledged as collateral.

unsecured short-term financing: Short-term financing obtained without pledging specific assets as collateral.

valuation: The process that links risk and return to determine the worth of an asset.

value dating: A procedure used by non-U.S. banks to delay, often for days or even weeks, the availability of funds deposited with them.

variable growth model: A dividend valuation approach that allows for a change in the dividend growth rate.

vertical merger: A merger in which a firm acquires a supplier or a customer.

voluntary reorganization: A petition filed by a failed firm on its own behalf for reorganizing its structure and paying its creditors.

voluntary settlement: An arrangement between a technically insolvent or bankrupt firm and its creditors enabling it to bypass many of the costs involved in legal bankruptcy proceedings.

warehouse receipt loan: An arrangement in which the lender receives control of the pledged inventory collateral, which is warehoused by a designated agent on the lender's behalf.

warrant premium: The difference between the actual market value and theoretical value of a warrant.

weighted marginal cost of capital (WMCC) schedule: Graph that relates the firm's weighted average cost of capital (WACC) to the level of total new financing.

weighted average cost of capital (WACC): Reflects the expected average future cost of funds over the long run; determined by weighting the cost of each specific type of capital by its proportion in the firm's capital structure.

weighted marginal cost of capital (WMCC): The firm's weighted average cost of capital (WACC) associated with its next dollar of total new financing.

white knight: A takeover defense in which the target firm finds an acquirer more to its liking than the initial hostile acquirer and prompts the two to compete to take over the firm.

wire transfers: Telegraphic communications that, via bookkeeping entries, remove funds from the payer's bank and deposit them into the payee's bank, thereby reducing collection float.

work-in-process inventory: All items that are currently in production.

working capital: Current assets, which represent the portion of investment that circulates from one form to another in the ordinary conduct of business.

yield curve: A graph of the *term structure of interest rates* that depicts the relationship between the *yield to maturity* of a security (y-axis) and the time to maturity (x-axis); it shows the pattern of interest rates on securities of equal quality and different maturity.

yield to maturity (YTM): The rate of return investors earn if they buy a bond at a specific price and hold it until maturity. Assumes that issuer makes all scheduled interest and principal payments as promised. Compound annual rate of interest earned on a security purchased on a given day and held to maturity.

zero-balance account: A checking account in which a zero balance is maintained and the firm is required to deposit funds to cover checks drawn on the account only as they are presented for payment.

zero (or low) coupon bonds: Bonds that are issued with no (zero) or a very low coupon (stated interest) rate and are sold at a large discount from par.

zero-growth model: An approach to dividend valuation that assumes a constant, nongrowing dividend stream.